One Man's London

By the same author

In Search of Blandings

One Man's London

N. T. P. MURPHY

HUTCHINSON
London Sydney Auckland Johannesburg

This edition first published in Great Britain
by Hutchinson, an imprint of Century Hutchinson Ltd,
Brookmount House, 62–65 Chandos Place, London
WC2N 4NW

Century Hutchinson Australia (Pty) Ltd,
89–91 Albion Street, Surry Hills, NSW 2010

Century Hutchinson New Zealand Limited,
PO Box 40–086, Glenfield, Auckland 10,
New Zealand

Century Hutchinson South Africa (Pty) Ltd,
PO Box 337, Bergvlei, 2012 South Africa

British Library Cataloguing in Publication Data

Murphy, Norman T.P.
One man's London.
1. London. Visitors' guides
I. Title
914.21'04858

ISBN 0–09–173711–7

Phototypeset by Input Typesetting Ltd, London
Printed and Bound in Great Britain by
Mackays of Chatham Ltd, Chatham, Kent

CONTENTS

TO CHARLOTTE

without whose patience this book would never have been written

ACKNOWLEDGEMENTS

This book is a personal view of one part of London. It is the area of London most visitors come to see and where, by chance, I spent many years. I took my first photograph of London in 1944 from the steps of St Paul's, looking out over the bombed wastes of the City. I have been collecting anecdotes and books about London ever since.

Many London enthusiasts will recognise some of the stories because they come from Stow, Walford, Larwood, Cunningham, Timbs and William Kent, Weinreb and Hibbert, the writers to whom every London historian owes a debt of gratitude. Some of my information has been gathered over forty years from the London Day By Day column (now 'Peterborough') of the *Daily Telegraph*.

For the rest of my information, I spent years asking questions of office-keepers, doormen and caretakers and I have taken up the time of foremen on building sites who would have preferred to get on with the job rather than answering my queries. To all these and the other Londoners who have tried to answer my questions over the years, my thanks are due.

FIRST ♦ WALK

Whitehall

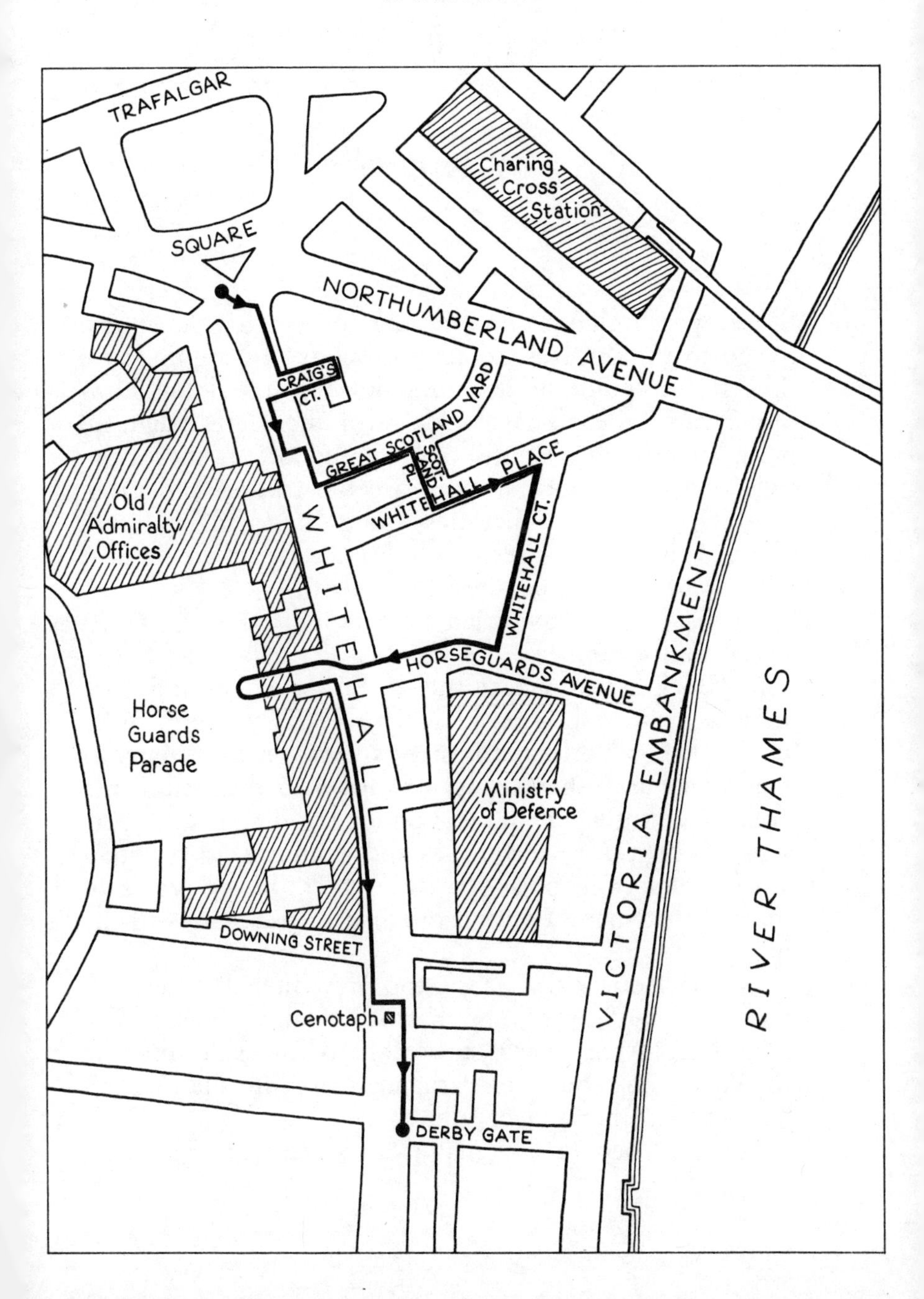

FIRST ♦ WALK

Whitehall

Every year millions come to London to visit the shops, to go to the theatres, to see the sights of a capital city. Every year guide-books are published describing London's famous landmarks. Many of them are delightful with superb illustrations but, all too often, they omit two important factors. Why are the palaces and other landmarks there? What lies along the roads between them? It is along the seemingly featureless streets that the history of London can best be traced.

In this book I have tried to show how the sights that every visitor admires, the Houses of Parliament, Piccadilly, Buckingham Palace and the rest, are of even greater interest if we ask – why? Why was it put here? Why is it still here? Along the streets between these famous landmarks are other sights, unknown to the visitor and equally unknown to most Londoners. There are doorways, lamp-posts, kerbstones and windows, each with a story, each contributing to the two thousand years of history that make London one of the great cities of the world.

We start our walks at the top of Whitehall where the traffic of the Strand joins that of Trafalgar Square. The Admiralty Arch guards the Mall to one side and the towers of the Houses of Parliament rise into the London haze at the other end of Whitehall.

For most people Whitehall is the street from which we

are governed, where faceless civil servants decide our destinies. There is much more to Whitehall than that and we shall see some unusual aspects of it on our walk. The first is that the junction of Whitehall and Trafalgar Square is not Whitehall; it is Charing Cross.

This is the real Charing Cross and has been so since the thirteenth century. When Edward I was fighting the Scots in 1291, his beloved Queen Eleanor died and Edward brought her body back to London for burial in Westminster Abbey. The funeral procession travelled slowly and Edward erected a memorial cross at each stopping place to show where the cortege had rested. He placed the last one here at the bend in the road at the small hamlet of Charing.

The cross stood for three hundred and fifty years until the Puritans took it down during the Civil War as a hated symbol of the monarchy and the old religion. A Victorian version stands in the forecourt of Charing Cross station, erected as a public relations exercise in 1865.

The Centre of London

If you ask six people where the centre of London is, you will probably get six different answers. Some will nominate Hyde Park Corner or Cornhill, basing their case on the old mile posts still found around London – 'Four Miles to Hyde Park Corner' or '2 Miles to The Standard at Cornhill'. Others will choose St Paul's Cathedral or the Guildhall in the City of London on the reasonable grounds that these two buildings were the hub of the old City. Another popular choice is Piccadilly Circus, probably because the newspapers used to describe it so often as 'The Heart of Empire' or 'The Heart of London'. They are all wrong. The centre of London is here on the site of the old Charing Cross.

In the middle of the road is a traffic island on which stands the equestrian statue of Charles I. A brass plate is set in the ground behind the statue. It is from this point that all distances are measured; this is the centre of

London. It is more than two hundred years since Dr Johnson said 'the full tide of human existence is at Charing Cross', but things have not changed much since. It is still one of the busiest places in London and, as with so many of the things we will see on our walks, we must ask – why?

Away to the east, along the Strand, is the old City of London. The Romans found a British settlement there and turned it into a walled city. For a thousand years that was all London was – the 'Square Mile' surrounded by its walls with fields, woods and rough tracks around it. Then Edward the Confessor became king and had a dream that changed London for ever.

Whether it was a dream or merely a bad attack of conscience, we don't know. But we do know that Edward, who became king in 1040, was a very pious man and had made a vow to make a pilgrimage to Rome. With the problems of kingship in the eleventh century, uprisings, wars, and rebellions, it was clear that if Edward made the journey, he would never return as king. There were plenty of rivals to make sure of that. Edward's vow lay heavily on his conscience and eventually, either because of the dream or on the advice of his councillors, he sought absolution from it by promising to build a great church in honour of St Peter.

It so happened that there was already a small monastery dedicated to St Peter down at Thorney Island (we call it Westminster today). Edward decided that should be the site of the new abbey. He also decided that its completion would be achieved more quickly if he supervised the project himself. He therefore took his councillors, his treasury and his retainers out of the City down to Thorney Island and set up his Court in a new palace beside the abbey.

The great church we now call Westminster Abbey was completed in 1066, just in time for Edward's funeral. He left behind a new Royal church with a palace beside it. When William the Conqueror defeated Harold at Hastings, he chose the palace at Westminster as his seat of government. It retains the same role today.

Although Edward had taken the Court down to Westminster, that did not mean that everybody else had to move. The merchants and traders of the City saw no reason to shift. They had their markets and businesses established within strong walls; the religious convictions of the King were no concern of theirs. The City merchants stayed where they were and still remain.

Charing Cross is the half-way point between the trade of the City and the legislators at Westminster. Until the Embankment was built a hundred years ago, this was the only road between them. The City men came here to find out news of taxes and legislation, Parliamentarians came here for news of trade, markets and banking. This has been the centre of London for more than a thousand years.

The brass plate set in the pavement is not here just to settle antiquarian arguments. As with many of the features on our walks, there is a sound financial reason. Policemen and civil servants working in central London are paid an allowance to cater for the extra living costs involved. To obviate disputes on where 'central London' is, the brass plate was set here to mark the centre of the six-mile circle within which the Civil Service pays the London allowance.

The Statue of Charles I

The statue of Charles I was commissioned by Lord Weston in 1633 from the Huguenot sculptor Hubert LeSueur, whose name can be seen on the horse's left forefoot. It is an excellent representation of the king. It is also an early example of public relations since Charles, who was only five foot four inches in height, is deliberately depicted as an impressive six foot. It was the first equestrian statue in England and caused a stir when it was erected in Covent Garden. It was taken down by the

Puritans during the Civil War and sold to be broken up for scrap.

That is what happened to it officially. Unofficially, the man who bought it took the long view. He was a brazier by trade, with the appropriate name of Mr Rivett. Rivett hid the statue and made a nice profit by selling thimbles, knives and scissors supposedly made from the metal of the statue. The Parliamentarians bought them as a memento of their victory over the hated monarchy; the Royalists bought them equally eagerly as a souvenir of their late King.

When the monarchy was restored in 1660, Rivett made another profit by selling the statue to King Charles II. It was set up here on the site of the old Charing Cross to look down Whitehall to the spot where Charles I had been executed. There was some delay before it was erected since the site was needed for more urgent business. Charing Cross was where proclamations were made and executions carried out. When Charles II returned, revenge was taken on the men who had sentenced his father to death. In one of the immortal understatements of English literature, Pepys wrote:

> I went out to Charing Cross, to see Major-General Harrison hanged, drawn and quartered; which was done there, he looking as cheerful as any man could do in that condition.

The plinth, designed by Christopher Wren, is made of Portland stone. Looking closely at the stone, one can spot the sea-shells that show the stone's origin as a marine deposit.

The statue has always needed protection from the traffic that roars around it. The black bollards beside it with the cypher of William IV on them were placed here in 1836.

The location of the statue is an excellent example of British compromise. It stands at the top of Whitehall, a monument to the only king Parliament executed. At the other end of Whitehall, in Parliament Square, is a statue of Cromwell, the man who executed him.

Whitehall

Whitehall is not one street; it is two and was originally three. There is a Whitehall street sign on the corner building but it has only been there since 1931. Until then everything within a hundred yards of here was officially Charing Cross. The postal address 'Charing Cross' came to include parts of Trafalgar Square, Northumberland Avenue, Northumberland Street, both sides of the Strand, Admiralty Arch, the upper section of Whitehall and Spring Gardens. The numbering of the buildings became so chaotic that the Post Office submitted an official complaint in 1929 after which the present system of house numbering was adopted.

The shops and banks that line the upper section of Whitehall are on the site of the original hamlet of Charing. The ground beyond them was monastic land till the Archbishop of York acquired it in 1245 and made it 'York Place', his official London residence. It remained York Place till the time of Cardinal Wolsey. When he became Archbishop in 1514, he extended York Place till it far outshone Henry VIII's Palace at Westminster.

Although Wolsey was the most powerful man in the country, he was unable to secure papal agreement to Henry's divorce from Catherine of Aragon and fell from power. His estates were confiscated and Henry, who had long coveted York Place, moved in only five days after Wolsey had left. Shakespeare tells us how the name was changed:

> You must no more call it York Place, that's past;
> For since the Cardinal fell, that title's lost
> 'Tis now the King's and called Whitehall.

It was in 1529 that Henry VIII came here with his Court, leaving the two Houses of Parliament behind at the Palace of Westminster, where they still sit. Since the Court in those days included the King's Ministers and Departments of State, they came to Whitehall as well.

When the Palace of Whitehall was burnt down in 1698 the Court moved again, but this time the Ministers and their officials stayed where they were. Whitehall has been synonymous with the Civil Service ever since. It is three hundred years since a king ruled from Whitehall but we shall see reminders of those times all the way along this walk.

Craig's Court

Craig's Court is a narrow alley twenty yards down the left-hand side of Whitehall. At the end of the alley is a quadrangle with a fine eighteenth-century building on the far side. This is Harrington House, built in 1702, a monument to the fire that destroyed the Palace of Whitehall four years before.

While the authorities were clearing the Whitehall Palace site, the Earl of Harrington bought this piece of ground and built the house. He did it as an investment for the future because he was confident that the Court would return to Whitehall. In those days, it was still the King who appointed ministers, bishops and all the other officials. By building a house next door to the Court, the Earl hoped to be in a good position to obtain lucrative appointments for himself and his family.

Unfortunately it did not work out the way he had hoped. The Court never came back, but the Earls of Harrington hung on. They did not move out till 1917, by which time this had become almost the last private dwelling in Whitehall.

The south side of the quadrangle is overlooked by the back of a large Victorian building. This was part of Old Scotland Yard, the original police headquarters. Because of its proximity, Craig's Court was for many years the home of private detectives in London. Officers retiring from the Force would set up here and rely on their friends around the corner to send them cases.

The most important feature of Craig's Court is the alley that runs down to Whitehall. Long thin granite slabs abut the kerbs on either side. They date from the days when the horse was the only means of transport around London and every cart and carriage had iron rims on its wheels. Tarmac was useless because the narrow iron rims cut it to pieces and strong stone like granite was needed to take the traffic.

These granite setts show how narrow the alley was and it was this narrowness that changed the appearance of London in the eighteenth century. In those days, London had no pavements. It is difficult to imagine today, but horses, coaches, carts and carriages were restricted only by the walls of the houses themselves. Pedestrians were at risk as soon as they stepped out of their front door. Some people put posts a few feet out into the road to create safer access to their house or shop; this is why some pubs still have names like the Blue Posts. With these exceptions, walking in London was a dangerous and messy business. 'To keep to the wall' was the aim of every pedestrian, away from the horse-dung and filth that covered the streets.

By 1762, Londoners had had enough. The Westminster Paving Bill was tabled in the House of Commons and received universal support, except for one vital point. It was agreed that the streets of London were a disgrace. It was also agreed that pavements should be built to protect pedestrians from wheeled traffic. What was not agreed was – who was to pay for it? One half of the House of Commons felt that householders should pay for their own pavements. The other half felt that it was too great a burden and that somebody else should foot the bill. They argued for weeks until Craig's Court settled the question.

One day the Speaker of the House of Commons, Mr Onslow, came to visit the Earl of Harrington. We don't know why he came but we do know that the alley was even narrower than it is now because the buildings came right up to the kerbstones we are looking at.

The Speaker's coach was one of the largest in London (it can still be seen in the Royal Mews). After Mr Onslow completed his business with Lord Harrington, he entered his coach, the horses pulled round and the coach became firmly wedged between the narrow walls of the alley. All efforts to move it forward or back proved fruitless. Eventually the furious Speaker had to be extricated through the roof. He went straight down to the Commons, resumed his chair in the Chamber and gave his casting vote in favour of the motion – that all householders in Westminster became responsible for providing pavements outside their dwellings. That is how London got its first pavements and the immediate results can be seen on the other side of Whitehall.

The Arrowheads

The pavement on the other side of Whitehall runs down from the bank on the corner past the Whitehall Theatre to the colonnaded screen of the Admiralty. The edge of the pavement is protected with granite kerbstones. At intervals of every fifteen yards, the kerbstones are marked with an arrowhead. There are seven along this stretch of pavement.

Map-readers will recognise the arrowhead as the sign of the Government survey, used to mark fixed points for map-making. This does not explain the arrowheads on the kerbstones whose origins go back to Queen Elizabeth I.

People who have served in the Armed Forces will remember that every piece of military equipment whether it be a rifle or a tea-spoon is marked with this arrowhead or 'pheon'. It has been marked with the arrowhead since the sixteenth century when England was fighting the Spanish. Like all the Tudor monarchs, Elizabeth kept a close eye on expenditure and became exasperated by the 'losses' of equipment in her army. She ordered her Master

General of Ordnance (still an appointment in the Army) to do something about it.

The officer concerned was Sir Henry Sidney who thought of the idea of putting a distinctive mark on every piece of equipment. He chose the pheon (arrowhead) from his family crest and the Armed Forces have used it ever since.

When the famous Paving Act of 1762 was passed, the Admiralty, like everybody else, had to provide a pavement outside their building. Since they were a Government department properly mindful of the need to save public money, they decided that if kerbstones were to be bought, they should be strong, long-lasting kerbstones. Since the strongest stone was reckoned to be Aberdeen granite, they sent someone off to Scotland to order it.

In the eighteenth century, ordering and delivering a load of cut stone from Scotland was a matter of months rather than weeks. To ensure that the stones that arrived down here in London were the same as those ordered in Aberdeen, the Government arrowhead was carved on them at the quarry. The stones are still here, a tribute to both the hard-wearing qualities of Aberdeen granite and the prudence of the Admiralty officials two hundred years ago.

The Board of Green Cloth

The administration of justice in mediaeval England was somewhat erratic. There were no policemen, few judges and law enforcement worked on the principle that might was right. A landowner with more men-at-arms than his neighbour tended to succeed in any legal dispute between them.

The maintenance of order around the Royal Household was a different matter and the Board of Green Cloth was created for the purpose in the fourteenth century. The Board, named after the covering of the table at which it sat, exercised jurisdiction over the area known as The Verge of the Court, i.e. the Royal Palace itself and the area around it. One of its responsibilities was the licensing of nearby taverns and theatres.

Although the Court left Whitehall after the fire of 1698, the Board of Green Cloth still exercises its authority within the area of the old Palace. The taverns and theatre in this part of Whitehall are still 'within the Verge of the Royal Palace' and attend the Board of Green Cloth every February to obtain renewal of their licences. The rule also applies to new businesses. Ten years ago a bookmaker applied for permission to open a betting-shop in Whitehall; he was startled to receive a summons to Buckingham Palace to prove he was a proper person to conduct a business within the historic precincts of a long-vanished Court.

The Admiralty

The Admiralty is a pleasant building set around a cobbled courtyard. It has an impressive row of columns supporting a heavy pediment. Designed by Thomas Ripley in 1726, it was the first office in London designed for a specific Government department. This is where the Lords of the Admiralty planned the campaigns that won the British Empire through the eighteenth and nineteenth centuries.

It comes as a surprise to learn that, for fifty years, the Admiralty was known as 'the shame of London'. It is a rare person who would pick up the mistake today but our ancestors knew more about Classical architecture than we do. Every London guide-book written before 1820 refers to this building as 'a disgrace to London' or 'a mockery of architecture'.

The guide-books knew what most of do not, that a classical column (Corinthian, Doric, Ionic etc) does not depend solely on the capital at the top. The correctness of style also depends on the ratio of height to width. The columns on the Admiralty frontage are Ionic which means they should be a good deal shorter.

When the Admiralty officials approved the plans for

the building, they did not realise that the choice of Ionic columns meant the pediment (the triangle over the columns) would be level with the top storey. As soon as they realised the pediment would block off all light from the rooms behind it, they instructed Ripley to make his columns taller. Ripley protested but the Admiralty officials were not going to pay good money for candles and oil to light a room just because of some fanciful architectural whim. The pillars were taken up to their present height and the whole of London laughed the Admiralty to scorn. As a guidebook of 1806 said:

> Never were such strange pillars seen. No building in London ever suffered from such a strange frontage as this.

The Admiralty could not knock down their new building, whatever anybody said about it, but they could do something.

The corner of Great Scotland Yard across the road is the best place to admire the attractive screen the Admiralty erected to hide their notorious pillars from public view. Designed by Robert Adam in 1761, it has two unusual features. The first is the hippogriffs, the fabulous animals on either side of the centre arch. They are horses with the head of a griffin and the wings of an eagle.

The other unusual feature is the ships carved at the ends of the screen. The one on the right is an excellent representation of a Roman galley. The ship on the left appears to be the same, until one notices the cannon projecting from the side. It is an optical illusion. The two carvings represent what were in 1761 the oldest and newest types of naval vessel, a Roman galley and a Royal Navy frigate. Their remarkable similarity is simply due to the angle at which the sculptor depicted them.

When the Admiralty was built in 1726, the authorities took full account of its special purpose. This was where naval strategy would be planned and, in the naval warfare of the eighteenth century, that depended on the wind. It was no good ordering fleets to the Mediterranean or sending frigates to blockade the French if the wind was in the wrong direction. That is why there is an ornate wind-compass on the wall of the Admiralty's great Board Room.

On the Admiralty roof, to the left of the triangular pediment, there is a small black square of metal moving slowly to and fro in the wind. It is the old Admiralty weathervane still sending its message down to the wind-compass in the Board Room below. It was this simple device that governed the planning and strategy of the Royal Navy for a hundred years, till steam drove the sailing ships from the seas.

Great Scotland Yard

Great Scotland Yard is the first of the three 'Scotland Yards' in London, a fact that often causes confusion amongst Sherlock Holmes enthusiasts. It takes its name from the Kings of Scotland who had their London embassy here from Saxon times. It was the largest of three streets on the site but Middle and Little Scotland Yards have long gone. As an embassy it counted as foreign territory and theoretically it still is. Although the kingdoms of England and Scotland were joined under James I, the diplomatic status of the embassy was never formally rescinded. A good lawyer could still make a case for Scots law to apply here.

This was the northern limit of the sprawling mass of buildings that made up the old Palace of Whitehall. After the palace was burnt down in 1698, some dwellings were erected here for Court officials while they assessed the damage and carried out surveys of the site.

Across the street is a pleasant little house, set back behind the Clarence Tavern. There has been much argument as to when it was built and who lived in it. There is a tradition that Christopher Wren, then the Surveyor of the King's Works, made it his official residence after the fire. Most historians pooh-pooh this belief, likening the story to the many old inns which claim that 'Queen Elizabeth slept here'. Perhaps they are right, but a few years ago a seventeenth-century water-tank with the initials CW emblazoned on it was taken out of the cellar. Oral tradition may not be infallible but it is foolish to ignore it.

Great Scotland Yard became famous in 1829 as the headquarters of the newly-formed Metropolitan Police. Their main office was on the left where the large Victorian building now stands. There were stables just beyond, a licensing office for the cabs and coaches that thronged the London streets and more offices on the right. The police moved out in 1892 but left behind a telling reminder of their time here.

The Clarence Tavern on the corner of Great Scotland Yard and Whitehall has a peculiar architectural feature. On the end wall is an enormous arch in the brickwork. It seems to have no purpose or practical function whatsoever. It is clearly not a doorway, it is far too big to be a window. It is a memorial to a bomb outrage of a hundred years ago.

Irish terrorism is not a modern phenomenon. In the 1880s the Fenians were planting bombs all over London; one of their biggest was here outside the police headquarters. In those days there was an archway over the Whitehall entrance connecting the Clarence to the building on the other side. The explosion caused such damage that the arch had to be taken down and that enormous curve on the wall shows where it used to be. The Clarence did quite well out of the affair. The landlord charged the sightseers threepence a head to view the havoc, did tremendous trade in the pub and more than recouped the cost of the damage.

Immediately beyond the large Victorian building on the left is another which has steel shutters covering its unprepossessing doorway. There are small round windows on the first storey; like the archway on the Clarence, they seem to fulfil no apparent architectural purpose.

This large block was built in Victorian times and land in London was expensive even then. If we remember that a couple of carriages and the horses to draw them occupied far more space than two motor cars would today, we have the clue to those small windows. Coaches and horses take up room, but horses can do one thing coaches cannot. Horses can walk upstairs and this is what happens here.

This is now a police stable used by the Mounted Branch. If you are here at the right time of day, you will see two mounted policemen come down the road and ring for the shutters to be raised. After they have gone inside, they dismount and lead their horses up the steep ramp to the first floor. It is a most unusual sight, to see horses slowly walking upstairs to their stables which are lit by those small windows above us.

We turn right here, under a large arch over the road. From a spot beneath the arch, it is possible to see the full height of the red-brick building beside the police station. On its roof is a single tall tower. It is an unusual structure, too small to fulfil any normal domestic purpose. It is too tall and thin to be an integral part of the building.

The clue lies in the large windows on the ground floor. They were built as doors when this was a Victorian fire station. Since the Victorians did not have radios or telephones, every fire station had a man on watch to raise the alarm. The tower was the lookout point when this would have been the tallest building in this part of London.

The War Office

The archway leads into Whitehall Place with the Old War Office across the road. It is a big, swaggering edifice built at the end of the Victorian era when Britannia ruled the waves and one sixth of the land as well. There are 2½ miles of corridors in the building with not a right angle amongst them. It looks like a square but it is a quadrilateral, built to fit within the angles of the streets around it.

Although the Victorians were quite happy to spend money on a building like this, they were equally conscious of the need to protect the public purse. The top right-hand corner is decorated with a pair of figures. On the opposite left-hand corner is another pair. They are the first of the many allegorical statues we will see on our walks and these are better than many. London is full of figures representing concepts like Mercy, Charity or Wisdom. Unfortunately it is often impossible to tell which Victorian semi-draped maiden is meant to represent what. With these at least it is possible to relate their form to their significance.

The figures up on the right are Truth and Justice; those on the left are Fame and Victory. Immediately around the corner to the left is War, one figure looking at a skull, the other wearing a helmet. At the far end from War is Peace, which comprises Sorrow (the widow and child) and Joy (the winged messenger). There are four figures on each wall producing a total of sixteen figures for the building.

This was where the Army Board showed their regard for the public purse. Perhaps like their Lordships of the Admiralty a hundred years before, they felt that artistic integrity could be carried too far. Whatever the reason, they came to the practical conclusion that they didn't really need sixteen figures. Since it was impossible to see more than three sets of figures at a time, why bother with the full set? They ordered four pairs of figures and told the sculptor to do two copies of each. Which is why, if one makes the effort to walk all the way around the War Office, each figure will be seen twice. The Army Board were right; nobody ever notices.

Whitehall Court

Our walk follows Whitehall Place down to the left and turns right at the first corner into Whitehall Court. Whitehall Court may not be great architecture but it certainly catches the eye. Built at the height of the Gothic revival, it is surmounted by a riot of pinnacles and spires.

Up to 1870 there was a muddy river-bank here. After the Embankment had pushed the river back, it was possible to build this tremendous edifice. The left-hand section is the National Liberal Club, built by Waterhouse in 1884 and opened by Mr Gladstone himself. By looking through the windows it is possible to see the famous glazed tiles that cover every wall. Perhaps it was the tiles that misled Lord Birkenhead who, though never a member, came here to use the lavatories. When challenged he expressed great surprise that it was a club and not a public convenience.

The roof-line consists of an impressive array of towers and turrets. They are picturesque although one must feel sorry for the servants who had to live in them. The tower in the middle is worth a second glance because this is where our official spy organisation started. Admiral Mansfield Cummings, the original 'C', made this the first MI6 office back in 1907.

The St Margaret's Boundary Mark

At the far end of Whitehall Court, twenty yards short of the last building, is a small blue metal plaque set against the left-hand wall three feet above the ground. The plaque is a parish boundary mark, the first of several we shall see on these walks. It goes back to the earliest form of local government in London.

Till the Reformation in 1532, the church provided schools and hospitals, repaired the roads and supplied food and shelter for the poor. With the closure of the monasteries, this burden fell on the parishes. Each elected its own councillors to the Vestry (so-called because they met in the church vestry). They raised the parish tax (the

'Parish Rate') on every householder and struggled with all those difficulties of administration they could not persuade somebody else to look after. They exercised their authority for a surprisingly long time. The London County Council was not created till 1889 and the parishes kept some of their powers till well into this century.

The result was that, for nearly four hundred years, it was in everybody's interests to know which parish they lived in. In rural areas it was easy but as London became more crowded, marker plaques like this were needed. It was important that the plaques were put in exactly the right place because it meant money. Some parishes were wealthy through bequests or legacies and therefore placed little burden on their parishioners. Other parishes, not so lucky with their endowments, had to levy a heavy rate.

This mark displays a portcullis and the letters 'SMW'. It is the boundary mark of St Margaret's Westminster, the parish church beside the Abbey. There are two reasons why it is here. When Henry VIII confiscated the Palace from Cardinal Wolsey, he built two great gates across the road through Whitehall and laid out the palace garden between them. But he omitted to take into account the strong sense of tradition of his subjects.

The parish church and parish burial ground for this part of London was at St Margaret's. There was a small chapel, St Martin-in-the-Fields, by Charing Cross but this had no graveyard. As the population around Charing Cross grew, Henry found that more and more funeral processions were coming down Whitehall, through the palace gates and across his new Privy Garden.

Funeral processions were not a feature that anybody wanted to see walking regularly across his garden, especially when London was undergoing one of its periodic plagues. Henry saw no reason to move from his new palace but even he could not stop people burying their dead in their parish burial ground. A masterly solution was found – a new parish church. St Martin-in-the-

Fields was upgraded to become the parish church for those who lived north of the gate, while St Margaret's continued to look after those to the south. Since the new parish had to be able to levy parish rates, a boundary was necessary and this plaque marks it.

Although the parishes had lost much of their authority by the time Whitehall Court was erected, there was another reason for making sure the old boundary was maintained. There had been a landing stage here until the Embankment was built. Little is known of it but tradition says that the parish either owned it or took a percentage of the landing fees. One way or the other, it was a valuable asset to St Margaret's Vestry and we can be sure that when this building was erected, the Vestry would be extremely anxious to show exactly where their jetty had been. It was quite possible that the Embankment might be washed away one day so, just in case, they made sure their marker was put back here.

The Eccentric Earl

Great Scotland Yard behind us has a theoretical claim to be considered Scottish territory. The corner of Horse Guards Avenue just past the St Margaret's boundary mark is literally Scottish territory; we are walking on Scottish soil (though it is covered by English tarmac).

In 1760 this site was bought by the Earl of Fife for his London house. The Jacobite Rising had taken place only fifteen years before. As a result of the repressive measures taken after Culloden, the Earl had developed a deep hatred of England and the English. For some reason he had to come to London but resolved not to tread on English soil unless he had to. He ordered a shipload of soil and gravel to be sent to London, covered this area with it and had a house built on top. When it was completed he came down by sea, landed at the jetty here and conducted all his business from this spot – on Scottish soil.

The Centre of Whitehall

This corner is the centre of Whitehall. Around us are buildings from four centuries. The Victorian grandeur of the War Office is on the right; across the road is the Horse Guards building of 1760, looking like a drawing from a child's picture-book. On the far left is the seventeenth-century Banqueting Hall and immediately beside us on this corner is the Ministry of Defence, very clearly of this century.

The Defence Ministry building has little to be said for it, although it is the only Government office with its own chapel. Its construction began in the 1930s but it was not completed till after the war. The large figures over the entrance are known to those who work here as 'The Two Fat Ladies'.

The original intention was to have four figures, two at this north entrance and two at the other end, representing the four Elements – Earth, Air, Fire and Water. Only these two figures, Earth and Water, were completed and there has been much discussion over the years as to which is which. Nobody seems to know and rumour has it that even the sculptor, Sir Charles Wheeler, admitted he had forgotten. Perhaps they are destined to become one of London's mysteries.

The Defence Ministry is difficult to enter but, by written application, it is possible to see the old Whitehall Palace wine cellar which lies forty feet below us. The Victorians called it 'Oliver Cromwell's cellar', but it is now 'The Henry VIII Wine Cellar' – another misnomer which the author tried to get rectified when he worked here. Wolsey built Whitehall Palace; all Henry VIII did was to confiscate it, but it would be wrong to call it the 'Wolsey Wine Cellar' either.

The cellar was built back in the fourteenth century, a hundred years before Wolsey was born. He used its thick wall to support the arches of his extension of the cellar. Henry VIII's men-at-arms drank here as did Elizabeth's sailors, and the Ministry staff still use it for parties. It is a nice thought that the soldiers and sailors of Queen Elizabeth II still take beer in the cellar where their predecessors did four hundred years ago.

The Horse Guards

We cross Whitehall to visit the Horse Guards, passing the statue of the Duke of Devonshire in the middle of the road. It is one of London's minor ironies that the centre of Whitehall is occupied by a statue to the only man who turned down the job of Prime Minister not once, but three times.

Every day crowds gather at the Horse Guards to watch the Life Guards (in red) or the Blues and Royals (in blue) make picture-books come to life. They are archaic but they are splendid. They are Whitehall's biggest tourist attraction but few tourists ask the question – why are they here?

The official answer is that this building was for a hundred years the office of the Commander-in-Chief. Like so much in London, the real reason goes back long before that. Although the Tudors and Stuarts had no standing army (shortage of money made sure of that), they lived in turbulent times. Every royal palace had its guards and sentries and they needed somewhere to sleep. We know that Henry VIII had a jousting-ground here and that a guard-room was built on it in 1649. When Charles II came back to Whitehall to become King in 1660, he put two troops of mounted guards here. They have been here ever since. The Palace of Whitehall that they guarded has gone, the Commander-in-Chief left here long ago but this is still a military establishment.

The Horse Guards was built in 1750. It was criticised at the time, probably because it bore such a close resemblance to the previous guardhouse that Charles II knew. Above it is the clock which was for fifty years the most accurate in London. It is still maintained by the firm which made it two hundred years ago.

We walk across the courtyard and under the archway

which is open to pedestrians but closed to vehicles. Only those fortunate enough to possess the 'Ivory Pass' can drive through and it is a privilege given to very few. Even Pitt, at the height of his power during the Napoleonic Wars, was unable to grant the favour to one of his supporters. He compromised by giving him a peerage instead.

In the middle of the ceiling in the archway is another demonstration of the importance of parish boundary marks. A black line separates the parishes of St Martin-in-the-Fields from St Margaret's Westminster. Even the Commander-in-Chief had to pay his parish rate. It was well worth his while to show that although half his headquarters lay in the 'new' (and therefore poorer) parish of St Martin's, the other half lay within the old, well-endowed (and therefore less heavily rated) parish of St Margaret's.

The Horse Guards Parade is where Henry VIII reviewed his army in 1535 and the ceremony of Trooping the Colour is still held every year on the Sovereign's birthday. Down in the left corner of the parade-ground is a small dark doorway. It is barred now but used to be a useful short cut through to Downing Street.

This is the Treasury Passage, running under the old Treasury the Tudors brought to Whitehall. The far end comes out alongside Henry VIII's Royal Tennis Court in Downing Street. Pepys knew the Passage well and there is some evidence that Shakespeare used it too. It is the setting for one of Whitehall's best stories.

The walls are coloured white to lighten the dark passage. It is not known when they were first painted but they were certainly done in 1898. Because so many eminent gentlemen used the passage to Downing Street and the Treasury, a sentry was put here to warn people of the wet paint. His cry of 'Keep to the left, gentlemen, keep to the left' became famous but the reason was soon forgotten. He remained on duty till 1914 when someone in authority realised the paint had had sixteen years in which to dry.

We retrace our steps to the Horse Guards archway. On the right is an enormous mortar known as the Cadiz Memorial. It was sent here by the Spanish in gratitude for Wellington's victory over the French at Salamanca in 1812. Its installation here gave rise to many bawdy jokes. The Prince Regent and his mistresses were the subject of constant caricature and the arrival of the mortar on the Parade sparked off a series of obscene cartoons of which the mildest showed crowds admiring 'The Prince's great thing in the Park'.

Just beyond the Horse Guards arch is another large cannon, called the 'Turkish gun'. Made in 1524, it was captured during the Egyptian campaign against Napoleon and installed here in 1801. It is a splendid piece of artillery but achieved notoriety when it nearly became the largest assassination weapon in the world.

A couple of years after the gun had been placed here, a man with the appropriate name of Captain Despard formed a conspiracy to assassinate the King while he was reviewing troops on Horse Guards Parade. The cannon, loaded to its full capacity with grape-shot, was to let fly at the Royal coach as it trundled across the parade ground. The conspiracy was discovered in time, which was just as well because a gun this size loaded with grape would have blown the coach into a thousand pieces.

Two lamp-posts stand beside the Horse Guards archway. Because this is Crown property they are painted black and they bear the cypher GIVR (George IV). They were erected in 1822, just a few years after the first demonstration of gas lighting in London. They are not particularly beautiful but they deserve our attention because they are the oldest working gas lamps in the world.

The great doors have hung in the archway for centuries. Just behind them is one of London's more unusual architectural features. Beside the hinge of the gate, closing the angle in the stonework, is a spiked iron bar about three feet from the ground. There are others in the angles and corners of the courtyard on the way back to Whitehall. They are to be found all over London on old buildings. They date from the days when there were no public lavatories in London and protected the angles of walls more effectively than the notices still sometimes seen: 'Commit No Nuisance'.

The Banqueting Hall

We leave the Horse Guards and turn right towards Westminster. Across the road is the pride of Whitehall, the Banqueting Hall, the only complete structure left to us from the old Palace.

In 1600 at the end of Elizabeth's reign, the Palace of Whitehall consisted of a jumble of two- or three-storeyed thatched wooden buildings spread over a quarter of a mile, interspersed with an occasional larger hall of brick or stone. Twenty years later, when James I had his court here, he decided to build a new palace to equal that of the French king at Versailles and commissioned Inigo Jones to design it for him.

Jones designed an incredible range of buildings that would have covered nearly a square mile, but shortage of money (always a problem with the Stuart kings) meant that only the Banqueting Hall was completed. It was a turning-point in English architecture. The perfect proportions, the high, symmetrical windows and the tall pilasters set between them are very familiar. There are buildings like this all over England: banks, Town Halls, stately homes, elegant houses in cathedral cities. They are all copies or derivatives of the Banqueting Hall, the first building in England in the Palladian style. It is also the first in the country designed as a double cube; the length is twice the height and width (110ft long x 55ft high x 55ft wide).

Inigo Jones introduced a third innovation with his stonework, the Portland stone facing that we see all over London today. It was first used here because it was Inigo

Jones who recognised the characteristic that makes it ideal for London. Portland stone washes itself, or rather, has the property of being cleansed by rain. This is why it is so white on the open areas but black under the window sills and in protected corners.

The Banqueting Hall became the glory of the Palace spread around it. When the Tudor and Stuart kings had gone and fire burnt the Palace to the ground in 1698, the Hall escaped to remind us of two events that changed the history of England. Built by the first Stuart king (James I 1603–1625), it also saw the execution of his son (Charles I) in 1649, whose statue stands at the top of Whitehall.

For a couple of hundred years there has been argument over the precise location of the scaffold on which Charles lost his head. Disraeli declared that it was a topic of conversation always to be avoided since it was both boring and pointless. Maybe he was right, but in the last century they tried to settle it by putting a plaque under the centre window to mark the spot.

A few years ago, the plaque came down because the historians changed their minds. It is now believed that the execution took place in front of the doorway at the left-hand end of the building. The author agrees because he has seen further evidence to support the theory.

The stonework above the doorway is a different colour from the main Hall. This short section used to be a connecting corridor from the older Tudor buildings and, although it has been faced with Portland stone, the facing has never been satisfactory. It has had to be renewed twice in the last thirty years and each occasion revealed a Tudor wall with a doorway visible in the middle. The wooden framework is still there and shows signs that it was fitted in a hurry. This is where the scaffold stood on which Charles met his death.

The Hall is open to the public and is well worth a visit. The painted ceiling by Rubens is the finest in the country and Charles gave him £3000 and a gold chain for it. It is Whitehall's bitterest irony that the last thing Charles saw before his death was the superb painting he had commissioned to commemorate the death of his own father.

On the left-hand end of the roof is the second memento the Hall has for us. At the Admiralty, we saw a weathervane that helped to win an empire. Here we see one that lost a kingdom. That fine gilt weathervane was put up by James II. He was the last Stuart king, a Roman Catholic who had antagonized the whole country with his attempts to restore the old religion. By 1688 things had reached such a state that Parliament asked William of Orange to come over to take the throne.

James knew that William's army could not sail until the wind blew from the east so he set up this weathervane to give himself warning.

For three months the wind blew steadily from the west and James was safe. One night the vane swung round to show what Londoners called for a hundred years 'the Dutchman's wind' and James and his family left Whitehall for ever.

The Privy Garden

Beside the Banqueting Hall is the Royal United Services Institution with the third Whitehall weathervane above it. Like the Admiralty vane, it commemorates the winning of an empire. It shows an Indian sepoy firing a cannon and marks the battles that brought India under British rule.

The next building is Gwydyr House. It is a Government office now but worth a glance because of the fine lamp-holder in front of it. The twentieth century is the age of electricity, the nineteenth century was the age of gas but Gwydyr House (1772) goes back to the days of candles, oil-soaked rags and torches.

When a reception was to be held in the house, a footman came out and clambered up a ladder to ignite a basket filled with rags soaked in oil. This illuminated the doorway for the guests who arrived by sedan chair, escorted by link-boys. Link-boys were street urchins who walked in front of the chair, lighting the way with a burning brand. When they reached their destination, the brand was extinguished in one of the link-snuffers beside the fire-basket. There are still link-men in London though their duties have changed. Covent Garden Opera House uses the term for the attendants and doorkeepers who escort patrons to their cars.

There is a statue of Sir Walter Raleigh on the stretch of grass beside Gwydyr House. He was a courtier, soldier, explorer and writer who became a favourite of Elizabeth I. The statue is modern but the site is an appropriate choice. The patch of grass is where the Privy Garden of the old Palace used to be; by a happy coincidence it was in the Privy Garden that Raleigh was first presented to Elizabeth.

Set against the wall of the Defence Building, behind Raleigh, is a statue to Field Marshal Montgomery. Opinions vary on its merits but it does have one unusual distinction. Instead of the full name and title seen on most statues, this has the single bold nickname – MONTY.

A semi-circular portico spans the pavement on the right. It belongs to Dover House built in 1758 by James Paine. It was the home of the Duke of York of nursery rhyme fame and of Lord Melbourne, Victoria's first Prime Minister. It is now the London home of the Scottish Office.

Fine staircases built into a great house to show off the owner's wealth and position are common. What is uncommon is to see a house built to show off a staircase, which is what happened at Dover House. When the Duke of York came here in 1797, the building was very different. The main house was set back from the road with a wing down either side of a central courtyard, rather as the Admiralty does today.

The Duke called in Henry Holland to improve the building and Holland, in Pevsner's words 'contributed the most elegant piece of architecture to the whole of

Whitehall'. What he did was to fill the entire courtyard with a great staircase and build the new Dover House around it. In a palace in Florence there is a staircase by Michelangelo built to such perfect proportions that, from a distance, it is impossible to tell whether it is five or twenty-five feet high.

The same effect can be seen through the glass doors of Dover House. The magnificent staircase fills the entire hallway. The only clue to its height is the piece of furniture on the upper landing. Perhaps the optical illusion stems from the curve of the steps or the proportions of the hallway. Whatever the reason, it is a superb piece of architecture and provides the setting for the second Dover House story.

The bicentenary of Byron's birth was celebrated while this book was being written. Everybody remembers his stormy love affair with Lady Caroline Lamb; many will remember the film made a few years ago about the unhappy pair. One of the scenes in the film showed Lady Caroline, distraught with passion, rejecting her husband's pleas and running down the great staircase to join Byron. The scene was not imaginary. It is exactly what happened and this is the great staircase down which she fled.

Downing Street

Downing Street is Whitehall's best-known offshoot. The threat of terrorism has closed it to the public but some of its features can be seen from the entrance. There is an opening twenty yards along to the right. If the Prime Minister is away and the street is open, the pathway repays a visit. It leads down to a piece of Tudor London; a quadrangle formed from the back wall and viewing galleries of Henry VIII's tennis court with the corridors of Elizabeth's Treasury behind them.

Historically, Downing Street is the most appropriate address for the Prime Minister's residence. Robert Walpole (1676–1745), the first Prime Minister in the sense we use the term today, was the first to move into No. 10.

The point of the story is that, until twenty years ago, the term Prime Minister was an unofficial term. The proper title for the incumbent was First Lord of the Treasury. Since the Treasury, the senior Department of State, is the large building on the corner of Downing Street, it is correct to say that the Prime Minister lives over the shop.

The name Downing Street is also considered appropriate by those with low opinions of politicians. It is named after George Downing whom Pepys described as the greatest rogue in Christendom. Educated at Dublin and at Harvard (he was the second Harvard graduate), Downing was employed by Cromwell during the Protectorate to spy on Charles II on the continent. He became a double agent, persuading Charles to employ him to spy on Cromwell.

At the Restoration of 1660, he made sure he came out on the right side and was rewarded with a knighthood and this piece of land. He proceeded to erect houses on the site and, typically, built them very badly. The interiors have had to be completely rebuilt twice since his time.

One needs good eyesight to appreciate Downing Street's next unusual feature. The junctions at the top of the drainpipes where they meet the guttering are shaped into square rainheads. It is the pleasant custom, when these have to be replaced, to emboss them with the initials of the current incumbent. That is why the rainheads at the corner of No. 10 have the initials 'HM' on one and 'DM' on the other, showing the work was done during the tenure of Harold and Dorothy Macmillan.

The initials over the end house, No. 12, are 'CH'. No. 12 is the office of the Government Chief Whip and the initials are those of Charles Harris. He came to the Chief Whip's office early in this century as a very temporary private secretary. He became so good at his job that both political parties agreed he should retain the post, no matter which party was in power. He stayed at No. 12

for more than forty years. His initials were placed on the rainhead at his retirement when he had become the longest serving official in Downing Street's history.

When the Foreign Office was built on the left side of Downing Street, a set of statues was placed on its walls including a copy of a Roman figure called the Headless Boy. After the last war repairs were carried out to restore the bomb damage the building had suffered. The repairs were done very well; too well in one case. When the official surveyor came round to check, he found that someone had put a head on the Headless Boy. The problem is that it seems to have been left there, because the author has been unable to identify it.

The Foreign Office runs down Whitehall towards the Cenotaph. It is a pleasant building but was once the centre of a tremendous architectural battle. When the decision was taken to rebuild it in the 1860s the authorities were greatly exercised whether it should be in the Gothic style, recently revived by the building of the Houses of Parliament, or in the plainer Classical-Italianate style.

The Prime Minister, Palmerston, was a confirmed classical enthusiast. When Sir George Gilbert Scott produced a design for an ornate Gothic building, Palmerston rejected it out of hand. Barry went away and produced a 'modified' Italo-Byzantine design which Palmerston promptly rejected again with the comment that it was 'a regular mongrel affair'. This time Scott realised that Palmerston meant exactly what he said; he immersed himself in books on the Italian style for three months and produced the Foreign Office we see today.

Scott's original Gothic design was not wasted. He used it to build St Pancras Station, described by Piper as 'a pinnacled castle in a Grimm's fairy story'. We should be grateful to Palmerston for sticking to his guns; St Pancras and the Houses of Parliament together would have been far too rich a mixture.

The Cenotaph

The Cenotaph is the name most people give to the impressive block of stone in the middle of the road. It is another of London's misnomers because the Cenotaph (Greek for 'empty tomb') is the flat altar-slab on the top. The obelisk is simply a plinth to support it.

It is an unusual structure; contrary to appearances there is not a single straight line on it. All the vertical planes are curved imperceptibly outwards because it is built on the principle of *entasis*. It was the Greeks who discovered that if a column is built with vertical lines, it will give the appearance of narrowing in the middle. The compensation of a curve outwards makes it look straight. That is why there are no straight lines anywhere on the Parthenon; even the floor surface is curved upwards to allow for the illusion.

The second feature on the Cenotaph that is often missed is that, though it is a war memorial, there is no religious symbol to be seen on it. The reason is that it was built as a memorial to the dead of the British Empire which included many creeds other than Christianity.

The most unusual thing about it is why it is here at all. There are many sites in London more suitable; in front of Westminster Abbey or St Paul's would seem far more appropriate. Like many of the landmarks we shall see around London, it came here by accident.

After the First World War was over, preparations were made for a Victory Parade through London. It was to be a tremendous affair with soldiers, sailors and airmen from all over the Empire as well as contingents from America, France, Belgium and all the other Allied nations. Someone suggested erecting a temporary monument on the route to commemorate those who died and the Prime Minister, Lloyd George, approved the idea.

The architect Edwin Lutyens was given ten days to design and erect a temporary catafalque. Made of wood, canvas and plaster, it was completed the night before the ceremony. To everybody's surprise, it became the focus of the Parade. Every contingent saluted it as they went by as did every spectator. It was a great success and Lloyd George was no fool. It was promptly announced that the trial Cenotaph had been the success the Government had hoped and it was to be built in a permanent form immediately.

John Burns

We cross the road to the other side of Whitehall where the numbering of the houses becomes somewhat confused. No. 85 stands next to No. 54 because Whitehall becomes Parliament Street at this point. The Red Lion pub on the corner of Derby Gate looks across to the archway over King Charles Street, which was erected in 1907, the year after the great Liberal election landslide.

The Liberals came to power because many Conservatives had joined them over the question of Free Trade, as had the handful of Labour Members of Parliament. One of the Labour members was John Burns, who had been a fiery politician in his youth, taken part in the great demonstrations of the 1880s and had become known as 'The Man With The Red Flag'. Burns entered Parliament in 1892 and earned respect for his honesty and integrity. The Liberal administration of 1906 invited him to join the Cabinet, an offer he accepted after some hesitation. He was made Minister for Local Government with his offices in the building across the road.

When the plans for the archway were drawn up the following year, someone had an idea. The figures over the archway represent classical gods and goddesses who, when one thinks about it, did little except eat, drink nectar and argue with each other. The bearded figure in the top right-hand corner is Vulcan the smith-god, the only one who worked with his hands. Since John Burns, whose office was next door, was the first working man to join the 'gods' of the Cabinet, they used his face and figure to portray Vulcan. It is an accurate likeness; an unusual tribute to an unusual man.

Charles Dickens and the Red Lion

A chapter in Dickens' *David Copperfield* describes the twelve-year-old hero's miserable existence working in a bottling factory. It is a direct memory of Dickens' own unhappy childhood when he was alone in London. In a pathetic scene he recounts David celebrating his twelfth birthday by coming to an inn in Whitehall and asking for a glass of their best ale. The landlady came to the counter to query the order, heard the reason for it and gave him his glass of beer free with a motherly kiss for his birthday.

That is exactly what had happened to Dickens at the Red Lion on his own twelfth birthday. Dickens never forgot their kindness to a little boy and the Red Lion has not forgotten him either. The pub has been rebuilt, but above the second window is a bust of Dickens looking down.

Scotland Yard

The last Whitehall story concerns Scotland Yard, just around the corner in Derby Gate. The complex of red-brick buildings is called the Norman Shaw Building nowadays but for millions of people it will always be the 'real' Scotland Yard. The police came here in 1892 and left in 1967. Their stay coincided with the golden age of detective stories; this is the Scotland Yard of John Appleby, Roderick Alleyn and George Gideon and all the other heroes whose exploits thrilled us for fifty years.

The police have gone but they left behind our last story. The building on the right, just inside the gate, used to be Cannon Row Police Station (the barred windows of the cells can be seen down to the right). The main section of Scotland Yard is of bright red brick but this building is black granite. The irony is that it is Dartmoor granite, quarried by the convicts to make this building for the men who caught them. It is Whitehall's last joke.

SECOND ♦ WALK

From Trafalgar Square to the Embankment and Westminster Bridge

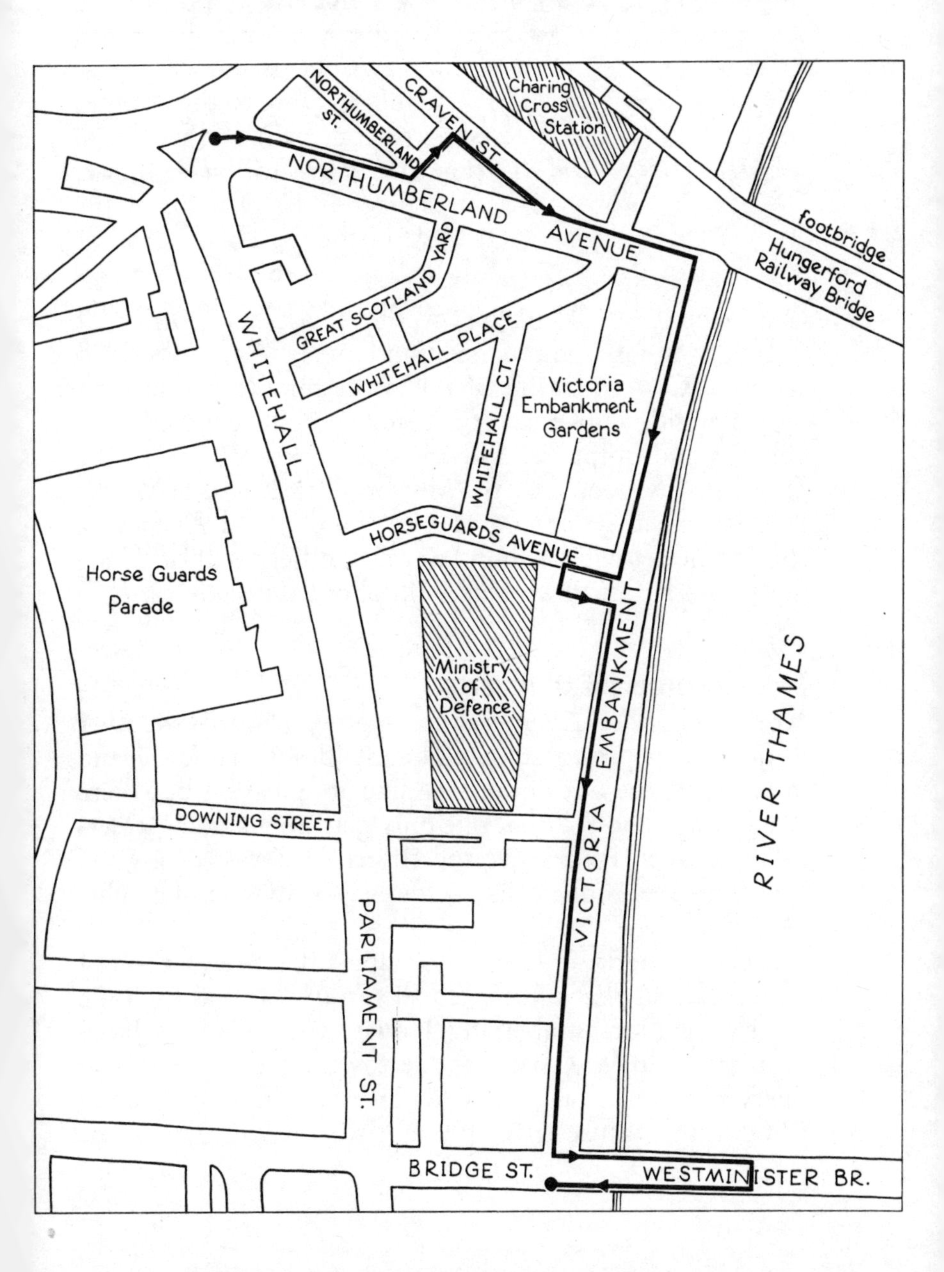

SECOND ♦ WALK

From Trafalgar Square to the Embankment and Westminster Bridge

Our Second Walk begins at the south-east corner of Trafalgar Square, where the Strand joins Northumberland Avenue. On the traffic island in the middle of the road is a splendid lamp-post. It is black and gilt, covered with cherubs and dolphins, and has the marks 'VR' and 'AD 1878'. It was erected by the Metropolitan Board of Works to celebrate the opening of Northumberland Avenue; a similar model will be found at the southern end of Charing Cross Road which was built about the same time.

Northumberland Avenue

Northumberland Avenue running down towards the river is not an inspiring street. The buildings are large and impressive, the trees on either side are pleasant but there is a dullness about it that one only gets in 'planned' streets like this one. To achieve the cheerful interest of a good London street, one needs a difference in styles and heights of buildings.

Northumberland Avenue occupies the site of the last of the palaces that once lined the Strand. It was till 1876 the site of Northumberland House, a tremendous Jacobean (1603) palace that was the town house of the great Percy family. It was so large and fortress-like that visitors to London confused it with the prisons at Newgate or the

Marshalsea, which did not amuse one of its eighteenth-century owners, the famous 'proud Duke' of Somerset.

The Duke had strong views on the respect that should be paid to him, especially from his own family. He inherited Northumberland House from his first wife and married again but soon had to remind his new wife of her position. At a reception the new Duchess was unwise enough to seek to attract his attention by touching him on the arm. He turned on her instantly: 'Madam, my first wife was a Percy, and she would never have taken such a liberty.'

His daughters were never allowed to sit in his presence and he maintained this regime till his last illness. Waking one night, he discovered that one of his daughters, overcome by exhaustion after nursing him constantly for weeks, had fallen into a doze on a chair beside his bed. The Duke was so outraged by this affront that he rallied just long enough to alter his will and reduce her inheritance by £20,000.

In 1874 the authorities bought the Northumberland House site, which stretched down to the river. It cost them £500,000 but it is the only recorded occasion when a new street in London made a profit. The sites down either side were immediately bought by entrepreneurs who wanted to build hotels and wanted to build them fast. The railway hotels catering to the thousands now able to visit London had set a fashion and land for new hotels was at a premium. The Grand Hotel occupied the left-hand corner and the large building on the right, now called Northumberland House, used to be the Victoria Hotel.

Although the Savoy was the first to introduce Parisian luxury to London's great hotels, the Victoria played its part in revolutionising English social manners. In the nineteenth century respectable families did not stay in hotels; they took 'a house in Town' for the Season and did their entertaining there. Hotels like the Victoria changed all that. If you wanted to entertain in the grand manner, it was far easier and cheaper to let a hotel do it for you.

In the 1880s the Prince of Wales set the seal of Royal approval on the idea by accepting an invitation from Mrs Lily Langtry ('the Jersey Lily') to dine at the Victoria. It was the first time that Royalty had entered a hotel publicly and it was a shock to London Society (Queen Mary did not enter a hotel officially till 1923). The Victoria was tremendously proud of the event. Although it has not been a hotel for fifty years, the façade still shows the entrance to the Edward VII Rooms.

The new building on the left covers the site of the Constitutional Club, which numbered P. G. Wodehouse amongst its members. He made it Lord Emsworth's London club and introduced it in his novels under the name 'The Senior Conservative'. At the end of the new block Northumberland Street comes in from the left with the Sherlock Holmes pub on the corner.

The Sherlock Holmes was the first of London's 'theme' pubs. The etched windows show scenes from Conan Doyle's novels and the bar has Holmes miscellanea around the walls. There is a superb reproduction of the sitting room of 221B Baker Street at the top of the stairs.

The sitting room, originally created for the Festival of Britain Exhibition of 1951 on the South Bank, was brought here when the Exhibition was over. It was an excellent choice because the previous name of this pub was the Northumberland Hotel; every Sherlock Holmes enthusiast remembers that was the address Conan Doyle gave the unfortunate Mr Baskerville in *The Hound of the Baskervilles*.

Between the Sherlock Holmes and the bank to the right is a little alley. A few yards along it is an extraordinary doorway, Moorish in design, made of bright yellow and green tiles. At one time the whole building looked like this, the doorway is the last trace of the Turkish baths that used to occupy the site. There were dozens all over

London in the last century, but they have now been replaced by saunas, which share the same slightly immoral connotations that Turkish baths used to have. Conan Doyle used these baths often (his club was just around the corner in Whitehall Court) and they appear in the Sherlock Holmes saga.

Craven Street

The alley leads into Craven Street, a London backwater where one can step back in time with hardly any effort. The eastern side is a uniform line of late eighteenth-century buildings, each with a delicate iron balcony. The balconies do not look too stable today but they were an innovation when these houses were built. Craven Street has several claims to fame. The first is a few yards up to the left, at No. 39. Dickens made it the home of Mr Brownlow in 'Oliver Twist', where Brownlow secured the confession by Monks that cleared Oliver's name.

At No. 36 is a plaque recording Benjamin Franklin's stay in the middle of the eighteenth century. Franklin spent much of his life in London and was involved in almost every controversy of the time. We will look at some of them later on when we visit Fleet Street and the Royal Parks.

No. 36's other claim to fame is that it was once the office of the Society for the Relief of Persons Imprisoned for Small Debts. This very worthy organisation was founded by the well-known London clergyman Dr William Dodd. Unfortunately, although the reverend doctor was a brilliant preacher admired by such luminaries as Johnson and Garrick, he was not so clever in organising his own financial affairs. The Society suffered a severe setback when Dodd tried to relieve his own very sizeable debts by forging a cheque for £4000, for which he was hanged at Tyburn in 1777.

The eighteenth century is still a strong influence in Craven Street. At No. 34 Mr Kakouli still makes uniforms for Sheriffs, whose ceremonial dress of tail-coat and steel buttons are exactly what Franklin and Dodd wore two hundred years ago. At No. 32 is a plaque recording Heinrich Heine's only visit to England in 1827. That was the year he created the Lorelei legend, with the poem about the siren who lured ships on to the rocks of the Rhine by her singing.

Craven Passage leads down to the railway arches, made famous by Flanagan and Allen in their song 'Underneath the Arches'. The pub in the alley has been here for nearly three hundred years. Its name, the Ship and Shovel, goes back to the time before the Embankment was built when the river-bank lay only a few yards away. This is where the barges came to unload coal and gravel. On the side of the pub furthest from us is a small round window to enable the dockers to see when the tide turned to bring their next cargo upstream.

No. 27 Craven Street was the home of James Smith, joint author with his brother Horace of *The Rejected Addresses*. When the Theatre Royal at Drury Lane was being rebuilt in 1812, the management announced a competition for the address to be given at the grand opening. The whole of London talked of the competition and the whole of London knew, or thought they knew, which famous poets and authors had put in entries. *The Rejected Addresses* was the Smith brothers' version of the unsuccessful submissions. Horace Smith wrote brilliant parodies in the style of Thomas Moore, Walter Scott and Bowles; James produced imitations of Wordsworth, Southey, Coleridge, Cobbett and Byron. *The Rejected Addresses* went through seven editions in three months and became one of the most famous parodies of the nineteenth century.

At that time Craven Street was well-known for the number of solicitors who had their offices there as well as for the coal jetty at the bottom. A friend of James Smith's once tried to score off him by describing his residence thus:

In Craven Street, Strand, the attorneys find place,
And ten dark coal barges are moored at its base;
Fly, honesty, fly! Seek some safer retreat,
There's craft in the river and craft in the street.

Smith replied immediately:

Why should Honesty fly to some safer retreat?
The lawyers are just at the top of the street,
And the barges are just at the bottom.

There are still solicitors at Smith's old house although Craven Street has not seen a coal barge for a hundred years.

The next house, No. 26, still possesses one of the original door knockers in the shape of a lion's head that were once a feature of the street. It was a Craven Street doorknocker that Dickens used in *A Christmas Carol.* He made it turn into Marley's ghost, the first warning to Scrooge to mend his ways. Dickens knew Craven Street well from his unhappy period in the blacking factory just through the arches behind us.

The Playhouse Theatre at the bottom of Craven Street is not one of London's most famous theatres but it has an unusual history. It is another of London's 'mistakes'; it should not be here at all.

In the 1880s an enterprising gentleman named Mr Sefton Parry looked at this empty site and at the railway line and railway bridge that ran above it and made some discreet inquiries. He found, as he had suspected, that the railway had plans to increase the number of station platforms, which meant they would need extra ground. He also calculated that the railway would have to pay far more for the site if a business was already operating there. He bought the ground and built a theatre on it.

The first part of his plan worked perfectly. The theatre was built in 1882, the railway made their offer soon afterwards and Mr Parry rejected it as insufficient. Unfortunately for him, the railway decided that its engineers had sufficient skill to build the new platforms on the existing supports. Rather than pay the sum Mr Parry wanted, they went ahead and built over the top of the theatre.

Mr Parry found himself the owner of a theatre he didn't want, which the railway didn't want and which, for a few years, nobody else seemed to want either. He made the best of things and started a new career as a theatrical producer. That should have been the end of the story, but in 1905, the theatre achieved fame when it fulfilled all too literally the expression 'to bring the house down'. Unfortunately this was achieved not by the enthusiasm of the audience, but through a mistake of the railway authorities.

A careless workman employed on repairing the platform above the theatre cut through one of the main crosspieces. A quarter of Charing Cross Station came through the roof, destroying the theatre and killing five people in the process. Whether Mr Parry was still around to collect the compensation is not known, but the theatre was rebuilt and went on to become the favourite of Gladys Cooper who was manager here for nearly twenty years.

The Embankment

The theatre stands on the Embankment, the greatest feat of civil engineering in London's history. It is often difficult to visualise a city before a new road was built but there are hundreds of pictures showing what this part of London looked like in the early nineteenth century. This area was covered with wide mudbanks stretching up to the bottom of Craven Street behind us. Small wooden jetties extended over boggy marshes, covered twice a day by the incoming tide. Christopher Wren had proposed an Embankment in 1670 and a Colonel Trench nearly carried the idea through in the 1820s but nothing was done until the Government was forced to a decision in 1858, the Year of the Great Stink.

Although the Embankment provides what London had needed for centuries – a second road leading west out of the City towards Westminster – its original purpose was to settle once and for all the problem of London's sewage. By the middle of the nineteenth century, London had completely outgrown the mediaeval sewage systems it had relied on for so long. For hundreds of years Londoners had simply used cesspits built behind or even within their houses, producing conditions of filth and squalor unbelievable today.

In the 1830s and 1840s, the use of private cesspits was forbidden and pipes were laid to bring all the sewage down here to the Thames. The intention was that the flow of the river would take all the sewage out to sea but it soon became clear that the idea was not going to work. When the sewage reached the Thames it stayed there, moving slowly downstream on an ebb-tide and returning on the flood. The flood-tides also filled the sewage pipes, blocking their flow and forcing new sewage back into the main system. The result was a series of cholera epidemics throughout London for twenty years.

The new engineer responsible for sewage disposal, Bazalgette, realised the mistake that had been made and put forward the project of building an embankment. By laying a large pipe on the land side of such a wall, sewage could be trapped before it entered the river and taken downstream to proper disposal facilities at the mouth of the Thames.

As with so many reforms, the idea was turned down because of the cost. However, the smell became worse and the 'Great Stink' from the Thames became so bad that the House of Commons had to suspend its sittings in hot weather. Some historians date the decision to build the Embankment from the day in 1858 when Disraeli was overcome by nausea in the middle of a speech and dashed from the Chamber, closely followed by the man he had been attacking, Mr Gladstone. Bazalgette's idea was approved at long last and the Embankment was started in 1864 to be completed six years later.

Bazalgette was a far-sighted man who realised what

other advantages there would be. London would get its first new road for hundreds of years with the added advantage that it could be built without the restriction of houses hemming it in on either side. Traffic from the City to Westminster could at last travel along a straight route and the new Underground railway could run beneath the new roadway without having to pay heavy compensation to the owners of the property above.

There is a memorial to Bazalgette on the balustrade across the road with the appropriate Latin tag *Fluvium in vincula posuit* (He put the river in chains).

On the left is the railway bridge whose name has caused confusion since it was built. Some maps call it the Hungerford Bridge, others call it the Charing Cross Railway Bridge. Both are correct because, legally, there are two bridges here, not one. Before the railway station was built at Charing Cross, the site was occupied by the Hungerford market, named after the Earl of Hungerford who built it as a rival to Covent Garden back in 1692. It never achieved the same popularity although it staggered on till the middle of the nineteenth century.

Brunel built the Hungerford Suspension Bridge to provide access to the market in 1845 but his bridge was dismantled when the railway company took the site over for Charing Cross Station. It wasn't wasted, however. It was taken down to Bristol to become the Clifton Suspension Bridge and Brunel's circular piers were left to help support the new bridge.

Although Hungerford Bridge had been in place only nineteen years, Londoners had become used to walking across the river here and the railway proposal caused an uproar. The railway company was forced to give way and built the only railway bridge in London with a pedestrian footpath. The footpath is, officially, still Hungerford Bridge while the remainder is known as the Charing Cross Railway Bridge.

The bridge is continually being repaired. Shipping has to be warned when work is in progress and this is done by dangling a bundle of hay on a rope below the centre span. No one knows why this is the warning sign, but every bridge in London uses it and the custom is known to go back to the Romans.

It may be as old as the word 'Thames' itself which is now known to predate the Romans, the Celts and even the tribes before the Celts. It should be spelt as it is pronounced, but a Dutch map-maker inserted the letter 'h' by mistake in the sixteenth century and the error has been copied ever since.

Around the corner of the gardens that stretch towards Westminster is the memorial to Samuel Plimsoll, the man who invented the Plimsoll Line and stopped the scandal of the coffin ships.

In the nineteenth century shipowners were sending vessels across the Atlantic grossly overloaded and claiming compensation for them when they sank. After a fierce campaign in Parliament, Plimsoll managed to force through his proposal that every British ship should have lines marked on the hull to show how heavily it can be loaded. (These are the lines painted on a ship's side with letters alongside each. WNA and SNA stand for Winter North Atlantic and Summer North Atlantic.) An example of the Plimsoll line can be seen on the monument.

The gardens behind the Plimsoll memorial pass under the spiky grandeur of Whitehall Court, which we looked at in the First Walk. The path through the gardens passes the statues of Outram, Bartle Frere and Tyndale to Horse Guards Avenue at the far end where the Earl of Fife built his house on Scottish soil. On the far side of the road is one of the four sets of river steps left behind after the Embankment was built. These steps, built by Christopher Wren for Queen Mary in 1691, were the last addition to the old Palace of Whitehall which was burned down a few years later.

Cross the roadway to the river side of the Embankment. There are large grilles set at intervals in the pavement through which mysterious pipes and cables can be seen carrying electricity and telephone wires. At either end of each chamber is an aperture giving access to a further tunnel. It is possible to walk under this pavement all the way from Westminster Bridge to Blackfriars.

The dolphin lamps on the balustrade caused controversy when they were erected and Ruskin led the opposition to them. Each lamp has a serial number on the base which makes them useful reference points.

The seats on the pavement are the 'Cleopatra seats' named after the famous Needle further along the Embankment. They have been placed on platforms to allow people to see over the Embankment wall and there are two 'generations' of them. The seats have always been popular with Londoners who want to sit and watch the river traffic but, unfortunately, they have also been popular as objects to throw into the river. The original seats were placed here soon after the Embankment was built and their numbers diminished over the years, especially during Mafeking Night and the Armistice celebrations.

When the Queen celebrated her Silver Jubilee in 1977, someone had the excellent idea of commemorating the occasion by replacing the missing seats. The copies are exact and it would be impossible to tell which are new and which are the originals except for one thing. All the new seats have a brass plate beneath them to identify the donor. The seat between lamps Nos 50 and 51 was presented by the Institution of Electrical Engineers; the seat opposite lamp No. 52 is an original model and has no plate on the platform. The next two, towards Westminster, were donated by British Airways and the Gas Corporation and they are followed by another of the old models near lamp No. 57.

It was on one of these seats that Bismarck so impressed the Foreign Office in the 1880s. Bismarck had come to London to negotiate some delicate diplomatic business and, as part of his itinerary, was taken to visit Barclay's Brewery in Southwark. At the end of the visit, he was offered a drink from the famous half-gallon tankard filled with their strongest special brew. The normal practice was for the visitor to take a token swallow and hand it back. Someone on the brewery staff was unwise enough to tell the Iron Chancellor that few men had managed to drain the tankard and walk out of the room unaided. Bismarck looked at him, grunted and swallowed the whole half-gallon.

Unfortunately, the same busybody then felt impelled to tell him that no one had ever managed to do it twice. Bismarck looked at him again, held out the tankard, ordered it to be filled, drank it, thanked his hosts and walked slowly to his carriage amidst tremendous applause from the brewery workers. As the party was travelling back along the Embankment, Bismarck suddenly announced that he was drunk, stopped the carriage, walked to one of these seats and told his secretary to wake him in half an hour.

While his staff and the Foreign Office officials waited patiently, he slept for the specified time, was woken by his secretary, resumed his journey to Downing Street and spent the rest of the day out-manoeuvring the awed British diplomats on every point they made.

The Embankment is one of three in London. The Albert Embankment is across the river and Bazalgette built another at Chelsea upstream. This is the Victoria Embankment which received the name after an embarrassing royal incident.

When they were building the Embankment Queen Victoria was going through her long period of mourning after the death of her beloved Albert. Her determined grief and reluctance to allow any enjoyment or relaxation at the Court antagonised not only the Prince of Wales (whom she blamed for Albert's death) but also many of her people. The papers called her the 'Widow of Windsor' from her determination to impress her sorrow on all around her.

Although she kept the reins of government tightly in her own hands, refusing to let her son play any part in it, there were some roles for which he was eminently suited and to which not even the Queen could object. These tasks included the official opening of the hundreds of bridges, railways and enormous Town Halls which were rising all over nineteenth-century England. The authorities felt that the Prince of Wales was the best person to open this splendid new embankment and decided to name it after him.

Since the Queen insisted on vetting all Royal engagements herself, a deputation waited upon her to inform her of their plans and to seek her gracious approval. She approved the idea of the Embankment, she approved the idea of her son opening it and was then informed of the third suggestion – that, since the Prince was to open it, it should bear his name. There was a dreadful silence; Queen Victoria glowered at the deputation and her voice hardened. 'What?' she said. 'Has England then no Queen?' So of course the deputation immediately explained that they hadn't felt bold enough to make the request, but of course if Her Majesty was gracious enough to let her name be used . . . So it was the Victoria Embankment that the Prince opened in 1870. When one thinks about it there are few Prince of Wales bridges or railway stations but many named after Victoria.

The incident is not unique. It was recently revealed that the *Queen Mary*, in her time the largest ship afloat, was also named by accident. Cunard had always given their liners names ending in 'ia' – *Lusitania, Berengaria, Mauretania*, etc. In the 1930s, the directors decided to call their new wonder-ship *Victoria*.

Since it was a royal name, royal approval had to be given and the directors waited upon George V and asked permission to name their splendid new ship after 'one of England's best-loved Queens'. The King was delighted with the request and interrupted them: 'Mary will be delighted. I'll go and tell her now.' Like the deputation to Queen Victoria before them, the Cunard directors could think on their feet. That night the shipyard painters worked overtime to change the name on the bows from *Victoria* to *Queen Mary*.

At the end of the massive white block of the Ministry of Defence across the road is London's newest police station, opened by Mrs Thatcher in 1985. It is the old Cannon Row station, moved from the Whitehall side of Scotland Yard to this spot. It should be Canon Row from the Canons of Westminster Abbey who lived here before the Reformation but, like the spelling of Thames, there seems little chance of changing the error now.

Across the river is the palatial length of County Hall, the headquarters of the Greater London Council and of the London County Council before that. There was a tremendous struggle to get it built and it took twenty-four years to complete. It is an impressive building, and one of the reasons for placing it here was because the County Council was jealous of the powers of Parliament and wanted to assert its own authority.

County Hall has a romantic story attached to it. Some four or five hundred years ago, a travelling pedlar came to the church authorities at St Mary's Church at Lambeth with an unusual request. If he left a legacy to the church, would they allow a window to be put up after his death, showing the pedlar and his dog? This was considered to be against canon law since dogs have no souls but, such was the earnestness of the pedlar's pleading, the church authorities agreed. In gratitude to them, the pedlar left the church an acre of ground, known as Pedlar's Acre.

That is one version of the story. Another is that the pedlar's dog found some buried treasure in a field. The pedlar bought the field, prospered and left the land to the church on condition he and his dog were commemorated. The window was erected in St Mary's, where it remains, and the church became owner of a piece of waste ground by the river. The buried treasure version draws some substance from the lines scratched on a window of the pub that stood on the site a hundred years ago:

Happy the pedlar whose portrait we view,
Since his dog was so faithful and fortunate too;
He at once made him wealthy, and guarded his door,
Secured him from robbers, relieved him when poor.
Then drink to his memory, and wish fate may send
Such a dog to protect you, enrich, and befriend.

Apart from a small rent from grazing, the church made little profit from Pedlar's Acre till the London County Council found the acre lay right in the middle of the site for their new hall – and they paid the church £81,000 for it.

On the right is the original New Scotland Yard, now used as office accommodation by Members of Parliament. From 1892 till 1967, this was the headquarters of the Metropolitan Police. The office of the Commissioner was on the second floor in the turret that sticks out at the corner. With this exception, the rule used to be the lower the rank, the higher the office. There were no lifts in the building and it was felt that junior ranks were better able to climb all the stairs to the offices at the top.

Like several other buildings in London, Scotland Yard was originally intended to be something else. In 1877 Queen Victoria's son, the Duke of Edinburgh, came here to lay the foundation stone of the National Opera House, one of the many National Opera Houses that have been started in London but never completed. The project folded after a year and Norman Shaw was invited to build the present block for the police. He designed many buildings in London but this was the one of which he was most proud. He let it be known that if he was considered worthy of a memorial plaque after his death, he would like it placed here, and the tablet on the wall shows that his wishes were respected.

His request for a memorial helped to solve a problem later. When the police moved out in 1967, they took the name New Scotland Yard with them and the authorities were faced with the question of a new name for the building. Because it was to be used by Members of Parliament, dozens of politicians' names were suggested, each of which provoked opposition. To avoid political prejudice, it was decided to ignore the parliamentary connection and simply name it the Norman Shaw Building after the man whose name was already on it.

The pavement on the river side of the Embankment widens at this section to allow for the steps leading up to the bridge from the water's edge. The juxtaposition of two of the 'Cleopatra' seats here repays inspection. It is either a happy coincidence or a sly comment by the official who set them here. Opposite lamp No. 60 is a seat with a plaque showing it was provided by Gerry Cottle's Circus. Beside it is the seat presented by the House of Commons. The implication is obvious whichever political party one supports.

The reason for the Cottle's Circus donating a seat at this spot is that circus families go back a long way, and Cottle's have a connection with Astley's, the first permanent circus in England. Astley's flourished from 1769 to 1862 in Westminster Bridge Road, just the other side of the river. During the 1850s the original equestrian turns became interspersed with more and more mini-melodramas and variety turns. Takings dropped off and a new manager came in to put things right. Knowing what the audience came to Astley's to see, he worked to one principle: Astley's needed less dialogue and more equestrian acts. All views to the contrary were met with the reply, 'Cut the cackle, and get to the 'osses.'

The roadway slopes up to Westminster Bridge, the second on the site, completed in 1862, the year of Queen Victoria's Silver Jubilee. A plaque in the middle of the bridge commemorates the event. It was from this spot that Wordsworth looked downstream to St Paul's dominating the London skyline and wrote:

Earth has not anything to show more fair:
Dull would he be of soul who could pass by
A sight so touching in its majesty:

The view he admired lasted another hundred and forty years till the present tower blocks put an end to it.

The first Westminster Bridge, completed in 1750, was a landmark in London's history. Since the time of the Romans there had been only one bridge in London – London Bridge running from the City into Southwark. The early bridges were made of wood and, in 1014, Ethelred and Olaf of Norway burnt the bridge to divide the Danish forces on either bank. This was the origin of 'London Bridge is falling down'.

The first London Bridge to be built of stone was started by Peter of Colechurch in 1176 and stood till 1832, the famous bridge with shops and houses and the heads of traitors stuck on pikes at the southern end. In the 1740s London Bridge provided the only crossing before Putney Bridge and most of London's freight and food was moved by water, making the watermen and boatmen a powerful body.

It was because of this dependence on the river that East Enders still use the phrase 'Up West' for the West End of London, since it is upstream from the City. The reverse phrase is now only found in America where 'Down East Maine' recalls that London merchants trading with America had to send their ships eastwards downstream before they could turn west to the Atlantic.

The monopoly of the watermen was eventually broken by the Duke of Grafton in the 1740s. He was a keen foxhunter who became tired of taking hours to get to his horses and kennels in Surrey before he could start hunting. When a Bill was put to Parliament to build a second bridge across the Thames at eight hundred, he threw all his influence behind it. The bridge was built in 1750 and the Duke was able to enjoy his hunting.

Beyond St Thomas's Hospital upstream are the grey towers of Lambeth Palace. This has been the home of the

Archbishops of Canterbury for eight hundred years. It was restored a century ago but the gatehouse and tower date from the fifteenth century. Matthew Parker, the original 'Nosey Parker', is buried in the Palace chapel. He was the first married Archbishop of Canterbury and, although Elizabeth I was a strong Protestant, the Reformation was too recent for her to feel happy about married bishops. When she dined at Lambeth Palace, she made her views clear when she thanked Parker's wife for her hospitality:

'Madam, I may not call you. Mistress, I am ashamed to call you. Yet though I know not what to call you, I thank you.'

Although the Reformation meant that the Archbishops no longer accepted the authority of Rome, they still retain some unusual powers derived from Papal authority. Because all schools and universities were originally run by the Church, all academic distinction stemmed from the Pope. Since the Archbishop was the Pope's representative, the power to confer academic degrees in England was delegated to him. Henry VIII confirmed the privilege after the break with Rome and the Archbishop still bestows the 'Lambeth degree' in his own right.

Turn back towards Westminster and look at the Embankment wall rising from the water. There is a lion's head every twenty yards, with mooring rings hanging from their mouths. They are part of London's flood-warning system and every policeman on duty near the river keeps a close eye on them. Although the Thames barrage has reduced some of the risk, the phrase 'When the lions drink, London's in danger' still holds good. If the water reaches the lions' mouths, the Thames is at danger level and the Underground and all the Thames tunnels are closed.

Back at the corner of the Bridge, on the Embankment side, is a little green turret set in the corner of the pavement. It is the Westminster tide recorder which measures the depth of water at this point. The recording mechanism can be seen by climbing the steps at the side and looking through the window.

Above the turret is the statue of Boadicea in her chariot, the Warrior Queen who rose against the Romans and burnt London in 61AD. When it was commissioned in the 1850s, Prince Albert expressed royal approval by lending the sculptor two horses from the Palace stables to act as models. It does have one fault. As soon as it was unveiled in 1902, the absence of any reins to control the stampeding horses led to a series of jokes about women drivers.

The statue still causes comment because the authorities cannot decide who it belongs to. In 1987 it was due for cleaning but the question of payment was raised. The City of Westminster claimed it belonged to the old Greater London Council; the successors of the Greater London Council felt it belonged to the Thames Water Authority because the foundations go below the waterline. The Thames Water Authority considered it was clearly the responsibility of the City of Westminster. All three authorities agreed that the Department of the Environment was involved; the Department took a different view. At the time of writing, the Westminster City Council has reluctantly agreed to maintain the statue on a 'temporary basis'.

THIRD ♦ WALK

Along the South Side of the Strand

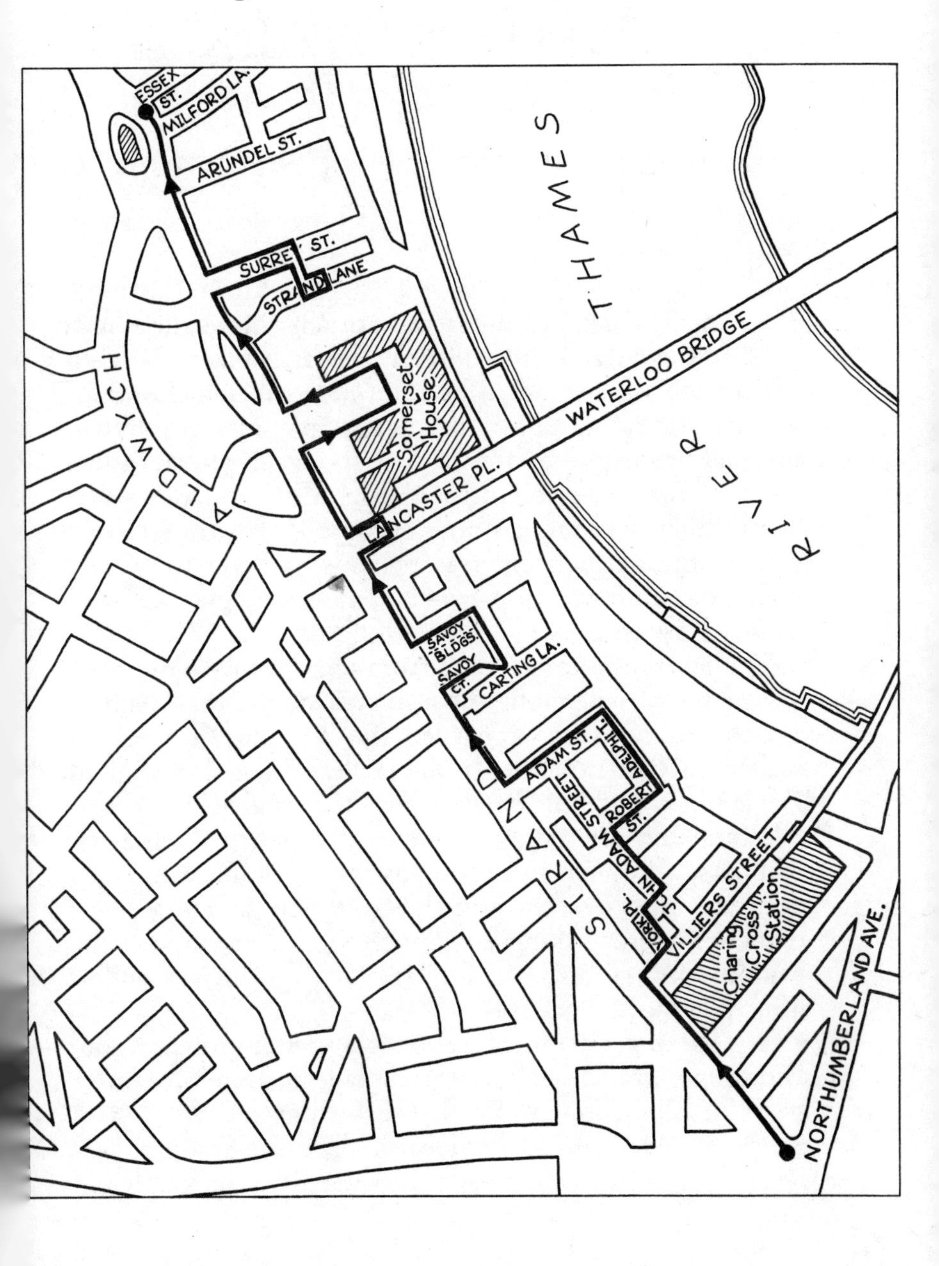

THIRD ♦ WALK

Along the South Side of the Strand

The Third Walk begins at the corner where the south side of the Strand runs into Trafalgar Square. Disraeli considered the Strand to be the finest street in London. Despite the ravages of modern development it still has an unusual atmosphere. It is not a shopping street, nor a street of offices; it is not the theatrical thoroughfare that Shaftesbury Avenue has now become. It has, in its time, been home to such diverse residents as Peter the Great of Russia, both the Emperors Napoleon and even Charles Edward Stuart.

The Strand takes its name from what it originally was, a river-bank lying along the northern side of the Thames. To the east Ludgate guarded the entrance to the old walled City of London. In the lawless days of mediaeval England, the territory between the walled City and Westminster offered little security to normal citizens. Robbers, vagrants and footpads were common but not even the most desperate of thieves would attack a priest or churchman. Taking advantage of this immunity, the bishops and abbots of England set up their London houses along the Strand.

The list of ecclesiastical residences is an impressive one. Along the Strand and Fleet Street lay the London houses of the Archbishop of York, the Bishops of Worcester, Salisbury, Durham, Norwich, Carlisle, Llandaff, Chester, Bath and Wells, Coventry, Exeter, Peterborough and

St David's, as well as those of the Abbots of Cirencester, Faversham, Tewkesbury and Winchcombe. There have been no bishops here for four hundred years but they left a surprising number of memories behind them.

When Henry VIII took control of the Church of England in 1535, he confiscated most of the Church's property and redistributed it amongst his favourites. That produced a second set of names that still line the Strand and the last of these aristocratic palaces did not vanish till late in the nineteenth century, when Northumberland House was taken down.

There is little to see along the first section of the south side of the Strand. The old ABC tea-shop at No. 10, between Northumberland Street and Craven Street, has long gone. It was the first tea-shop in England, started by the Aerated Bread Company in 1861. The temperance movement threw its weight behind the idea in an attempt to stop drunkenness and the tea-shop has been with us ever since.

The modern Charing Cross stands outside the railway station. It is a Victorian reproduction of the Eleanor Cross that had stood for three hundred and fifty years where Charles I now rides his horse at the top of Whitehall. This copy was erected in 1865 by the railway company as a public relations exercise. The proposal to build a railway station so near the centre of London caused much disquiet at the time and the Cross was put up to show the railway company's respect for the historic site.

The Cross is a useful lesson in understanding commemorative statuary. Figures were often carved in the same stylised form and it is usually the hands of the statue that indicate the sculptor's intention. Queen Eleanor who died in 1290 was revered as a queen and as a charitable, religious woman; the statues round the column show her in those roles. Where the figure has a purse in her hands, she is represented as giving alms to the poor. Where she is shown holding a small building, she is remembered as the founder of a church or monastery. On the other four figures she is shown as queen, signified by her royal crown.

The station and the hotel to the left of it may look familiar. They started a fashion when they were built in 1863 by E. M. Barry. This was the first major building in England to have artificial stone facing and helped to popularise the florid French Renaissance school of architecture. One of the practical advantages of the style was that the high-pitched roofs gave space for two extra floors. Dozens of hotels were built around London in imitation of this one.

Villiers Street turns down beside the station; York Place runs off to the left after a few yards. A small plate on the right-hand wall records that York Place was originally called 'Of Alley'. In 1237 this site was the town house of the Bishops of Norwich, but eventually became the property of the Duke of Buckingham. In 1670 the Duke sold the site to one of the greatest of London's building speculators, Nicholas Barbon. Barbon made a fortune from his speculations by methods that were irregular even by the standards of the seventeenth century. There was public consternation after his death when it was known that his will specifically stated that none of his outstanding debts were to be paid. In his spare time he made another fortune by founding the fire insurance industry (the Great Fire of London was still a recent memory). His relaxation was the study of political economy and the opening paragraphs of Karl Marx's *Das Kapital* quote Barbon's definitions of commodities and use value.

Although Barbon made a great deal of money from buying Buckingham House, he had to abide by the conditions set by the Duke. These were that the streets built on the site were to bear the Duke's name – George Villiers, Duke of Buckingham. So Barbon built George Court, Villiers Street, Duke Street, Of Alley and Buckingham Street. Duke Street has gone but when the authorities renamed this small passage York Place some years ago, they were astonished to discover how many people remembered the story – so the Of Alley plate was retained.

At the end of York Place, a turn to the right brings us into John Adam Street. A few yards along on the left is George Court with the George pub that has been here since 1675. Contrary to outward appearances, much of the building dates from that time. It has been refurbished recently but the splendid staircase in the middle of the new large bar is still the one that Barbon built three hundred years ago.

The pub looks down on to York Buildings. A few yards down the Buildings on the left is a roadway through one of London's most famous labyrinths, the Adelphi arches. The road through the cellars is called Lower Robert Street and leads to the Savoy Hotel and the Embankment beyond.

The Arches have lost most of their magic because they have become a car-park and are now well lit. Till a couple of years ago, they consisted of mysterious dark doorways and gloomy cellars, justifying all the stories that used to be told about them. Corpses were often found here in the last century and a sinister old-clothes establishment, tucked away in one of the dark corners, was known to local residents as Fagin's Den. They adopted the name from Dickens's *Oliver Twist* and they were more accurate than they knew. Dickens played here as a boy with a companion named Bob Fagin. When he wrote *Oliver Twist* thirty years later, he simply associated the sinister gloom of the cellars with his boyhood friend.

When the site was cleared in the 1930s, the surprised owners found at least three inhabitants whose existence they had never suspected, including one old lady who had kept cows here for some twenty years.

The next turning on the left is Durham House Street, once the home of the Bishops of Durham. The red brick building on the corner (16 John Adam Street) has a blue plaque to Thomas Rowlandson the engraver. For some reason it makes no mention of the other figures of the past who lived in the old house. Simon de Montfort, the founder of Parliament, occupied the site in 1258; it was Catherine of Aragon's lodgings in 1502. Cardinal Wolsey stayed here in 1518, while he built Whitehall Palace. He was followed by Anne Boleyn, Lady Jane Grey and Sir Walter Raleigh.

Every schoolboy knows the story of Raleigh smoking his pipe and having water thrown over him by the servant who thought he was on fire. Scholars have dismissed the anecdote out of hand, but it is now known that the story is based on an incident that occurred in the turret room of old Durham House.

The Adelphi

The road slopes up to the Adelphi, constructed in the 1770s by Robert Adam and his brothers. They took a lease on what was then a steep river-bank and built an immense platform supported by stone arches going down into the mud. On top of the platform they built a block of superb houses, overlooking the river.

The Adelphi (classical Greek for 'brothers') caused a sensation. Instead of the normal red brick facing, the Adam houses were covered in plaster. They were adorned with tall plaster pillars, covered in decorative mouldings and painted red and green. The Adelphi was based on one of the few survivals of Roman domestic architecture, the Palace of Diocletian at Split in Yugoslavia. It introduced a form of decoration into English buildings that has been followed ever since.

The centre block of the old Adelphi was knocked down in 1936 but the buildings at the end of the street show what it used to look like. Nos. 1 and 2 Robert Street at the top of the slope were the first purpose-built flats in England. To the right, towards the river balcony, a plaque on the wall of the end house tells us that J. M. Barrie, John Galsworthy and Thomas Hardy were all residents here.

Directly across the road from Barrie lived Bernard

Shaw, who scandalised his neighbours by his telegraphic address ('Socialist, London'). They became friends and used to conduct conversations from their windows across the street. If the windows were shut, then cherry-stones or biscuits were used to attract each other's attention.

No. 3 Robert Street seems to have been popular with literary men. In 1917. Granville Barker lived on the ground floor with Barrie above him, while John Galsworthy occupied the top storey. In the same year one of Barrie's dinner parties was interrupted by a Zeppelin raid, and he and his guests went up on the roof to watch. It was fortunate the bombs did not drop on the Adelphi that night or England would have lost most of its literary establishment. The party consisted of Barrie, Shaw, Hardy, H. G. Wells, Arnold Bennett and what the diarist present calls 'several other writers'.

Robert Street was a late addition to the Adelphi design. There should have been one wide block all the way across the frontage but Thomas Coutts the banker had his office in Durham House Street at the northern side. The Adam brothers were in severe financial difficulties when they built the Adelphi and Coutts was in a position to lay down conditions. He stipulated that whatever they built should not interfere with the view from his office across to the Surrey hills – so the plans were swiftly altered to allow this short street to be built.

This did not solve the brothers' financial troubles. A government lottery had to be authorised to raise funds and London local workmen proved so expensive that cheaper labour was brought from Scotland with a bagpiper who played all day to encourage them. Unfortunately the Scots discovered what the local rate of pay was and went on strike so the Adam brothers sent them all home and imported Irish labourers instead. The stipulation was that none of them should be able to speak English, so that they would be unable to find out what the London rate of pay was. The theory worked for twenty-four hours, by which time the Irish population of London had ensured that each newcomer knew exactly what the rates should be.

Walk along beside the balustrade, with the new Adelphi to the left. This is where Dr Johnson walked as he mourned the death of his old friend David Garrick, who lived in the centre house overlooking the river. A few doors away lived the man who left his name to the English language – Jack Robinson. In the 1780s Sheridan was a Member of Parliament, famous for his stinging attacks on the corruption of the Government administration. The chief object of his attacks was Jack Robinson, Secretary of the Treasury, who allocated Government appointments.

Under Parliamentary rules, Sheridan could not mention Robinson's name but one day his patience broke. Under constant taunting from the Government benches: 'Name him! Name him!', Sheridan replied, 'Name him? Yes, I could name him. I could name him as easily as I could say Jack Robinson.'

At the end of the ugly new Adelphi block, turn left back towards the Strand along Adam Street. No. 7, on the right, is the best survivor of the original Adam design. It is covered with typical Adam decoration, tall plaster pilasters, the Adam coat of arms on the pediment and the oldest decorative motif in Europe on the door-frame – a bull's head that goes back to the Minoan palaces of 3000 BC.

The Royal Society of Arts building on the left was designed for them by Robert Adam in 1774. The Society saw Dr Johnson's only known attack of stage-fright. Called upon to address the members, the great lexicographer who was famous for his eloquence and readiness to express an opinion on any subject, stood up, stammered ten words and left the room in confusion.

The Society's lecture theatre contains a set of pictures by the eccentric eighteenth-century painter James Barry. They depict great events in the world's history and the final panel includes all the people Barry felt had improved human knowledge, including his contemporaries Johnson, Burke, Goldsmith and Fielding.

Barry was a brilliant artist but a man of considerable temper. When Benjamin West painted the Death of General Wolfe at Quebec, the characters were shown in contemporary dress. The tradition of the time was that Roman dress should be used for all such pictures and Barry was shocked by the precedent set. He promptly did his own version of the scene only to have it turned down by the Royal Academy, of which he was a senior member. It was a magnificent picture, full of horses, regiments and guns; the difficulty was that every single character was portrayed in the nude. Barry's eccentricity may have been hereditary. His daughter pretended to be a man so successfully that she rose to become Inspector General of Military Hospitals; her sex was not discovered till her death in 1865.

At No. 9 Adam Street a ceiling painting by Angelica Kauffman can be seen through the window of the first floor. She was a founding member of the Royal Academy in 1769 and this is one of the few places in London where her work can be seen in its original location.

Adam Street leads back into the Strand and a turn to the right brings us to the locked gate at the entrance to Ivybridge Lane. The Lane has been closed for nearly forty years. The reason it has not been built over is probably because nobody knows who it belongs to. It has been here for at least six hundred years and marks the course of one of the many streams that crossed the Strand down to the river. Since nobody wanted running water through the middle of their house, this narrow alley was left open. When the watercourse eventually dried, it became a useful shortcut down to the river-bank. Charles II used it to escape from Parliamentary soldiers during the Civil War.

Just past Ivybridge Lane is the gloomy dignity of Shell-Mex House. It stands on the site of what was the largest hotel in Europe, the Cecil Hotel, built in 1896 by Jabez

Balfour, one of the great Victorian con-men industrialists. The building costs came from his Liberator Permanent Building and Investor Society but, as was said at the time, the Society wasn't quite permanent enough and was certainly much too liberated. Balfour was found guilty of misappropriating £8 million and went to prison for 14 years.

This was once Salisbury House, one of the many bishop's palaces that lined the Strand. We would not call them palaces now; they looked more like a cavalry fort in the American West. They were built around a central quadrangle with wooden or stone walls for protection. The wall facing the Strand had a strong gatehouse in the middle and stables and servants' quarters lay on either side of the courtyard. The bishop's house stood on the far side looking down to the river. Access to the water was by a gate built in another wall on the river-bank. That is why the old steps we will see are called watergates, rather than jetties or water-steps.

After the Reformation, the bishops were replaced by Court favourites such as Elizabeth's Walsingham, Burleigh and Essex. When they left, the buildings were taken over by squatters or small shop-keepers who occupied separate sections. None of them was bold enough or wealthy enough to buy the entire site so the central courtyard remained open. In some cases, as at Shell-Mex House, it has remained open ever since.

No. 84 Strand, just beyond Shell-Mex House, has a long, narrow interior dating from its years as a newsreel cinema, while No. 85 marks the border between St Martin-in-the-Fields and the Duchy of Lancaster. Above the window of No. 85 is a small red plaque with three lions on it. It shows that we are crossing the boundaries of the old Savoy Palace that passed to the Duke of Lancaster (the second title of the Sovereign) in 1345. The Savoy Chapel, the last remnant of the old palace, still ranks as a 'Royal Peculiar' which means that it does not come under the jurisdiction of the Bishop of London.

The lamp-post in the middle of the road directly opposite No. 85 is one of the famous 'lilies of the Strand', a nickname they acquired as soon as they were erected in 1899. All the previous London lamps had pointed upwards, following the natural direction of the oil or gas flames that lit them. When the incandescent gas-mantle was invented, flames could be directed downwards and these were the first lamps to utilise the discovery. Their elegant drooping curves resembled lilies and the name stuck because of the association with the popularly-derided Art Nouveau movement of the time.

The lamp opposite No. 85 has the number '2038' on a small metal plaque four feet from the ground. It resembles the other lamps along the Strand, painted in the Westminster colours of black, white and blue, but the base of this lamp was specially made for this spot. It is a parish boundary mark. One side has St Martin giving his cloak to the beggar, the other displays an anchor and the letters 'SCD'. It shows that this is the boundary between St Martin-in-the-Fields and St Clement Danes. The lamp is the only one of its kind in London.

The Savoy

A courtyard on the right leads to the Savoy Hotel and Savoy Theatre, both built by Richard D'Oyly Carte with the money he made from the Gilbert and Sullivan operas. He built the theatre in 1881 and made it the first to be lit by electricity, a move which horrified the fire authorities of the time. The stretch of pavement by the theatre should be hallowed ground among social historians because it saw the first queues in England. The operas were so popular that the police complained about the crowds and Carte had to employ attendants to keep them in order. He came up with the idea of the queue, little thinking that he was introducing what was to become a permanent feature of British life.

The hotel caused a sensation when it was opened in 1889. While his rivals were building hotels with one bathroom for every hundred guests, Carte told the architect to provide seventy bathrooms for the Savoy. The architect was incredulous – was this to be a hotel or an aquarium? But Carte got his bathrooms and ensured the success of the hotel by going to Paris and engaging the greatest hotel manager in Europe, César Ritz. Leaving nothing to chance, Carte then secured the legendary Escoffier as head chef and completed the coup by providing music in the dining room under the baton of Johann Strauss himself.

Carte did everything he could to make the Savoy stand out from other hotels; the Savoy staff are still proud of their long list of 'firsts'. It was the first hotel to provide supper after the theatre, to provide dancing for its guests, to have passenger and service lifts, to install telephones in bedrooms and to have private bathrooms. The first commercial broadcast to America was made by the Savoy Orpheans, with Signor Marconi himself attending to the technical details. It is well known that Escoffier invented the *Pêche* Melba here in honour of the soprano's performance in *Lohengrin*. What is not so well known is that the first dry Martini in England was poured here and that the whisky sour was invented in the Savoy bar.

The Savoy has always attracted an international clientele. In deference to American guests, tomatoes were provided here when they were still regarded with deep suspicion elsewhere in England. If for any reason guests find themselves sitting down thirteen at table, then the Savoy will provide a fourteenth guest in the form of an ebony cat called Casper. Jascha Heifetz took bagpipe lessons on the roof from Harry Lauder and Tetrazzini expected the Savoy to cope with her pet crocodile as well as the Pekinese and parrots she brought with her.

The figure above the canopy represents the man who gave his name to the site, Count Peter of Savoy, who was given the land by Henry III in 1264. The correct name for the canopy he stands on is a marquise. The word originally came from a wide overhang built to allow the wife of a French marquis to alight at her front door without getting wet. The term was then transferred to the small canopy at the entrance to a general's tent. When the word was adopted in England, it was used to describe the tent itself and, because it sounded as though it was plural, we decided to call it not a marquise but a marquee.

The hotel stands on historic ground. Around the forecourt, which is also a survival of the mediaeval layout, is a series of chrome panels giving the history of the site. The forecourt is the only place in England where the traffic drives on the right; the Savoy had to get a special Act of Parliament passed to do it. The reason is not, as many suppose, to make American visitors feel at home. It is more practical than that. If traffic drove in on the left, the line of carriages and cabs coming to drop people off at the theatre blocked the entrance to the hotel. By keeping traffic on the right, the hotel entrance is kept clear.

Steps lead down from the courtyard into Carting Lane. At the bottom of the steps are some iron railings running downhill. The railings end at the famous Carting Lane sewer gas lamp, which can be distinguished from its fellows by the thickness of its pillar. Contrary to popular belief, it does not run on sewer gas. What it does do is to draw the sewer gases upwards by the heat induced by the gas-flames. Over two hundred were installed in the 1890s, but this is the only model left.

The roadway runs uphill through a dark tunnel underneath the Savoy. Half-way through the tunnel, grilles on the left give a glimpse of enormous generators. This is the Savoy's power station, the oldest in the country, if not in the world. D'Oyly Carte installed it in the 1880s and it has provided electricity for the hotel and theatre ever since. It supplied the power for the BBC when they were 2LO and enabled the Savoy Chapel to become the first church in England to use electric light.

After the Second World War, the Savoy found itself in the Gilbertian situation of playing host to the commissioners assembled to work out the nationalisation of the electricity industry. The commissioners spent months on their task, brought the whole industry under their control and then found themselves faced with an electricity bill from the Savoy power station, whose existence they didn't even suspect.

A passage leads up the dark slope of Savoy Buildings towards the Strand, passing the site of the house where William Blake saw his visions in the 1820s. Simpson's stands beside the top of the alley. Founded in 1818 as a salon for chess players, it has become famous for the excellence of its meat, which the carver still wheels to the table for the customer to choose his cut. It is mentioned often in the Sherlock Holmes stories and the chess pieces on the tiles around the doorway show it has not forgotten its origins. The rook, pawn and knight shown here are commonplace now, but it was at Simpson's that they were first adopted. Up to 1849 chess pieces could be any size or shape, leading to confusion whenever tournaments were held. Eventually the famous Howard Staunton gave his name and approval to the design we recognize today and it became standard across the world. One of the sets used by Staunton is in the foyer.

Simpson's retained its independence till 1904. In that year, a careless labourer working on the extension of the Savoy put his pick through Simpson's wall and brought half of it down. The Savoy were clearly liable but carried the matter off with their usual panache; they took the easy way out and bought the restaurant.

No. 107 Strand is a new building but, from 1760 till the last war, it was occupied by Burgess's Fish Sauce shop. It became famous for its anchovy sauce and Lord Byron was such an enthusiastic customer that he referred to it in a poem. It was also Byron who spread the fame of the shop round England by pointing out that the rapid repetition of 'Burgess's Fish Sauce Shop' was a far better test of sobriety than 'British Constitution'. Burgess's are still in business elsewhere and take great pride in being the only surviving firm to have advertised in the first edition of *The Times* in 1785.

A close neighbour of Burgess was Harris's Sausage Shop. William Harris was an ebullient Victorian who was proud of his shops, wore full evening dress all day long and sported the largest diamond tie-pin in London. He always carried a few pounds of his sausages with him to hand out as tips and he ensured his name was not forgotten by naming his seven sons William I, William II, William III, William IV, etc.

It was on this stretch of pavement that Mr Hetherington was arrested on January 15th 1797 on a charge of creating a breach of the peace. Mr Hetherington's offence was that he 'wore a structure on his head calculated to frighten timid people'. He was trying out the world's first top-hat.

Savoy Street, on the right, leads down to the Savoy Chapel, all that is left of the Savoy Palace that John of Gaunt and Chaucer knew. It also leads to an easy confusion of street names because Savoy Street leads to Savoy Hill, Savoy Steps, Savoy Row, Savoy Way, Savoy Court and Savoy Buildings.

After Peter of Savoy left, the site reverted to the Crown and was given to Henry, first Duke of Lancaster. When the dukedom was assumed by the monarch, as it still is, the Savoy remained as ducal, not regal, property. This eventually led to a lengthy legal dispute in the eighteenth century in which the King brought a case against himself as Duke of Lancaster to try and decide in which capacity he owned it.

Although it has been heavily restored, the Chapel is still royal. It is the chapel of the Victorian Order (Queen Victoria paid for the restoration) and, as part of the Duchy of Lancaster whose boundary marks we still see around these streets, 'God save the Queen' is not sung here. The words are 'God save the Duke'. In the side vestry is a plaque in memory of H. V. Esmond, the only memorial in London showing a man smoking a cigarette.

The next turning off the Strand is Lancaster Place. Thresher & Glenny occupy premises thirty yards along on the right. They began as hosiers in the Strand in 1694. They left their old shop beside Somerset House a few years ago, but they can still provide the measurements of such customers as Lord Nelson and George III, Swinburne, Tennyson and Buffalo Bill. Garibaldi led his Redshirts in a Thresher & Glenny shirt and they even supplied the Mikado (Emperor) of Japan with underwear (which must have been lucrative since he wore a new set every day).

Walk back to the Strand and cross Lancaster Place. The Victorian building on the corner, No. 133 Strand, was built for an insurance company and the decoration shows the moral virtues used to impress their customers. A beehive beside the doorway has hard-working bees flying around it, while the stern statement 'Nothing Without Labour' reinforces the point. Over the doorway the company relaxed slightly to show off what we must assume was their modern office equipment and the contentment of their workers. Four cherubs are shown talking down speaking-tubes while another managerial cherub listens in above them.

Somerset House

Fifty yards along the Strand, past Balls Brothers, the oldest winehouse in London, is the grandeur of Somerset House. It was originally the site of the houses of two more of the Strand bishops, Chester and Worcester. Lord Protector Somerset seized it after the Reformation and built a palace on the site using building materials from St Paul's and St Mary Le Strand just down the road. He would have taken the furniture and stone from St Margaret's church in Westminster as well but the parishioners turned out in force with bows and pikes to stop him.

The palace was confiscated by the Crown after Somerset's death and became a dower house for the Queens Consort. It fell into disuse in the eighteenth century and the Somerset House we see today was built in 1775. The reason was that the young King George III found himself patron of nearly every learned society, each of them looking for Royal assistance of a practical kind. At the same time, various Government departments were outgrowing their rented offices around the City and were looking for something bigger. After years of discussion it was decided to rebuild Somerset House and solve both problems. The Royal Academy, the Royal Society and the Society of Antiquaries were given the wing overlooking the Strand while the Navy, the Stamp Office and the Duchy of Cornwall got the rest.

Chambers was the architect and young Thomas Telford worked on this Strand frontage. It may have been Telford who placed some of these decorated keystones in position along the frontage. They represent the rivers of England with the Ocean in the centre. The Thames is the head crowned with swans, garlands and flowers but the rest have to be identified by guesswork. They are the Humber, Mersey, Dee, Medway, Tweed, Tyne and Severn but, after forty years, the author has been unable to discover which is which. Above them, four Romans represent Prudence, Justice, Fortitude and Temperance (desirable qualities in any Government office) and above them yet again are the Royal Arms of England supported by Fame and Genius.

Somerset House is open to the public and is certainly well worth a visit. Immediately inside the gates, two doorways lead to the side wings. Over the left doorway is a bust of Isaac Newton showing where the Royal Society met from 1780 to 1856. This is where Herschel, Watt and Humphrey Davy came to tell their colleagues of their discoveries. Through the doorway on the right, surmounted by a bust of Michelangelo, Chantrey, Lawrence, Reynolds, Wilkie and Turner attended meetings of the Royal Academy.

The quadrangle is one of the most peaceful places in London. The parked cars are the only indication of the twentieth century. The lamp-posts date from the early 1830s and the carvings beside the doorways represent the Government departments for which they were built. In the middle of the quadrangle is an unusual memorial to the civil servants who died in the First War. From a distance, the flags that flutter around it are life-like but closer inspection shows them to be plaster.

Somerset House must be the only Government building to have a cemetery in its basement. Charles I's widow, Henrietta Maria, lived here and her household were all French Roman Catholics. Since Catholicism was forbidden, there was nowhere in London where they could be buried. A private graveyard had to be dug in the grounds of the old house. Five of her courtiers are still here, down in the cellars, their memorial plaques neatly lined along the wall. The cellar they are in is now used for unwanted furniture – it is called the Dead Room.

A few yards beyond the gateway is an extraordinary memorial to George III. He is depicted as a Roman emperor leaning on a rudder with Neptune towering over him. Queen Charlotte attended the unveiling and made it quite clear that she did not admire the figure of her late husband. She turned to the sculptor, John Bacon, and asked him bluntly: 'Why did you make so frightful a figure?'

Bacon produced what must be the finest reply ever made by a sculptor to a disappointed client. He bowed low and replied:

'Madam, Art cannot always effect what is ever within the reach of Nature – the union of beauty and majesty.'

The next opening on the right is the gateway of King's College. It was founded in 1828, not from a desire to spread knowledge, but rather to ensure that knowledge was spread the right way. University College London had been founded two years before to provide a university education for those non-Anglicans whose religious beliefs debarred them from attending Oxford or Cambridge. Public opinion promptly decided that it was a nest of atheists and free-thinkers, christening it 'the godless college of Gower Street'.

The forces of orthodoxy rejoined by founding King's College as a rival institution. It started with what must be the most powerful set of trustees the country has ever seen. They included the Duke of Wellington, both Archbishops and no less than thirty Anglican bishops, who kept a close eye on the subjects taught and insisted that all members of the staff were practising Anglicans. The quadrangle dates from the nineteenth century and occupies the site of the house of another Strand bishop, the Bishop of Chester.

St Mary's Le Strand

Directly across the road is St Mary's Le Strand, one of the two churches that has blocked or enhanced the Strand, depending on your point of view, for five hundred years. It had its own graveyard for centuries but, in the 1840s, the scandal of bodies and rotting coffins piled on top of each other became too much and the site was cleared. When the crypt was opened, the church had to be evacuated for a week to let the gases disperse.

From the entrance of King's College, the position of the old vaults can still be seen. 'Vault 14' and 'Vault 15' can be read in faint letters along the wall. Vault 16 provides the information that this is where Mary Thresher was buried in 1823, a member of the Thresher & Glenny family we looked at in Lancaster Place. On the wall of the church itself is an inscription of 1807 telling parishioners about the new parish pump. It informs the public that the well is 19 feet south of the notice, is 7 feet wide and 28 feet deep.

Although the Strand traffic is heavy, there may be a couple of taxis parked in front of the church. They are continuing an old tradition because this was the first cab-rank in England, where Captain Bailey installed four coaches for hire in 1625. Coaches were rare in those days. They originated at Kocs in Hungary (hence 'coach') and the Earl of Rutland brought the first one to England in 1555. At the time they were considered the height of decadence and, although Queen Elizabeth had one made in 1564, she refused to use it till she went to St Paul's to give thanks after the Armada victory of 1588.

There has been a church here since 1147 but Protector Somerset knocked it down to provide building materials for his Somerset House and, despite all his promises to rebuild it, nothing was done for two hundred years. The present building was designed by James Gibbs as the first of the fifty new churches authorised by Queen Anne. It was Gibbs's first major work and shows strong traces of his architectural training. The ceiling and porch are remarkably similar to those designed by Carlo Fontana, under whom Gibbs trained in Rome and the steeple bears more than a passing resemblance to those built by Christopher Wren.

It was to have been the most remarkable church in England because the plans stipulated a column at the front two hundred and fifty feet high (Nelson's Column is only 186 feet). The column was to support a statue of Queen Anne, whose Act of 1711 enabled the church to be rebuilt, but she died before the church was finished. It was then quietly agreed that the flattery of such an enormous memorial was no longer required and the column was never built.

The stretch of pavement east of King's College was the beat of Louis Napoleon (later Napoleon III) when he was enlisted as a special constable during the Chartist riots of 1848. Follow it around into Surrey Street, past the Aldwych Underground Station, where the peculiar dark purple tiles were chosen to make the new (1904) station stand out from the buildings around it.

Forty yards down Surrey Street, past the splendid Victorian splendour of the old Norfolk Hotel, is an alley to the right. The steps at the end lead down to Strand Lane and the Roman Bath over which controversy has raged for a hundred years.

The bath is, in theory, open to the public but gaining entrance is a complicated matter. By pressing the light switch at the side, it is possible to see the small pool that Charles Dickens knew as a child and remembered in *David Copperfield*. It is now believed that the bath was constructed in the sixteenth century and fed from the waters of the holy well that stood in the Strand. The confusion over its name arose from the narrow bricks which certainly resemble Roman work in their size and colour.

Strand Lane used to run from the Strand to the river-bank and, like Ivybridge Lane, was probably an old watercourse. The burial ground of St Clement Danes used to be here and the building straddling the alley is the oldest police station in London. It used to be the parish watch-house, where the constables assembled and where malefactors were brought to await trial. Directly under the watch-house, three parish marks show how careful our ancestors were about their boundaries. The mark on the left wall states that the boundary of St Mary Le Strand is 7 feet 8½ inches to the East. On the other side, St Clement Danes marks its boundary with two plaques, one of which states its territory extends 1 foot 10 inches to the West.

There was good reason for this precision. St Clement Danes is a very old parish and received many charitable endowments over the centuries. One bequest specified that it was to provide a meal for the poor of the parish at Christmas; another provided decent burials for paupers. The result was that, as Christmas drew near, the population of the parish increased alarmingly. Eventually a system of tickets was introduced which could be obtained only by regular attendance at the parish vestry. St Mary Le Strand was a far poorer parish and would certainly have given their paupers every encouragement to die on the other side of the parish boundary. Perhaps that is why the watch-house was here, to stop too many corpses being dumped in their territory.

The next section of the Strand passes the enormous new office block built on the estate of the Duke of Norfolk. The family were given the site after the Reformation and retained ownership till 1973. However, there is still a ducal memory here because the Duchess and her daughters were asked back to plant the trees in the middle of the quadrangle.

The roadway curves right to sweep around St Clement Danes to the corner of Essex Street where this walk finishes. The Fifth Walk returns to Charing Cross by way of the Embankment; the Seventh Walk takes us along Fleet Street and through the Temple.

FOURTH ♦ WALK

Along the North Side of the Strand

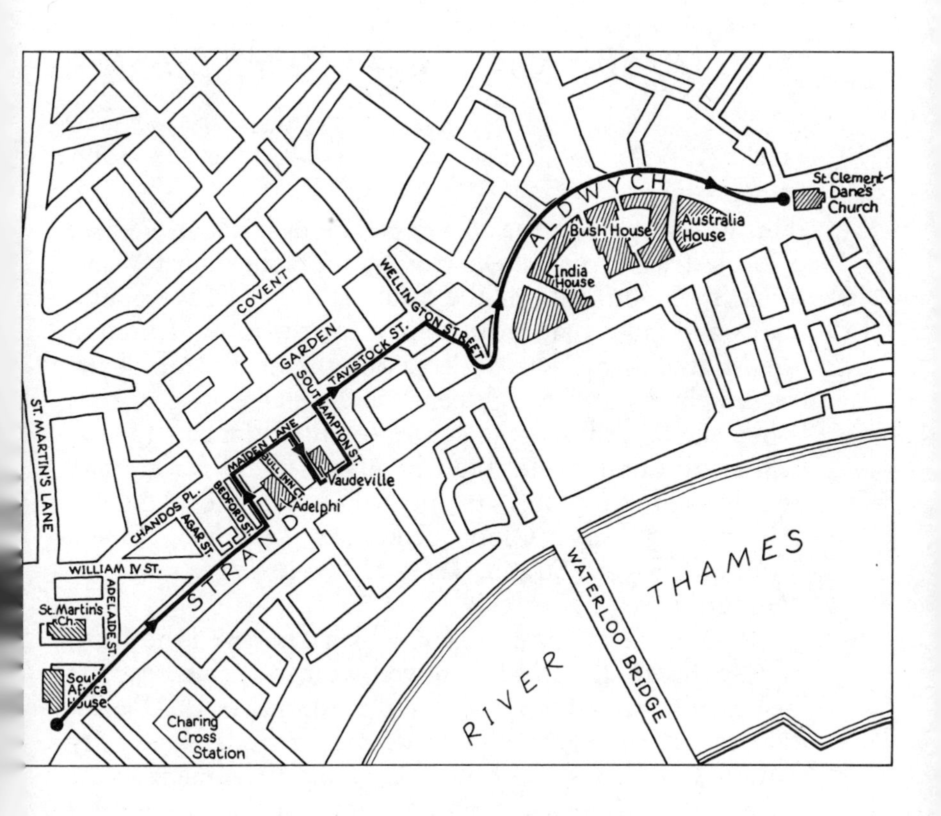

FOURTH ♦ WALK

Along the North Side of the Strand

This walk begins on the corner of Trafalgar Square, where South Africa House meets the Strand. The Third Walk, along the south side of the Strand, looked at the courtyards and lanes that recall the bishops who lived here in the Middle Ages. This walk, along the north side of the Strand, looks at the eighteenth and nineteenth centuries when the Strand was the centre of entertainment for the whole of London. In 1890 it possessed no fewer than thirteen of London's twenty theatres: the Adelphi, Aldwych, Gaiety, Globe, Lyceum, Olympic, Opéra Comique, Savoy, Strand, Terry's, Tivoli, Toole's and the Vaudeville.

After the Great Fire of 1666 which destroyed the City, those who could afford it moved west to the new streets being built around St James's and St Martin-in-the-Fields, while the merchants and tradesmen rebuilt their City houses and offices. With the Court and Parliament established at Westminster, this left the Strand as the border between the City and what was becoming known as the West End.

The saying in the nineteenth century was 'Commerce stays east of Temple Bar and Fashion lives west of Leicester Square'. In between was the Strand, full of theatres, pubs, restaurants and cafés. As late as 1890, it was held that no shop stood a chance of success in the Strand unless it sold food or drink. The music-hall song 'Let's

All Go Down The Strand' summed up the way Londoners regarded it.

The corner of South Africa House has a splendid carving of a winged springbok, done in 1934 by Charles Wheeler, who based the idea on the five-thousand-year-old golden winged oryx in the Louvre. The office block beyond it is modern but its wall still carries the name borne by every building on the site since the fourteenth century – Golden Cross House.

The inn that stood here for centuries took the name from the original Eleanor Cross in the middle of the road behind us. It was from the Golden Cross that the Pickwick Club started their immortal adventures, with Mr Jingle's warning to keep their heads down as the coach passed under the inn's low arch. The grisly story he recounted of the lady who was killed because she forgot to duck is perfectly true. The incident had happened only a few years before and Dickens, like every other Londoner of the time, remembered it vividly.

The Queen's Bankers

Along the Strand, at the angle of Duncannon Street, are the famous 'pepper-pots' that decorate the end of the Coutts' Bank block. The pepper-pots are part of the façade built by Nash when he rebuilt this end of the Strand in 1831. It is the only surviving Nash design for commercial premises and there was a tremendous outcry when Coutts wanted to rebuild in the 1970s. They were forced to keep the façade but London lost two of its smallest pubs. One of them was 'The Final', so named because its licence stipulated that it had to close within half-an-hour of the final curtain coming down at Toole's Theatre which stood beside it.

Coutts' Bank has been in the Strand since 1692, when it was founded across the road where Charing Cross Station now stands. Its address then was 'At The Sign of The Three Crowns In The Strand Next Door To The Globe Tavern', the words still printed on its cheques.

The Royal Family have kept their account here since the eighteenth century and Sheridan, Walter Scott and Dickens followed their example. Thomas Coutts was a personal friend of George III and, after a visit to Rome, it was he who told the King of the financial hardship of the last Stuart claimant to the throne, Henry, Cardinal Duke of York. When the French occupied Rome in 1798 and confiscated the Cardinal's property, King George arranged for an annual allowance of £4000 to be paid to him through Coutts'.

The royal links are still strong. During the great amalgamation of the English clearing banks in the 1920s, Coutts' became part of the National Provincial group and would have lost its name if George V had not intervened. A director called on the King to inform him of the proposed change of name and to assure him that there would be no other alteration in the bank's service. The King cut him short: 'We don't bank with the National Provincial anything. We bank with Coutts'.'

Three or four times a week a small horse-drawn carriage comes clopping round Trafalgar Square to draw up in front of the bank. It has no badges or crests and very few of the tourists who photograph it realise that it comes from the royal stables carrying correspondence between the Queen and her bankers. It gives a picturesque touch to London's streets as well as the practical advantage of exercising the royal horses and accustoming them to busy traffic.

The bank is proud of its traditions. All the male members of staff are clean-shaven and wear frock-coats, following rules laid down in the last century. There are still members of the family in the bank; the chairman in 1974 was the appropriately-named Mr Money-Coutts.

The interior is magnificent although its finest feature, the Chinese wallpaper, is inaccessible to the public. When the bank stood across the road in the eighteenth century Lord Macartney, Britain's first Ambassador to China, sent some rolls of Chinese wallpaper to Thomas Coutts.

The paper has hand-painted landscapes and scenes from Chinese life and was the first to be seen in Europe. The bank was very proud of it and hung it on the walls of the Directors' Room. When the bank moved to this side of the Strand in 1904, experts were called in to remove it from the old building and re-hang it here. When the block was rebuilt in the 1970s, the process was repeated. Although the architect was given a free hand with the design, he was given exact instructions on the size of the Directors' Boardroom. It must be the only bank in London planned around two-hundred-year-old sheets of wallpaper.

The Strand is one of many London streets whose numbering causes difficulties for visitors. Coutts' Bank, for example, is at No. 440 while the buildings across the road are Nos. 38–50. Streets were not numbered in London till the end of the eighteenth century; even then it was a matter of choice since many people could not read. Houses were described as 'the second on the left past the third alley by the Red Lion' or by the signboards that hung outside them. It was from the widespread use of signboards that the expression came 'He hangs out at . . .' to describe where someone lived. As the numbering system became more common, two systems were used. The City and the older streets in this part of London numbered their houses consecutively – up one side and down the other; the newer streets used the 'odd and even' method, which allowed more flexibility.

It was not until 1855 that the 'odd and even' system became standard and then it was too late for streets like the Strand to change. It is still a common occurrence for visitors to walk nearly a mile up and down the Strand looking for an address just across the road from their starting point.

The old signboards that stuck out at right angles from every shop and business establishment were a perpetual danger to passers-by. They were banned in 1762 although, as can be seen everywhere in London, pubs, pawnbrokers and banks continue in the old way. When the authorities tried to enforce the rules in their case, they were informed that the pubs and pawnbrokers needed distinctive signs because the poor could not read, and the banks were so wealthy it would not be politic to annoy them.

Epstein's Statues

At the end of the Coutts' block, across Agar Street, is Zimbabwe House with the row of figures below the eaves that caused uproar in Edwardian London. When the British Medical Association made this their headquarters in 1907, the architect commissioned the young sculptor Jacob Epstein to produce a frieze around the building. It was Epstein's first major commission in England and he decided on a row of figures representing the Ages of Man, emphasising the changes in physique brought about by adolescence, maturity and old age.

The nude male figures were complete in every detail and their unveiling, only seven years after the death of Queen Victoria, produced a storm of protest. The papers spoke of decadence and immorality, questions were asked in Parliament, respectable ladies refused to enter the Strand and the offices across the street replaced their windows with frosted glass so that their female clerks could work without embarrassment.

One story is that the 'controversial appendages' were removed by the Rhodesian High Commission when they took over the building in the 1930s, because the figures gave a misleading impression of the inhabitants of the Colony! What really happened is just as amusing. About twenty-five years after the figures were installed, parts started dropping into the street below. Unfortunately, they were the most embarrassing parts, broken off by rain which collected in crevices and then froze. Rather than face a law-suit, the details of which would make him the laughing-stock of London, the High Commissioner had the figures 'pruned' to their present shape.

The opticians Dollond & Aitchison, at No. 428, have been in the Strand since 1750; they list both Nelson and Wellington amongst their customers. The building is nearly a hundred years older than the firm. The nondescript plaster exterior hides a structure of 1670 and the showroom upstairs still has the original Carolean fireplace.

Next to Dollond & Aitchison is a narrow alley called Harvey's Buildings. It is dark and dank, ending in a small depressing courtyard below an incongruous stained glass window that illustrates how fittings installed by one occupant can puzzle subsequent residents.

When Zimbabwe House was being refurbished, the author met an official in this courtyard trying to identify the heraldry on the window. The explanation that it had been installed by the British Medical Association led on to the solution of another puzzle, the acoustics of the hall inside. Members of the audience in the middle of the hall were being heard far more clearly than the speaker on the platform.

What subsequent occupiers had not realised was that the hall was built for anatomy lectures given from a dissecting table in the middle of the hall. The architect had installed a rounded echo-roof in the centre of the hall, well-suited for the doctors, but annoying to other speakers ever since.

A few yards past Bedford Street, the façade of the Royal Society of Arts can be seen across the road (see Third Walk). This is the best spot to admire Adam's frontage with the medallions of cherubs whose painting and musicianship symbolise the aims of the Society. It is also the only place where it is possible to see Adam's engineering skill in reconciling four different street levels – the Strand, Durham House Street, John Adam Street on the other side and the Embankment which can be reached through the archway below the cherubs.

The narrow entry of Exchange Court, beside No. 419 Strand, follows the line of one of the dozens of streams that once ran across the Strand. It is the first of many alleys we shall see in this part of London unchanged since Dickens walked them as a boy.

The words court and alley have become interchangeable now but alleys, from the Norman French 'aller', used to mean a path between buildings too narrow for vehicles, while a court, a small enclosure, comes directly from the Latin when the Roman shepherds grazed their sheep in small enclosures – 'cortes' – on the Latium hills. In the early fourteenth century, the City formalised the situation by stating that streets had to be broad enough for three armed knights to ride side by side and alleys wide enough to allow two men to roll a barrel of wine along them.

Half-way up the Court the pavement widens to form a small courtyard surrounded by neat white-painted buildings, overlooked by a flagpole and clock on one wall. It has an air of almost military neatness because this was until recently the headquarters of the Corps of Commissionaires, one of those organisations peculiar to England which combine charity with efficiency.

After the Crimean War, a Captain Walter was shocked to find how little provision was made to assist ex-servicemen. He thought of the idea of employing time-expired soldiers and sailors to act as messengers and watchmen and, in 1859, he recruited seven old soldiers to form the Corps of Commissionaires. Walter brought his minute organisation to the public eye by marching his seven men down to Westminster Abbey for a special service. He also persuaded his brother to publicise the Corps' existence. Since the brother was editor of *The Times*, the Corps started its life on an excellent footing and grew to become a feature of English life. The family connection continued for 116 years till the last Walter resigned from the post of Commandant in 1975.

The little courtyard was the parade-ground of the original commissionaires where they were inspected each morning before going off to their duties. The offices on the left were the headquarters and orderly room; the two buildings on the right were rest-rooms with two small plaques to show they were built in 1902 and 1910.

Another alley on the right leads back to the Strand behind the building that used to be one of Yates's Wine-bars. Built for serious drinking in the days when the Strand was thronged every night with pleasure-seekers, it was constructed around the single narrow bar that is still one of the longest in London.

Exchange Court leads up to Maiden Lane, past the boundary mark on the wall that shows we are entering the parish of St Paul's Covent Garden.

Maiden Lane

Maiden Lane was originally a country lane, named after a small shrine to the Virgin Mary that stood at the junction at the far end. The building on the Exchange Court corner stands on the site of Turner's birthplace; the house immediately beyond it was once the Cider Cellars, an all-night tavern famous for its singing which Thackeray frequented often and remembered in *Pendennis*.

The Lane was part of the Duke of Bedford's Covent Garden estate and access was restricted till late in the nineteenth century. Anyone who took a cab from the Strand to Holborn had to decide whether to pay a toll to pass through the estate or take the longer route round the outside. Many of the tolls were abolished in the 1880s although the streets did not become public rights of way for another ten years.

A wall closed this end of Maiden Lane until 1857, when it was taken down at the personal request of Queen Victoria. She used to attend performances at the Adelphi Theatre and entered by a private door in Maiden Lane to avoid the crowds in the Strand. The narrowness of the Lane meant the Royal carriage was unable to turn around, so the Duke of Bedford was informed that Her Majesty would be grateful if the wall could be removed to allow her to drive through. The Duke took it down at once but made sure that a barrier across the road stopped lesser mortals from using it. Even though the barrier is long gone, the entrance is still so narrow that only one vehicle can pass through at a time.

A few yards along to the right is the stage-door of the Adelphi Theatre with the Royal coat of arms that commemorates Victoria's use of this back entrance. The Adelphi has been here since 1806, staged the original *Tom and Jerry* in 1821 and the first Negro Minstrel show in 1839.

In 1897 this stage-door was the setting of a murder that shocked London, when a madman stabbed 'Handsome Bill' Terriss, one of London's leading actors. Terriss's ghost was seen here often on winter evenings until the 1950s, when a psychical research paper solemnly reported that it had moved to Covent Garden Underground Station.

Beyond the Adelphi stage-door, past Nos. 16 & 17 which are late seventeenth century, Bull Inn Court runs back to the Strand. The Court was for centuries the home of England's oldest secret detective service, the Post Office Special Investigation Department, originally founded around 1555 to track down treason and heresy. There has been a pub down at the end for just as long, although the present building is Victorian.

The pub at No. 13 Maiden Lane has been here since 1692, while Rule's across the road started in 1798. It is now the oldest restaurant in the West End. Every noted figure of the nineteenth century dined here and Rule's prize a theatre programme given to them by Dickens after one of his amateur productions. To the right of the main entrance is a side door especially built for Edward VII so that he could entertain his lady friends in private.

A plaque on the right records that Voltaire lived here in 1727 when he was a frequent visitor to the Old Bedford Head across the road at No. 41, one of the most historic taverns in London. The Old Bedford Head, recently re-named 'the Maple Leaf', has been here since the time of Queen Anne and was a favourite resort of Robert Walpole and Alexander Pope. The latter mentioned it twice in his poems:

> When sharp with hunger, scorn you to be fed,
> Except on pea-chicks at the Bedford Head?

The pub retained its place in London's social history in this century by providing an upstairs room for a young Charlie Chaplin to practise acrobatics and by being the first pub in the country to install an espresso coffee machine.

Turn down the steps of Lumley Court towards the Strand. On a dark rainy evening this is one of the most sinister places in London, far closer to the 1880s than the 1980s. High walls on either side, steep slippery steps and flickering gas-lamps evoke the days of Dickens or Sherlock Holmes.

The new office building at No. 399 Strand, beside Lumley Court, is the site of Romano's Restaurant, the centre of Bohemian night-life at the end of the last century. It was the outrageous behaviour of Romano's habitués and their ladyfriends that gave the decade the name 'the Naughty Nineties'. Although their ghosts have long gone, it is still possible to re-enact the famous bet that poor Romano himself lost not once, but twice.

One night, one of the many customers who owed the 'Roman' money, bet him that it was possible to tell the time from the Law Courts clock down at the other end of the Strand while standing outside the restaurant doorway. The 'Roman' considered, thought of the two churches that block that end of the street and took the bet. The party trooped out to the pavement here and the 'Roman' discovered that the illuminated Law Courts clock was (as it still is) very visible, beside the two churches.

A month later, the 'Roman' tried to retrieve his money and bet another of his clientele that he could check his watch by the Law Courts clock from his own doorway. The customer, a journalist who had dropped in from his Fleet Street office, looked at him oddly, grinned and took the bet. Romano led the way outside to find to his horror that the clock was invisible. He took the party across the street and even persuaded them to walk fifty yards down the Strand, but to no avail. He paid his money and, while the winner celebrated inside, the 'Roman' walked disconsolately down to the Law Courts. It was only when he arrived there that he discovered what the newspaper man had known all along, that the lamp inside the clock had been undergoing repairs for a week.

Southampton Street which connects the Strand to Covent Garden takes its name from one of the courtesy titles of the Dukes of Bedford. W. S. Gilbert was born where the Post Office stands now and Vincent Van Gogh stayed here in 1883 for what he said was the only happy year of his life.

A building constructed of peculiarly coloured bricks stands a few yards up on the left-hand side. It was built in 1855 as an advertisement to show that coloured bricks were no more expensive than the normal red or yellow but the fashion never became popular.

The ornate baroque clock on the right of the street was designed by the architect Edwin Lutyens for Sir George Newnes. The building was then the centre of Newnes's magazine empire and *Tit-Bits*, *The Strand Magazine*, *The Wide World* and *John O'London's Weekly* were published here.

Newnes had a particular reason for employing Lutyens to design the clock. The building on the far corner, just beyond Newnes's office, was until recently the offices of *Country Life* magazine built by Lutyens in 1904. It was Lutyens's first major commission in London and the *Country Life* people were extremely proud of it. George Newnes felt they had gained an advantage over him but, since he had just built new offices himself, he could not afford to knock them down and start again as they had.

He compromised by getting Lutyens to design this ornate clock. His intention was that it would impress everybody so much as they walked up the street, they would not notice the new *Country Life* building beyond it. Since he saw no reason to disguise his patronage of the arts, he specified that the numbers on the dial should be replaced by the letters G-E-O-R-G-E-N-E-W-N-E-S which remained there till a few years ago.

The dark church on the corner where Maiden Lane enters Southampton Street stands on the site of Robert Boyle's laboratory, where he formulated Boyle's Law. Charles II came here to admire his experiments; the furnace Boyle used in his work on the transmutation of metals was still in use when the old building was pulled down in 1885.

Immediately beyond Maiden Lane, at 27 Southampton Street, is David Garrick's house, where he lived at the peak of his career from 1749 to 1772. The glass in the windows, however, cannot be earlier than 1755. The date can be set exactly because it was the year Garrick presented *The Chinese Festival.* Although he was the most admired actor in London, *The Chinese Festival* was a disaster; to make sure he appreciated the fact the audience came here after the show and broke every window in the house.

Tavistock Street runs to the right past the corner block designed by Lutyens in 1904. It is a perfect example of his so-called 'Hampton Court Wrenaissance' style and the carvings of animals and birds are now all that is left to remind us of the *Country Life* magazine which commissioned it. We shall look at Covent Garden in another walk, but this is the best place to see the motto of the Dukes of Bedford which became famous as a popular song in the 1970s. Across the road, on the attic roof of the old Jubilee Market building, is the Bedford crest and the motto 'Che Sera Sera'.

The office on the corner of Burleigh Street has an enormous coat of arms to show it was once the local office of the Metropolitan Board of Works, which looked after the sewers, streets and lighting of London for much of the nineteenth century. Adjoining it in the angle around the corner is one of London's ugliest buildings, the old rectory of St Paul's Covent Garden, designed by Butterfield in 1859.

Some of the original Tavistock Street houses are at the far end, beyond the Wellington Street crossing. London's oldest street sign can be seen from the pavement outside No. 15. Just below the roof-line of No. 34 across the road is a small oblong plaque with the faded inscription 'Yorke Street 1636'.

The Bookmakers' Club

We retrace our steps and turn downhill into Wellington Street. On the left, at the corner of Exeter Street, is the impressive doorway of the old Victoria Club, the activities of whose members were once followed as eagerly by one section of London society as others followed the political activities of the Carlton and Liberal Clubs.

Until betting shops were authorised a few years ago, it was illegal to take cash bets off the course. The result was a thriving industry of bookmakers and their runners devoted to making sure that punters could place their bets, legal or not. Since so many Londoners came to the Strand for their amusement, it was an ideal place for bookmakers to carry out their trade, employing runners to take bets at every street corner and using quiet corners of pubs to work out their winnings and make up their betting books.

The difficulty for the would-be client was to find a bookmaker in the Strand crowds. It was to meet this problem that bookmakers started wearing the conspicuous clothing still called 'bookies' tweeds'. At a time when everybody wore black, grey or a daring dark blue, tweed suits of orange and green checks made identification easy. Their 'loud' clothing (so-called because it was considered to shriek to the Heavens) certainly brought them more business but also made it easier for the police to keep an eye on them.

The solution was to have their own club where they could settle with each other in private and, over the doorway, is a relief carving of the animal on which their fortunes were based – the racehorse. The club became an important institution in the racing world. While the Jockey Club decided on runners and the organisation of race-courses, the Victoria Club became the official source of starting prices – a much more important matter so far as millions of gamblers were concerned.

The Victoria Club also became famous for the high level of betting that took place amongst the members themselves. The bookmakers were immensely proud of their billiard table which had been made for Queen Victoria and the members played each other for enormous sums. The club championship used to take weeks to complete because the entire membership gathered to watch, staking large sums on the result of each stroke.

Henry Irving's Theatre

The frontage of the Lyceum Theatre dominates the bottom of Wellington Street. The first Lyceum was built in 1771 and Madame Tussaud held her London waxworks exhibition here in 1802. Rebuilt in 1816 by Samuel Beazley, it was burned down a few years later and Beazley came back to re-build it in 1831. The enormous portico dates from that period. It was probably at that time that the nasty spikes were inserted around the bottom of the pillars, an effective device for preventing vagrants from using the bases as seats.

This is the portico that Henry Irving knew when he played here from 1871 to 1902, breaking every theatrical tradition and proving that Shakespeare could be a financial success. He was a perfectionist and drove his staff to distraction in his search for dramatic stage effects. When his rehearsal of *Macbeth* was interrupted by a tremendous clap of thunder that shook the building, he shouted into the wings: 'Excellent! Excellent! That's exactly what I wanted. Make sure you do it again tonight.'

The theatre was rebuilt in 1903 although the portico was retained from sentiment. It was then taken over by the Melville brothers, two of the most unusual characters in London's theatrical history. Unlike most theatrical managers who flaunted their wealth as a sign of success, the Melvilles made a point of impressing everybody with their poverty.

They scrimped on everything they did, used old plays and sets discarded by others, paid minimum wages and acted as their own producers and writers. In 1920 they disagreed on what to do with the Lyceum and, since neither would give way, it remained empty for three years. Although they shared the same office, they refused to speak to each other during that period, conducting all business through their unfortunate assistant whose desk was brought in to stand between theirs. Despite this, they provided London with a series of successful shows and pantomimes for thirty years. They died within a year of each other as two of the wealthiest men in England.

Around The Aldwych

Just around the corner of the Strand is a pub named the Samuel Beazley with a clock in the shape of a beer barrel on the wall outside. This was installed a hundred years ago to provide both an advertisement for the pub and a social service at a time when few people possessed watches. The 'new' electric light that illuminated the clock face had the further advantage of indicating when the establishment was open for business.

A door in a corner of the bar connects with the back stage of the Lyceum, enabling the theatre staff to drink with the minimum of inconvenience and, presumably, assuring the pub of a regular clientele. The man after whom the pub is named was an entrepreneur of extraordinary energy. He was an architect who built Irving's theatre and his financial affairs were as complicated as his private life. His epitaph can be seen inside:

Here lies Samuel Beazley
Who lived hard and died easily

The Aldwych

The impressive bank across the road to the left is Inveresk House, built as the headquarters of the old *Morning Post* which merged with the *Daily Telegraph* in 1937. It was a newspaper of such respectability that it made *The Times* look like a yellow scandal sheet. Around the corner of Inveresk House stretches the Aldwych, the semi-circle of roadway built at the turn of the century to join the newly-widened Strand to Kingsway, the broad road cut to connect the Strand to High Holborn.

Until Charing Cross Road and Kingsway were built, there was no main road north from the Strand. Every vehicle travelling to Holborn had to wind through a series of narrow lanes like those we have just looked at or pay tolls to drive through the Bedford estate.

The big office block across the road stands on what was till 1957 the site of the Gaiety Theatre. This was the home of the Gaiety Girls, so many of whom married peers of the realm that the House of Lords became known as the 'actresstocracy'. A plaque just around the corner commemorates the old theatre and another, a few yards beyond, commemorates Marconi's first public broadcasts in 1922.

The first theatre on the left is the Strand which has changed its name five times in its eighty years. Intended to replace a previous Strand Theatre, it opened as the Waldorf in 1905, became the Strand in 1909, changed its name to the Whitney in 1911 when it was bought by Mr F. C. Whitney and reverted to the Strand again in 1913. It staged the first performance of *Arsenic and Old Lace* in 1942.

A plaque beside the Strand Theatre commemorates Ivor Novello, who died here. The next section of the Aldwych is occupied by the Waldorf Hotel whose best feature should be viewed from the other side of the road.

When Kingsway and the Aldwych were planned at the turn of the century, the British Empire was at its zenith. The widening of the Strand and the building of the Aldwych gave the authorities the chance to emulate the ideas of Nash a hundred years before. The Strand was to become an Imperial Highway starting at Australia House, then running past India House, Rhodesia House and New Zealand House to Canada House and South Africa House in Trafalgar Square. (Montreal Place running alongside India House shows where Canada House would have stood if they had not moved into the College of Physicians building in Trafalgar Square.)

The general idea was carried out and, while the embassies of foreign nations lie to the west of Trafalgar Square in Mayfair and Belgravia, most of the offices of the old Imperial territories are to be found around the Strand.

India House, the most decorative of all the Commonwealth buildings, was built by Sir Herbert Baker in 1930. He went to India for inspiration and brought workmen back with him to carve the intricate stonework and tracery that adorn the interior. The word 'INDIA' over the entrance is in English, Urdu and Devenagari characters while each of the twelve Indian provinces has its own badge. The roundels on the wall represent Bengal (a tiger), Bombay (a ship), Madras (a fort), United Provinces (fishes and a bow and arrow), Punjab (five rivers and the sun), Central Provinces (snakes), Bihar and Orissa (the Bodhi Tree), Burma (a peacock), Assam (a rhinoceros), Delhi (an elephant), Baluchistan (camels) and the North West Frontier (a moon over a gateway).

From the entrance of India House, look across to the Waldorf Hotel which recently achieved popularity by reviving tea-dances, an almost forgotten feature of London social life. The Waldorf's best external feature is the set of cherubs along the frieze below the roof. It is a pity that they are not lower where they could be seen more easily. Some are singing, some painting and some are playing musical instruments. Perhaps the most amusing are the pair fifth and sixth from the right. One is carving a bespectacled bust with a mallet much too heavy for him which is clearly about to slip from his outstretched hand. Directly behind the sculptor another small figure, clutching a doll, is looking horror-struck at the disaster about to occur.

Beside the Waldorf Hotel is the Aldwych Theatre whose close resemblance to the Strand Theatre stems from their being built as a pair by the same architect. From 1925 to 1933 this theatre was famous for the Aldwych farces. It is now the London base of the Royal Shakespeare Company. It was built in 1905 for Seymour Hicks and his wife Ellaline Terriss, one of the most successful married couples in musical comedy. Their shows always opened with Seymour Hicks as the first character to appear on stage, while his wife was always the last.

If the plot did not fit that arrangement, it was altered till it did. Ellaline Terriss was already an experienced actress when she opened the Aldwych in 1905, but she lived long enough to take her bow at its diamond jubilee and to send goodwill messages to the cast for a further five years after that.

The enormous building looking up Kingsway is Bush House, built in 1919 by an American, Irving T. Bush. He intended it to be an exhibition centre of all the goods manufactured by the firms which had their large offices along the new Kingsway. As a sop to fears that he was about to emulate Lord Astor and take over the London property market, Mr Bush erected the two figures of Britain and America over the portico, dedicating the building to the friendship of the English-speaking peoples.

The figure on the right (America) lost an arm from a bomb in the last war and, at the suggestion of the American Embassy, it was left unrepaired for thirty years as a token of joint sacrifice and mutual suffering.

The new arm on the figure was fitted in 1977. An American visiting London during the Queen's Jubilee celebrations decided to make his own contribution to the occasion by restoring the damage. To ensure that it was an all-American job, he had the arm carved in America and brought over a mason to instal it.

Bush House has two other interesting features. The first is the lettering used for the words 'BUSH HOUSE' in the title and 'PUSH' and 'PULL' on the big doors. The capital letter 'U' is represented by 'V', the correct form since the rounded version was not officially accepted into the English language till 1961. The other idiosyncrasy stems from the fact that Mr Bush was a Mohammedan. To the right of the main entrance is a space filled with columns; the centre column of the right-hand row has deliberately been left with an uncarved capital to meet the dictum that 'perfection is an attribute of Allah; it is impiety for man to achieve perfection'.

From Bush House, Kingsway stretches northwards with the same dullness of architecture that we saw in Northumberland Avenue. Kingsway was opened in 1905 to relieve the appalling traffic conditions of Victorian London and to replace Chancery Lane and Drury Lane as the main axis for traffic coming south to cross the river.

A clue to the boring similarity of the office blocks along Kingsway is in the names they bear, each reflecting the Imperial style and period in which they were built – York, Alexandra, Prince's, Central, Windsor, Crown, Regent, Kingsway, Victory, Connaught, Africa and Imperial House. The close resemblance of the buildings to each other is explained by the fact that the same firm of architects designed twelve of the sixteen along the street.

From the same spot it is possible to see how the semicircle of buildings that form the Aldwych have a similar uniformity, but to a much lesser extent. A competition was held for a single design for the whole Aldwych. Competitors were told to use the Imperial Palladian architectural style and were given a predetermined building height. Hundreds of designs were produced but the judges could not agree on an overall winner. They compromised by taking the best dozen entries and asked each architect to design one building each. The result is the façade stretching around the Aldwych, uniform in height and architectural style, but with each building trying to outdo the others in its decorative detail.

Follow the curve of Bush House round to the right and turn down Melbourne Place, the wide passage that separates it from Australia House. At a point twenty yards down the left-hand side, stop and look at the wall opposite. Above the third row of windows are three plaques, difficult to spot because they are the same colour as the brickwork. They represent a miniature Test Match. The one on the left shows a kangaroo while the right-hand plaque is of an English lion. The centre panel shows a ball taking off the bails of what is clearly an English wicket since the grim-faced wicket-keeper is wearing an Australian cap. It is one of London's best architectural jokes.

From the upper end of Melbourne Place, Australia House curves round to its enormous entrance surmounted by the bronze sculpture of the Horses of the Sun. The two groups of statuary on either side of the doorway represent Australia past and present. Burke and Wills are shown exploring the barren interior; the other side shows the same land cultivated for sheep and corn. The Australian Government insisted that every plank, brick and bag of cement used to construct the building should be shipped from Australia. The only English material is the facing of Portland stone to match its neighbours.

St Clement Danes

Beyond Australia House is the church of St Clement Danes. The legend is that Alfred the Great granted this area outside the City walls to those Danes who had married English women and wished to remain in England. Historians used to dismiss the theory as mere folklore but recent excavations along the Strand have shown that the original church stood in the centre of a large Viking settlement.

The clock is blue and gold, following the edict of Henry VIII (see Fourteenth Walk), while the weathervane displays the anchor that appears on all the parish boundary marks. The symbol was chosen because St Clement was martyred by being tied to an anchor and thrown into the sea. Wren built the present church in 1679 and the parishioners were so pleased with it that they voted to send him a barrel of wine as well as his fee.

Some years later the church was the centre of a tremendous scandal when someone noticed that the altar cloth, supposedly depicting St Cecilia, bore an astonishing resemblance to the wife of the Jacobite Pretender. Since the Rising of 1715 was a recent memory, this caused great excitement and the Bishop of London had to intervene, ordering the cloth to be removed.

Dr Johnson was a regular attender here and his favourite place in the church is still pointed out. The list of rectors on the wall includes William Webb-Ellis, the man who founded the game of Rugby football when he picked up the ball and ran with it 'with a fine disregard for the rules of the game . . .'

St Clement Danes is now the RAF church. Every Allied squadron that took part in the Second World War is commemorated by 750 slate slabs set in the floor. The bells still play the old nursery rhyme 'Oranges and Lemons' and, since the 1920s, the children of the local school come here every March to a special service and take an orange and a lemon home with them afterwards.

Each service here is announced by a single calling-bell with an unusually high note. It is the church's proudest possession, cast in 1586; it rang out when Elizabeth I came by on her way to St Paul's to give thanks after the defeat of the Armada.

Outside the church is a statue to Lord Dowding, who commanded the RAF forces which won the Battle of

Britain. The statue was unveiled in 1988 and a close inspection of the plinth shows that an error was made in the list of Dowding's decorations. The 'CMG' (Companion of the Order of St Michael and St George) had to be altered from the non-existent 'GMG' originally carved by the mason.

A small open space looks down Fleet Street behind the east end of the church. A plaque commemorates the old Holy Well that was given its title before the Conquest and the splendid ornate lamps in black and gold match the Gothic grandeur of the Law Courts.

Beside the church is a statue of Dr Johnson. Opinions vary on its artistic merit but it is unique in London. A number of memorials around London were privately sponsored by admirers or followers of the person portrayed but none of them is such an individual effort as this. The man who proposed this statue secured permission from the authorities to erect it and then went on to design it, carve it, fix it in position and even carry out the unveiling ceremony.

The versatile enthusiast was Percy Fitzgerald, writer, London historian and amateur sculptor who felt Fleet Street was incomplete without a statue of its greatest resident and decided to do something about it. Since he was prepared to undertake the work and pay any costs himself, the church authorities were quite happy to let him place the statue here and Fitzgerald persuaded Princess Louise to perform the unveiling. Unfortunately, the death of Edward VII cancelled all Royal engagements and the Princess was unable to attend – so he went ahead and did it himself.

FIFTH ♦ WALK

Essex Street, Cleopatra's Needle and Buckingham Street

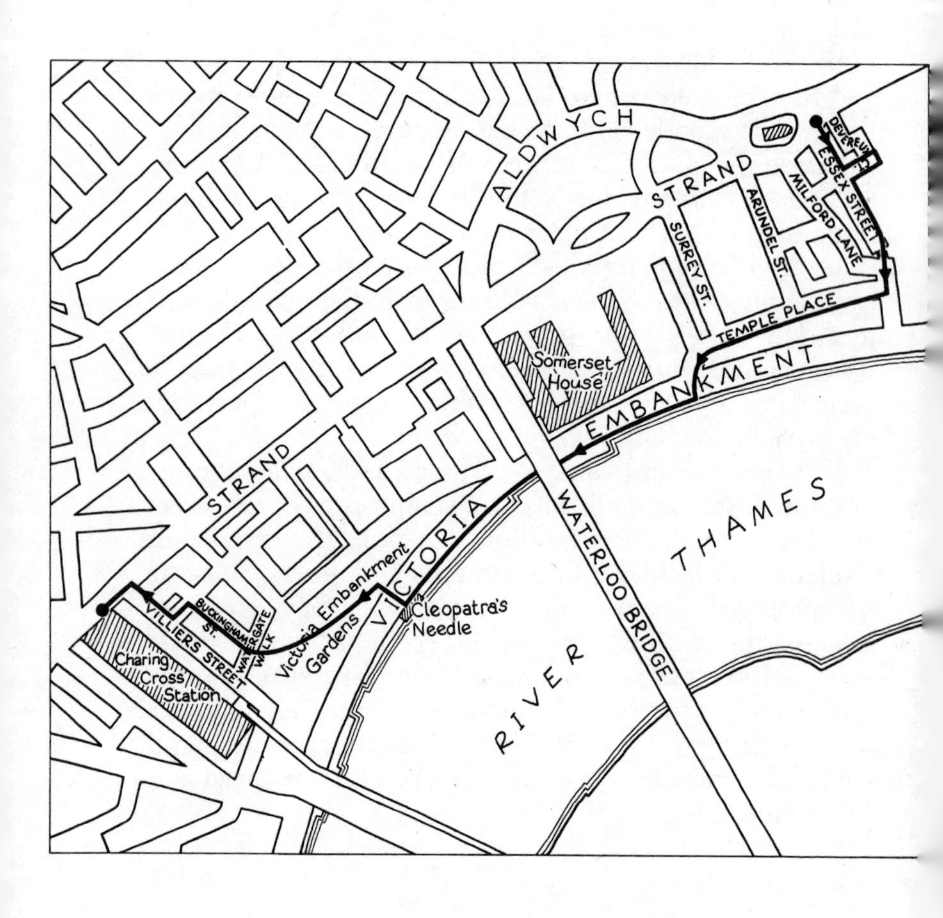

FIFTH ♦ WALK

Essex Street, Cleopatra's Needle and Buckingham Street

Essex Street runs south from St Clement Danes to the river. It was once the Outer Temple, the part of the Temple that lay outside the City boundaries. The Bishop of Exeter had his London house here in 1320 and the narrow entrance to the street shows where his gatehouse stood.

The Bishop lost the site after the Reformation but the new owners did not prosper. The Duke of Norfolk was given the site first and he was executed for his conspiracy with Mary, Queen of Scots. He was followed by Robert Dudley, Earl of Leicester, who was arrested for poisoning Nicholas Throgmorton here in 1571. The next tenant, Elizabeth's favourite Robert Devereux, Earl of Essex, was executed after the uprising of 1601.

His son, the third Earl of Essex, became a general in the Parliamentary army and died here in 1646. In 1670 Nicholas Barbon bought the site as one of his many speculations and laid out the street as we see it today.

Essex Hall, a few yards down on the right, has been dedicated to religion for over eight hundred years, ever since the Templars built a small church here in the twelfth century. When the Bishops of Exeter came here, they used it as their domestic chapel. In 1774 it became the first Unitarian church in England. The congregation at the first service included Benjamin Franklin, who seems to have been involved in just about every controversy in London at the time.

Opposite Essex Hall is a Victorian building with some splendid plaster heads on the frontage. Their significance is lost on the passer-by today but they were put there as an advertisement for *The Portfolio* art magazine who built the office in 1884.

No. 40, now occupied by the Edgar Wallace public house, is the most historic site in the street. In the eighteenth century it was the home of Lady Primrose, who demonstrated her strong Jacobite sympathies by giving shelter in 1747 to Flora Macdonald, the girl who had helped Bonnie Prince Charlie to escape after the Jacobite Rising of 1745.

In September 1750 No. 40 was the setting for one of the odder incidents of London's history, the secret visit of the Prince himself. The Young Pretender stayed with Lady Primrose for five days, during which he was received into the Anglican church at St Mary Le Strand and walked amongst the crowds in The Mall. The reason for his visit is still a mystery. His presence in London was discovered by the authorities but no action was taken to arrest him. King George II, showing great magnanimity to the man who had nearly dispossessed him five years before, ordered him to be left alone: 'When he gets tired of England, he will leave it.'

A few years later a pub called the Essex Head was built on the site although the 'Head' itself is around the corner. The landlord had been a servant of Dr Johnson's friend Mr Thrale and Johnson promptly founded Sam's Club here to encourage trade. It remained the Essex Head till 1976 when it was renamed the Edgar Wallace. The ceremony was performed by Wallace's daughter Penny who was too tactful to point out that her father had been a teetotaller. The present building is Victorian but, as with many pubs on old sites, the cellars are much older. Those below the Edgar Wallace may well be those in which Lady Primrose kept her claret for the Prince two hundred years ago.

Devereux Court leads around the corner to the Devereux Tavern. In 1652 this opened as the Grecian Coffee House which became a meeting place of London society for a hundred years. The Royal Society and Royal Academy used to dine here after their meetings at Somerset House and even the Privy Council met here on occasion.

It was renowned for the heated political discussions of its patrons. These occasionally led to blows and high words, but the most serious argument was over the correct placing of the accent in a Greek word. Two young men became so incensed over the question that they came out to the alley and continued the argument with their swords till one lay dead.

On the far side of the pub, up on the roof-line, is the 'Essex Head' itself, a bust of Robert Devereux, third Earl of Essex, who gave his names to these streets. Underneath the bust is an inscription: 'This is Devereux Court 1676'. The Grecian was refurbished and renamed in 1843 as the Devereux Tavern but kept its character. At the time of writing it is still a splendid example of a pub of Dickens's day.

We return to Essex Street and turn down towards the river. The street was bombed during the war but has been so well restored that it is difficult to tell which are the houses Barbon built in the 1670s. Nos. 11, 14, 19 and 34 are original and Nos. 32–35 date from the 1750s. The ornate frontage at Nos. 36–39 was built in 1892 as an advertisement by a publisher who wanted to show up his staider rivals on either side.

At the bottom of the street is another of the Thames watergates, showing where the river came before they built the Embankment. The splendid gateway was originally erected by Barbon in 1680 as an architectural feature as well as providing a landing-stage for the food, fuel and materials that would be needed by the residents.

With only one bridge over the Thames till 1750, it was far cheaper to have deliveries made by water. The tolls for every handcart and barrow trundling through the City streets were prohibitive.

The Temple gardens lie to the left of the watergate steps. The Knights Templar gave the Temple their name in 1162 and it has been the home of the barristers of the Inner and Middle Temple since the fourteenth century. The guidebooks state that all trace of the Outer Temple outside the City boundary vanished when the bishops came to Essex Street six hundred years ago. However, one single vestige remains. At the bottom of the watergate steps the brickwork is broken by a vertical course of grey stone. It was here long before Nicholas Barbon erected the gate in 1680; it was probably here when Queen Elizabeth came to visit Essex four hundred years ago. It is the last of the old Outer Temple and the arrowhead mark cut on the stonework shows that it still has a use today as a reference point for the surveyors.

The path from the watergate runs into Temple Place. The building on the corner was constructed in 1895 by the American millionaire William Waldorf Astor as his London estate office. Astor, whose family had made one of the greatest fortunes in the world from the American fur trade and property development in New York, came to England in 1890 to cut a tremendous figure in London society.

The building is one of the most luxurious in London. It cost Astor a quarter of a million pounds to build. It is said that he specified that every type of wood and mineral known in the world was to be used. He secured the finest mason in England to do the stonework; Starkie Gardner, the iron craftsman, cast and forged the grilles and screens by hand. Columbus' ship, the *Santa Maria*, in gilt copper surmounts the roof. The building is closed to the public, but inside there are pillars of solid ebony and the artist who carved the figures to stand on the newel posts of the staircase was so proud of them he kept them in his bedroom till he died. There is nothing, however, to prevent us entering the forecourt to admire the two cherubs beside the steps who are busy on the telephone.

Temple Place leads up the slope to the new Howard Hotel named after the Dukes of Norfolk whose estate this was for so long. A few yards beyond the hotel is a shabby wooden hut on the left. They seem unlikely adversaries but, for some months, this small shack played David to the Goliath of the enormous new block across the road.

Up to 1914 the majority of London's cabs were horse-drawn. There were several models – hansoms, growlers, four-wheelers – but with all of them the driver was exposed to the weather. In 1874 some philanthropists started the Cabmen's Shelter Fund to erect small shelters like this one where the cabmen could rest and get a meal. The idea received Royal support and members of the theatrical profession were enthusiastic donors (Sir Squire Bancroft gave the shelter that stood in Leicester Square till 1988). The shelters are vanishing from the streets of London now but the survivors can be recognised by their dark green paint and the letters 'CSF' (Cabmen's Shelter Fund) carved over the windows.

The new block on the right stretches up to the Strand. Its development took years to plan and cost millions to build. Four streets were demolished, to be replaced by enormous office buildings around a centre quadrangle with this hotel forming the southern side. It was only when the hotel was nearing completion that the developers realised they had overlooked something. In a scene reminiscent of an Ealing comedy of the 1950s, they found that the entrance of their splendid new hotel was blocked by this small wooden shed.

The developers immediately applied for the shelter to be moved but found that might was not necessarily right. The taxi-drivers pointed out that their shelter was a good deal older than the hotel; it had been there since 1880 and there was no good reason why they should move it.

If the planners, architects and developers hadn't bothered to do their homework properly, so much the worse for them. The eventual happy outcome was achieved by someone with the commonsense to ask the taxi-drivers politely if they would accept the inconvenience of the shelter being moved a few yards along the road, on condition that the hotel paid for the move and accompanied it with a donation to the Shelter Fund. And that is what happened.

Our walk follows the curve of Temple Place down towards the river, past the statue of Brunel on the corner and crosses the traffic of the Embankment to the pavement on the river side.

The next building on the right is Somerset House. The parapet railings mark the terrace where George Eliot and her publisher used to walk together. The enormous archway below is the old watergate where barges delivered their loads direct to the Somerset House cellars. The mooring rings show where they tied up.

If you travel along this route by Underground, you may have noticed that the trains seem to run more smoothly along two sections, under the Temple behind us and under Parliament Square up ahead. The reason is that when the Underground railway was designed it was naturally viewed with great suspicion. When permission was sought to lay this line along the Embankment, Parliament and the lawyers were powerful enough to lay down conditions. The conditions they set for the section that ran under their property was that vibration should be minimised and the railway company was forced to lay a special foundation of tan and bark.

The engineers laid the specified foundation but made it clear that they did so under protest, since precautions were entirely unnecessary. They were wrong. When the first train ran through this section half the Portland stone facing fell off this side of Somerset House.

Waterloo Bridge was erected in the 1940s to replace Rennie's bridge of 1817. The old bridge was considered by many to be the most beautiful in Europe and there was an outcry when it was taken down in the 1930s. The name of the bridge is another heartening example of popular opinion overruling officialdom. When Parliament authorised the building of the bridge in 1810, it decided that it would be called the Strand Bridge. This was the name used until it became known that it was to be opened by the Duke of Wellington on the second anniversary of the battle of Waterloo. Public opinion then decided that Waterloo Bridge was the only possible name and Parliament had to pass a hurried Act to change its original decision.

In those days bridges charged tolls to cover their costs and the opening of Waterloo Bridge saw the introduction of the world's first automatic turnstile. The Duke arrived for the ceremony, made his speech and cut the tape. Then, to show everybody how it worked, he went over to the machine, solemnly put his penny in and walked through.

When the bridge started to show signs of age in 1924, a temporary metal structure was built alongside and this was used till 1942. In that year there was enough of the present bridge completed to allow the temporary structure to be dismantled and it disappeared from public view. It reappeared two years later in the most dramatic fashion. When the Allies invaded Germany, the Remagen bridge was the only one left standing over the Rhine. It allowed initial crossings to be made but collapsed very soon afterwards.

The temporary Waterloo Bridge had been carefully stored for just this purpose. It was ready in a special train only a few miles from the Rhine, was installed in a week and became the main traffic artery of the Western Front.

On the other side of the road are steps leading up to the bridge from the Embankment. A few feet up on the left-hand wall is a small plaque showing that we are back within the boundaries of the old Savoy Palace. Under the bridge itself is a remnant of Rennie's old bridge and a viewing platform with a useful diorama showing the buildings to be seen from this spot.

Beside the viewing platform is a floating station of the River Police. We saw an old parish watch-house in Strand Lane but this is the oldest police station in continuous use. The River Police were started in 1798, thirty years before the Metropolitan Police, and they have had a station at this spot ever since. They still have the job of picking up the suicides who have jumped off the bridges but they no longer enjoy the perquisites of Dickens's day. Newspaper readers in his time used to be puzzled as to why all the corpses seemed to be found on the southern side of the river. The reason was that boatmen always landed bodies on the Surrey bank in those days because the authorities on that side paid 50 pence for each body brought ashore. The City on this side paid only 35 pence.

Through the bridge there is another set of gardens on the right. The corner building by the traffic lights is the Institution of Electrical Engineers. It has a small garden in front, the corner of which had for fifty years a telephone box unique in England. It was the only one painted green instead of the standard red.

When public telephone boxes were introduced in the 1920s they were painted bright red because their primary purpose was to enable the public to call for the police and fire brigade. When the Post Office turned up to instal a box on this corner, the Electrical Engineers were not at all happy. There was a tree standing at this corner and the Engineers saw no reason why it should be spoilt by a nasty red telephone kiosk. After long negotiations the box was installed, but it was painted green to match the tree.

The mystery is how did the Electrical Engineers persuade the Post Office to change the colour of just this one call-box? Perhaps pressure was applied in the background; there must have been a great many electrical engineers among the senior ranks of the Telephone

Department. Maybe it is better not to speculate. In any event the green box sat here happily till the 1970s, when a passer-by (the author) noticed that the tree beside it had died. Luckily, he knew the story and was able to warn the Institution. Without a tree to blend with, the telephone box need not be green – so the Institution took immediate action and planted another tree before the Post Office noticed. (At the time of writing the kiosk has vanished, demolished by a lorry. The Institution intends to put a statue of Faraday there instead.)

The next monument on the river balustrade commemorates Sir Walter Besant. It is the only memorial in London showing someone wearing pince-nez. Besant's official job was Secretary of the Palestine Exploration Fund but his ambition was to publish a complete history of London before he died. He spent thirty years on the task but saw only four volumes issued; the remaining twenty came out after his death.

The lamp-posts along the Strand show St Martin giving his cloak to the beggar, because they are in the parish of St Martin-in-the-Fields. The lamp-posts along the Embankment commemorate the fact that it crosses the boundaries of two Cities, London and Westminster. Both were fiercely jealous of their independence, but the Embankment was such an enormous project that the authorities dropped their normal rivalry. That is why the lamps here have a large badge surmounted by a female figure with the arms of the City of London under one arm and the badge of the City of Westminster under the other. They occur nowhere else in London.

Cleopatra's Needle stands a few yards to the west of three boundary marks on the balustrade marking the rival claims of the Savoy, St Clement Danes and St Martin-in-the-Fields.

There must be more anecdotes about Cleopatra's Needle than any other monument in London, starting with the fact that it has nothing to do with Cleopatra. It is doubtful if she ever saw it. It was originally erected in 1450 BC by Thothmes III, the great Pharaoh who introduced chariots and cavalry into the Egyptian army. He is remembered by the hieroglyphics in the centre. Two hundred years later, Rameses II added further panels, claiming equal credit for his kingship, and the first recorded use of the phrase 'King of Kings' appears on his inscription.

Augustus Caesar moved it to Alexandria in 23 BC, seven years after Cleopatra's death, and set it up outside her old palace. Londoners had never heard of Thothmes or Rameses but they had heard of Cleopatra. Whether the historians liked it or not, Cleopatra's Needle is what Londoners decided to call it.

The first attempt to bring it to England was made by Abercrombie in 1801 after he had defeated Napoleon's army. That failed and nothing was done till Mehmet Ali offered it to George IV as a Coronation gift in 1820. Nothing came of that offer nor of the similar offers made to William IV in 1831 and to Victoria after that. When further offers were refused in the 1850s and 1860s, the Khedive decided to sell it. Human nature being what it is, this changed the Government view entirely. Wasting public money bringing a large lump of stone to London was one thing. Letting somebody else dispose of it was quite another.

From learned societies, enthusiastic public support and an element of Government funds, the money was raised to build a special coffin-shaped container to bring the obelisk to England. It arrived at last in 1878 having caused the death of six seamen after it broke adrift in the Bay of Biscay. Its unloading in London brought to a head all the heated arguments on where it should be placed.

One body of opinion felt it was not worth erecting at all because it looked so like a factory chimney. The academics urged that the forecourt of the British Museum was the best site, where it would provide an excellent introduction to the Egyptian antiquities. Another traditionally-minded group remembered Nelson's connection with Egypt and wanted it placed in front of the Naval Hospital at Greenwich. The Round Pond in Kensington Gardens was another suggestion, on the grounds that the obelisk would look as it did by the banks of the Nile. A splinter group urged that the pond in St James's Park was the obvious place. A sixth party felt it should be sited at the Adelphi, to emphasise its classical design.

The engineer responsible for bringing the obelisk to London was quite firm in his view. The only place for the obelisk was beside the Houses of Parliament in Parliament Square. He felt so strongly about it that he went to the expense of having a full-size replica made of wood, painted and carved with hieroglyphics, and installed it in Parliament Square to win over public opinion. The replica appeared in every illustrated paper of the day and led to confusion for twenty years afterwards as visitors to London looked for it in vain around Westminster.

The Parliament Square proposal would certainly have been the final choice if the directors of the Metropolitan Underground Railway had not intervened. They pointed out that 160 tons of granite was not perhaps the best thing to place on top of their new underground railway, since they could not guarantee that it would not drop straight through the roof. Matters reached a stalemate until the Metropolitan Board of Works tentatively offered this site on the Embankment. Nobody really liked the idea but nobody could think of any good reason against it. And that was enough to settle the question.

It was common practice to place a memento under the foundations of important buildings, a custom that goes back to primeval offerings to the gods. The Needle was no exception and the Victorians made a special effort for it. The result was that they needed two caskets, not one, because underneath the Needle rest:

an Imperial measure of a foot length,
an Imperial pound weight,
a bronze model of the obelisk,

a copy of the *Engineering Journal* on vellum, describing the method of setting the obelisk in place,
some jars of Doulton ware,
a piece of stone from the obelisk,
a complete set of Imperial coinage including an Indian rupee,
a translation of the hieroglyphics,
standard gauges down to one thousandth of an inch,
a portrait of Queen Victoria,
copies of the Bible in various languages,
Bradshaw's Railway Guide,
a razor,
a case of cigars,
a set of tobacco pipes,
a box of hairpins and ladies' ornaments,
a child's feeding bottle,
a set of children's toys,
a model of the hydraulic jack used to raise the monument into position,
specimens of wire rope and submarine cable,
a map of London,
copies of national newspapers,
photographs of twelve English beauties,
a two-foot rule,
a London directory,
a copy of *Whitaker's Almanack*.

Yet even with all this preparation, planning and organisation, something went wrong – and it is still wrong today. It is an obvious error but, so great was the secrecy and drama over the final preparations, nobody noticed it till the dreadful moment when the monument was unveiled. The contractor had put the sphinxes the wrong way round. Sphinxes are meant to face outwards, guarding a monument. These break tradition by facing towards it, and officialdom spent a long time looking for someone to blame. Eventually it was decided to brazen the matter out and the official view is that the sphinxes do not face the wrong way; they face inwards to distinguish them from those elsewhere!

The morning after the ceremony a notice was found hanging across the front of the Needle. The author was never discovered but Londoners appreciated his succinct summary of all the excitement:

This monument, as some supposes,
Was put up in the time of Moses.
It passed in time to the Greeks and Turks
And was put up here by the Board of Works.

The steps at the Needle make it one of the few places on the Embankment where it is possible to walk down to the river. It is the best labelled monument in London with no fewer than six explanatory plaques giving its history. It is a pity that none of them mentions that it spans the history of recorded warfare from the introduction of cavalry by Thothmes, through the cannonades of Abercrombie's army in 1801, up to the scars it still bears from the air raids of both World Wars.

The new Embankment seats around the Needle include three presented by the famous stationers, W. H. Smith and Son, and one presented by the Savoy Hotel. The Savoy looms across the roadway to the right of the Shell-Mex clock so the siting of their seat is appropriate enough. The reason for the W. H. Smith seats being here is not quite so obvious.

Cross the road from the Needle into the Embankment Gardens. The W. H. Smith connection with this part of London started when the firm opened shops in the Strand in 1820. In 1851 the firm secured the contract for the bookstalls on the London and North-West Railways. Smith was a strict Methodist and his main reason for tendering was to prevent the sale of what he called 'cheap French novels of the lowest class'. In 1868 he was elected to Parliament by the Strand Division and became involved in the controversy over these gardens.

There had been much discussion over what to do with the old mudbanks won from the river when the Embankment was built. Gladstone considered factories and offices should be built here, so that the Government could recover some of its expenditure. Smith had been a strong advocate of the Embankment for years and led the opposition, taking the view that it should become a garden for the public. He won his case; they are called the Victoria Embankment Gardens but we have W. H. Smith to thank for them.

Smith is probably best remembered today as the original of Sir Joseph Porter, First Lord of the Admiralty in Gilbert & Sullivan's *Pinafore*. Smith was made First Lord in 1877 and even the Queen queried the appointment. Smith was a kind and considerate man and many felt he was thoroughly unsuitable for such a warlike position. This is the aspect that was satirised so cruelly in *Pinafore*. The irony here is that the profits from *Pinafore* and other comedies built the great hotel that looms over these gardens that Smith created. Even more ironic, while Smith has no memorial here other than the three seats across the road, Sullivan's memorial is twenty yards to the right of the gateway and Gilbert's is nearby, beside Hungerford Bridge.

This corner of the gardens is the best place to appreciate the feat of Esmond Drury in 1953. Two Americans staying at the Savoy argued whether it was possible for a fisherman to cast a fly from the roof of the Savoy over the gardens and Embankment into the river. They took their question to Hardy's the famous fly-fishing firm, who in turn put the matter to Drury.

Drury had no head for heights but agreed to try, so long as he was given a safety-line firmly attached to a chimney. He came here one Sunday morning and, with the assistance of a friendly policeman down below to stop the traffic, he proved the feat was possible.

The gardens are full of statues and memorials, although the siting of Robert Burns's statue attracts some comment. Remembering Burns's liking for whisky, it seems odd to see him beside Wilfred Lawson, the famous temperance advocate, and Robert Raikes, the founder of Sunday Schools.

At the western end of the gardens the path bends right to the old York Watergate. This is the best known of the four surviving watergates and was built for the Duke of Buckingham in 1626.

The path at the top of the steps is the old Watergate Walk that Canaletto painted two hundred years ago. Along to the left, steps lead down to a cellar. This is Gordon's Wine Cellar, run for three hundred years by a Free Vintner who had the right to sell wine free of an excise licence. Chesterton and Hilaire Belloc came to the cellars to drink sherry and write their articles amongst the pillars and arches that have been here since Buckingham's day. Under the eaves of the same building is the small flat where Kipling wrote *The Light That Failed* in 1891.

To the left of the steps at the end of the Walk is a small, brick lodge. It was built originally for the porter whose job it was to keep out beggars and vagrants when this was one of London's smartest addresses. In the middle of the eighteenth century the lodge became famous when it was revealed that the occupant, Hugh Hewson, was the original of Hugh Strap the faithful companion of Roderick Random, the eponymous hero of Smollett's novel.

Buckingham Street immediately above the Watergate is best seen on a foggy October evening when the mist from the river softens the electric light. It is not as historic as Whitehall nor as grand as Pall Mall, but its short length has seen more famous men than any street of its size in London. Built by Barbon in 1675 after the Duke of Buckingham had gone, it has changed little over the centuries.

The first house on the left, No. 14, was the home of Samuel Pepys from 1688 till 1701. When he left, Harley the Lord Treasurer (Prime Minister) to Queen Anne, moved in and Swift and William Penn dined with him here. Harley was followed by Lord Torrington, the man who captured Gibraltar in 1704.

The house was rebuilt in 1791 and Humphrey Davy rented the cellar to work on his experiments to prevent corrosion in ships' hulls. The painter William Etty took the ground floor in 1824 and moved to the top storey a few years later. Clarkson Stanfield, another painter, moved into Etty's old rooms and painted sunsets over the Thames in the company of Turner and Flaxman.

The new building on our right, No. 15, has an even more exotic history. Peter the Great of Russia stayed here in 1698 and astonished London with his capacity for brandy. His farewell to King William consisted of a single 'Thank you' in broken English and a brown paper parcel thrust abruptly into William's hands. William was even more startled by the discovery that the bag contained the second largest ruby in Europe. Henry Fielding, the playwright and novelist, moved into the house in 1735, and Dickens came to live on the top floor in 1833. He remembered it fondly and used it in *David Copperfield* years later.

No. 12 is original and Pepys lived here before he moved to No. 14. John Evelyn and Newton came here to dine with him and the staircase they used can still be seen through the doorway. Later residents at No. 12 include Cromwell's daughter and the novelist Benjamin Farjeon.

In 1766 No. 10 was shared by two of the greatest thinkers of the eighteenth century, David Hume and Rousseau, while Peg Woffington, the most beautiful actress of the day, lived at No. 9. Across the road, at No. 21, Samuel Taylor Coleridge started writing *Wallenstein* next door to 'Strata' Smith, the father of modern geography.

Somewhere at the top of the street lived the most unexpected resident of all, Napoleon Bonaparte, who stayed here in 1791. He came to offer his services to the British

Army but was rejected. What might have happened to the world had he been accepted is something to ponder on while we walk around the corner to Charing Cross Station and the end of this walk.

SIXTH ♦ WALK

The North Side of Fleet Street With Diversions

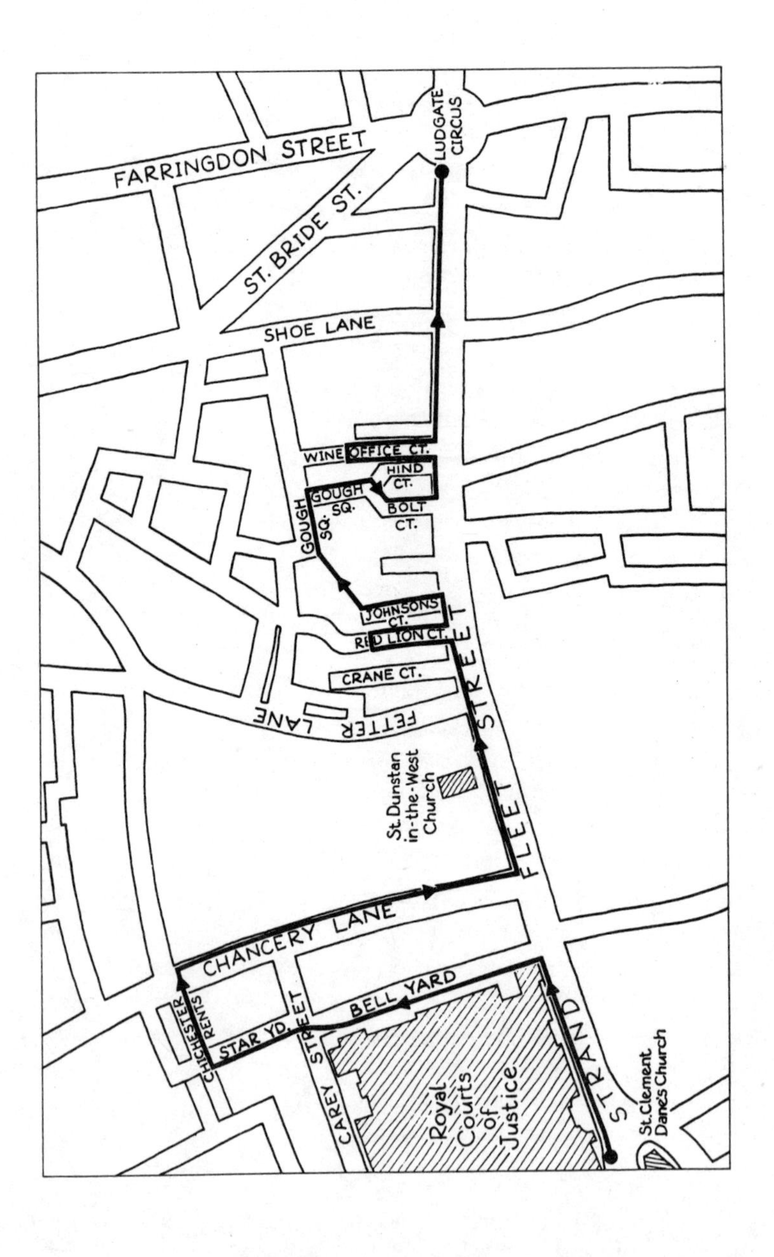

SIXTH ♦ WALK

The North Side of Fleet Street With Diversions

The Sixth Walk begins on the north side of the Strand beside St Clement Danes and looks at the section of London where lawyers and publicans have plied their trade for nearly five hundred years.

The barred road beside us is all that is left of Clement's Inn, one of the old Inns of Chancery, while the Law Courts 'the last gasp of the Gothic Revival in England', tower ahead of us.

In the middle of the road, on the island running eastward from St Clement Danes, is a public lavatory marked by ornate railings. The spiked and fluted ironwork is not just there for decoration; it was considered by the authorities to be a very necessary advertisement.

Public lavatories of a sort existed in London in the early fifteenth century, installed by no less a person than Dick Whittington. They lasted only a few years, and for a long time the only provision for Londoners was squalid shacks built over the many ditches and streams that ran through the City of London. These soon clogged any watercourse running below them, and building reduced the number of streams as more and more houses were constructed within the crowded City walls.

Cesspits dug beside or even inside houses were the main provision till the middle of the last century. People unfortunate enough to be caught short while walking the streets made use of any corner or shelter they could find – hence the 'Commit No Nuisance' rails seen around many buildings in Westminster (see First Walk).

The result was that there was a living to be made by providing facilities for the public in need. Those who plyed this unusual, if necessary, trade were known as 'human lavatories'. Their equipment consisted of a very large cloak and bucket. The bucket was used while the customers concealed themselves from passers-by in the cloak, after which a fee was then taken by the provider of the useful service.

In the 1840s the ban on private cesspits and the construction of main sewers made the present self-flushing water-closet a practical method for householders, and dozens of different styles were shown at the Great Exhibition of 1851. The combination of modern engineering and efficient sewage pipes meant that the authorities could install public lavatories. The first, built beside the Royal Exchange in 1855, was followed by others all over London during the next thirty years. They were the pride of the local authority, although some writers pointed out that it had taken London fifteen hundred years to achieve what had been commonplace amongst the Romans.

The next step was to persuade people to use them. That is the reason so many public lavatories have such ornate ironwork and Victorian lamp-brackets. They are there to try and lure in the Londoners of the 1870s who were reluctant to spend the penny entrance fee (the origin of the phrase) and suspicious of the lavatories below ground level, since liquids do not flow uphill.

The Law Courts

Only the Victorians could have built the tremendous edifice known as the Law Courts and have the confidence to break with a tradition that had lasted a thousand years. Since the laws of the land were decided by the king, only the king could administer justice and the court of justice was wherever the king happened to be. As time went by the king delegated the function of deciding cases to judges and for many centuries the senior court, the Court of King's Bench, sat at Westminster Hall. It took its name from the King's Court and was considered as part of the Royal Household. The executive and judicial functions of the State have been separate for a long time but, in law, it is still treason to kill a judge when presiding in a court since he represents the sovereign.

By the middle of the last century the old Hall at Westminster (see Fourteenth Walk) had become grossly overcrowded and the decision was made to move the courts to a new building. Because of the publicity and scandal that had attended the choice of design of the Whitehall offices and the Palace of Westminster only a few years earlier, there was tremendous interest in the project and designs were submitted by every leading architect of the day. As with many such competitions, the authorities made things more complicated by their inability to state where the new Courts were to stand. Apart from the Metropolitan Board of Works and the parish vestries, there were over a hundred boards, committees and local organisations to be consulted.

When the eventual winner, G. E. Street, was chosen, he was promptly instructed to produce another design for a site on the Embankment. Having done that, he was told that the Law Courts were to be in the Strand after all, but on a smaller area than that originally planned. The Strand site was probably chosen by the lawyers who made sure they were on the committee to decide its location. It is sited neatly between the Inner and Middle Temple to the south and Gray's Inn and Lincoln's Inn to the north, ensuring that every barrister can reach it easily from his chambers. It connects legal London in one continuous strip from Theobalds Road in the north to the banks of the Thames.

Street decided to use a special size of brick and specified that those used in the construction should be 10 × 5 × 2½ inches as opposed to the standard 9 × 4½ × 3ins.

He used 35 million of them with 62,000 tons of Portland stone to provide the facing we see today and, because London was in the middle of a long building strike, the bricks were laid by Germans brought from Hamburg.

The Courts are open to the public and what is probably the only public bar in a court building is just off the great Hall. The Hall itself is as Street designed it but very little of the remainder follows the proportions of his original design. The specifications were constantly changed and he was instructed to accommodate more and more rooms within the same area.

The official appointed by the Metropolitan Board of Works to supervise the project, Acton Smee Ayrton, made Street's life a misery by insisting on screening every one of the 3000 drawings and plans Street produced. Ayrton was notorious for cutting costs whenever he could and his ruthlessness was a byword amongst architects and designers of the day. Only one succeeded in exacting revenge; that story will be told in the Eighth Walk.

Street's death from overwork and worry in 1881 before the building was completed was widely attributed to Ayrton's interference. The narrowness of the corridors, staircases and lobbies that spoil the interior today is certainly due to Ayrton's influence.

The Law Courts is the only secular building in London to have a statue of Christ on top of it. It is not there to provide divine guidance for the lawyers who work here; it is one of a set of four law-givers placed above each side of the building. Christ overlooks the Strand, Solomon is on the west front, King Alfred is on the east and Moses looks down on Carey Street on the north side.

Three of our oldest legal ceremonies take place in the Courts each year. The Lord Mayor comes here to be sworn into office by the Lord Chief Justice and, every October, the Corporation of the City of London comes to pay its Quit Rent to the Crown for a piece of ground near Chancery Lane on which a forge once stood. The rent is six horse-shoes and sixty-one nails which have been paid by the City since 1118. The City pays the Crown another rent of a billhook and hatchet for a piece of land called The Moors in Shropshire. To make sure these are in working order, the City Solicitor solemnly chops some faggots with them in front of the Queen's Remembrancer, as his predecessors have done since 1211.

The Killer Clock

Below the towers on the Strand frontage is the Law Courts clock which, when it was built, was the most accurate in London. Nowadays everyone has access to the correct time but in the nineteenth century it was as much a topic of conversation as the weather is today. People in this part of London made a point of checking their watches daily against this clock in the same way that people in Westminster used to keep a window open to compare their clocks with the chimes of Big Ben.

The clock achieved more publicity when the authorities tried to procure a second model with the same accuracy. There was no record of the maker's name and it required some investigation to discover that it had been made by an Irish carpenter who enjoyed making clocks in his spare time. He was known to have made every ratchet, wheel and spring by hand but, since he could neither read nor write, the secret of the clock's accuracy had died with him.

In 1950 the clock was in the news again when it killed a man in a particularly unpleasant manner. A workman was carrying out routine cleaning when his tie became entangled in the mechanism. The escapement moved as he struggled to free himself, jerked him off balance and he choked to death as he swung above the Strand.

Temple Bar

At the eastern end of the Law Courts is Temple Bar, which marks the limits of the City of London. In the twentieth century there is little excitement in walking by it, but this has been a boundary between the City and the rest of London for over a thousand years. It still serves a practical purpose. Ever since William the Conqueror gave the City its charter on the small scrap of parchment it still treasures, the City has guarded its rights jealously against Parliament and Crown alike.

When the Queen pays an official visit to the City, she halts at Temple Bar to be welcomed by the Lord Mayor. Up to 1877 when Temple Bar was still a gateway across the road, the gate was shut to show the City's independence. It was opened only on the command of the Lord Mayor after a Royal Herald had asked permission to enter. The same ceremony in a more simplified form takes place today; although it is always described as the Lord Mayor welcoming his Sovereign, he is in theory giving her permission to drive through his City.

On a more mundane level the Lord Mayor can, and occasionally does, impose his own taxes on the City Livery Companies. The City has its own police force, a completely separate body from the Metropolitan Police whose jurisdiction surrounds the City. The Lord Mayor takes rank as an Earl while he is in office and he is the only permanent member of the Queen's Privy Council. While other Privy Councillors lose their appointment on the death of the Sovereign, the Lord Mayor's appointment continues since in theory the new Sovereign has no choice in his selection.

Although the Tower of London is a Royal fortress lying outside the City boundaries, the Lord Mayor receives a list of the Tower's passwords signed personally by the Sovereign. The rule was tested as late as 1883 when Queen Victoria was at Balmoral and a Court official decided it was unnecessary to bother her with such a minor matter. He signed the list himself and sent it to the Mansion House. The Lord Mayor took one look, caught the next train to Balmoral, walked up to the Queen, put the list in her hand with the words 'The City presents its humble duty' and marched out again. Victoria realised exactly what had happened and its constitutional importance. A courier followed the Lord Mayor down to London with the Queen's apologies and the list properly signed by the monarch as it has been ever since.

The question is often asked – why is Temple Bar the City boundary when it stands half a mile outside the City gate at Ludgate Hill? Although the City had walls and gates to protect it, these were insufficient on their own. Around any defensive position there should be an open space where an enemy can be seen and attacked with arrows and missiles. For this reason nobody was allowed to approach the City walls after dark and the Bars were physical barriers closed at sunset to prevent this happening. Since the City exercised military control over the space up to the Bars, they were able to claim legal jurisdiction over the same area.

The old Temple Bar that Christopher Wren built in the 1670s spanned the road in a single arch. By the late nineteenth century the traffic was so great that the Bar had become the worst traffic jam in London. It was dismantled in 1878 and now stands in the grounds of Theobalds Park in Hertfordshire. Like London Bridge, Temple Bar was a favourite place to display the heads of executed traitors to the populace. The last to be placed here were the heads of Jacobites executed after the 1745 Rising. One remained on its pole till 1772 when it was found on the pavement by a passer-by who sold it to the bank across the road. The bank kept it in their strongroom as a memento till the reign of Victoria.

The present monument in the middle of the road, erected in 1880, has become just as much of an obstruction as the old Temple Bar but at least it provides some interesting information. One panel shows Victoria on her way to the Lord Mayor's Banquet in 1837, the first time she entered the City as Queen; another shows her going to St Paul's with the Prince of Wales in 1872 to offer thanks for his recovery from typhoid fever. This occasion is commemorated because it was the last occasion she drove under the old Temple Bar.

The side of the plinth facing away from the City has a coat of arms supported by London's legendary giants, Gog and Magog, while the eastern face asserts the City's jurisdiction by reminding passers-by that the centre line of the old gateway stood 3 feet 10 inches to the south of the mark shown on the plinth.

Temple Bar divides the Strand from Fleet Street and the house numbers change accordingly, although Fleet Street's numbering is incomplete. Like some other streets in London it has no No. 13. There are 125 streets in the City of London, 73 lanes, 18 alleys and innumerable passages, avenues, ways, courts and squares but not a single road. The City fathers followed the strict rules of English and held that a road was a highway leading from one locality to another, whereas a street is a paved way flanked by houses along its length. That is why Blackfriars Road stops at Blackfriars Bridge and Farringdon Road becomes Farringdon Street when it crosses the City boundary.

Bell Yard leads off to the left just beyond the Law Courts. Before the Courts were built, the entire area consisted of alleys like this; the great hall of the Courts lies over the site of Butchers' Row where the Gunpowder Plot was hatched in 1605. Bell Yard has been here for five hundred years and the great bell suspended from the wall marks the site of the pub that once stood here. The Yard achieved notoriety in the early 1800s when the first edition of *Sweeney Todd* appeared, which placed Todd's establishment half-way along the alley. An unfortunate barber who traded here was forced to make a hurried move. The use of victims to make pies is completely fictional but the Sweeney Todd story had its origins in the criminal activities of eight lady barbers of Drury Lane, whose apprehension had been the sensation of London a century before.

The boundary between the City and Westminster does

not run in straight lines. It crosses Bell Yard from left to right, runs along the front of the buildings and passes through the middle of the block at Nos. 11-12. It is marked by a small plaque at each point high up on the wall.

Carey Street

Carey Street at the top of Bell Yard has given its name to the language, albeit in a modified form. Londoners have used the phrase 'to be in Queer Street' to describe someone's financial difficulties ever since the time the Bankruptcy Court moved to Carey Street two hundred years ago.

Carey Street runs left to the corner of Serle Street. All the buildings along it belong to Lincoln's Inn and a statue to one of the Inn's most illustrious members, Sir Thomas More, stands on the corner.

The Seven Stars pub at No. 54 has been here since 1602. The original name, 'The League and Seven Stars', commemorated the provinces of the Netherlands who were fighting the Spanish and had become heroes to Londoners. The Seven Stars appears in *Pickwick Papers* as the Magpie and Stump although its erstwhile neighbour, the Plough, was even more famous in Dickens's time for its landlord, John Gully, who became a Member of Parliament after many years as prize-fighting champion of England.

Two large stones on the pavement outside No. 55 mark the parish boundaries of St Clement Danes (with the anchor) and St Dunstan's in the West. Just beyond them is a jeweller's shop called The Silver Mousetrap. The firm has been in the trade since 1690 and takes its name from the silver mousetraps used in the eighteenth century when ladies wore enormous wigs powdered with flour. Since the wigs were kept on all night, mice were a permanent danger and silver mouse-traps were set around the pillow to catch them.

No. 60, the red-brick house at the eastern end of Carey

Street, was built in 1731 and is now the residence of the President of the Law Society. It stands on the corner of Star Yard which has a splendid example of one of the few Victorian cast-iron urinals left in London. Although the Victorians held their Queen in high regard, they had no scruples about using the royal coat of arms to advertise their wares and the panels of this urinal are covered with Royal crests.

Chichester Rents around the corner takes its name from the bishop who built it; Dickens placed Krook's rag and bottle shop in *Bleak House* where Nos. 8 and 9 now stand. The Rents leads into Chancery Lane which we follow down to the right towards Fleet Street.

Chancery Lane

No. 93 Chancery Lane is occupied by a firm which has supplied the Coronation robes for every British monarch since 1689. Ede and Ravenscroft have made ceremonial clothing since the seventeenth century and are the world's leading authority on the subject. They give advice on the correct order of dress for the Chancellor of the University of Hong Kong or the gown to be worn by a stipendiary magistrate in Lower Bengal. They have made robes for nearly every legislature and university in Africa and the gold lace on their robes still contains a proportion of the genuine metal.

Chancery Lane is one of London's oldest streets but there has always been some question into whose jurisdiction it falls. The southern end belongs to the City of London, the centre section belongs to the City of Westminster, while the northern end comes under the jurisdiction of the Borough of Holborn.

The confusion stems from 1232 when Henry III founded a chapel where the Public Record Office stands across the road today. It was later given to the Lord Chancellor as a repository for the records of the Court of Chancery. The two roles of the building, that of chapel and storeroom, continued for centuries. When the chapel was refurbished in 1784, the congregation found themselves sitting on lockers containing the court records. The old chapel was eventually taken down in 1895 to be rebuilt as the Public Record Office where the Domesday Book can be seen. The unusual dual function of the building has still not completely vanished. Students looking through the papers have to make their way around three large tombs in the middle of the floor, while the stained glass windows commemorate chaplains who preached here.

The City of London hesitated to claim that such a royal enclave lay within its borders, especially when Chancery Lane became the home of Cardinal Wolsey, the most powerful man in England. The upshot is that the City boundary loops across the Lane, swinging round to exclude the Public Record Office before running north again to Holborn.

Chancery Lane still has links with the Lord Chancellors of the past. The topping-out ceremony of the new office block up Chancery Lane behind us was performed by the owner of the site, the Premier Baronet of England. The baronet was Sir Edmund Bacon and the property has been in his family ever since it was bought in 1560 by Sir Nicholas Bacon, Lord Chancellor to Elizabeth 1.

The dignified building at No. 113, opposite the Public Record Office, belongs to the Law Society. It is the headquarters of the solicitors of England and Wales. Built in 1831, it has a fine lamp-holder over its doorway but its most distinctive feature is the splendid lions that sit on top of the railings in front of it. These are copies of the lions Alfred Stevens did for the British Museum, which have been imitated up and down the country ever since.

When the Museum authorities were planning their forecourt in 1852, they commissioned Stevens to design a figure of a lion to sit on top of the pillars of the railings. They specified that the lions were to be 24 inches high and fit within a base 14 inches square. Stevens realised that only a seated lion would fit those requirements and produced these models which the Museum installed. They became immensely popular and are still to be seen on gateposts of thousands of homes.

It has only recently been discovered that the figures are fakes. Stevens found that lions never sit in this position and, rather than admit he could not fulfill the commission, he borrowed a friend's cat, modelled it and put a lion's head on top.

No. 122 Chancery Lane occupies the site of Izaak Walton's house and stands beside the alley of Andrew's Crosse which takes its name from the inn that once belonged to the Priory of St John of Jerusalem.

Fleet Street

On the right-hand corner, where Chancery Lane runs into Fleet Street, is Attenborough's the jewellers, who occupy an ornate and colourful building of 1883. It was built at a time when Victorian shopkeepers vied with each other in the splendour of their frontages, paying their customers the compliment of assuming a high degree of artistic appreciation. Attenborough's frontage has two such artistic allusions although it is doubtful if their significance is appreciated today.

On the Fleet Street side of the shop is a figure of a page-boy, which stood at the Alexandra Palace till the fire of 1867. The figure represents Kaled, the faithful attendant of Count Lara in Byron's poem 'Lara'. Attenborough bought it because Byron's poems had a revival in the 1880s and most educated Londoners knew the lines:

> They were not common links that formed the chain
> That bound to Lara, Kaled's heart and brain.

The significance of the allusion was that Attenborough's best-selling line was their extra-strong watch chains.

As well as selling jewellery, Attenborough was a pawnbroker with a steady trade amongst those gentlemen of the West End whose social position was not matched by their bank balances. All such delicate transactions were conducted over a counter in a corner of the shop, a circumstance that led to the famous greeting Attenborough received one day at Ascot from an impoverished peer of the realm: 'Mornin', Attenborough. Never seen your trousers before.'

The second advertisement depended on a knowledge of Latin for its proper appreciation. On the corner of the building is the bracket where the pawnbroker's sign of three golden balls used to hang. Immediately above the bracket it is just possible to read the Latin motto *Sub Hoc Floresco* (Under this sign I prosper). Since the common term for putting goods into pawn was to 'hock' them, the pun was much enjoyed by those of Mr Attenborough's customers who had a classical education.

The corner of Clifford's Inn Passage a few yards to the left is where John Rokesmith took Mr Boffin aside and offered him his services as secretary in *Our Mutual Friend*. The passage leads to the gateway of Clifford's Inn, the oldest Inn of Chancery (1340), which stood here til 1934. In its later days, it ceased to have any connection with the law and Samuel Butler wrote *Erewhon* and *The Way of All Flesh* during his time here. There was much opposition to the Inn's demolition and the developers were persuaded to leave this gateway. It is dated 1766, while the initials 'PWM' commemorate William Monk who was Principal of the Inn when the gate was built.

St Dunstan's in the West

St Dunstan's in the West, so-called to distinguish it from the other St Dunstan's in the City, has been here since 1185 although most of the present building dates from 1833.

The head carved on the left of the doorway is that of William Tyndale, the translator of the Bible into English, who was St Dunstan's rector in 1528. The head on the right is of John Donne, the metaphysical poet, who became rector here in 1624 before he was appointed Dean of St Paul's. His monument in St Paul's, the only one to survive the Great Fire of 1666, is a macabre carving of Donne wrapped in his funeral shroud. In order to prepare himself for death, Donne commissioned and posed for the carving and kept it at his bedside till he died.

Above the doorway is the famous St Dunstan's clock with the giants who beat the bell with their clubs every quarter of an hour. The clock, made in 1671, is one of the oldest in London and was inspired by the clock in the Piazza San Marco in Venice. It was the first clock in London to show minutes on the dial, to have two faces and to strike on the quarter-hour.

The clock used to be one of London's tourist attractions; nearly every writer of the eighteenth and early nineteenth century wrote of it. Goldsmith brought the Vicar of Wakefield here to admire it, David Copperfield brought his nurse to see it and Walter Scott mentioned it in *The Fortunes of Nigel*. The Marquess of Hertford bought the clock in 1830 for his house in Regent's Park and it did not return till 1935, when Lord Rothermere bought the house and restored the clock to its original position.

Because of the shape of the site, the church is octagonal, one of the three in London built on a north–south axis rather than the normal east–west. At the time of writing, it provides facilities for worship to an unusual variety of denominations including the Old Catholic Church of Utrecht, the Assyrian Church of the East, the Roumanian Orthodox Patriarchal Church and the Coptic Ethiopian Church.

Despite rebuilding in the last century, the church has kept many of the old monuments. Over the door halfway down the left-hand side, a tablet makes a laconic comment on the legal profession with the statement that it is:

> To The Memory of Hobson Judkin Esq
> The Honest Solicitor . . .

Over in the far right corner a plain plaque, with a rapier carved on either side, remembers Alexander Layton, a fencing teacher. The plaque reads:

> His thrusts like lightning flew, more skilful Death
> Parried 'em all, and beat him out of breath.

The small courtyard outside the church is all that remains of St Dunstan's churchyard, once famous for the booksellers who thronged it. Richard Pynson lived here in 1483 and produced *Dives and Pauper*, the first book published in Fleet Street; the first English tragedy *Gorboduc* was sold here in 1565. Izaak Walton, who lived around the corner and was churchwarden of St Dunstan's, sold *The Compleat Angler* here as well as his life of Donne.

In the corner of the courtyard is a statue of Queen Elizabeth I. It is the second oldest statue in London (the oldest is that of Alfred the Great in Southwark) and is the only contemporary statue of any Tudor monarch. It was carved in 1586 and installed on the front of Ludgate, where the Queen rode under it often on her visits to the City. When Ludgate was pulled down in 1760, the statue was saved and brought here to St Dunstan's.

The statue's third distinction is that it is the only statue in London with a private income. Lady Millicent Fawcett left a sum of money in 1929 to provide for its cleaning and maintenance.

Unfortunately, like other elderly ladies on a fixed income, the Queen now has financial problems and more funds are needed to care for her properly.

In an alcove below the Queen are three other statues from the old Ludgate. Their age is uncertain, possibly sixteenth century, and they represent the legendary King Lud himself (after whom Ludgate was named) and his two sons. No one knows who King Lud was but his name was used for the west gate as early as 1160. Folklore claims that he founded the City centuries before the Romans came.

Fleet Street

Fleet Street was the home of printing and newspapers for five hundred years, from 1483 when Richard Pynson came here, till a few years ago when the newspapers moved to the East End. Although the printers came simply to join their fellow-tradesmen, the newspapers set up here as a matter of practical convenience. From 1712 till 1855 newspapers were taxed and every copy had to be stamped at Somerset House before it could be sold. This section of Fleet Street was the obvious place for newspapers, set between the printers' presses already here and Somerset House along the Strand.

At the beginning of this century, there were over forty daily newspapers being produced here as well as six hundred weekly publications, every one of which tried to advertise its name on the front of its offices. Now the Press have left Fleet Street the jumble of names and trade signs has started to fade away. In some cases the advertisements have proved more durable than the publications; the red-brick wall beside St Dunstan's will advertise the departed *Dundee Courier* and *The People's Journal* until it is painted over or demolished.

A few yards past St Dunstan's, at 184 Fleet Street, is Hen and Chickens Court whose delightful rustic name has no known explanation. At the end of the Court is a single decrepit building – the old Vestry house of St Dunstan's parish. Neale's Mathematical School was founded here in 1777 and, although its age has made it unsafe for use, it is one of the few buildings left in Fleet Street that Dr Johnson, Pope and maybe even Donne himself would recognise. With Nos. 184 and 185 Fleet Street that guard it, it forms the oldest group of buildings left in Fleet Street. It was here that the Great Fire of 1666 stopped, halted by the brick buildings around St Dunstan's.

The recent widening of Fetter Lane has destroyed all traces of the old Peele's Hotel that had stood here for centuries but Crane Court, a few yards further on, is a pleasant introduction to the Fleet Street that Dr Johnson and Boswell knew.

The first editions of *Punch* were printed at No. 3 Crane Court and the end building, No. 7, replaces the house where the Royal Society had their first meetings in the reign of Charles II. Isaac Newton ordered a lamp (the light of knowledge) to be lit over the doorway whenever the Society met and King Charles himself, Prince Rupert, Pepys, Boyle and every scientist of the seventeenth century walked up this narrow alley to discuss their discoveries with their fellows. Some of the seventeenth-century houses built to replace those burnt in the Great Fire are still here with parish boundary marks of St Dunstan's and St Bride's on their walls.

The next turning on the left, Red Lion Court, still leads to the Red Lion tavern that gave the Court its name in 1592. On a misty evening, it recreates the London of the eighteenth century as vividly as the alleys off the Strand recall the London of Dickens or Sherlock Holmes (see Fourth Walk). Red Lion Court and the next five alleys off this side of Fleet Street all lead to Dr Johnson's house in Gough Square, although the route can be tortuous.

No. 18, the house at the first corner of Red Lion Court, is still much as it was when rebuilt after the 1666 Fire by the speculator Nicholas Barbon, whom we have met before (see Third Walk). Barbon was christened 'If-Jesus-Christ-had-not-died-for-thee, thou-hadst-been-damned Barbon' but was known by his family as Nick, although his colleagues and many of his tenants preferred simply to call him 'that Damned Barbon'.

Wren is reputed to have played some part in the design and the house still has an original powder room where the ladies of the eighteenth century went to have their hair looked after. The first circulating library in England started here in 1745 and, until a few years ago, this was the home of Taylor & Francis the printers. They took over the business of John Valpy, the printer who came here in 1820 to publish the 144 volumes of the Delphin Classics. It was Valpy who erected the sign that still hangs on the wall – a lamp with the motto *Alere Flammam* (Fuel the lamp (of learning)).

It is possible to walk right through to Holborn from Red Lion Court but our tour takes us back to Fleet Street, with the reflection that the majority of London's thoroughfares were as narrow as this till the Victorians started widening the streets in the 1840s. Even in the 1980s it is possible to walk two miles due north from the Embankment along alleys and courts like this, free from vehicle traffic.

Dr Johnson

The next entry along Fleet Street is Johnson's Court, which is not named after the Doctor, even though he lived here for some years. The Court has always been connected with Radical journalism. Theodore Hook started the magazine *John Bull* here in 1820 and ensured its success by publishing a scurrilous libel on Queen Caroline for which he was promptly taken to court in a case which brought the magazine all the publicity he had planned. In 1864 the Radical paper *The National Reformer* was published here and the same office saw the birth of the Rationalist Press Association.

This time our walk does go through to Gough Square, by way of the right-hand far corner of Johnson's Court and through to the left-hand corner of the alley beyond. No. 17 Gough Square is famous as the home of Dr Johnson from 1746–59 when he compiled his English dictionary. It is now a museum visited by thousands every year, although most of them miss two unusual architectural features. The woodwork in the house is white and yellow American pine, brought back as ballast from the colonies when this house was being built in the 1690s.

The other unusual feature is the brick from the Great Wall of China. In Boswell's *Life*, Johnson said that it would be a wonderful thing to travel around the world and that he wished he could see the Great Wall of China. As a tribute to his memory, Lord Northcliffe procured a sizeable stone from the Wall and installed it here in 1922.

There are five ways from Gough Square back into Fleet Street; our route is from the right-hand corner down the narrow alley and right again into Bolt Court where Johnson died in 1784. His house at No. 8 is long gone but No. 3 was the home of his friend Dr Lettsom. A well-known physician of the time, he is now best remembered by the verse that commemorates the bold signature he used on his prescriptions:

If any folks applies to I,
I blisters, bleeds and sweats 'em;
If after that they please to die,
Well, then – I Lettsom.

Our walk turns left along Fleet Street, past the doorway that covers old Three Kings Court and Hind Court beyond. No. 146 Fleet Street, the site of Radford's which has sold tobacco on this corner for two hundred and fifty years, stands on the corner of Wine Office Court.

Wine Office Court was originally the entrance of the town house of the Bishop of Peterborough. The cellars of his house are still under the Cheshire Cheese whose licence goes back to the 1660s. The tavern, renowned as the haunt of Johnson and of Dickens after him, maintained its reputation by the famous puddings which were served each winter for a hundred and sixty-four years up to 1939. The puddings, large enough to serve ninety people, took sixteen hours to cook and the ingredients included steak, mushrooms, larks, oysters and kidneys.

The pudding season started on the first Monday in October and the first cut was ceremonially carried out by such famous men of the day as Stanley Baldwin, Dean Inge, Jack Dempsey and Conan Doyle. Another attraction of the inn was the parrot which celebrated Armistice Night in 1918 by giving its famous imitation of a champagne cork popping four hundred times before falling over in a faint. Its death in 1926 was reported in every major newspaper around the world.

No. 6 Wine Office Court, beyond the Cheshire Cheese, is the site of the house where Oliver Goldsmith wrote *The Vicar of Wakefield*. He suffered considerable financial hardship and once, when the bailiffs were in the house, had to call on Johnson for help. His only asset was the manuscript of *The Vicar* which Johnson took and sold within an hour for fifty pounds.

The romantic frontage of No. 143–4 Fleet Street has annoyed every architectural historian ('tastelessly and mercilessly Gothic, even to the windows') but reflects perfectly the taste of the man who built it. Although it has always been used as an office, the building was erected by Sir John Tollemache Sinclair as a memorial to the queen whose statue stands in the niche of the wall – Mary, Queen of Scots.

Sir John, an eccentric in the grand tradition, felt that Queen Elizabeth's statue at St Dunstan's should be matched by this memorial to the Queen she executed. To build this office block and instal the statue was only one of his architectural foibles. On holiday near Chamonix, he saw a beautiful hillside with a lake below it, bought them both and had a series of picturesque ruins built to enhance the landscape. When he was satisfied with the final appearance, he invited his friends from all over Europe to a party to celebrate the beauty of the scene – and left it the following morning for ever.

His attempt to ensure that Queen Mary would be remembered by those inside the building as well as by those outside can be seen by stepping through the doorway. On either side of the steep staircase is a large stone panel hanging precariously from the wall, commemorating the unhappy Queen's virtues.

Peterborough Court at 135 Fleet Street takes its name from the Bishop of Peterborough to whom it once belonged. Although all the other prelates lost their

London houses during the Reformation, this piece of land remained in the possession of the diocese till 1863.

The Daily Telegraph, whose office occupied the site, was founded in 1855 in a Colonel Sleigh. He took advantage of the abolition that year of the Stamp Tax on newspapers to conduct a private vendetta against the War Office and the Duke of Cambridge.

Unfortunately he saw little need for such things as advertising revenue or experienced staff and went bankrupt in a few months. The paper was revived by the new owner J. M. Levy and achieved success as a single sheet costing a penny and even greater success when it doubled its size but remained at the same price.

The *Telegraph* has moved from No. 135 but left a couple of unusual features behind it that can best be appreciated by crossing the street. Above the doorway are two winged messengers showing how the paper carried its news across the world. It is an impressive carving but the way the sculptor depicted the straps on the sandals has enabled rival newspapers to claim that the two figures are firmly tied together and would therefore be unable to travel very far.

Behind the tremendous clock is a small balcony which was grassed over, justifying the *Telegraph*'s claim that it had the only lawn in Fleet Street. At the corners of the building are two masks representing Journalism Past and Future. They were carved in an unusual way by an unusual artist. The sculptor, Sam Rabin, was a man of many parts. He was an East End wrestler who took up sculpture and painting and he carved these two faces *in situ*, working seventy feet up in the air on a scaffolding platform. It is recorded that his main difficulty was not the height he was working at but being unable to step back to check his work. This meant that every time he wanted to see how they looked at a distance, he had to climb down the scaffolding, cross the street to this spot, see what he had done and then climb all the way up again to carry on with the next section.

Beyond the *Telegraph* building is Shoe Lane followed by the black-and-chrome *Daily Express* building which caused a sensation when it was built in 1931. A few yards further on Poppins Court is still marked by the Sign of the Popinjay, the badge of the Abbot of Cirencester who had his London house here eight hundred years ago.

The last house on this side of Fleet Street should be viewed from the other side of the street. It dates from 1873 and, like Attenborough's shop at Chancery Lane, its interest lies in its frontage.

When the Victorians were building the British Empire, every campaign and battle was reported by newspaper correspondents who started their journeys from this building – the old head office of Thomas Cook. Cook was another of the great Victorians who seemed to create world-famous enterprises by accident. He was a lay preacher and temperance enthusiast who ran the first excursion in England in 1841 when he hired a special train to take a party of temperance enthusiasts from Leicester to Loughborough for a shilling a head.

In 1852 he organised the first conducted tour of Europe and consolidated his position as the main travel agent in the country by running excursions to Paris for the Exhibition of 1855. By 1884 his firm was working for the Government, arranging the transport for General Gordon and 18,000 men to travel to Egypt; a couple of years later Cook's were called in to arrange similar facilities for another force to go and rescue them.

Cook felt his office should reflect the scope of his firm's activities and the result is the splendid row of heads looking down on to Fleet Street. They represent all the races of the world and include Indians, Hottentots, Greeks, Chinese, Bushmen and Esqimaux.

The severity of the line of heads is more than offset by the delightful carvings of cherubs at each corner, as amusing as any in London. It is not known whether they are meant to represent Cook's customers travelling happily around the world or the famous Cook's agents who looked after them in the role of guardian angels.

At the top of the building cherubs gather around a globe planning their journey, working out their route with maps and compasses, while the carvings over the doorways show the journey completed. In the bottom right corner, the cherubs rest after their travels against a globe supported by models of the railway engines and steamships that had carried them.

St Paul's looms over Ludgate Hill (see the Eighth Walk) and the traffic shows how Ludgate Circus has been for centuries one of London's busiest junctions. England's first daily newspaper, the *Daily Courant*, was published here in 1702 and this corner saw the first postal pillar box in 1855.

Before the age of motor-cars, when horses were the only form of transport, London's streets were filthy places, covered with horse-droppings and debris of every sort. As a result, crossing-sweepers were important members of the community. The sweepers adopted a corner or section of road and swept it clean to allow a clear passage. They were little more than beggars since their only reward was the occasional farthing or halfpenny tossed to them.

The crossing at this corner was swept by Charles McGhee, an old coloured man nicknamed 'Brutus Billy' or 'Timbuctoo'. The house overlooking the crossing was the home of Alderman Waithman whose young daughter took pity on the old sweeper. She made it her business to see he had a piece of bread each day or a bowl of soup when the weather was cold. When the old man realised he was nearing his end, he sold his 'beat' and died within a few weeks. He left Miss Waithman the respectable sum of £700, all the money he had managed to save over the years – a touching episode with which to end this Walk.

SEVENTH ♦ WALK

The South Side of Fleet Street,
St Bride's Church and the Temple

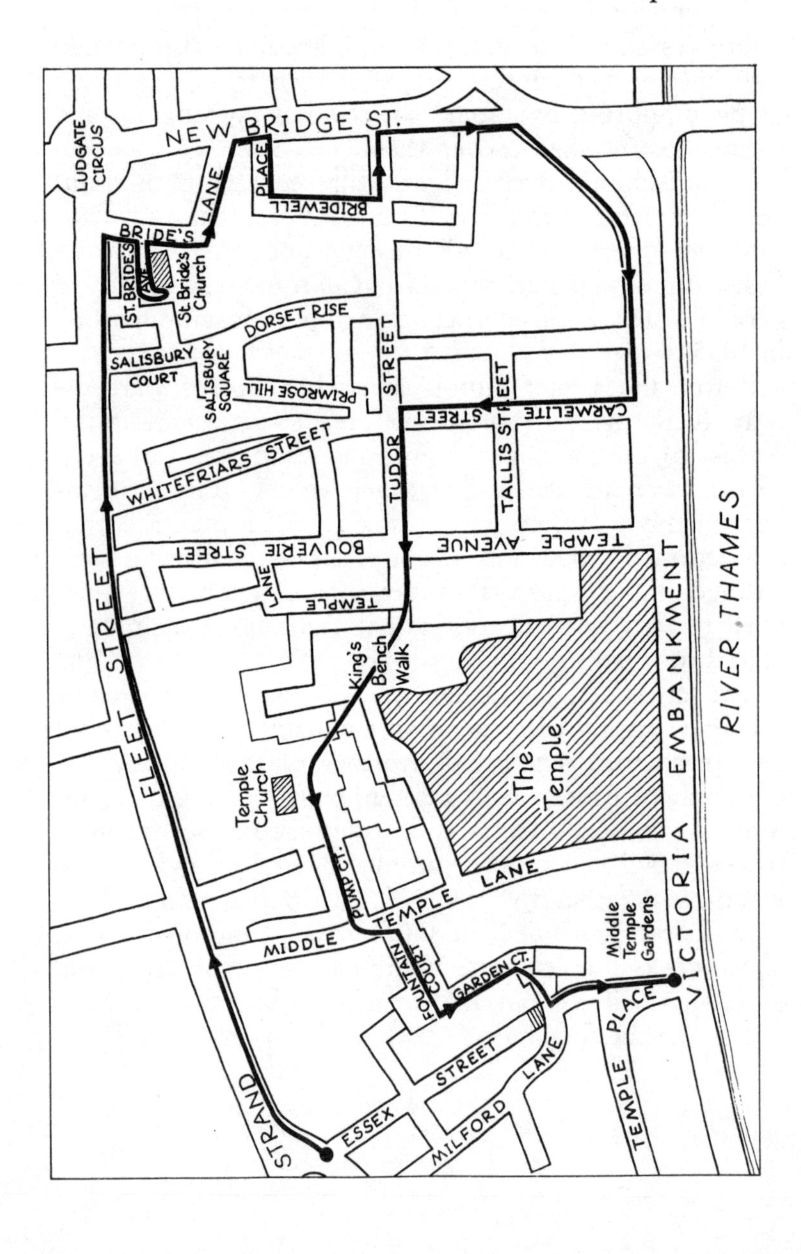

SEVENTH ♦ WALK

The South Side of Fleet Street, St Bride's Church and the Temple

The Seventh Walk begins at the corner of Essex Street in the Strand, where the Fourth Walk finished, and looks at the banks and taverns of Fleet Street that have been here for centuries and at the Temple that lies behind them.

The roadway curves round St Clement Danes church towards Fleet Street. The second building on the right, 213 Strand, is the George Tavern, nearly three hundred years old. Its heyday was the eighteenth century when Fleet Street and Covent Garden were the resort of wits and politicians and every group had its particular haunt.

The George was a favourite of Sir Robert Walpole, George I's Prime Minister, who was in the company one night when an anti-Government mob came along the Strand, carrying an effigy of Walpole to be burnt at Tower Hill. A group entered the George seeking subscriptions for its cause and asked everyone present to make a donation. Walpole realised that a refusal would be dangerous, if not fatal, and gave generously to his opponents' cause. He justified the action later with the remark that he considered the Government of Britain was well worth the half-guinea he had given.

Walpole showed more generosity in the George than Sir James Lowther did later. Sir James, one of the wealthiest men in England with an income of £40,000 a year, was also one of the meanest. He confirmed his reputation when, after a long evening in the tavern with his friends, he returned the following morning to spend an hour upbraiding the landlord for having given him a bad half-penny in his change the night before. He refused to leave till he received a good one and never entered the George again.

Devereux Court beside the George leads down to the Devereux Tavern that we looked at in the Fifth Walk, and a few yards more bring us to Twining's tea shop at 216 Strand, which has been here since 1706. James Bone, the London historian, used to make a point of ensuring that his American friends did their shopping in London at establishments founded before 1776 and always brought them to Twining's where Queen Anne and Christopher Wren used to buy their tea. Queen Anne's addiction to tea was well known and she drank so much of it that her physicians attributed her death to that dangerous beverage, though Londoners attributed it to brandy.

There are many shops in London established in the eighteenth century, but Twining's is the oldest to occupy the same site and to be run by the same family (the tenth Mr Twining is now in charge). The alabaster Chinese figures over the doorway have been here since 1787, which was about the time Twining's contributed to a change in English social habits. The import duty on tea was very high and five times as much was smuggled tax-free as entered the country legally. William Pitt the Younger asked Twining's views on the problem and Twining advised him to reduce the tax to a tenth of its current level. That would stop smuggling and the government would receive increased revenue from the extra imports. Pitt took his advice and found that his prophecy was correct; the Government gained sufficient money to fight the war with France and England became a nation of tea-drinkers.

At Nos. 222–225 Strand is one of London's most extraordinary banks with an entrance hall that would do justice to a cathedral. The interior is panelled with walnut and sequoia, interspersed with hand-painted tiles of Jacobean characters and chrysanthemums. The unusual decoration dates from the building's original purpose as a restaurant designed to outshine every other eating-place in London.

This is the site of the old Palgrave's Head, a tavern frequented by Ben Jonson and named after Frederick Palgrave who married James I's daughter Elizabeth and went on to become King of Bohemia. In 1880 two businessmen built the restaurant to match the new Law Courts rising across the road. They foresaw an influx of respectable county gentlefolk consulting their family solicitors, who would look for somewhere different from the seedy taverns and cafés that filled the Strand.

No expense was spared in filling the building with every form of decoration the owners could think of. Doulton designed the stoneware pillars and panels in the hall and provided the hand-painted plaques of the King of Bohemia and his bride. The tiles inside illustrate characters from Jonson's plays and the prize-winning blooms in the chrysanthemum class of the Royal Horticultural Show of 1882, the year before the restaurant was completed. (In those days the Show was held in the Temple Gardens just behind the building.) Despite all these attractions the restaurant never paid its way and was bought by the bankers in 1895, when the Press congratulated them on having bought 'the handsomest and most elegant bank in London' – a title it can still claim.

A few yards on, at Nos. 229–230 Strand, the Wig and Pen Club occupies a picturesque black-beamed building that is as old as it looks. Recent restoration has given it some anachronistic features but it was built in 1625 and is one of the few domestic buildings left in London from before the Great Fire.

The Wig and Pen Club stands just short of the City boundary, where the Strand becomes Fleet Street. Fleet

Street, which takes it name from the Fleet River which flows into the Thames below Ludgate Hill, has been the western road out of London since the time of the Romans who laid the paving-stones that can still cause problems when new sewers are being laid.

Like the Strand, Fleet Street's position outside the City walls meant that only clergymen dared live there but, while the Strand was the home of bishops, Fleet Street attracted monasteries. Three great religious houses occupied the southern side of Fleet Street, the Knights Templar at this western end, the Carmelites (Whitefriars) in the middle and the Dominican (Blackfriars) monastery at the far end.

Directly in line with the Griffin in the middle of the street is a boundary mark that is often missed because it lies on the pavement outside Child's Bank; it marks the limit of St Clement Danes parish which ends at the City boundary.

Child's Bank is the oldest in the country and predates the Bank of England by 130 years. Founded as a goldsmith's business in 1560 at 'The Sign of the Marigold', which still hangs outside the building, Child's found it profitable to lend money to its customers on the gold and silver they deposited. The idea of advancing money on this sort of regular basis had become common in Europe through the Italian bankers from Lombardy, after whom Lombard Street is named, and the Italian influence is still to be seen on every English banknote. The signature of the Chief Cashier is shown to be on 'behalf of the Govr. and Compa. of the Bank of England'; 'Compa.' is not an abbreviation of the English word 'Company', it stands for the Italian 'Compagnia'.

Oliver Cromwell had an account at Child's, as did Charles II and his mistress Nell Gwynne; the bank's records show that she was more often in credit than he was. Child's produced the first printed bank-notes in 1729 and appeared as 'Tellson's Bank' in *A Tale of Two Cities*. Till the 1920s a member of the family always lived in the bank to make any emergency advances and, although the present building dates only from 1879, it still possesses what Pevsner calls 'the quiet and stately manner of a West End Club'.

Child's stands on the site of the famous Devil Tavern, where Ben Jonson presided over the Apollo club. He drew up the rules of the club in 1624, inscribing them on a board in gold letters. They are still in the bank, in the Directors' room, with the famous bust of Apollo that stood over the doorway of the club.

The next lane on the right passes under the Middle Temple Gateway which has been here since the Templars came in the twelfth century. Although the present gateway was rebuilt in 1684, it gives an excellent idea of what the entrance to the old bishops' palaces along the Strand must have looked like, a massive double gate built for defence and set in a strong wall.

Above the gateway is one of London's oldest lamps adapted through the centuries to fit each new style of lighting. The iron basket in the centre was originally built to hold tarred sticks and was supported on brackets curving away from the wall to prevent the building from catching fire. In the eighteenth century, the basket was replaced by a metal container full of liquefied fat or whale oil which fed a wick protected by a glass globe. When gas became available in the early 1800s, the familiar four-sided glass lamps were introduced with the fish-tail gas flare at the bottom. When the invention of the gas mantle enabled the flame to be pointed downwards, the gas pipe was simply taken around to the top of the lamp, and the same piping is now used to carry the wiring of the modern electric switches.

The small lodge under the gateway was once occupied by Benjamin Motte the bookseller and it was here, in 1726, that Jonathan Swift sold him the copyright of *Gulliver's Travels* for £200. Because Swift was then Dean of St Patrick's Cathedral and *Gulliver* was such a bitter satire on the government, he adopted the pseudonym of Richard Sympson.

The house on the eastern side of the Gateway, No. 8, became a printing-house in 1544 and continued in the same use till this century when Butterworth's, the law publishers, left it to move to Chancery Lane. Until a few years ago it was a bookshop and completed a record of over four hundred years in the same trade.

No. 15-16 Fleet Street (the confusion arises because No. 15 stood directly behind No 16) is Simmond's Bookshop, five storeys high but only ten feet wide, the same width it was in the reign of Henry VIII. The Rainbow coffee-house, opened in 1656 as the second in England, stood on part of the site, although it was nearly closed down the following year when indignant neighbours reported the owner 'for the evil and noxious smelles' issuing from the establishment. He persevered, however, and coffee continued to be sold at the Rainbow till 1973.

The Inner Temple Gateway next to Simmond's Bookshop has been here since 1184 although the splendid Gatehouse itself, which is open to the public, was built in 1610. There is doubt concerning its origins but the name of Prince Henry's Room certainly refers to James I's elder son. One version is that the room was built especially for the Prince as an office for the Duchy of Cornwall; another states that it was simply an extension of the tavern next door and adopted the royal title to attract trade. The carved woodwork and panelling are original as is the splendid plaster ceiling.

A plaque on the wall of No. 18 Fleet Street commemorates the founding of the Automobile Association in 1905, when they adopted as their livery the colours of their patron, Lord Lonsdale of Lonsdale Belt fame. The Bank at No. 19 has been here since its foundation in 1650 and still displays its original Sign of the Three Squirrels.

The Cock Tavern at No. 22 is the oldest in Fleet Street trading under its original name. Founded in the reign of Henry VIII, it stood on the opposite side of the street till 1877. Samuel Pepys frequented it and tried to seduce Mrs Knipp here after a lobster supper. Dr Johnson, Dickens, Carlyle and Tennyson were customers and the Cock's owners were immensely proud of the lines in Tennyson's poem 'Will Waterproof's Lyrical Monologue At The Cock':

> O plump headwaiter of The Cock,
> To which I most resort,
> How goes the time? 'Tis five o'clock,
> Go fetch a pint of port.

When Tennyson became Poet Laureate, hundreds of people dined at the Cock to see the head-waiter in question who was indeed extremely corpulent. All enquiries on his recollections of the poet were met by the comment that he 'did not remember the gent'.

When the old Cock Tavern was bought for rebuilding in 1877, the owners simply moved across the street, bringing their treasures with them. Their last act before leaving the old building was to send Tennyson, then nearing the end of his life, an Elizabethan tankard as a memento of the old house and the fame he had brought to it.

The carved figure of the 'Cock' itself, traditionally ascribed to Grinling Gibbons, stands behind the bar (it used to be on the customers' side till the author advised the landlady of its importance). The chimney-piece and side-board from the old tavern are in the restaurant upstairs. They are beautiful pieces from the early seventeenth century and one has to be very blasé not to get a thrill from putting down a glass of claret on the side-board that Pepys, Addison, Dickens and Tennyson used for the same purpose.

It was in the Cock and the other Fleet Street taverns that the word 'tip' acquired its meaning as a gratuity for a waiter. It originated in the notices that used to be displayed stating that a small additional payment would help 'To Insure Prompt Service'.

No. 32 Fleet Street was the site of Wynkyn de Worde's printing press, who moved here in 1500, having learnt his trade under Caxton. He published nearly eight hundred books and the printing business continued up to the time John Murray bought it in 1762. Murray's did not move to their present site in Albemarle Street till 1812, so it was to this shop that Lord Byron came when they published his *Childe Harold* which caused such a sensation. Murray sometimes found his visits a nuisance because Byron, who took fencing lessons, would use the books as his targets when showing the passes and lunges he had learnt, often with serious results to the bindings.

At No. 37, Hoare's Bank still has the Golden Bottle outside, the sign of the tavern in Cheapside where the firm started in 1672 before moving here in 1690. Hoare's is the last of the old private banks and the partners still include members of the family. Mitre Court further east was the scene of execution in 1733 of Sarah Malcolm, who was found guilty of murdering three women in the Temple. Following the normal practice of deterring others from following her example, the execution was carried out at the entrance to the court, the nearest public place to where the crime had been committed.

El Vino's, the wine-bar at No. 47, is considered by many to be the real centre of Fleet Street. Founded in 1879, the wineshop moved to Fleet Street during the war. The bar became famous in the 1960s because of its refusal to serve women at the bar, an ironic complaint because El Vino's had welcomed women during the war and had, as an act of courtesy, provided stools at the bar specifically for them. However, this kind gesture resulted in such a clutter of gloves, handbags and umbrellas on the bar that the male customers complained there was no room for them.

Since El Vino's still wanted to show every courtesy to their female clientele and save them the embarrassment of jostling for position at the bar, they introduced the rule that ladies would be served at tables. The courtesy was taken to be discrimination and the matter was decided by the Court of Appeal only in 1982 after a series of ugly scenes in one of which, 'The Battle of Fleet Street', the proprietor was nearly strangled by a lady forcibly asserting her rights.

Serjeant's Inn commemorates the Serjeants at Law, legal practitioners who were mentioned in Chaucer's *Canterbury Tales*. By the fourteenth century they had acquired a monopoly of the legal profession in England and all judges were appointed from their ranks. Their status, however, became anachronistic after the law reforms of the nineteenth century and the last appointment to the rank was made in 1875.

Salisbury Court, at No. 81 Fleet Street, was the birthplace of Samuel Pepys (a plaque on the left marks the site). The Court leads into Salisbury Square, once the centre quadrangle of the town house of the Bishop of Salisbury, who acquired the site from the Carmelites. Samuel Richardson (1689–1761) lived here over his printing press and wrote *Pamela*, the first modern English novel. The Square has been recently 'developed' but No. 1 still looks as it did in Richardson's day. The obelisk in the middle commemorates Alderman Robert Waithmain who lived on the corner of Ludgate Circus and whose daughter's kindness to the old negro street-sweeper we read of in the Sixth Walk.

At the beginning of the nineteenth century, Salisbury Square was the scene of a book-burning ceremony when Mrs Clarke, the spurned mistress of the Duke of York, decided to tell all and an eager publisher printed 10,000 copies. On the eve of publication day, the Duke decided the publicity would be too damaging, placating Mrs Clarke by paying her debts and giving her a pension of £400 a year. Every copy of the book was piled in a heap in the centre of the square and burnt under the eye of the Duke's solicitor.

It is possible to leave the square by several different routes since alleys lead out from every corner, but we turn back into Fleet Street, turn right past No. 85 where *Punch* used to be published to No. 91 Fleet Street, once the office of *Bell's Weekly Messenger*. Mr Bell was the publisher and printer who should be remembered for his brave decision to discard the old 'f' sign for the letter 's' and to use the latter exclusively, a change that made every subsequent book published in England easier to read.

St Bride's Church

Turn right into Bride Lane and right again at the first corner. The pub on the corner, the Old Bell, was built just after the Great Fire of London in 1666. Although tradition errs in claiming it was erected exclusively for Christopher Wren's workmen as they built the imposing church above us, they were certainly among its first customers.

St Bride's Church, the pride of Fleet Street, was badly bombed in the last war but has been beautifully restored. It has the tallest spire of any of Wren's churches, 226 feet high, although a further 8 feet were lost when it was struck by lightning in 1764. This led to the controversy that raged all over England, similar to the famous argument of the people of Laputa in *Gulliver's Travels* of a few years before – should a boiled egg be opened at the blunt end or the sharp end? The St Bride's question that divided the nation was – since the splendid spire needed a lightning conductor, should it be a lightning conductor with a pointed end or a blunt end?

Every section of society entered the fray and King George himself was the leader of the blunt end party. The sharp end faction was led by the American Benjamin Franklin and their famous debate on the question led to allusions in the newspapers to 'good, honest, blunt King George' and his defeat by 'sharp-witted Americans'.

Franklin's name crops up in every discussion of scientific discoveries in London in the mid-eighteenth century and his entry into the lightning conductor controversy in

London was only to be expected. Although his sense of diplomacy kept his argument with the King on a polite level, he had a certain advantage since he had invented the first lightning conductor twelve years before, a feat which won him membership of the Royal Society of London.

His reputation as 'the wisest American' was well-deserved since he made a success of any project he undertook. At 15 he wrote, edited, printed and published his own newspaper, at 20 he produced tracts on philosophy, and at 26, he wrote and published *Poor Richard's Almanac*, making his fortune from it. He went on to found America's first circulating library, organised its first fire brigade and invented a wood-burning stove that is still in use today; he developed the first efficient bi-focal spectacles and, after discovering the positive and negative elements of electricity, produced the first effective lightning conductor.

He returned to America and went into politics, helping to draft the Declaration of Independence, but he left St Bride's with an efficient lightning conductor that lasted till the bombings of 1940.

Everyone who sees it compares St Bride's steeple to a wedding cake but very few realise that the resemblance should be the other way round; traditional wedding cakes are copies of the steeple. In the early nineteenth century a pastrycook called Mr Rich, who lived nearby, decided to make a special cake for his daughter's wedding. He had the happy inspiration of basing the 'bride's cake' on St Bride's Church and produced a confection of sugar and marzipan that copied the tiers and pillars of the steeple. He died in 1811 but the fashion he began has remained popular ever since.

The spire's second claim to fame is its peal of bells. The first peals were rung in this spire by England's oldest bell-ringing society, The Ancient Society of College Youths who were founded in 1637 and still have a complete list of all their members. (The 'College' concerned was founded by Dick Whittington in 1422.) In 1717 the Youths rang the first peal of Grandsire Caters on St Bride's bells and came back in 1726 to ring the first ever set of Bob Maximus. The secretary of the time recorded with pride that 'every ringer went home in his own carriage'.

During the post-war restoration of the church, excavations carried out in the crypt confirmed that many of the legends of the church's antiquity were true. Traces of no fewer than seven previous churches were found, as well as a Roman building, and evidence was found of a connection with St Bride (Bridget) that folk-lore had kept alive for nearly two thousand years. The significance of the legend is that Bridget was the Christian version of Brigit, the Celtic goddess whose shrines were built beside wells. The well at St Bride's was a London landmark for a thousand years and is still remembered by the word 'Bridewell'.

The crypt is open to the public and the church is well worth a visit. On the wall beside the font is a small monument to Virginia Dare, the first English child to be born in America, and a panel nearby has a delightful tribute to Christopher Wren. Besides being the architect who gave London so many of its finest buildings, Wren was a mathematician and scientist and was Professor of Astronomy when he was asked to make a survey of St Paul's Cathedral. The verse on the panel appeared in *Punch* in 1928 and makes a pleasant change from the mournful sonority of so many memorials. The opening lines are:

Clever men like Christopher Wren
Only occur just now and then.
No one expects
In perpetuity,
Architects of his ingenuity.
No, never a cleverer dipped his pen
Than clever Sir Christopher – Christopher Wren.

The well that produced pure water for so many centuries and gave its name to the original pagan shrine has now gone. It was famous for its capacity and ran dry only once in its history, during the Coronation celebrations of 1820, when the taverns and eating-houses of Fleet Street exhausted its supply trying to cater for the crowds that poured into London.

There is a small garden on the Fleet Street side of the church. Walk along it, with the church on your right, to a spot about ten feet short of the railings at the end. The old well lies under the raised bed; the author was fortunate enough to be here when it was last uncovered in 1949 by workmen repairing the bomb damage.

The last story concerns the small fountain in the garden. St Bridget/Bride, after whom the church is named, was reputed to have the enviable power of turning water into beer. Cynics have said that this is the reason her church is so popular with journalists. While history offers no firm evidence of the saint performing the feat, the present church authorities have kept the tradition alive by changing water into wine! During a period of severe frost a few years ago, they became anxious about the water in the fountain freezing and, taking the line that the old ways are the best, they added a sizeable quantity of white wine to the water to keep it flowing.

The Bridewell

The path that runs back past the Old Bell bends right at the corner and passes under the retaining wall of the churchyard. About ten yards on, a patch on the wall shows where the spout of the old well used to be. At the bottom of the alley, one path leads up a flight of steps to the right and goes on to Salisbury Square and the Temple. Our walk follows the path to the left into New Bridge Street, passing the St Bride's Institute on the right.

The old Palace of Bridewell extended from the Institute down to the river. Like the Tower of London, the Normans built it originally as a fortress to defend the City with the secondary purpose of defending themselves if the City attacked them. Henry VIII enlarged it to make a Royal palace and entertained Charles V, the Holy Roman Emperor, here in 1522. His son, Edward VI the Boy-King, had no use for it and presented it to the City of London as a hospital and refuge for beggars.

Over the years the emphasis changed and a school was established on the site of the present Institute while the main part of the building became a women's prison, which is what the word 'Bridewell' has indicated ever since. Destroyed in the Fire of 1666, it was rebuilt and remained a prison till 1855.

One of the prisoners was a well-known brothel-keeper known as Madam Cresswell. She died in Bridewell and left the sum of £20 to the chaplain on condition that he conducted her funeral service and 'spoke well of her in his address'. Because of her notoriety the will was widely discussed and half London turned up at the funeral to hear what the chaplain would say.

The clergyman gave a general discourse on life, death and mortality ending with the words:

> I am desired by the will of the deceased to mention her and to say nothing but what is well of her. All that I shall say therefore is this – that she was born well, lived well and died well; for she was born a Cresswell, she lived in Clerkenwell and she died in Bridewell.

Although the Bridewell Institute now occupies a Victorian building it is still a charity, founded by the statutes of Edward VI, and the old courtroom of the prison it later became is still inside. It is now governed jointly by the City Corporation and the Guild of St Bride's, a body which holds an annual service in the church as it has since receiving its charter in 1375.

New Bridge Street was for many years the widest in London. Built in 1764 to give access to the newly-built Blackfriars Bridge, its contrast to the narrow lanes that make up so much of the City is explained by the fact that it covers the Fleet River and the lanes that used to be on either side. The Fleet is still there underneath, visible through the open manhole covers in the middle of the road; it is still possible to walk along its course underground from Blackfriars Bridge up to the base of Hampstead Hill.

The river was navigable up to Holborn till the reign of Elizabeth but deteriorated into an open sewer and rubbish tip in the following century. During an attempt to clean it during the reign of Charles II, some Roman remains were found and the King came to inspect them. He was presented with a Roman penny discovered on the site and was so struck by it that he used it as a model for the first modern English copper penny, persuading the Duchess of Richmond to pose for the figure of Britannia that appeared on every penny for three hundred years.

No. 14 New Bridge Street, built in 1802, is all that remains of the old Bridewell Prison. The arch of the old gateway is decorated with a head of Edward VI who gave it to the City. Bridewell Place runs down the side of the building and bends to the left.

The red-brick Victorian building in the right-hand corner, No. 2 Bridewell Place, used to be the old rectory of St Bride's where, for two hundred years, the rector paid the City of London £1 a year to cross his own doorstep. He did so because Bridewell Place follows the line of the old Palace wall built by Henry VIII. When Edward VI gave it to the City, parts of the palace were knocked down but the old wall was left. Bridewell Place was constructed inside it and the rectory was built outside with a doorway in the wall for the rector. Although the wall was eventually demolished, the space it had occupied still belonged in law to the City which meant the rector continued to pay rent for the doorway in the long-vanished wall till the 1950s, when a new rectory was built. The line of the old wall can still be traced on the paving stones.

Although most accounts of Bridewell state that it ceased to be a prison in 1855, that is not strictly correct. When the new block down the left of Bridewell Place was being excavated in the 1970s, sections of the old Palace of Henry VIII were discovered at the bottom end. An archaeological survey was done but the section nearest Fleet Street was ignored. When the Bridewell prisoners were transferred to Holloway in 1855, the City Chamberlain retained the right to put unruly apprentices into Bridewell. The question is – where would he have put them?

The author discovered the answer by accident when he saw the underground car-park in the northern corner being cleared and noticed two cellar doors of remarkably strong construction. Inside were two Victorian cells and the records should now show that, although Bridewell may have lost its prisoners in 1855, it did not lose its cells till 1973 (and the author was the last person to occupy them).

At the bottom of Bridewell Place the road runs left back into New Bridge Street, The section of London immediately across the road is called Blackfriars after the Dominicans whose monastery stood here from 1278 to 1538. We will see the only remaining section of their buildings on another walk but there is an unusual memorial to them across the street.

The Blackfriars pub, a remarkable example of Art Nouveau architecture, is so narrow and so tall that its stability seems doubtful. Its main attractions are the panels above the windows which show a series of alcoholic friars engaged in various aspects of the brewing trade. On the panel advertising bottled beer the friars are busy bottling, while the panel extolling draught beer shows friars busy among barrels. The other agreeable feature is the series of directions given so that no passer-by can be in doubt as to where the appropriate entrance is. One friar, for example, points a finger firmly to the Saloon Bar door and the panel excludes any confusion by stating that it is '9 yards' away.

Blackfriars Bridge, like Waterloo Bridge, Eros and Cleopatra's Needle, is another heartening example of popular opinion defeating officialdom. Parliament decided that the first bridge on this site, opened in 1769, should be called the William Pitt Bridge after the Prime Minister, but Londoners christened it Blackfriars Bridge and that has been its name ever since. The bridge spans the outlet of the Fleet River (which can still be seen at low tide by craning over the balustrade). Like the other three road bridges within the City boundaries, Blackfriars Bridge was erected at no cost to the Government, taxpayer or anyone else.

Up to 1750 London Bridge was the only one across the Thames below Putney. Because of the importance of the bridge to the City, wealthy merchants left money to assist in its upkeep and the tolls exacted to cross the bridge were put into a fund, opened in 1209, to keep the bridge in good repair. Over the centuries the Bridge House Estates invested their money carefully in the City and acquired sufficient capital to build and maintain the present Blackfriars, London, Southwark and Tower Bridges.

New Bridge Street joins the Embankment at Unilever House. This was the site of De Keyser's Royal Hotel, once the smartest in London. De Keyser's was one of those success stories which show how the Victorians were not so class-conscious as is sometimes supposed. De Keyser came to London from Belgium as a penniless waiter, worked his way up to become manager of a hotel, then built the largest hotel in London on this site. In 1887 he became the first Catholic Lord Mayor of London since the Reformation. The hotel prospered but Fashion moved west and the site was sold to Unilever, who erected the present building in 1930. The architectural decoration tends to conceal the lack of windows on the ground floor, a feature intended to protect the occupants from traffic noise but adding a slightly sinister touch to the building's appearance.

The next building along the Embankment was, until 1986, the City of London School whose frontage has been retained. Like Blackfriars Bridge it is an example of the respect the City Fathers devote to the bequests entrusted to their charge. In 1422 John Carpenter, a colleague of Dick Whittington's, left property to the City authorities to pay for the education of four boys. Although the bequest specified only four boys, the City followed the spirit rather than the letter of the trust and increased the number of pupils as the bequest grew in value until they had sufficient funds to build this school in 1883.

The Victorian Gothic building beyond the school is Sion College, a society and library for Anglican clergymen within the City of London, founded in 1624 with the laudable aims of 'the maintenance of truth in doctrine, love in conversing together and for the repression of such sins as do follow men'.

Carmelite Street, named after the monastery that used to stand here, runs up from the Embankment. The first doorway on the left is part of the old *Daily Mail* offices; the silver-bronze doors date from the time of Alfred Harmsworth who built the largest newspaper empire in the world. They are a modern version of the Baptistery doors of Florence and each panel shows a stage in the making of a newspaper.

Carmelite Street, once the home of the newspaper industry, is now being converted to new uses. At the junction with Tudor Street, pause before turning left towards the Temple. Ahead is Whitefriars Street, and the romantically-named Hanging Sword Alley runs off at an angle to the right. A few yards directly in front is Britton's Court in which a small crypt survives from the old Carmelite Priory. Although the crypt is the only remaining chamber from the Priory, the foundations of the old monastery, six feet thick and set deep in the ground, still cause problems to the demolition firms working in the area.

The Temple

Tudor Street runs westwards, crossing Bouverie Street (famous as the home of *Punch*), to enter The Temple at King's Bench Walk. The Temple has been a separate enclave acknowledging the authority of neither the City of London nor of Westminster since the Knights Templar came here in 1162. Founded to protect pilgrims travelling to the Holy Land, the Templars took their name from their first quarters on the site of Solomon's Temple at Jerusalem. They became a powerful Order of warrior knights but, as their fame and wealth grew, they attracted enemies and were eventually disbanded in 1312.

The lease of their property was given to lawyers for a hostel (hence the name Inn for the Inns of Court) and the lawyers have been here ever since. The reason they adopted the site so readily was because Henry III had founded a school of law at Oxford and, in order to encourage students to attend it, had forbidden the teaching of law within the City of London. By moving to the Temple, theoretically outside the City boundaries, the lawyers evaded the edict.

This refusal to accept the authority of the City continued over the centuries and three attempts by the Lord Mayor to enter the Temple were defeated by force. All appeals by the Lord Mayor to the Crown proved fruitless since, whenever the King asked for legal advice, the Temple lawyers always put their point of view. One of the Lord Mayors, who had been physically evicted from the Temple grounds, did get his own back when a fire broke out in the Temple and he stopped the City fire brigades from entering. His revenge was short-lived because the Templars went to their cellars and put the fire out with beer.

The question of jurisdiction remained dormant till 1911 when a death occurred in the Temple; the City Coroner arrived to hold an inquest but the gates were locked in his face. Even the Temple's rates bill was, and maybe still is, excluded from normal legislation; a contribution is made to the relevant authorities based on the lawyers' own assessment of what they should pay.

The Temple is divided into the Inner Temple, that part nearer to the City and the Middle Temple, the section that stands to the west. The Outer Temple has now vanished from history, save for the few stones left in a wall at the bottom of Essex Street. Both the Inner and Middle Temple joined in a common anxiety over their right to this section of London and spent a long time trying to acquire a freehold from the Crown. When James I arrived in England in 1603, they were at last able to purchase the freehold. To make sure that it was safe from a Royal change of mind, they promptly buried the document under the altar in the Temple church. They left it there for the next three hundred years till they considered their position was secure.

King's Bench Walk, designed by Christopher Wren in 1677, still has some of the iron rings to which horses were tied and these remained in use till the early part of this century. A recent proposal to remove them was defeated by those members of the Inn who pointed out that they had proved very useful during the last petrol strike when some lawyers rode their horses to the Temple as their forebears had done.

Walk across King's Bench Walk, aiming half-right to the passage through to the next courtyard. This is Church Court, with the Inner Temple Library and Hall on the left and the Temple church on the right, looking much as it did when the Knights Templar built it back in 1185. It is one of the five round churches in England, built by the Templars in imitation of the Holy Sepulchre in Jerusalem. It was consecrated by no less a person than Heraclius, Patriarch of Jerusalem, while on a visit to England to urge Henry II to join a Crusade.

Despite bombs, restoration and Victorian 'improvements', the church is little changed and the west doorway is exactly as it was eight hundred years ago, while the two-ton door itself has been here since before the Armada. The bombing destroyed some of the old pillars but they were replaced by the same Purbeck quarry that had supplied the originals seven hundred years previously.

The circular section is the original church and the nave to the east was added in 1204 making 'the Oblong and the Round'. The effigies of the Knights Templar in 'the Round' include two men, the Earl of Pembroke and Lord de Ros who were at Runnymede in 1215. In one corner of the church, in the thickness of the wall, is a tiny penitential cell where a Knight was left to starve to death for disobeying the orders of the Grand Master. The organ, installed in 1670, was a favourite of Purcell's. It was chosen only after tremendous competition between two organ builders, Renatus Harris and Father Schmidt. It was eventually decided in favour of Schmidt by Judge Jeffreys who was the Temple's best musician.

When James I gave the freehold to the lawyers, he specified that the Inner Temple should look after the southern half of the church, while the Middle Temple should maintain the northern side. The condition is still obeyed and members of each Inn can be distinguished by the side on which they sit. The Paschal Lamb on one side of the altar marks the Middle Temple side; the winged horse to the right shows where the Inner Temple sits.

The chaplain, who enjoys the splendid title Master of the Temple because his appointment goes back to the Knights Templar who were a religious Order, is appointed by the Crown and is independent of the Bishop of London. This led to some confusion in the religious turmoil of the seventeenth century, when sermons in the morning were given by a fervent Royalist High Anglican Master while the evening service was taken by the Reader, appointed by the lawyers, whose views leaned heavily towards Calvin and republicanism.

In the last century, the Temple was blessed with a Master who took his duties very seriously and became deeply concerned by the morals of some of the younger members. In particular he took exception to the young ladies who visited barristers in their chambers at night. After deep reflection, he worked out a system to stop the wicked habit. He ordered the Gate porter to make every lady sign her name in book, together with the name of the gentleman she was visiting. The system lasted one day. When the porter brought the book to him, the Master opened it to find that twenty-seven young ladies had entered the Inn the night before and each had named the Master as her host.

The Cloisters lie directly south of the church. Since they belong to the church rather than to either Inn there was a tremendous dispute when they were burnt in 1688. The Inner Temple wanted them restored exactly as before; the Middle Temple, at the suggestion of our old friend Nicholas Barbon who had a financial interest, wanted them enlarged to provide extra accommodation.

Eventually the question went to arbitration, the extra accommodation was agreed and Christopher Wren was called in to design it. He found the Templars difficult since they insisted on having the traditional pillars of the cloisters replaced whereas Sir Christopher saw no reason for them. With the building methods he was using, pillars were no longer needed. The lawyers insisted, so Wren gave them the pillars they wanted, but proved his point by leaving the pillars a good inch short of the roof so that they supported nothing at all. The gap was filled only a few years ago when the ceiling was repainted.

Directly west of the Cloisters, Pump Court leads to Middle Temple Lane. To the right is Middle Temple Gateway which we passed on the outside; from this angle we can admire the wooden-framed houses that stand beside it. An inspection of the wooden window frames shows how the Great Fire spread so quickly, since the flames jumped easily up the City house-fronts from the frames set flush with the wall.

This section of Middle Temple Lane looks on to Fountain Court, with Middle Temple Hall on the left. With the Temple Church, this Hall is the pride of the Temple. Begun in 1562, it was completed in 1570 and, although it suffered some bomb damage, it is still one of the finest pieces of Tudor architecture in London. The double hammer-beam roof and the spectacular screen date from the days of Queen Elizabeth I who came here to attend the first performance of *Twelfth Night* on 2nd February 1601, when Shakespeare himself appeared in a small part.

The long table on the dais is 29 feet long, made from a single piece of oak presented by Queen Elizabeth. Near it is a small table which is given the correct name of a cupboard, i.e. a board on which cups were placed, that was made from the hatchway of Drake's *Golden Hind*.

One thing no longer seen in the Temple is the horn-blower who blew a call every night to summon the students to dinner. The Templars were called to their meals by horn back in the twelfth century and the tradition of the horn-blower lasted from that century to this. A few years ago the horn was broken and, unbelievably, the governing body of the Inn felt it was unnecessary to keep the tradition alive. A protest by the author was met by the reply that the Temple felt it was inappropriate in the twentieth century.

From Fountain Court, where Dickens had his lovers meet in *Martin Chuzzlewit*, there are two exits. One leads through New Court, built in 1675 by Barbon who made a nice profit selling it to the Middle Temple, and returns us to Essex Street by the Devereux pub we saw earlier.

A better way is down towards the river and the Embankment, along the path that comes out at the bottom of the Essex Street steps. Walk out of the gate and turn sharp left. After a few yards, look back at the building inside the railings. On the corner, facing the river, are some magnificent painted parish boundary marks showing that we have left the City and re-entered Westminster. A few yards further on, a raised bank of earth shows the route of the Underground Railway through the Temple gardens. The Templars insisted it was built there as a condition of the railway passing through their grounds. If the Thames were to overflow, the bank would make a useful flood-barrier for the Temple gardens.

EIGHTH ♦ WALK

Ludgate Hill to St Paul's and Blackfriars

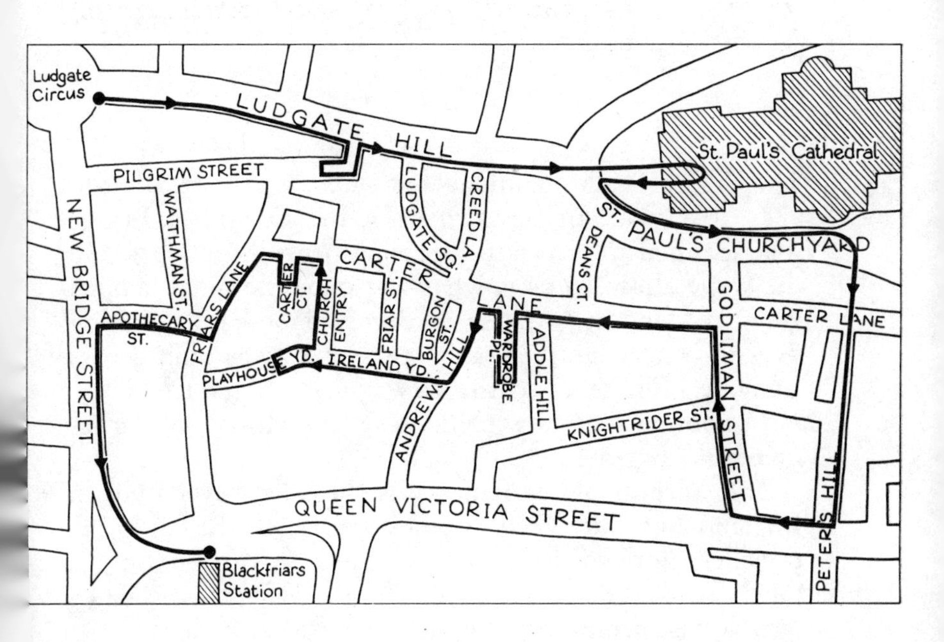

EIGHTH ♦ WALK

Ludgate Hill to St Paul's and Blackfriars

The Eighth Walk commences at Ludgate Circus, built in 1874 to replace the crossroads at the Old Fleet Bridge that spanned the river still flowing beneath our feet. Up the slope ahead of us is what was once the most famous view in London – the great dome of St Paul's soaring over the City. Until the railway viaduct was built across Ludgate Hill, this was the view tourists came to admire in London as they now come to see the Houses of Parliament and Big Ben.

The spire of old St Paul's was the tallest ever built in England and, like Wren's dome after it, was the landmark travellers looked for as they approached London. St Paul's could be seen from the North Downs, the Chilterns, even from the Hampshire Downs sometimes; it was the highest building in London till the planning regulations were relaxed in the 1960s.

When the old cathedral was burnt down in the Fire of 1666, London expected to see another spire in its place. Wren's dome was the first to be built in England and caused a sensation. The idea was promptly copied by every English designer; the domed lids of the silver coffee pots and teapots of the Queen Anne period are imitations of the new feature of London's skyline.

Our walk goes up the right-hand side of Ludgate Hill where it is easy to see why the Romans chose this spot for the western gate of the City. Anyone attacking from this direction had to cross the Fleet River under a hail of arrows, then advance uphill against the fortified City walls. As the City grew, Temple Bar became the first line of defence, far enough away to ensure that no military force could approach the City without warning, but near enough to ensure that the guard could get back within the City if danger threatened.

The Lud Gate, one of the four City gates erected by the Romans, was restored by Alfred the Great and rebuilt in 1215, the year of Magna Carta. Built like a fortress with towers and battlements, the massive gatehouse became a City prison and was rebuilt again in 1586, when the statue of Queen Elizabeth now at St Dunstan's was placed on it. It was finally demolished in 1760. One trace still remains at the corner of Pilgrim Street, about thirty yards off Ludgate Hill. The large grey stone that protects the angle of the building from vehicles cutting the corner too sharply, performed the same function for the Ludgate towers four hundred years ago.

Ludgate Square, a few yards further on, must be the smallest square in London. It is a narrow alley leading round to Creed Lane. A notice under the arch in splendid Victorian copperplate script announces firmly that 'This Wall and Archway are Private Property. Anyone Posting . . .' and the rest is silence.

Creed Lane, next on the right, takes its name from the processions and open-air services that the Cathedral clergy conducted before the Reformation. Celebrations at Easter and other Feast Days included processions around the precincts of the Cathedral with halts at intervals to recite certain prescribed prayers. These are commemorated at Creed Lane, Paternoster Square, Sermon Lane, Ave Maria Lane and Amen Court.

St Paul's

St Paul's was founded in 604 by Ethelbert, the Christian King of Kent, who appointed Melitus as the first Bishop of London. Although English law holds that all legal ownership of land dates from 1066, the cathedral recently proved its title to the oldest land-tenure in England, a farm at Tillingham in Essex which it has owned since 606AD.

The area in front of the cathedral was once the churchyard and the bishop had to build a wall around it in 1284 to prevent the City authorities from taking it over. Although such incursions on the Cathedral's property are now unlikely, the diocese maintains a single wooden barrier standing by itself on the left of the forecourt. It is the last City toll gate, marking the old route to Cheapside around the back of the Cathedral. In 1874 the City authorities tried to buy the roadway and abolish the toll, but the Cathedral refused and the gate stands here just to make the point. It is solemnly opened for official processions even though it could be easily passed on either side by any driver who cared to do so.

The statue of Queen Anne in the middle of the Square has been here since 1712 when it was erected to commemorate completion of the Cathedral. Contemporary opinion was not favourable. When the Queen died childless two years later, leaving the country with another problem of constitutional succession, Londoners satirised both her childlessness and her liking for strong drink with the rhyme:

Brandy Nan, Brandy Nan,
You left us in the lurch.
Your face towards the brandy-shop,
Your arse towards the church.

The figure of the Queen became so worn that it was replaced by the present statue in 1886, carved by Richard Belt. Belt was renowned as much for the irregularity of his private life as for his artistic skill. Soon after he was given the commission, he was arrested and convicted on a charge of fraud. Because of the urgent need for a new statue, plus the fact that the authorities were reluctant to spend more money commissioning another one, he was given special facilities to complete the job in prison. It has the dubious distinction of being the only statue in London carved by a convict serving his sentence.

The figures around the statue are original and represent Queen Anne's jurisdiction as it was considered to be in 1712. Since the Kings of England claimed title to the throne of France, a claim maintained till the reign of George IV, France is shown as the figure with a cap on her head; Ireland is the lady with the harp and England holds a trident. The fourth figure, representing America, shows a woman wearing the clothing and head-dress of an American Indian chief, a costume which the sculptor had seen the year before when four Indian chiefs came to London to offer their help in the war against the French.

The statue has received little critical acclaim but Queen Victoria had a high regard for it. When arrangements were being made for her Diamond Jubilee in 1897, the proposal was made to move Queen Anne to enable the royal carriage to drive straight up to the front of the Cathedral. Victoria was horrified at the idea: 'That would never do! One day there will be a statue of me in London and someone might want to move that – and I should not like that at all.'

At the bottom of the steps, a plaque marks the spot where Victoria celebrated her Jubilee of 1897, when she came to St Paul's but stayed in her carriage while the Service of Thanksgiving was enacted on the steps in front of her.

Wren's masterpiece was built over a period of 35 years by one master-builder Thomas Strong. Wren came regularly to superintend the work, even though he was engaged from 1666 onwards in building fifty other London churches. He saw his son perform the task of laying the last stone in the lantern in 1710.

It is the partnership of Wren and Strong that gives St Paul's the feeling of unity that is stronger here than in any other cathedral in the country. It is even more remarkable if we remember that Wren produced the design when he was 33 years old, a Professor of Astronomy at Oxford, whose only previous architectural work had been the design of a doorway at Ely Cathedral and a memorial chapel at Cambridge.

He realised the cost was going to frighten people and, to ensure that his design was not altered by Parliament, he did not follow the normal practice of building the Cathedral in sections but started on the entire ground plan so that every level went up stage by stage. This meant that the first service could not be held till 1697 but he persevered even though Parliament voted his annual salary of £200 should be reduced by half. He did not receive the arrears till 1711 when he was 80 years old.

There are plenty of guide-books to the Cathedral and this walk looks only at some of its more unusual aspects. The first is the memorial to John Donne, which he posed for himself, the only monument from the old Cathedral to survive the Great Fire of 1666. It stands south of the choir, a sinister figure in a shroud with dark smoke stains still on it. (See Sixth Walk.)

Across the nave is the extraordinary monument to the Duke of Wellington, so large that it is easy to confuse its columns with the cathedral pillars. The Duke himself lies in the crypt beside Nelson, but his monument took fifty-six years to complete and is a saga of controversy and delay. It was designed by Alfred Stevens, whose seated lions we saw in Chancery Lane (see Sixth Walk) and he regarded it as the culmination of his career, which indeed it turned out to be, although not in the way he hoped.

Stevens was an enthusiastic and skilful sculptor who introduced a dramatic exaggeration into his carving that found little favour with his critics. He accepted the commission for £14,000, although it was clear that the sum would be insufficient even to pay for the materials he would need. He took the job very seriously, but felt that it would be wrong to rush it and drew money from the Cathedral architect as and when he needed it. It was not until the entire amount had been disbursed that a formal inquiry found that Stevens was penniless, scarcely half the monument had been completed and the castings and masonry work still had to be done.

The Cathedral authorities passed the matter over to the official Surveyor of Works, Acton Smee Ayrton, who had already become notorious amongst architects with his harsh treatment of G. E. Street, the designer of the Law Courts in the Strand (see Sixth Walk). Ayrton at once issued a writ calling upon Stevens to produce the monument within thirty days. This was clearly impossible but Ayrton saw no reason to wait and served a further writ of execution, seizing Stevens's studio, tools and all his models and designs. After appeals to Mr Gladstone from every architect and sculptor in the country, Stevens was allowed to continue the work but died a short time later with the monument still incomplete.

Thirty years after Stevens's death, John Tweed was called in to finish the monument by casting the missing top section, the figure of Wellington on his famous charger Copenhagen. This led to further controversy since many people felt the figure of a horse had no place in a sacred building. It was finally erected in 1912, sixty years after the Duke's death; it is still the only equestrian statue in an English church.

Stevens died a disappointed man but he had managed to take his revenge. Below the equestrian statue are two groups of figures. One shows Virtue keeping Vice beneath its feet, the other shows Truth plucking out the tongue of Calumny. As soon as it was placed in position the features of Calumny were immediately recognised by Londoners as those of Stevens's tormentor, Acton Smee Ayrton.

The figures around the dome representing the life of St Paul were painted by Sir James Thornhill, who had to work on scaffolding to do it. One day, moving back to inspect his work, he went so far that his horrified assistant realised a shout would send him to his death.

With great presence of mind his assistant seized a brush and daubed it across the panel; Thornhill's convulsive start of fury brought him safely back on to the scaffolding.

The mosaics in the dome were done in the nineteenth century. The figure of St Mark is another portrait of the Labour politician John Burns, who appears as Vulcan in the archway over King Charles Street (see First Walk). Burns came to inspect the work and reminded the artist that the Apostles were rough working men, not the aesthetic figures being portrayed. They found an office nearby in which Burns stripped off and posed for the rest of the morning. The artist told his friends of the incident and Burns was asked back again by Sir William Richmond to pose for another figure in the Carnarvon window in the north aisle.

The prebendal stalls bear the name of the estate, or prebend, with which the stall is endowed. Some have familiar names like Islington, Hoxton, St Pancras but one is named after a piece of land in Suffolk given a thousand years ago and now vanished under the North Sea. It is the sixth stall on the right and bears the legend *Consumpta per Mare* (Consumed by the Sea).

The crypt is the burial place of heroes and artists. Wren lies here as do Sullivan, Parry and Landseer. Many of the memorials have copies of the artist's best-known work; Lutyens's Cenotaph marks his tomb, Landseer is remembered by a sculpture of the famous 'Shepherd's Dog', Gilbert's Eros is shown and Frampton has Peter Pan on his plaque.

The ornate 18-ton funeral carriage specially built to bring Wellington's body to the Cathedral attracts most attention from visitors, but the most unusual tomb is that of Nelson. Nelson, who had a premonition that he would die at sea, had his coffin made from the mast of the *Orient*, a French warship sunk at the Battle of the Nile. (The *Orient*'s other claim to fame is that the captain's son who perished in the battle was the original boy who 'stood on the burning deck'.)

The coffin lies inside an enormous sarcophagus which pre-dates Nelson by three hundred years; it was commissioned by a cardinal and stolen by a king. When Cardinal Wolsey was Chancellor in 1521, he brought Benedetto da Rovezzano from Florence to carve this black marble tomb in which Wolsey intended to be buried, continuing in death the splendour in which he had lived. The tomb was completed but was confiscated by Henry VIII in 1529 who decided to make use of it himself when the time came. It was carefully stored at Windsor but was forgotten by the time Henry died. It remained there until 1804 and was re-discovered just in time to act as Nelson's final resting-place.

St Paul's Churchyard and the College of Arms

The paved open space in front of the Cathedral and the road that circles around it are both called St Paul's Churchyard, which confuses visitors who expect to see tombstones and grass. The roadway was once lined with bookshops selling missals and prayerbooks to the pilgrims attending the great religious ceremonies. The tradition of book-selling continued after the Reformation and the move of Stationers' Hall to the top of Ludgate Hill confirmed the Churchyard as the centre of London publishing. John Newbery came here in 1745, published Dr Johnson's and Goldsmith's books and was the first to print books for children. He produced *Little Goody Two Shoes*, written by Goldsmith, in 1765 and followed it with the first edition of *Mother Goose Rhymes*, to which Goldsmith also contributed.

The road runs left around the south side of the Cathedral to the Information Centre. If the hour strikes on the Cathedral clock, the chimes will be those of Great Tom, the bell cast by the Whitechapel Bell Foundry, established in 1420. The foundry has provided most of London's church bells over the centuries and many that we still hear today rang peals to celebrate the victory over the Armada. Great Tom weighs 5 tons but its companion, Great Paul, is a giant of 17 tons whose unmistakable deep tone can be heard every day at 1 o'clock.

This is one of the best areas of London for the amateur archaeologist because every roadworks or excavation repays a close look. The sides of any holes dug in central London resemble a layer cake, twentieth-century tarmac on the top, Victorian granite or concrete below and a level of mixed rubble and red brick from the Stuart or Tudor period below that. Sometimes the bottom of the hole has pieces of orange tiles from the Roman occupation.

The level of London's streets rose by an average of six inches a century and traces of London's three great fires can often be seen when deep foundations are being dug. The damage done in the Blitz of 1940–41 is only too apparent in the bomb-sites still common around London, while the Great Fire of 1666 left a blackened layer about six inches thick often found just below cellar level. If a deep excavation is being dug, a thin line of red ashy soil about ten or twelve feet down marks the level of London when Boadicea put it to the torch in 61AD.

Peter's Hill runs down towards the river past the building on the corner with a mysterious plaque of a cross and circle. It marks the boundary of the cathedral property. Sermon Lane, running parallel just a few feet away, leads to the corner of Knightrider Street and the old Horn Tavern that Dickens knew. He was friendly with the landlord and deliberately advertised the tavern when he made Mr Pickwick a customer in *Pickwick Papers*. The present building dates from the eighteenth century but there has been an inn here for hundreds of years before that. The Heralds met here while they restored the damage done to their College in the 1666 Fire.

At the bottom of the hill is the broad sweep of Queen Victoria Street, built in 1867 to extend the line of the Embankment roadway up to the Bank of England. Christopher Wren proposed exactly such a route in 1667 but it took two hundred years for the City authorities to realise he was right.

On the right is the dignified red-brick building of the College of Arms behind splendid wrought-iron gates. Built in 1678, it houses the three Kings at Arms: Garter, Clarenceux and Norroy; six Heralds: Richmond, Somerset, Lancaster, Windsor, Chester and York and four Pursuivants: Rouge Dragon, Blue Mantle, Portcullis and Rouge Croix.

The College was given the authority to grant arms in 1484 and its jurisdiction is wider than many realize. Twenty years ago a city in the Midlands decided to create its own coat of arms without the College's permission. It was fined a considerable sum of money by the Court of Heraldry which was especially re-convened for the first time in two hundred years.

The Heralds have included some notable eccentrics, one of whom, William Oldys, was appointed Norroy King at Arms because the Duke of Norfolk admired his biography of Walter Raleigh. Oldys was an excellent genealogist but achieved notoriety by his drunkenness: he was 'rarely sober in the afternoon, never after supper'. He spent his evenings in the Bell Inn beside the Old Bailey, employing a watchman to ensure he was delivered back to the College before midnight. Entry after that time meant an automatic fine of sixpence.

It was in the Bell, as he watched a fly drinking from his beer-mug, that he wrote the lines for which he is now best remembered:

Busy, curious, thirsty fly,
Drink with me and drink as I;
Freely welcome to my cup,
Couldst thou sip and sip it up
Make the most of life you may;
Life is short and wears away.

Both alike are mine and thine,
Hastening quick to their decline;
Thine's a summer, mine no more,
Though repeated to threescore;
Threescore summers, when they're gone,
Will appear as short as one.

Across the road is the City of London Boys' School on its new site. Beside it is an unusual set of sculptures looking down on the road, seven huge aluminium heads representing the Seven Ages of Man.

Along Shakespeare's Carter Lane

Godliman Street runs up beside the College of Arms to a junction with Carter Lane, one of the oldest streets in the City. For some reason Carter Lane has been left undisturbed by the developers. The buildings are Victorian but retain the proportions of their predecessors and the bends and twists of the narrow roadway would be familiar to Dickens, Johnson, even to Shakespeare. There are many pleasant closes and churchyards left in the City, but Carter Lane and the area of Blackfriars through which it passes give a better impression of mediaeval London than anywhere else.

Bell's Yard on the left is occupied by a telephone exchange now but the Bell Inn that stood here was a favourite of Shakespeare's and of Dickens after him. It was from the Bell Inn that Richard Quyney wrote the only letter to Shakespeare that has survived.

The splendid Deanery in Dean's Court was built by Wren and the front door carved by Gibbons gives on to a hallway deliberately built large enough to hold diocesan meetings. The dignified frontage has one flaw. It may be an optical illusion, but the building looks as if it is imperceptibly 'melting'; the window ledges either side of the doorway seem to slope slightly downwards.

In the angle of the wall by the Deanery is a stone cornice carved with minute letters. It lists the Cathedral officials responsible for building the St Paul's Choir School which stretches around the corner and along Carter Lane. The façade has a fresco of divine praises in Latin and the building is a perfect example of what Betjeman called High Church Victorian Italianate.

Wardrobe Place stands on the site of the King's Wardrobe, built in 1350 by Edward III. Robes of State were kept here as well as clothing for the servants and retainers of the royal household. In 1604 Shakespeare received 4½ yards of scarlet cloth from the Wardrobe so that he could march with the other members of the King's Company of actors in the procession for James I's official entry into the City.

In 1720 the Wardrobe was converted into the delightful square we see today. Birds sing in the trees that stand amongst the cobbles and one of the old houses on the right has the only flexible link-snuffer in London, swinging from a bracket by the door.

A few yards past Wardrobe Place is the section of Carter Lane that justifies its title as the 'last village street in the City'. Five mediaeval streets meet at crazy angles, making it difficult for anything larger than a Post Office van to negotiate the corners. Every corner has solid iron bollards dating from the days when an iron-shod cartwheel could tear down the angle of a timber house-wall. Seeing the difficulty that even taxis have in pulling around these narrow lanes, the bollards are just as necessary today.

The house with bright blue shutters has two small plaques marking the ward boundary of Farringdon Within. It stands at the top of St Andrews Hill, which we follow down to the first turning on the right. A fine merchant's house flanks St Andrew's Church which has been here since 1325. The postbox in the wall has been decorated by somebody who felt it would be improved by picking out the initials of King Edward and King George in bright yellow.

We follow Ireland Yard to the right where Shakespeare

bought a house in 1613 under a conveyance that can be seen in the Guildhall Library. The house stood just west of Friar Street, beside the steps to the churchyard where a small section of wall is all that remains above ground of the Blackfriars monastery.

The monastery which gave its name to this part of London stretched from Ludgate in the north to the river-bank below us and as far as the Fleet River to the west. Founded in 1278, it became one of the largest religious houses in the south of England. Parliament met here in 1311 and 1450 and the Emperor Charles V of Germany was lodged here when he came to visit London in 1522. After the Dissolution this small site was saved for the parish church of St Anne's which stood here till it burned down in the Great Fire.

Ireland Yard opens out into Playhouse Yard where the Blackfriars Theatre stood when Shakespeare joined Burbage. Burbage had brought his company here to escape from the Puritans of the City who had no jurisdiction over the old monastery grounds. The company stayed here for ten years, then moved over the river to the Globe. Their old theatre here was eventually pulled down by the Puritans during the Commonwealth.

There is little to see in Playhouse Yard now, though the black building on the right has an unusual curving side wall bearing a remarkable resemblance to the bastion of the old City wall that once stood here. The *Observer* newspaper on the left occupied Printing House Square, where the King's Printers set up their presses in 1627 and which became famous around the world as the home of *The Times* from 1785 to 1974.

We turn up Church Entry where a small dignified building on the right shows that, although St Anne's church had disappeared by fire in 1666, the parish had kept going long enough to need a new vestry in 1906. There were clearly plenty of funds for the task because the stone at the bottom right corner shows the architect was Sir Banister Fletcher.

Church Entry leads back into a section of Carter Lane even narrower than that we walked along before. It makes it very easy to appreciate the dangers of London's streets when narrow thoroughfares like this were full of horse-drawn vehicles, all trying to squeeze past each other, driving over such pavements as existed and forcing pedestrians to jump into any doorway handy.

Carter Court, a small bare yard at the end of a dark archway, is derelict now but a dozen families once lived here. The right-hand wall of the passage has not changed since it was built about 1670. Rough wooden panels protect the plaster and brickwork and the strong post at the far end still takes the weight of the timber-framed structure.

Apothecaries' Hall and the Livery Companies

Carter Lane finishes dramatically at a small plateau looking out over the valley of the Fleet to western London. Ludgate Broadway, surely the narrowest broadway in London, is on the right and the new building to the left has a badge showing that it belongs to the Society of Apothecaries around the corner. Blackfriars Lane leads around to the left past a Victorian pub clinging to the slope, the only survivor of the bombs that fell here in 1941.

Apothecaries' Hall has been here since 1684 and candidates still come here for examination because the Apothecaries are one of the few Livery Companies still offering qualifications for their craft or 'mistery'.

There are ninety-four Livery Companies in the City, all of them descended from the mediaeval trade guilds, an early form of closed shop. No one could practise a trade in the City unless he was a member of the relevant Company and the Lord Mayor and officials of the City were, and are, always elected from their ranks. The Companies grew rich and powerful over the centuries and, although the restrictions of trade no longer apply, they still exercise great influence. Their income nowadays is spent on maintaining the almshouses, schools and hospitals founded by past members.

Although the old rivalries have faded away and the apprentices of the Companies no longer fight each other in the streets, two Companies still vie for theoretical seniority and their struggle has been immortalised in a figure of speech. In the fifteenth century the Merchant Taylors' and the Skinners' Companies each claimed that they were the sixth in order of precedence and the Lord Mayor was asked to arbitrate. His decision was a masterpiece of compromise; each Company would be sixth one year and seventh the next. The two Companies accepted his ruling and still obey it but the rest of London regarded the matter as being as confused as ever and the phrase 'being at sixes and sevens' was born.

Few of the old privileges of the Companies remain though a member of the Vintners' Company can still sell wine without a licence in certain parts of London. The Vintners and the Dyers share with the Crown the ownership of all swans on the Thames, going out on the water every year at the famous Swan Upping ceremony to mark their birds.

The Companies adhere faithfully to the conditions of their bequests. One Company offers its guests drinks after dinner with the mysterious words, 'Do you drink with Sir George or Lady Jones?' The phrase originates with a Liveryman who enjoyed his brandy and left a sum of money to the Company so that his fellows could enjoy it as well. His widow felt that brandy had contributed to his death and, convinced that gin was a far healthier drink, she left an equivalent sum on condition it was used to purchase that beverage. If you prefer brandy, you 'drink with Sir George'; if you want gin, you 'drink with Lady Jones'.

The courtyard of the Apothecaries' Hall is open to the public and the coat of arms over the doorway represents Apollo flanked by two unicorns. Unicorns were chosen because drinking cups made of their horns were believed to have the magical power of rendering all poisons harmless. Unfortunately unicorns were difficult to find so rhinoceros horn was used instead – and it is a mediaeval impression of a rhinoceros that Apollo bestrides on the badge.

There was tremendous rivalry between the Apothecaries and the Physicians. Lawsuits were brought by each Company against the other, followed by prosecutions to decide whether or not the Apothecaries were allowed to diagnose illnesses or the Physicians should be allowed to sell drugs. The House of Lords eventually settled the matter in 1723 and gave the Apothecaries the rights they enjoy today, including the authority to set the examinations still taken here at the Hall.

Blackfriars Lane runs down to Blackfriars Station, built in 1886. The station served the south coast and Channel ports, advertising the destinations of its trains on a series of stone panels outside the entrance. The Blackfriars panels became famous, not for the names that were carved on them, but the order in which they were set out. Small suburban stations were mixed with the great capitals of Europe, a juxtaposition that tickled Londoners' sense of humour. The decision in 1977 to rebuild the station and destroy the panels brought protests from all over the country. The authorities relented and some of the originals can be seen in the new booking-office.

From Blackfriars, according to the panels, you can still travel direct to Antwerp or Ashford, Gravesend or Darmstad, Naples or Cologne, Westgate-on-Sea or St Petersburg. It makes an incongruous ending to our short walk from Ludgate Circus.

NINTH ♦ WALK

Ludgate Circus to St Bartholomew's Hospital and the Old Bailey

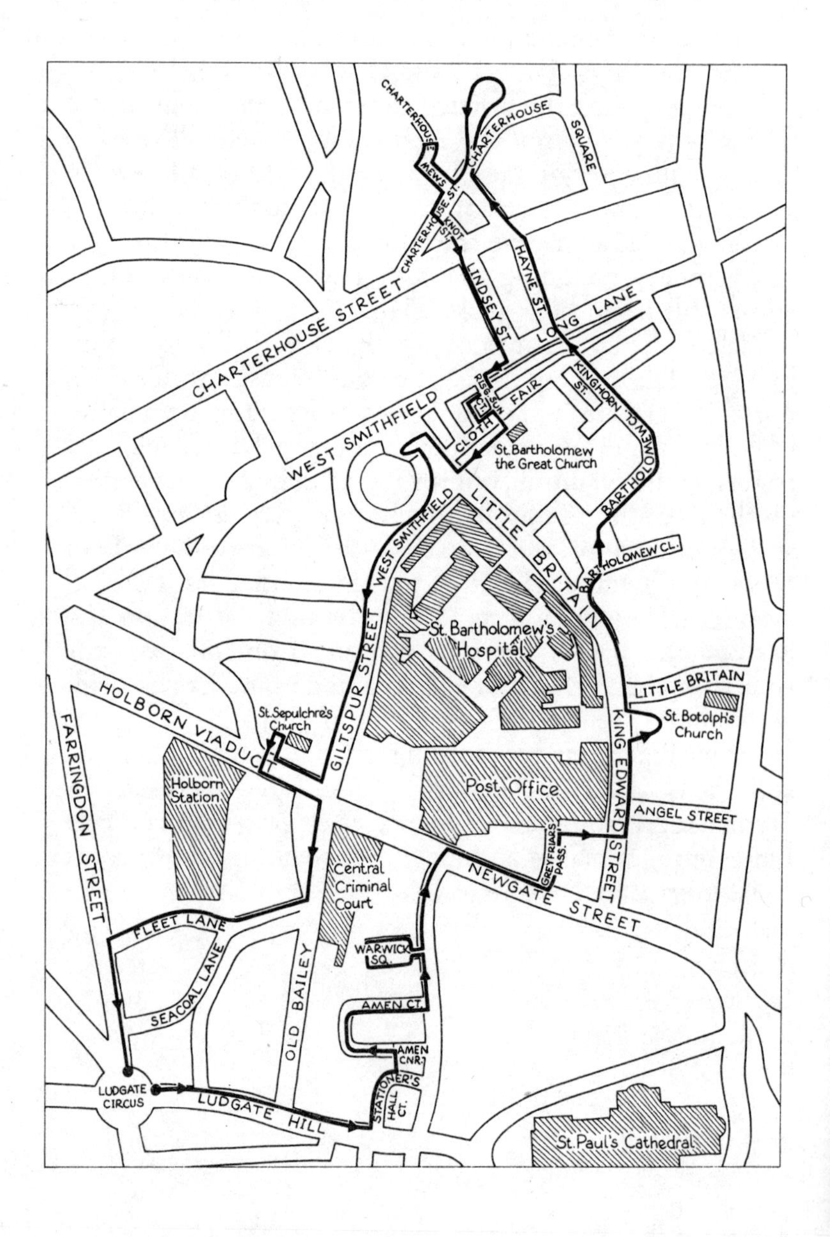

NINTH ♦ WALK

Ludgate Circus to St Bartholomew's Hospital and the Old Bailey

This walk begins at Ludgate Circus as the Eighth Walk did, but looks at another part of the City of London. This time we walk up the left-hand side of Ludgate Hill past the two fierce heads over the windows of the King Lud Tavern which, like the statue we saw at St Dunstan's in Fleet Street, depict the king as a pre-Roman chieftain.

A small opening on the left just beyond the railway bridge is all that remains of Belle Sauvage Yard, the courtyard of the ancient inn that Dickens described as the headquarters of Sam Weller's father in *Pickwick Papers*. Built immediately outside the City wall, the Belle Sauvage was one of London's great taverns, acting as the terminus for travellers from the west. Pocahontas stayed here in 1617, and in 1683 the inn drew customers with its exhibition of 'A Rynoceros lately brought from the West Indies'.

The church of St Martin's Ludgate Hill, built just inside the old City wall, is not the most famous of Wren's churches but some authorities consider it his best design. It is tucked into the side of the hill on a difficult site and its slender spire was built as a perfect contrast to the great dome of St Paul's behind. The font is seventeenth century and has a Greek palindrome inscribed around it (*Niyon anomhma mh monan oyin* – Cleanse my sin and not my face only), copied from the inscription at St Sophia in Istanbul.

The church's proportions make it very nearly a cube. The main door was carved by Grinling Gibbons, the master-carver of the seventeenth century, whom John Evelyn discovered and introduced to Wren just in time to join him in rebuilding fifty-three of London's churches after the 1666 Fire. The door has Gibbons's trademark, a small carved peapod which is shown open, indicating that Gibbons had been paid for the commission by the time he carved it. A closed pea-pod meant that payment was still due.

No. 34–40 beyond the church is a large ornate Victorian building with a ram's head over the door, protected by an enormous shell canopy. It shows that the building stands on ground owned by the Stationers' Company who are just around the corner in Stationers' Hall Court. The Stationers were established in 1403, chartered in 1577 and have been on this site since 1611. They rank 47th in the order of precedence of the 94 City Livery Companies and, until 1911, every book published in England had to be registered with them.

The Company was originally authorised by the Crown as a useful agent in the fight against heresy and they were given the right to 'search any shop, house or chamber for books published contrary to statutes, acts or proclamations', which were then solemnly burnt here at the Hall. For two centuries they controlled education in England since they had the monopoly of publishing almanacks, primers and psalters.

This authority carried with it an equal responsibility. In 1632 they published the famous Wicked Bible, in which a printer had omitted the word 'not' from 'Thou shalt not commit adultery'. Archbishop Laud took them in front of the Star Chamber and fined them heavily. The Stationers exercised their right to burn books as late as 1829, when they disposed of Mrs Clarke's reminiscences of her life as the Duke of York's mistress. They retained the monopoly of printing almanacks even longer.

In the 1880s they decided to publish *Old Moore's Almanack* (first published in 1699) without the astrological predictions which they felt made a useful publication cheap and tawdry. The project was a disaster. Nearly every copy was returned and a commentator of 1892 records solemnly: 'they have not since dared to oppose the stolid forces of vulgar ignorance'.

The Stationers still enjoy a bequest left to them by John Norton in the reign of James I. Under the terms of his will an annual sermon is preached at St Paul's on Ash Wednesday and the Stationers enjoy cakes and ale after the ceremony.

A small gateway in the corner leads through to the Stationers' garden. It is a beautiful place; the luxuriance of its flowers and shrubs comes from the richness of the soil that has built up a high potash content over the centuries from the books burnt here.

Amen Court

An alley to the right of Stationers' Hall leads into Amen Court, a semi-circle of attractive houses built for the Canons and clergy of St Paul's Cathedral. No. 1 dates from the late seventeenth century and the link-snuffers beside the door match the bootscrapers beside the steps. These go back to the days when London's streets were inches deep in horse manure and debris. Unlike the modern bootscraper these have curved sides to allow dirt and dung to be cleaned off the side of one's shoe as well as from the sole.

R. H. Barham wrote *The Ingoldsby Legends* at No. 1 but its most famous resident was Sydney Smith the clergyman, who was London's greatest wit. Smith was one of the most popular men of his time and when Lord Grey (father of the Earl Grey whose favourite mixture of tea is still so popular) became Prime Minister in 1830, one of his first statements was 'Now I shall be able to do something for Sydney Smith.'

Smith (1771–1845) never received the preferment his intelligence deserved, but he enlivened London society for forty years, although his tongue made him enemies among his ecclesiastical superiors. Which bishop, for example, could feel easy promoting a vicar who was only too ready to produce such remarks at a duchess's dinner-table as:

'As the French say, there are three sexes – men, women and clergymen.'

'I have, alas, only one illusion left and that is the Archbishop of Canterbury.'

'What a pity it is that we have no amusements in England but vice and religion.'

'How can a bishop marry? How can he flirt? The most he can say is "I will see you in the vestry after service".'

'I am just going to pray for you at St Paul's, but not with any lively hope of success.'

The row of old houses leads past a garden in the centre of the Court. Most of the high wall that protects the Court is Victorian, built to separate this haven of ecclesiastical quiet from the old Newgate Prison. The wall follows the line of the old City fortifications and, down in the left corner half-hidden by shrubs, a section of rough stones marks the old mediaeval wall the Normans rebuilt. The lower section is even older; the bottom three courses were laid by the Romans nearly two thousands years ago. There are other sections of Roman wall in London but this is the only one still fulfilling its original purpose.

Follow the Court round towards the second gateway. Children's toys on the grass and a climbing-frame add a homely touch to a peaceful scene that seems a hundred miles away from the bustle of London. The houses in this part of the Court are Victorian but the sundial in the middle of the lawn pre-dates them by a century. The old water-tanks used by the clergy before the days of running water have been preserved as flower tubs. Three of them by the gateway are dated 1669, 1716 and 1750.

From Warwick Lane to the Charterhouse

Amen Court leads back into Ave Maria Lane, one of the street names around St Paul's that commemorates the old Catholic processions around the Cathedral. A few yards to the left the street becomes Warwick Lane, named after Warwick the Kingmaker who lived here in 1450. His house was big enough to accommodate the six hundred retainers who accompanied him on his visits to London. For anybody else the number would be excessive but Warwick, who had deposed and installed two kings, dared not come to London with a smaller army.

Warwick Square, where Hogarth lived, is now the Lord Mayor's entrance to the Central Criminal Court where he still sits as of right, a privilege now unique to the City of London.

Cutlers' Hall has elephants supporting the coat of arms outside, reflecting the importance of ivory to the cutlery trade. The Hall stands beside the large doorway set in the wall which is the prisoners' entrance to the Old Bailey.

The gardens across the road at the Newgate Street junction mark the site of the old Greyfriars (Franciscan) Monastery that stood here from 1225 to 1552. The Franciscans were enormously popular and those London citizens wealthy enough to do so left them large bequests for permission to be buried in the churchyard in Franciscan robes, a move intended to ease their path into Heaven.

By 1306 the monastery church had become the largest in England, over 300 feet long. Four queens are buried somewhere under the gardens beside us, including Queen Isabella, the infamous wife and murderer of Edward II. In another grave lies Richard Baxter, the dour Calvinist who preached against Charles I during the Civil War and the author of forty hymns including 'The Saints' Everlasting Rest'.

Although Baxter was imprisoned for his subversive views, he and his wife enjoyed much popularity. When his wife died, he wrote a broadsheet which sold extremely well entitled 'Last Words of Mrs Baxter'. Because of the pamphlet's success, the printer decided to write a sequel himself entitled: 'More Last Words of Mrs Baxter'. Baxter effectively stopped any success this might have had by issuing his own pamphlet consisting of the single sentence 'Mrs Baxter did not say anything else.'

After the Reformation, Edward VI allowed the City to use the old monastery building for Christ's Hospital School which stayed here till its move to Godalming in 1902. It still counts as a City school and the pupils return every St Matthew's Day (Sept 21st). They march through the City to take tea with the Lord Mayor, wearing the famous Blue Coat uniform and yellow stockings that date from their foundation in the sixteenth century.

The path bends round behind the ruined church to enter King Edward Street with the two enormous General Post Office buildings on either side of the road. A statue of Rowland Hill, notebook and pencil in hand, looks across the street to the loading-yards under the arch. The postmen who work here say his notebook is to take down the names of those arriving late for work. His successors Cecil Raikes and Arnold Morley are commemorated by two heads set either side of the great archway.

Beyond the Post Office buildings is a small churchyard, officially called the graveyard of St Leonard' Foster Lane, St Botolph's Aldgate and Christ Church Newgate Street, but better known as Postman's Park. Down in the left-hand corner are memorials to deeds of bravery, an idea of the sculptor G. F. Watts who set the first tablets here in 1900.

King Edward Street stretches down past the high walls of St Bartholomew's Hospital to a square on the right, called Bartholomew Close. The square is a depressing place, surrounded by a mixture of bomb-damaged warehouses and new office blocks, but it is one of the oldest parts of the City. Hogarth was born here and Milton hid here after the Restoration till he felt he was safe from arrest.

The building to the left with the large coat of arms over the doorway is the Hall of the Butchers' Company. The coincidence of St Bartholomew's Hospital standing between the Butchers' Hall and the Smithfield Meat Market has provided the Dean of the Hospital with a perennial joke with which to welcome new students.

Bartholomew Close swings round the right-hand corner to become Kinghorn Street, which runs past Newbury Street where the sundial on the end house has eccentric bolts to make it the most accurate in the City. The bottom section of Kinghorn Street crosses three lanes, Cloth Fair, Middle Street and East Passage which show their mediaeval origins in the size of the houses and the narrowness of the passages between them. From an archway at the end, Hayne Street leads straight down to the trees and grass of Charterhouse Square.

The Charterhouse

There are gracious eighteenth-century houses around the small square, but its fame stems from the Charterhouse itself on the north side. It is the last survivor of London's monastic foundations, apparently little changed since the Carthusians left it four hundred years ago to die for their beliefs. It is not open to the public because it is still the hospital for elderly gentlemen, the Charterhouse Brothers, that John Sutton founded in 1613.

From the courtyard just inside the fifteenth-century gatehouse, it is possible to admire the chapel and hall of the old monastery which became the home of the Duke of Norfolk after the monks had left. Queen Elizabeth was a frequent visitor and James I stayed here before his coronation; both of them would still recognise the cloisters and courtyards of the finest example of Tudor domestic architecture left in London.

Turn right outside the gatehouse and into Charterhouse

Mews a few yards along. In the First Walk along Whitehall we saw the eighteenth-century kerbstones of London's first pavements. In those days roads dipped downwards in the middle so the rainwater could, in theory, wash away the rubbish that collected. It was not until the Victorians introduced drains and sewers that the streets were built with the convex camber we know today. This mews is one of the very few places where the old type of roadway can be seen; just around the first corner the granite setts change to lines of cobbles sloping down towards the centre.

Leaving the Square by the gateway to the right, turn up Lindsey Street past the vast sheds of Smithfield Meat Market on the right. It is the last of the great London markets; meat has been sold here since 1173. For centuries the drovers brought their herds of cattle from all over England and the Norfolk farmers walked their geese and turkeys to London with the birds' feet covered in tar so that they would last the journey.

Rising Sun Court at the top of Lindsey Street leads into a maze of alleys that grew up around the mediaeval Priory of St Bartholomew. It retains the layout of thirteenth-century London with narrow courts and passages that meet and separate every few yards.

Turn right at the first corner of Rising Sun Court and follow Cloth Court around to the left. At the far end is a painted window, one of London's pleasant follies. At the beginning of this century, the building opposite was occupied by a firm of architects who became tired of looking at a blank wall. They reached agreement with the owners and commissioned B. D. L. Thomas to paint the delightful scene showing a Victorian sailor returning home. There are other *trompe l'oeil* paintings in London, but this is one of the best. John Betjeman, who once lived in the house, was very proud of it.

'Bart's' – the Churches and Hospital

Cloth Fair, on which the house stands, takes its name from the mediaeval Fair of St Bartholomew's that attracted cloth merchants from all over Europe. Until the Blitz of 1941, Cloth Fair had the oldest houses in London, fifteenth-century timber-framed buildings that jutted out so much that their roofs nearly met over the middle of the street.

The path through the churchyard across the road leads past the flat table-tomb on which the Butterworth Charity has been distributed for three hundred years. A service is held in the church every Good Friday, after which the rector comes to this tomb and lays out hot cross buns and sums of money to be distributed to poor widows of the parish.

The Church of St Bartholomew the Great (so-called because the smaller St Bartholomew the Less is inside the hospital itself) is London's oldest church, built in 1123 by Rahere, jester to Henry I. The unusual proportions of the church stem from the fact that this is only a remnant of the original structure which stretched right across the present churchyard into Smithfield. Rahere became the first prior and he lies in the sanctuary surrounded by the pillars and windows he saw built. His tomb became a place of pilgrimage and a small window opposite was erected by a later prior, Prior Bolton, where he could keep an eye on the pilgrims and ensure the services were properly conducted. It is marked by a rebus (a pun on the prior's name) which shows a bolt impaling a barrel (tun).

On the south wall is the 'miracle monument', the bust of Edward Cooke who died in 1652. The tablet beneath asks the passer-by to weep for him – 'or if yee find noe vent for tears, yet stay and see the marble weepe', which it will do in cold weather when the condensation causes drops of moisture to run down the cheeks.

Much of the church was destroyed after the Reformation. The remainder was used at various times as a blacksmith's shop, a fringe factory, a coal store and a printing press where Benjamin Franklin worked as a young man. He astonished his fellow-workers by drinking water instead of beer. Since this meant he always had more money than they had, he augmented his wages by lending them money for their beer, recovering it with interest at pay-day.

The church we see today was restored through the efforts of the rectors of the nineteenth century, some of whom beggared themselves in the process. It was they who bought back the old cloisters and recovered the seven-hundred-year-old door that still separates the cloister from the church.

The gatehouse, built in 1595, looks out over Smithfield – the 'Smooth field' where the knights held jousting tournaments in the twelfth century. It was at Smithfield in 1381 that Wat Tyler was stabbed by the Lord Mayor, when Tyler brought his rebels to London to confront Richard II. The young king's bravery on that occasion and his stirring address to the rebels is well known. What is not so well known is that Tyler was taken to the nearby hospital for treatment, which might have been successful if the Lord Mayor had not followed him in and finished off the job.

Smithfield became a place of execution in the thirteenth century and the first burning for heresy occurred about 1410. Men and women of all denominations died here, a practice that did not cease till the reign of James I when ten Catholics died at the stake. A plaque on the hospital wall commemorates the martyrs, although the actual place of execution is some twenty yards away in the middle of the roadway where the traffic bollards now stand. The ashes left from the burnings are only two feet below the tarmac and come to light every time a pipe or cable is laid here.

In the middle of the Square is a small garden with a roadway that vanishes down to what is now an underground car-park. For a hundred years this was the Smithfield Depot railway station which carried meat to and from the Market. It was one of the few depots in England correctly spelt with a circumflex accent over the 'o' of 'Depôt', an addition made by the medical students across the road.

The statue in the garden was erected as a monument to Peace but, because of the cornucopia under her arm, it has always been regarded as a memorial to Ceres, the goddess of fertility. When a gold ring was found in the market nearby in 1924, one of the porters pointed out that the figure of Fertility presiding over London's largest meat market was an unmarried woman. In order to regularise the position, the ring was welded on to her finger where it can still be seen, although it has been painted over for security.

The hospital of St Bartholomew's, known universally as 'Bart's', is the oldest European hospital north of the Alps. The hospital still has a record of the first patient of 1123, a man named Adwyne, who was cured of his 'enfeebled muscles'. Its staff have included Dr Lopez, Queen Elizabeth's physician, who worked here until he was executed for trying to poison her in 1594 and Harvey, who discovered the circulation of blood in 1619. Dr Potts, after whom Potts' fracture is named, was a Bart's man as was W. G. Grace, and a small plaque in the pathology laboratory records the first meeting of Holmes and Watson in *A Study in Scarlet*.

Bart's is the original of 'St Swithin's' in the *Doctor In The House* novels and the irascible Sir Lancelot Pratt in those stories owes something to Bart's most famous physician, John Abernethy (1764–1831), whose brusque and eccentric manner attracted the very patients it was meant to drive away. He used to prescribe the thin biscuits that bear his name as a slimming diet for those of his patients whose illness arose from over-eating, forbidding them sternly to eat anything else for the week or fortnight he felt appropriate.

It was Abernethy who outraged a duchess who had come to consult him about a sore shoulder which, she said, hurt her whenever she lifted her left arm. Abernethy's response was: 'Then what a fool you must be to lift it up.' To another London hostess who complained of depression, his advice was simply: 'Don't come to me. Buy a skipping-rope.' Even the Duke of Wellington received the rough end of his tongue when he sought priority of treatment over the other patients. Abernethy lost his chance of a knighthood when he refused to attend George IV, sending a message that his lectures to his students were more important.

The church of St Bartholomew's the Less stands just inside the hospital gateway because the hospital counts as a parish on its own. The square mile of the City had 73 churches before the Fire and Bart's used to claim to be the smallest parish. The hospital has grown so large it is doubtful if they could make the claim today.

The statue of Henry VIII over the gateway disappeared for a century when the Victorians covered the archway with a tiled front. It was forgotten till a bomb dropped in Smithfield in 1917 and blew down the tiles, revealing the statue behind them. Henry is commemorated as the second 'founder' of the hospital but, as in so many other instances, the statement is one of cautious sycophancy. All he did was to allow the hospital to continue its work after he had confiscated the priory to which it was attached, although he did pledge a royal donation of 500 marks a year – a promise that was never fulfilled.

The long western wall of Bart's leads down Giltspur Street, named after the Smithfield jousting tournaments, when newly-created knights were awarded a golden spur as a badge of rank. Cock Lane on the right has the famous figure of the fat boy on the corner, marking the spot where the Great Fire stopped in 1666. Londoners believed the Fire was divine retribution for their sins. Since the fire started in Pudding Lane and finished at Pie Corner, the sin was assumed to be gluttony.

In 1763 the whole of London society came to No. 33 Cock Lane to try to hear the famous ghost whose scratchings and knockings were the sensation of the day. Dr Johnson played a leading part in the investigation and eventually discovered that the eleven-year-old daughter of the house was responsible.

St Sepulchre's and the Old Bailey

Giltspur Street's last building before St Sepulchre's Church is the old parish watch-house with a tablet recording its building and re-building. Like the watch-house we saw beside the Roman bath in the Strand, it had a triple purpose. The watchmen assembled here before going off on their nightly rounds; it acted as a lock-up for those prisoners they apprehended and was so placed that an eye could be kept on the burial ground of the church next door to prevent corpses being stolen. The proximity of St Bartholomew's Hospital meant this was a constant problem; the anatomy teachers were always anxious for fresh specimens and paid a good price for bodies in good condition.

On the corner of the church railings, where Giltspur Street meets Newgate, is London's first Metropolitan Drinking Fountain, put here by the Temperance League in an attempt to counter drunkenness. It was installed in 1859 and the sharp reminder to users: 'Replace The Cup', clearly did not work because the cup is now secured by a strong chain. Like so many of London's drinking fountains it no longer works, although someone has enough respect for it to keep the metal-work highly polished.

The Church of the Holy Sepulchre, founded in 1137, stands beside the old north-west gate of the City, as does the Church of the Holy Sepulchre in Jerusalem. Because of the coincidence, it became the custom for knights setting out on a Crusade to come here to take their vows. The original name of St Edmund's quickly died out and the church assumed its present title.

Captain John Smith, the man saved by Pocahontas in

America, was buried here in 1631. A tablet commemorating his adventures opens with the modest words:

Here lyes one conquered that hath conquered kings,
Subdued large Territories and done Things,
Which to the World impossible would seem,
But that the truth is held in more esteem.

He is supposed to have killed three Turks in single combat when serving under the banner of the King of Hungary, but most of his fame rests on his own account of events.

Sir Henry Wood was baptised here in 1874, learned to play the organ in this church, and his ashes lie in the Musicians' Chapel underneath a stained glass window showing him conducting an orchestra.

St Sepulchre's stands across the road from the Old Bailey which was for seven hundred years London's most fearsome prison – Newgate. The Newgate, one of the original City gates, received its first prisoners in 1189 and the prison grew over the years. It was burned down in the Gordon Riots, was rebuilt and public executions were carried out here until 1866.

Under the will of Robert Dowe who died in 1605, the bell of St Sepulchre's was rung through the night before a Newgate prisoner was to be executed. The practice lasted for a hundred and fifty years till a parishioner asked for it to be suspended because his wife was seriously ill. By the time she had recovered, his fellow parishioners had become so used to the quiet nights they refused to let the custom be revived.

Mr Dowe's will also specified that, to reinforce the message, the church sexton had to stand outside the door of the condemned cell at midnight, ring his handbell twelve times and declaim:

All you that in the condemned hold do lie,
Prepare you, for tomorrow you shall die;
Watch all, and pray, the hour is drawing near

That you before the Almighty must appear;
Examine well yourselves, in time repent,
That you may not to eternal flames be sent.
And when St Sepulchre's bell tomorrow tolls,
The Lord above have mercy on your souls.

The last line was always shouted through the keyhole of the cell, in case the condemned man had missed any of the previous words of comfort.

The Central Criminal Court was erected in 1903 on the site of the old prison but the rough-faced stones of the lower sections are still those of the old Newgate that Jack Shepherd knew. The figure of Justice was erected in 1907 and at least one person is known to have achieved the hazardous feat of sitting in the scales. Mr James Pratt performed the feat as a schoolboy in 1938, which he always felt led him to take up his later career as an official at the Old Bailey.

Dick Whittington

Fleet Lane runs from Old Bailey, down under the railway to Farringdon Street. Just beyond the railway is a new office block, on the site of the old Fleet Prison where Mr Pickwick was incarcerated in *Pickwick Papers*.

The Fleet Prison stood here from 1170 to 1842, when a Congregational Chapel was built on the site and the prison became one of London's memories. When this new office block and its neighbour came to be built, the enormous crypt of the old prison was rediscovered. It took weeks to dig through it and the site foreman commented that he hoped his work would be in such good condition in eight hundred years' time.

Traces of the old prison can still be seen lying in a heap beside the narrow alley between the office block and railway. The pile of rubble consists of lumps of concrete, dark red Victorian brick and orange mottled brick from the Tudor period. Scattered amongst the rest are pieces of light grey stone; these were part of the old crypt floor, laid before Henry Fitzailwyn became London's first mayor in 1192.

Farringdon Street lies at the bottom of Fleet Lane with Holborn Viaduct to the right. The Viaduct was built in 1869 to save horses having to negotiate the steep banks either side of the Fleet River. It cost over £2 million, which shocked Victorian London which had seen the Houses of Parliament built for far less.

Turnagain Lane lies just below the Viaduct. Some historians believe this is where Dick Whittington made his fortune in the days when the Fleet River, that still flows below Farringdon Street, was navigable up to Holborn.

Whittington, who was mayor of London not three, but four times, became one of the wealthiest men of his time. A member of the Mercers' Company (there is still a Whittington in the Company), he financed Henry V's wars in France in 1415 and left a fortune that the City still uses to run the almshouses and schools he founded.

Turnagain Lane got its name from the time anyone walking down it to the banks of the Fleet River had to turn around and walk back up again, since the lane led nowhere else. Even though the river is now covered over, the name is still appropriate because the railway station now blocks the other end.

In the fifteenth century, tolls had to be paid for all merchandise brought into the City and goods arriving by water had to be transhipped on to small craft before they were landed at jetties. The charges for this transhipment were high. The tradition is that Whittington made his money by cutting out the middle-man, using his own small boats to bring his cargoes up the Fleet River to Turnagain Lane. Since the small boats were called 'cats', the word became associated with Whittington and 'Turnagain, Turnagain Whittington' hallowed by two hundred years of pantomime, perpetuates the association.

Caroone House stands a few yards down Farringdon Street towards Ludgate Circus, where this walk began. While Turnagain Lane is a reminder of one of London's greatest capitalists, Caroone House commemorates a very different philosophy. A small plaque to the left of the steps records the foundation of the Labour Party here in February 1900. It provides an appropriate point to conclude our visits to the City.

TENTH ♦ WALK

Around Holborn and Legal London

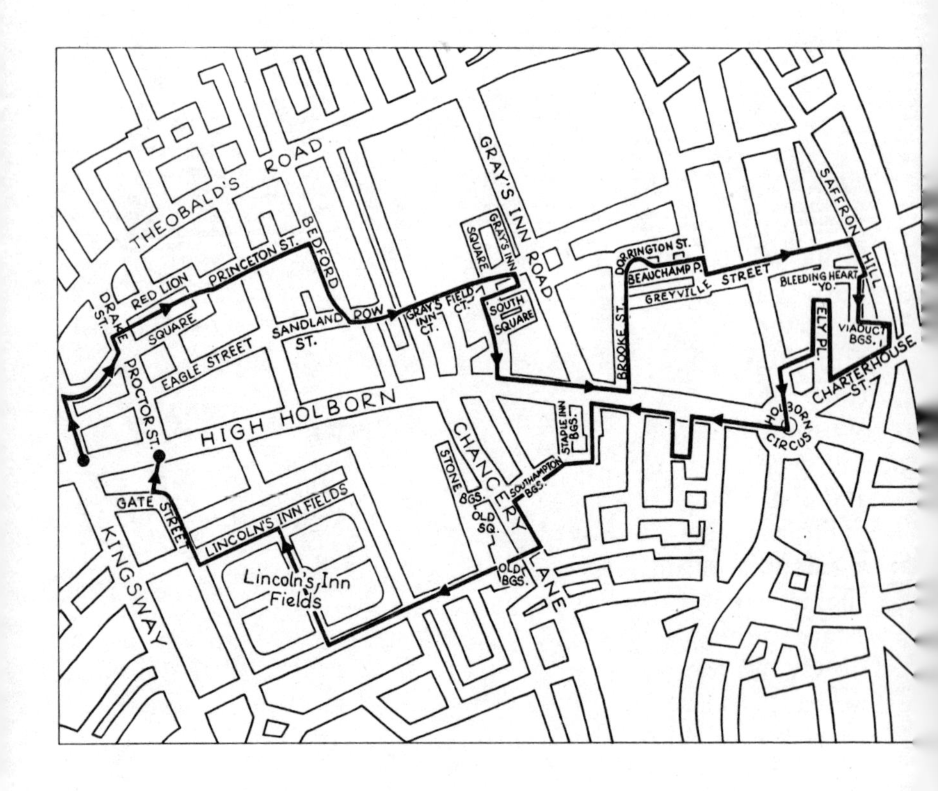

TENTH ♦ WALK

Around Holborn and Legal London

Holborn Underground Station, the start of the Tenth Walk, stands at the junction of Kingsway and High Holborn. Like the Strand, High Holborn was a main road from the old City of London to the west, but unlike the Strand, it remained open country till the fifteenth century. As the kings moved their Court successively to Westminster, Whitehall and St James's, London Society followed them along the axis of Fleet Street, the Strand and Pall Mall.

Holborn lay on the fringes of this gradual move westwards; this is reflected by the piecemeal development that characterises it. The Russells laid out their Bloomsbury estate to the north but most of Holborn, like Soho, grew slowly. In the nineteenth century it became a centre for writers, artists and immigrants from all over Europe, attracted by cheap accommodation and the proximity of the British Museum and new London University.

High Holborn, named from the high ground above the Hole Bourne stream, runs westwards to the junction with New Oxford Street, then bends southward to St Giles' Church. Centre Point, the skyscraper on the horizon, stands on the old St Giles execution ground, cursed by Sir John Oldcastle in 1417. Oldcastle, the original of Shakespeare's Falstaff, was burnt for heresy by Henry V and laid a comprehensive curse on those who burnt him and on the place where he died. When the CBI moved into Centre Point a few years ago, the newspapers remarked that no business had ever flourished on the site and felt the move boded no good for British industry.

Red Lion Square and Bedford Row

Southampton Row runs due north from High Holborn and the second turn on the right brings us into Red Lion Square. It is one of London's smallest squares, a mixture of Victorian and eighteenth-century houses set around a small garden of grass and shrubs. The Square, built in 1684, is another of Nicholas Barbon's enterprises but this project ran into opposition from the lawyers of Gray's Inn, who did not want to see the open ground beside their Inn covered with houses. They sought the protection of the courts but Barbon, for once, had bought the land perfectly legally and won the case.

The lawyers then decided on direct action. They came out from Gray's Inn, attacked his workmen and filled in the trenches. Barbon retaliated by hiring dozens of toughs, hid them in carts and sent his workmen in again. As the lawyers and students came out to repeat their assault, Barbon led the counter-attack and chased them back to the Inn with bruises and broken heads, after which he had no further trouble.

Red Lion Square became known for the progressive thinkers who came here. No. 17 saw the start of the Pre-Raphaelite movement; Gabriel Rossetti lived there in 1851 and William Morris and Burne-Jones moved in later. The landlord did his best to keep the establishment respectable by stipulating the models who sat for the artists should be 'kept under some gentlemanly restraint as some artists sacrifice the dignity of art to the baseness of passion'. The phraseology may sound archaic today, but the complicated affairs of the artists and their models justified his forebodings.

After the Pre-Raphaelites had moved on, the progressive tradition of the Square continued with the South Place Ethical Society, whose hall still stands in the north-west corner. Bernard Shaw lectured here as did Bertrand Russell and Fenner Brockway, both of whom are commemorated by statues in the gardens.

Princeton Street joins Red Lion Square to the eighteenth-century dignity of Bedford Row. Two lines of Queen Anne red-brick houses run northwards, with beautiful fanlights, perfectly proportioned windows and a variety of iron lamp-brackets and link-snuffers. It seems appropriate that the rules of whist, the staple card game of the Hanoverians, should have been drawn up in the 1730s at the coffee-house which stood at the corner.

Two small tombstones stand in front of Nos. 42–43, the only houses left from Barbon's time. The stones commemorate 'Little Whig' and 'Kitty Cat'. The residents have no idea when they were put here, but 'Little Whig' has a strong eighteenth-century flavour to it.

Because Bedford Row was built as a square, the numbers continue around the bottom of the street. No. 48 has a small plaque above the doorway showing that Miss Elizabeth Doughty lived here in 1824. Miss Doughty's house looks across to a splendid pump dated 1826. It was a parish pump originally but the shields and badges show this model was a co-operative effort by St Andrew's Holborn, the City of London and 'SP SWD', whoever they may have been.

Gray's Inn

A small gateway beside the pump leads into the wide sweep of Gray's Inn Gardens. Laid out by Francis Bacon in 1606, the long walks amongst the trees became the Inn's best-known feature and visitors to London were told they could recognise the four Inns of Court by:

> Gray's Inn for walks,
> Lincoln's Inn for wall,
> The Inner Temple for a garden,
> And the Middle for a Hall.

The path bends down to the right towards the Inn, past

a beautiful Regency house with delicate iron balconies that looks assif it should be on the sea-front at Brighton rather than in the centre of London. At the bottom of the path, large gates guard the avenues and lawns that stretch up to Theobald's Road. This is the northern boundary of 'legal London' that stretches unbroken to the Thames through Gray's Inn, Lincoln's Inn, the Law Courts and The Temple.

Walter Raleigh consulted Bacon in the gardens before his last, ill-fated voyage to the New World and Pepys used to bring his wife here after church to admire the fashions. At the far end of the left-hand walk, below the Mound that Bacon laid out to provide 'a prospect' over the countryside to the north, is the famous catalpa tree that tradition says he planted. It has lain on its side for the last fifty years and, since the normal life of a catalpa is a hundred and fifty years, the tradition is suspect. The Inn gardener does not defend the belief but points out that there are new shoots coming from the old root and so the present tree could well be the grandchild of the one Bacon planted.

Gray's Inn has been the home of lawyers since 1370, when they moved into the old house of Lord Grey, Chief Justice of Chester. The Inn has always been jealous of the independence of the judiciary, following the example of Sir William Gascoigne in the fifteenth century. He was the Chief Justice who refused to obey Henry IV's command to find Archbishop Scrope guilty of treason. He offended the King even more when he sentenced the King's son, the future Henry V, to a spell of imprisonment for contempt of court.

Relations with the Crown improved over the years and the Inn came into favour with Elizabeth I, probably because her councillors, Cecil and Bacon, were both members. The Queen came here often and her portrait still has pride of place in the Hall, where Shakespeare's *Comedy of Errors* had its first performance in 1594.

Cecil was remembered at the Inn for the revenge he

took on a fellow student who had cheated him out of every penny at cards. Cecil let a few days elapse, bored a hole through the man's ceiling, waited till he fell asleep and then addressed him from the room above in the deepest voice he could manage. In accents of doom he warned the man of impending death, certain damnation, and the necessity of making restitution to those he had wronged. The trick worked perfectly. The following morning Cecil received his money back from a frightened penitent who never gambled again.

A low archway leads into Gray's Inn Square, emerging beside a small wooden seat set in the wall. This was where the footmen used to wait while their masters consulted their legal advisers. The Hall, built in 1556, stands beside the Chapel of 1693. Both were bombed during the war but their panelling and glass had been taken down for safety. They have now been replaced and include a window escutcheon that dates from 1462 and the famous screen made from the wood of a Spanish galleon.

The passage beside the Hall leads into South Square, where the porter comes each night to ring the curfew. The original purpose of a curfew was not to keep people off the streets, but simply to act as a fire precaution in the days when London houses were built of wood with thatched roofs. The word comes from the Norman French *couvre le feu* and William the Conqueror ordered all church bells to ring curfew at dusk as a signal to householders to put out their fires and candles. A dozen London churches still rang the curfew in 1939, but now Gray's Inn and the Tower of London are the only places where the edict of the Conqueror is still obeyed.

Along Holborn to Saffron Hill

Gray's Inn Gate in Holborn is guarded by a porter wearing red livery. Each Inn of Court has its own colour; the Lincoln's Inn porters wear Lincoln green and the Temple staff wear black because the Knights Templar were a religious order. The Inn's Holborn Gate stands beside the City of York pub, which has been here nearly as long as the Inn.

The City of York was built in 1693, though the cellars and some of the roof beams go back to the fifteenth century. Dickens knew it well when he worked as a clerk at No. 1 South Square, Gray's Inn, and he described it in *Barnaby Rudge*. The unusual three-sided marble fireplace in the middle of the floor came from Gray's Inn Hall in 1815.

Beyond the junction of Gray's Inn Road to the left, Brooke Street runs up beside the incredible red-brick palace of the Prudential Assurance Society. The Prudential building, designed by Waterhouse in 1879, attracts admiration or scorn as the extreme example of the Gothic architectural revival in London that started with the Houses of Parliament forty years before. The building is inelegant but the workmanship is superb, and the street names carved on the corners are triumphs of the brickmakers' craft.

Brooke Street is now one of London's quieter thoroughfares but is famous for two events. In 1770 London was shocked to learn that the boy-poet Chatterton had committed suicide at No. 34, choosing poison rather than starvation as a means of dying. In 1890, at No. 20, William Friese-Green showed the first true moving film in the world, a fifteen-second scene showing his cousin and son walking in Hyde Park.

At the far end of Brooke Street is the gloomy church of St Alban the Martyr, built in 1861 by Butterfield, a rival of Waterhouse, designer of the Prudential building behind us. It used to be a matter of intense argument amongst architectural students as to which building was the uglier. St Alban's was usually adjudged the worse because of the depression induced by the gloomy purple bricks Butterfield favoured.

St Alban's, a missionary church deliberately built beside the last thieves' kitchen in London, became famous for its High Church practices. The 'Roman' liturgy went to such extremes that the Bishop of London was forced to bring prosecutions against the clergy. They persevered, however, and it is still difficult to distinguish St Alban's from the most ornate of Roman Catholic churches.

Greville Street runs along the back of the Prudential building, across Leather Lane, the busiest of London's street markets, to Hatton Garden. Hatton Garden became the centre of London's diamond trade in 1836. It grew in importance as diamond merchants fled from Europe to escape the revolutions of 1848 and 1870. Diamonds have always been the most portable form of wealth and 'the Garden' received another influx of traders during the 1930s when the German jewellers foresaw the consequences of Hitler's rise to power more accurately than the politicians.

Beyond Hatton Garden the road runs downhill towards the valley of the Fleet past Bleeding Heart Yard, whose dullness belies its romantic name. We turn up Saffron Hill to the right, climbing a flight of steps into Charterhouse Street.

The top of the steps brings us to another of London's invisible boundaries. The feeling of leaving one region and entering another is extraordinarily strong. This is what mediaeval London must have been like when every trade had its own quarter of the City and clustered around its own guild church. Behind us are the narrow streets and small shops of the jewellery trade; across the road the wide roofs of the Smithfield Meat Market stretch away to the Charterhouse and the centre of the City.

Ely Place

Charterhouse Street leads up to the right, to the lodge and gateway of Ely Place, whose legal status has been an idiosyncrasy of London for five hundred years. The Bishop of Ely built a house here in 1290, grand enough to lodge Philippa of Hainault before her marriage to Edward, and John of Gaunt lived here till his death in

1399. It was here that Shakespeare had him reflect on: 'This royal throne of kings, this sceptred isle. . . .'

The estate was confiscated by Henry VIII in the Reformation but the bishops continued to occupy the site. In 1576 Elizabeth I granted part of the land to her favourite, Christopher Hatton, after whom Hatton Garden is named. The bishop, Dr Martin Heton, objected strongly to this exercise of the Royal prerogative but Elizabeth had no doubts whatever on the question. She made Dr Heton fully aware of her views in the famous letter:

> Proud Prelate,
>
> I understand you are backward in complying with your agreement; but I would have you know that I, who made you what you are, can unmake you. And, if you do not forthwith fulfil your engagement, by God, I will immediately unfrock you.
>
> Elizabeth

Christopher Hatton moved in and took advantage of a vacancy in the see to build himself a new house in the grounds. It descended to his nephew, whose widow married Sir Edward Coke the famous lawyer. The marriage proved disastrous and eventually she locked him out of the house. Even though he was Chief Justice, the legal question of ownership of the house (Crown, bishop or Hatton family) was still so confused, he was unable to claim entry. By the time he managed to do so, he found his wife had vanished, taking with her every piece of furniture and silver in the place.

The bishops returned to their part of the property in 1660. In 1772 the last of the Hatton family died and the bishop claimed the Hatton house and garden back again for the diocese. This time the decision was made to settle the matter once and for all. The Crown took the entire estate back into its possession, built the present houses on the site and gave the bishop a new house in Dover Street, off Piccadilly (see Fifteenth Walk).

It was at this point that the City authorities intervened. They informed the residents of the new houses that they would be expected to pay rates to the City. The Crown's response was to rule that, although Ely Place was Crown property. it was administered (but definitely not owned) by the Bishop of Ely. It therefore formed part of the Diocese of Ely and was not part of the City of London! The result was that a member of Ely police force was detached for duty to the City of London police, who were unable to exercise their authority within Ely Place.

Even when the Ely policeman was withdrawn at the turn of this century, the residents clung to their old ways. A watchman walked the Place every night on the hour, repeating the time in the traditional way: 'Ten o'clock of a wet winter's night. . . . and this continued till the start of the Second World War. The custom was revived in 1945, but the six-year break had been too long. The residents had become used to sleeping undisturbed and London's last watchmen stopped their patrols a few weeks later.

Ely Place's status is still obscure and, in law, it lies outside the City of London. It is administered by a Board of Commissioners, the gates are still shut every night and the City Police enter only when invited to do so.

St Etheldreda's Church, on the left-hand side, is all that remains of the old episcopal palace. The church is named after a seventh-century saint, in whose memory relics and medals were sold at country fairs. As her name became shortened to St Audrey, the cheap, shiny trinkets gave the word 'tawdry' to the language.

The church was built around 1293 as a private chapel for the bishop, but rests on a much earlier foundation with some Roman stonework. There are several churches in England built before the Reformation which have now become Catholic again. St Etheldreda's is the only one that has been consecrated as a Catholic church three times.

It became an Anglican church after the Reformation

but reverted to the old Faith when the Spanish ambassador lived here. He used his diplomatic position to reconsecrate it so that Masses could be said for his household. It became Anglican again when he left, was sold to the Welsh Church in 1836 and eventually returned to the Catholic faith in 1874.

Half-way between the church and the gateway is a small, dark alley called Ely Court. It leads to a small pub, hidden amongst high walls. This is the Mitre, built originally in 1546 for the retainers at the bishop's palace. In one corner of the bar a glass partition protects an old tree-trunk. Tradition says that this is the cherry-tree around which Queen Elizabeth and Christopher Hatton danced when they celebrated his arrival at Ely Place. A more likely reason is that it marked the boundary between Hatton's land and that of the dispossessed bishop. This would account for its position in the corner of the pub, since it was unlikely the bishop would allow a tavern within his palace precincts.

The alley continues past the Mitre to come out in Hatton Garden, where the plaque at No. 5 records the stay of Mazzini. Mazzini came to London as a political refugee from Italy in 1832. He spent years in Hatton Garden, writing political pamphlets and organising the movement that eventually led to the reunification of Italy. In 1844 he nearly managed to bring down the British Government as well when he was able to prove they had been opening his letters and revealing their contents to the authorities in Italy.

Hatton Garden runs into Holborn Circus, where the traffic from six streets flows around the equestrian statue of Prince Albert, consort of Queen Victoria. The mounted figure used to be known sarcastically as the politest statue in London because the Prince, dressed in field-marshal's uniform, is shown returning a greeting by doffing his hat, rather than by saluting. The sculptor's critics were wrong on two counts. In the early nineteenth century salutes were indeed returned by doffing one's hat and, secondly, field-marshals do not salute with their hands.

Field-marshals are created rarely and such promotions are usually made at the end of an officer's career. The result is that they are not often seen in uniform with their special badge of office – the marshal's baton. It is with the baton that field-marshals return salutes, but there is an excellent precedent for this being little known.

After the Second World War, a ceremony at Westminster Abbey was attended by a group of newly-created field-marshals including Alanbrooke, Montgomery and Alexander. It was their first ceremonial appearance in their new rank and none of them was quite sure how to carry his new baton or what to do with it. To save them embarrassment, a shocked Guards sergeant-major took them behind the chancel after the ceremony for a quick course in the correct carriage and use of 'Batons, field-marshals for the use of'.

The plinth of Prince Albert's statue has a panel on the near side showing him laying the foundation stone of the Royal Exchange, while a seated angel at the front represents History. The sculptor's own historical sense is clearly suspect because, although the Prince died in 1861, the angel is shown reading a volume inscribed 1851–1862. The best part of the monument is on the far side. It is worth crossing over to see because it gives an excellent idea of the confidence with which the Victorians regarded those nations not fortunate enough to be British.

The panel illustrates the award of prizes at the Great Exhibition of 1851, in which Prince Albert had played an important part. The central figure of Britannia is shown presenting awards to the nations of the world with a Chinaman kneeling humbly before her. Other representatives from Britain's Empire assume similar attitudes of awe, while the European nations are portrayed in a slightly more dignified manner to acknowledge their higher level of civilisation. The scene is watched from one side by a tall, kilted Highlander who seems to be regarding the proceedings with amused contempt.

Barnard's Inn and Staple Inn

The narrow entrance to Barnard's Inn is on the south side of High Holborn, just beyond Fetter Lane. Like Clifford's Inn that we saw in Fleet Street (see Sixth Walk), it was an Inn of Chancery which prepared students for the four Inns of Court. At the time of writing it is being redeveloped but the old Hall of 1542 is still there around the first corner.

The Inn did not have its own chapel so the members attended St Andrew's Church nearby, where they had pews kept locked for their especial use. When the rector of St Andrew's, a Mr King, was made a Doctor of Divinity, the Inn sent him £2 as 'a remembrance of their high regard' for him. Mr King, affronted by the small sum, sent it straight back with the comment that he 'had expected a better remembrance than that'. The Inn, equally offended by the refusal of their gift, kept the £2 and sent him nothing at all. The rector retaliated by removing all the locks from the Inn's special pews. When the members of the Inn arrived at church the following Sunday, they found their pews already filled by parishioners (at the rector's instigation). They were forced to seat themselves ignominiously on the public benches at the back.

Dyers' Buildings, a few yards to the west, belong to the Dyers' Company and their badge appears on every doorway and gatepost. This was done not from pride of ownership, but from financial prudence. The early London fire brigades put out fires only when the householder could display an insurance badge on his house. The badges in Dyers' Buildings were to show the firemen that they were covered by the Company's block insurance policy.

The public lavatory in the middle of the road was one of the first to be built in London, in the days when the authorities were trying to persuade Londoners to use them. Every kind of device was employed to make them attractive and the foul-air pipe that rises from this lavatory has a cheerful cherub beaming down on the patrons.

The original fittings of this lavatory, now in the Victoria & Albert Museum, were of polished brass and mahogany with water-cisterns made of glass. They became famous in the 1920s when the attendant turned them into aquaria, putting different types of goldfish into each one. When the news got out, the authorities tried to stop the practice. The attendant was able to show that the fish attracted more paying customers than any other lavatory in London because everyone wanted to see what happened to the fish when the chains were pulled.

Staple Inn, just west of Furnival Street, is the pride of Holborn. It looks too antique to be genuine but it dates from 1378 and the timbered Tudor façade that looks down on Holborn was built in 1586, two years before the Armada. Customers to the shops have to watch out for the low lintels but this does not deter them from visiting Brumfitt's the tobacconist, where a Victorian gas cigar-lighter still stands on the counter for customers' use.

The history of the Inn is set out on a plaque under the archway, opposite the notice that bears the stern injunction;

> Old Clothes Men, Rude Children Playing and Horses are not allowed in the Inn.

The courtyard is as Dr Johnson knew it in 1759, when he lived at No. 2 Staircase and wrote *Rasselas* in a week to pay for his mother's funeral. 'No Nuisance' railings protect the corners from abuse, presumably from the rude children or old-clothes men. An 'antique' lead-covered pump stands beside the archway, but it is firmly dated 1937. The pump handle is also fake but a small brass tap tucked discreetly around the side produces an excellent stream of water over the cobbles.

In the middle of the courtyard, beside the tree-lined

path across the cobbles, is a small circle of stones set into the ground. They mark the old lost well of the Inn that reappeared dramatically in 1922. A girl was having her lunch beneath the trees when she felt her feet sinking into the ground. She managed to jump away before the surface caved in completely to reveal the old well-head, now marked by the inscription *Puteus Oppletus* (The Filled-in Well).

The Hall, now in the possession of the Institute of Actuaries, dates from 1580 and the archway beside it leads through to the small Dutch garden laid out in the seventeenth century. On the left is the part of the Inn made famous by Dickens in *Edward Drood*. His characters puzzled over the initials at the door, 'PJT 1747', wondering whether they stood for 'Perhaps John Thomas' or 'Perhaps Joe Tylor'. In fact they stand for John Thompson who was Principal of the Inn in that year.

Lincoln's Inn

The path swings round to the right, through the gate where an inscription marks the area of ground reserved by the Inn when it was finally sold in 1884. Beyond the gate Southampton Buildings run down to Chancery Lane and the gateway of Lincoln's Inn.

The Lincoln's Inn gate, one of the most picturesque in London, was erected in 1518 and rebuilt a few years ago using bricks especially made the same colour and texture as those they replaced. The great doorway and the doors themselves date from 1564 and Ben Jonson helped to repair them, 'working with his Horace in one hand and a trowel in another'. Jonson would have remained a brick-layer had not some gentlemen, as Fuller says, 'pitying that his parts should be buried under the rubbish of so mean a calling, did of their bounty manumize him freely to follow his own ingenious inclinations'.

Immediately inside the Gatehouse are Old Buildings which date from about 1490. The ground floor of No. 24

was the office of John Thurloe, Cromwell's Secretary of State. Cromwell came here in 1649 to discuss a plan to lure the young Charles II and his brothers back to England so that they could be assassinated.

During their talk, Cromwell suddenly discovered Thurloe's clerk, a man called Morland, apparently asleep in a corner. Cromwell drew a knife to kill him on the spot but Thurloe convinced him that Morland was really asleep. Morland was, however, wide awake and managed to get a warning to the King in France, for which he received a knighthood when Charles returned in 1660.

The Old Hall dates from 1490. In an incident that shows that young men do not change over the centuries, three students of the Inn were fined the sum of twelve pence each in 1552 for breaking a Hall window as they were 'playing with a balle when they should have been attending to their studies'.

The Old Hall was the setting for the Court of Chancery in Dickens's *Bleak House*, the novel in which he satirised the interminable proceedings of the Court. The story revolves around the case of Jarndyce versus Jarndyce which dragged on for years till the lawyers' fees consumed the entire estate. Dickens needed no exaggeration to make his point. The whole of London knew he was referring to the Great Jennings Case, which started in this Hall well before Dickens's birth in 1819 and did not finish till after his death in 1870.

New Square, just beyond Old Buildings, dates from the seventeenth century, just before the Window Tax of 1697 was imposed. The end wall of the left-hand block shows that no fewer than ten windows were filled in to avoid the tax. A notice on the wall warns against any infringement that would render the Inn liable to pay more money: 'This Wall is built upon The ground of Lincolne's Inn No windowes are to be brocken out without leave.'

The Chapel at the other side of the Square was built by Inigo Jones and John Donne preached the inaugural sermon in 1623. The Chapel bell, which is tolled at minute intervals for the death of a Bencher of the Inn, was presented by Donne. He brought it back from Cadiz where he had accompanied Essex on his ill-fated attack of 1596. The open undercroft of the Chapel, unique in London, was deliberately designed to give the students and barristers somewhere to walk in wet weather: 'to talk and confer for their learnings'.

The New Hall, just beyond the Chapel, is a Victorian building completed in 1845. G. F. Watts painted the great frieze for no payment other than the cost of materials but the Benchers were so pleased with it that they presented him with 500 sovereigns in a silver cup. There are thirty-one figures on the frieze and some are familiar. Watts used the features of many of his contemporaries for the figures, including Tennyson who appears as Minos, Sir William Harcourt as Justinian, while Holman Hunt represents Ina.

The staircase of the library was decorated with coats of arms which became covered with grime over the years. In the 1930s the Inn decided they should be cleaned and passed a resolution accordingly. The urgent necessity can be judged from the remark made by a senior member when a colleague mentioned the decision to refurbish the coats of arms. The senior member looked at him blankly: 'What coats of arms?'

The Inn's western gate has a parish boundary mark on the corner and is manned by porters wearing Lincoln green. The gateway gives on to Lincoln's Inn Fields, London's largest square and the site of the horrific executions of the Babington Plot conspirators in 1586. Building started around the square in 1641 and met with strong opposition from Lincoln's Inn. The lawyers were unable to stop the houses being built but managed to force the developer to leave the central space open as it is today.

The developer reluctantly agreed, but spread a story (which lasted for centuries) that the lawyers only wanted to keep the space open because they were all Masons and British Israelites who were going to conduct secret ceremonies in the Field, as it was of exactly the same dimensions as the Great Pyramid.

The Royal College of Surgeons moved into the southern side of Lincoln's Inn Fields in 1797, though most of their present building dates from the nineteenth century. Their old hall had been near the Old Bailey and bodies of executed murderers were normally given to the Surgeons for dissection. This frequently led to pitched battles between the relatives of the dead man as they tried to take the body away for burial, and the servants of the College asserting their legal right to the corpse.

The College's anatomical museum is famous and the skeleton of Jonathan Wilde is on show as well as that of the eight-foot Irish giant, which John Hunter acquired by bribing the undertaker. Many specimens were lost through bomb-damage in the war, including the bizarre remains of the first Mrs Van Butchell.

Van Butchell was an eighteenth-century surgeon/dentist/scientist who crossed the line between quackery and science so often it is difficult to classify him as either. He performed some remarkable cures but the eccentricity of his habits and his advertisements in the newspapers would certainly prevent him from practising medicine today.

When his first wife died, he had her body mummified and dressed in her wedding gown. The corpse was then set in a glass case in his hall, where she was solemnly introduced to all who entered. A few years later Van Butchell married again but his second wife made it conditional on the first wife's being removed. She was presented to the College Museum where she remained unburied for another one hundred and seventy years till German bombs finally disposed of her.

In the entrance hall of the College is a bronze monument by Gilbert, the man who sculpted Eros. It is the size of a table centrepiece and shows the heads of Dr and Mrs McLoughlin. The figures are separated by a small container containing the ashes of both, joined together in death as they were in life.

A path runs across the square from the College to the northern side, past the pavilion in the centre where a small brass plaque marks the spot on which Lord William Russell was executed in 1683. The path comes out opposite No. 13, once the house of Sir John Soane, now the Soane Museum.

Soane (1753–1837) was an architect who pioneered the Classic revival and built the Bank of England. He also started a collection of antiquarian curiosities and pictures that grew so large his family found themselves living in two rooms in the attic.

Soane therefore turned his architectural skill to the problem of storing his collection in the minimum space. His picture room, for instance, has a series of panels on the walls which open out like leaves of a book so the room contains enough paintings to fill a gallery three times its size.

The Museum, which now occupies most of Nos. 12, 13, and 14, is admired by architects as much for its design as for the exhibits within it. They come to see the devices he used to cram in all the objects he collected in a structure that became an amalgam of house, museum and studio. Nearly every feature of architecture appears somewhere including domes and convex mirrors used to alter perspectives. One room has the floor taken out, in imitation of the Dôme des Invalides in Paris, enabling the visitor to look down on the mummy of Seti which Soane considered to be the gem of his collection.

He even managed to squeeze in a Monument Yard and Monk's Yard at the back. These display the mediaeval statuary and masonry he acquired from the old Palace of Westminster, set out to make a completely fictitious cloister and tomb for the legendary Padre Giovanni.

Across the road from the museum is a monument unusual for its subject. Most Prime Ministers are remembered by a statue somewhere in London, but their wives are usually forgotten. In this case, it is the wife, not the husband who is remembered. The memorial is to Margaret Macdonald, wife of Ramsay Macdonald the first Labour Prime Minister, commemorating her work with London's orphan children.

At the corner of the square, glance down the houses along the western side. Powis House on the corner (No. 66) was rebuilt in the 1930s, but is a copy of the original house built in 1685. It was the London residence of the Duke of Newcastle, George II's Prime Minister, whose effectiveness in office was described by a contemporary: 'He loses half an hour every morning, then spends the rest of the day chasing after it.'

No. 58 was once the home of Nell Gwynne. Her first child was born here and Charles II acknowledged it by making him the first Duke of St Albans. In the nineteenth century, Dickens's friend and biographer John Forster lived in the same house; Dickens dined here often and tried out his short stories on the guests.

Gate Street, which leads north from the corner of the Fields, takes its name from the gate used to keep in the cattle that grazed the Fields till the last century. At the bend of the street is the Ship Tavern, established in 1549. The plaque on the corner records its history as a meeting place for Catholics to celebrate the Mass in secret. The site was chosen because it can be approached from four different directions.

From the Ship, both Great Turnstile and New Turnstile lead back to High Holborn, a few yards from the Underground Station where we started this walk.

ELEVENTH ♦ WALK

Around Covent Garden to Leicester Square

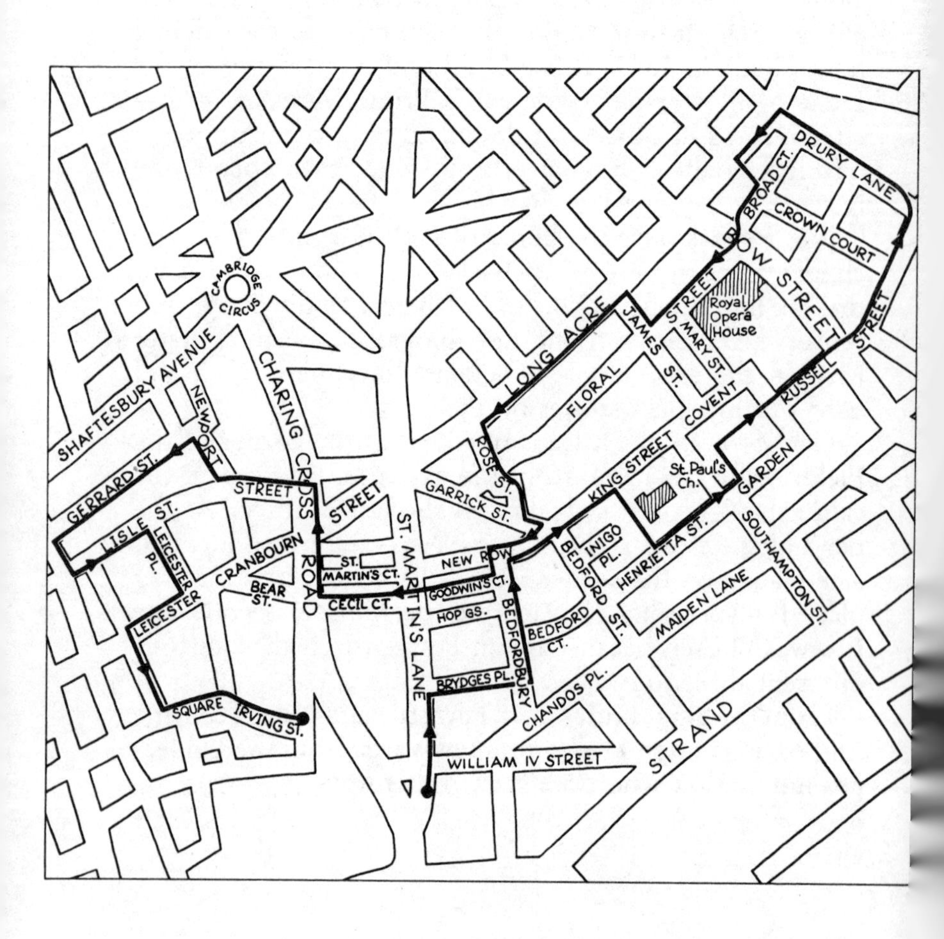

ELEVENTH ♦ WALK

Around Covent Garden to Leicester Square

The statue of Edith Cavell, the start of the Eleventh Walk, stands at the north-east corner of Trafalgar Square, where the traffic of St Martin's Lane meets that of Charing Cross Road. For centuries St Martin's Lane was the only road north from Whitehall, running from the corner where Whitehall meets the Strand. The lower section vanished when Trafalgar Square was built which is why the houses in the present Lane begin at No. 29.

When Charing Cross Road was built in 1877 to relieve the appalling traffic congestion in St Martin's Lane, the engineers installed an underground service tunnel like the one that had proved so successful on the Embankment. It provides access to the water-pipes, gas-pipes and sewers under the roadway and can be seen by looking down through the metal grille in front of Edith Cavell's statue. The tunnel runs from Charing Cross Station all the way to Oxford Street and every access grille has a small notice on the wall below to tell those working underground where they are. By peering down through the bars it is possible to see the words 'Edith Cavell' with the admonition 'No Smokeing' (sic) just visible beneath them.

From Brydges Place to King Street

A few yards up St Martin's Lane beyond the pub on the corner, once the shop of Mr Gibus, inventor of the folding top-hat, is Brydges Place. It is dark and sinister, the last survivor of the old rookeries and slums that covered this part of London till they were cleared to make room for Trafalgar Square and the National Gallery. Brydges Place is the narrowest alley in London; only one person can walk down it at a time and even an umbrella can cause one to get stuck between the narrow walls.

Half-way down the alley, a section of wall lower than the rest allows some light into the gloom. The reason for the sudden change in level is an 'Ancient Lights' sign on the opposite wall, once common in London but now rarely seen. The sign is on the back wall of the Marquis of Granby pub, known to Dickens when he worked at the blacking factory nearby. He remembered the name in *Pickwick Papers* and gave it to the pub in Dorking owned by Sam Weller's father.

The pub takes its name from the general who led the British army during the Seven Years War of 1756–1763. He was not a strategist, but paid great attention to his soldiers' welfare and his popularity led to dozens of pubs being named after him. His personal courage was legendary and the expression 'to go bald-headed' at something originated at the Battle of Warburg in 1760, when the Marquis led his cavalry in a counter-attack with such vigour that his wig fell off. An account of the time praises the bravery of the troopers as they 'followed the bald but undaunted head of their noble leader'.

The pub, originally known as the Hole in the Wall, has been here since the seventeenth century. It was a notorious den of thieves, kept by the equally notorious Mother Maberley, once the mistress of the Duke of Buckingham. The pub became famous in 1669 when Claude Duval, the original romantic highwayman, was captured here on information laid by Mother Maberley. She did very well out of it, receiving both a reward for his capture and a vast increase in trade from the sightseers who flocked to the pub.

At the end of Brydges Place, Bedfordbury leads up to

the left past the Lemon Tree, whose name dates from the seventeenth century when citrus fruits were a luxury and an orange was a treat to be sold in theatres by Nell Gwynne and her friends much as usherettes sell ice-cream today. This section of Bedfordbury is occupied by the Coliseum Theatre whose enormous wall runs down May's Buildings to St Martin's Lane.

The Coliseum, London's largest theatre, was built in 1904 for Sir Oswald Stoll. He was an impresario with big ideas who deliberately built the Coliseum to outdo Augustus Harris's Theatre Royal at Drury Lane. He gave the Coliseum the first revolving stage in London and provided lifts to take his patrons to the circle and gallery. The theatre had three restaurants, a roof-garden, its own post-box and even a short length of railway from the front door to the lifts that took Royalty and distinguished visitors to their seats with the minimum of inconvenience. The foyer still has a domed roof of mosaics copied from ancient Rome because Stoll intended his Coliseum to be to London what the Colosseum was to Rome.

Why the theatre is called the 'Coliseum' and not 'Colosseum' is uncertain. One version is that Stoll simply scribbled down the name and his staff were too frightened of him to point out the error. A contemporary recounts that Stoll had no idea of the correct spelling but saw no reason to admit it. He quickly learnt to counter any comments on the error with the remark that the spelling was deliberate, so no one could confuse his beautiful new theatre with what he referred to as the 'moth-eaten ruin in Rome'.

At the top of Bedfordbury, New Row leads into King Street at the corner where Moss Bros fitted morning dress and top-hats on nervous bridegrooms for nearly a century. Their clothes' hire service has become legendary and they recount proudly the story of the head of the firm who went to Ascot and, as he sat in the stand scanning the crowds, was greeted by an acquaintance with the words: 'Morning, Moss. Stocktaking?'

In 1989 Moss Bros moved across the road to the dignified building with the Westminster portcullis and Prince of Wales's feathers on the front. Built in 1780, this was the office of the Westminster Fire Insurance Company who put up the Prince of Wales's feathers when they sold a policy to George I's eldest son. At the far end of the ground floor is the old Court Room, which got its name in the days when no insurance payment was made without lengthy consideration and the Directors assembled for formal meetings to consider the risks of each policy they issued. The Room is splendidly proportioned but its remarkable feature is the false doorway. On the outside it appears to be two tall, narrow doors but the inside face is twice as wide to fit the proportions of the Court Room; an effect achieved by building a false second door on the inside wall.

No. 37 King Street, part of a row of early eighteenth century houses, is now the offices of the Royal Scottish Corporation, one of London's oldest charities started by the Scots merchants who came down to London with King James I in 1603. Their donations to provide assistance for their widows and orphans were placed in an enormous iron-bound chest called the Scots Box, which still has pride of place in the Corporation's boardroom.

The front door of No. 37 and the houses beside it are original, although they show remarkably little wear for their two and a half centuries of use. The reason is that they are made of mahogany, the first use of the wood in England. Around 1720, a Dr Gibbons of King Street was given some baulks of mahogany by his brother who had brought them back from the West Indies as ballast. The wood was too tough for the local carpenter to make furniture from it and the best he could do for Dr Gibbons and his friends was to make the doors that still hang here.

The Essex Serpent pub, across the road at No. 6, has been here since 1669 and commemorates the legendary cockatrice that terrorised Saffron Walden in the Middle Ages. The cockatrice killed with a glance from its eyes and was said to have depopulated much of Essex till it was challenged by a knight whose armour was so shiny that the reflection of its own eyes caused the monster's death. Beside the Essex Serpent is an archway leading into the churchyard of St Paul's, the only building left of the original Covent Garden.

Covent Garden and the Dukes of Bedford

After Henry VIII's Reformation, the bishops lost their houses along the Strand (see Third Walk) and the monastic holdings were seized by the Crown to be distributed to the King's favourites. The Howards were given the block around Arundel Street, the Duke of Somerset built Somerset House and, in 1552, John Russell, first Earl of Bedford, received the open land off the Strand where the monks of Westminster had grown their food – the Convent Garden.

In 1627 the fourth Earl paid the Crown £2000 for a licence to build an estate of houses 'for gentlemen and men of ability' and commissioned Inigo Jones to design it. There was a pause when the Crown fined the Earl another £2,000 for starting work before the licence had been officially issued but Jones completed Covent Garden, the first of London's squares, in 1631.

It was the beginning of the Bedford Estates that grew to include Bloomsbury to the north. Building proceeded so fast that Parliament queried whether one landowner should be allowed to own a fifth of London and the Estates made the Earls, later Dukes, of Bedford the richest men in England. The whole area was run as a private housing development for nearly three hundred years and access was restricted by toll-bars till the 1890s. Covent Garden was made an independent parish within the old parish of St Martin-in-the-Fields which still surrounds it.

In 1913 the Covent Garden estate was sold to an entrepreneur named Mallaby Deely for under £2 million pounds. A year later Sir Joseph Beecham bought the estate and his son Thomas was able to continue his musical career at Covent Garden with the security of his father owning the freehold.

The Bedfords have made their contribution to history in unusual ways. The present Duke revolutionised the 'Stately Homes industry' by his attractions at Woburn, while his grandmother 'The Flying Duchess' took up flying and speedboats in her middle years, setting world records in both till her death flying over the North Sea in 1937. Perhaps the family's most lasting claim to fame, if the least known, is the Royal Navy's blue uniform with white trim. They were the colours of the riding-habit worn by the fourth Duchess of Bedford which so impressed George III that he instructed the Lords of the Admiralty to adopt them for the crews of Royal ships.

When the Earl of Bedford commissioned Inigo Jones to lay out Covent Garden, he told him to build a church on the west side, but added that he wanted the church to be simple and cheap, to be little better than a barn, so Jones built him 'the handsomest barn in England'.

It was the first Protestant church to be built in London and this accounts for its simplicity of decoration. It became the burial place of painters like Lely, Kneller and Girtin and its proximity to the Theatre Royal started a connection with the stage that has now become its major claim to fame. Every wall is covered with memorials to actors of the nineteenth and twentieth centuries.

Ellen Terry's ashes rest in a silver urn on one wall beside the grisly monument to Charles Macklin the actor, whose tablet claims that he lived to the age of 107. He appeared at Drury Lane from 1733 till 1789, specialising in the part of Shylock. His memorial, a dagger thrust through a skull, commemorates his trial for murder in 1735 when he killed a fellow actor in just such a way in an argument over a wig.

The opening bars of Thomas Arne's most famous composition 'Rule Britannia' are inscribed below his monument which stands beside the plaque to William Bellamy.

Bellamy is remembered here as being the Father of the Whig Club of England, but he was better known as the caterer whose establishment beside the old Houses of Parliament became so popular that William Pitt's last words were: 'I think I could eat one of Bellamy's pork pies.'

The southern gate of the churchyard leads into Henrietta Street, past the crowned lamps in the churchyard that cause some people to think this is a royal church till close inspection shows they are not royal crowns but ducal (Bedford) coronets. Somewhere in the graveyard is the tomb of Claude Duval the highwayman, who was hanged at Tyburn after his capture in Brydges Place in 1669. He was tall, good-looking and entered folk-lore as the original romantic highwayman who returned jewellery to pretty women and stole a kiss instead. His gravestone had the inscription:

Here lies Du Vall: Reader, if male thou art
Look to the purse; if female to thy heart.

Henrietta Street has always been one of the quieter parts of the Estate and Jane Austen used to stay with her brother, who lived at No. 10. St Peter's Hospital for Stone, at No. 27, has been here for a century and is a relic of the days when hospitals specialised in specific diseases. It still concentrates on urinary complaints.

The Hospital stands on the site of the old Castle Tavern which played its part in the social history of England in 1772, when it saw the conclusion of the famous duel between Richard Sheridan and Captain Matthews. The cause of argument was Miss Linley, the young lady whom Sheridan married. He and Matthews met with swords near the Ring in Hyde Park but were interrupted by a crowd gathering and agreed to adjourn to a tavern in Piccadilly where they resumed their duel in the courtyard. Interrupted once more, they came to the Castle Tavern and continued till both were exhausted.

Although Sheridan had not yet become famous, the

duel caused a stir. Neither combatant was seriously wounded but both were covered with blood from head to foot. In an age when elegance was all, Society thereupon decided that the rapier was a messy way of duelling and turned to the pistol instead. Joseph Manton, the eighteenth-century gunmaker, always attributed his financial success to Sheridan's inefficiency with a sword.

Henrietta Street joins the Market at the corner by the public lavatories. These were rebuilt some years ago but the attendants' room is original; tradition has it that it was once part of the old church crypt. Until twenty years ago, one corner was occupied by a large cast-iron box. Nobody knew where it had come from or how long it had been there. It was about to be sold for scrap when a historian heard of it and did some research. He discovered that it was a plague oven installed by the church authorities in 1665 to burn bodies of victims of the Great Plague which started a few hundred yards away in Drury Lane.

The massive portico of the church overlooking the square provided the opening scene of Shaw's *Pygmalion*. Passers-by point out the tablet on the pillar that records the first Punch and Judy show in 1662 but few stop to wonder why this superb portico is here at all. The Earl of Bedford and Inigo Jones intended this to be the grand entrance from Covent Garden but they had not taken into account the views of Archbishop Laud. A High Church prelate with strong views on ritual, he believed that, whenever possible, altars should be at the east end of a church and doorways should be to the west, as indeed they normally are in Christian churches.

The Archbishop heard of Jones's outrageous idea just in time to stop the consecration of the church and forced him to fill in the portico, build the altar behind it and put the door at the other end.

The portico of St Paul's is the best spot from which to view the square laid out in 1631. Inigo Jones, the first to adopt the title of 'architect' in England, had been deeply impressed by the work of Palladio in northern Italy (see

First Walk) and designed Covent Garden in imitation of the Piazza d'Arme in Livorno.

Although the idea of a square surrounded by houses was common in Italy and France, Londoners had never seen one before and Jones's design was derided by his colleagues, particular abuse being heaped on the colonnaded walks around the three sides. The Earl's influence overrode all objections, however, and Covent Garden became the smartest address in London till the Fire of 1666 persuaded the aristocracy that the new estate around St James's might be a better place to live.

Jones called his design a 'piazza' because that was the word used to describe squares in Italy (Italian 'piazza' – French 'place') but Londoners decided that the word referred, not to the square, but to the arcades around it; they have called them piazzas ever since. Londoners also decided they liked the sound of the new word and Piazza Smith, Piazza Brown and Piazza Jones appeared in the local baptismal records for the next thirty years.

The church is all that remains from Jones's time, although the arcaded walk on the north side of the square was rebuilt by the Victorians to follow the old design. Its official name is still The Piazza. Orford House, which stands at the end of the piazza in line with the church portico, was built in 1710 and is the last of the Garden's great houses. It became a music-hall in the early nineteenth century and enjoyed such popularity that the Cabinet used to hold their meetings here.

Across the cobbles of the square is the Market Building, erected in 1830, with the faded advertisement on the right-hand pillar for 'Jas Butler, Herbalist, Seedsman, Lavender Water. . . .' The market that made Covent Garden famous was authorised by a charter of 1670 and, despite complaints over the years, lasted till 1974. As the original residents moved out at the end of the seventeenth century, their houses became gambling dens and brothels and Hogarth depicted the debauchery of the square in his 'Morning'.

By the nineteenth century the market had grown to become one of the sights of London. Ladies and gentlemen in full evening dress picked their way through piles of rotting vegetables to the Opera House or the Theatre Royal, while the famous licensing hours for the local pubs which opened at four in the morning made it a popular rendezvous for young men after the nightclubs had closed.

Thanks to the efforts of the residents and local authority, the Market is even more popular today and the old arcades and warehouses have been restored to make one of London's most attractive shopping centres.

At the far side of the central Market Building is an open concourse flanked by the green ironwork and glass of the Floral Hall standing beside the Opera House. The resemblance of the Floral Hall to the old Crystal Palace is easily explained; it was built from sections of the Crystal Palace left behind after its move from Hyde Park to Sydenham in 1864.

Drury Lane and the Theatre Royal

Russell Street looks the same today as it did when Boswell met Dr Johnson for the first time at No. 8, which now bears a blue plaque to commemorate the fact. No. 8 was then the home of Tom Davies the bookseller, renowned both for his good humour and the beauty of his wife. His house stood in the middle of what was London's Clubland for a hundred years, from the time of the Stuarts to the Napoleonic Wars.

The whole of London Society came to Russell Street to exchange news and gossip at three coffee-houses; Tom's, Button's and Will's. Button's, at No. 10, was presided over by Addison, and Pope, Swift, Steele and Colley Cibber came here daily to discuss their contributions to *The Tatler and Spectator*, which had been founded over the tables at Button's. Tom's, across the road at No. 17, was named after its owner Captain Thomas West, who killed himself by falling from the top window in a fit of delirium occasioned by gout. Smollett and Fielding came to Tom's to plan plays with Garrick and, after Dr Johnson and Joshua Reynolds had become habitués, Tom opened a membership list that included every duke and writer in London.

Will's, at No. 21 on the corner, was the senior of the three and is now considered to have been the first real London club. It was founded in the reign of Charles II and Pepys came here in 1664 to meet Dryden who presided over Will's till his death in 1700. A century later Charles Lamb came to live here with his sister Mary, whom he looked after all his life rather that commit her to the asylum where the authorities wished to place her.

Across the road is London's oldest theatre, the Theatre Royal, Drury Lane, which has been on this site since 1663. When Charles II came back as King in 1660, he recreated the Company of King's Players that the Puritans had disbanded and gave Killigrew the licence to open a new theatre on this site. Pepys came to the first play and later met Nell Gwynne who was, as legend says, an orange-seller here. Incidentally, the sale of oranges or any other fruit was soon restricted to the lower tiers; the actors discovered they made too effective a missile to be sold in the upper gallery. This restriction did not appear to affect their sale unduly. Mistress Mary Meggs, who had paid Killigrew £25 for the franchise to sell food at the theatre, sold it back to him later for £500.

Killigrew was followed by Rich, Colley Cibber and Doggett, who presented the Coat and Badge for which Thames watermen have raced since 1729. 'Rule Britannia' was played here for the first time in 1755, when Garrick was manager. He was followed by Sheridan, under whose direction John Kemble made his debut in 1783, founding the theatrical dynasty that has lasted till the present day. Grimaldi, Kean and Dan Leno appeared here and in 1879 Augustus Harris, whose bust stands outside the theatre, took it into its greatest phase with the most lavish shows and pantomimes that London has ever seen.

Harris was an extraordinary showman who took the lease of the theatre at the age of 27 with only £14 in his pocket. He set about reviving its fortunes by staging spectacles with casts of hundreds. He presented *Carmen* with real bulls, staged the Derby and the Grand National with real horses and started a tradition of Christmas pantomimes that is still legendary. He knew what his audiences came to Drury Lane for and his ideal scene consisted of cramming five hundred people on the stage, the more colourfully dressed the better.

When he staged *Ali Baba and the Forty Thieves*, he decided the numbers were too few and wanted to call it *Ali Baba and the Four Hundred Thieves*. His staff eventually convinced him that every child in England knew what the proper title was and that it would be foolish to change it. Harris reluctantly agreed and reverted to the usual name, but gave every thief a retinue of ten assistants so that he could present 440 ruffians to delight his audience.

The present building, the fourth on the site, was erected in 1811. The previous theatres had all been destroyed by fire and the opening of each was marked by a grand opening with a special address written for the occasion. Dryden wrote the address in 1674, Dr Johnson did the address for Garrick's debut and Byron wrote the lines for the opening of the present building. (This was the speech satirised by the Smith brothers in their famous *Rejected Addresses* – see Second Walk.)

The previous theatre had burnt down in 1809 when Sheridan had the licence and he dealt with the matter with his customary coolness. The news that the theatre was on fire reached him when he was sitting in the House of Commons and the Speaker offered to close the session so that he could leave. Sheridan dismissed the proposal out of hand with the remark that he saw no reason why any private calamity should interfere with the public business of the country.

Persuaded by his friends to leave the House, he came

to Catherine Street to find the fire had gained such a hold that the building was lost. He sat in the front room of the tavern opposite, where the Opera Tavern is now, ordered a bottle of port and watched the flames consume his theatre, with the comment: 'Surely a man may take a glass of wine by his own fireside.' It was a typical Sheridan remark. He was a brilliant speaker and dramatist but his indolence drove his actors to distraction. He used to leave writing his plays to the last possible moment and, on at least two opening nights, the complete cast was on stage for the first Act, while Sheridan sat upstairs writing the parts for the last scene, sending them down to the wings with apologies for the delay.

The theatre has its own ghost, The Man In The Grey Suit, probably the spectre of the skeleton found in a sealed chamber when they carried out some building work in the 1840s. He is known as Arnold and his sightings are so common they no longer cause comment amongst the theatre staff. He was seen by the entire cast of *The Dancing Years* and a clairvoyant, who came to a Drury Lane show three years ago, saw so many ghosts along the side-walls that she came back the next day to tell someone about it. As she recounted her story, she found that Arnold had followed her into the office and her description of him to the theatre historian confirmed all the previous sightings.

The grand foyer is unchanged after two centuries and the staff will still direct you up the 'King's Side' or 'Prince's Side' of the grand staircase. The tradition goes back to the eighteenth century when there were only two theatres in London and a Drury Lane First Night was an obligatory social event. The relationship of the first three Hanoverian kings with their sons was one of bitterness, and opponents of the Government always supported the Prince of Wales as part of their efforts to overthrow the Ministers in power. The King and his son always sat at different sides of the theatre and the King's Side and Prince's Side became synonymous with the Government and Opposition. An MP who wished to publicise a change of allegiance could either cross the floor of the House of Commons or walk up the wrong staircase at Drury Lane; the effect was the same.

The long colonnade leads down to Drury Lane from which the theatre takes its name, even though the entrance has been in Catherine Street for two hundred years. The colonnade was added in 1831 to provide protection for the crowds gathering for the evening performances. Nash had originally installed the pillars in Regent Street to form an arcade along the shop-fronts but they proved so unpopular that the Crown Commissioners had to take them down. Rather than waste them, George IV gave them to the theatre.

The stage door, two thirds of the way down the colonnade, is the most impressive of any London theatre. There are two tall, strong double doors decorated with roundels and lions' heads. The lions reflect the theatre's royal connections and the strength of the doors is a reminder of the Gordon Riots of 1780 when the theatre was attacked by the mob. Sentries were posted here immediately afterwards and remained till 1896, when someone pointed out that similar attacks had become unlikely.

Across the road is the Fortune Theatre, built in 1922. It has the distinction of sharing its site with the Church of Scotland. They form an unusual combination, especially since one of London's finest nudes stands over the theatre entrance. Although the entrance to the church appears to be beside the theatre, it actually runs through it along a covered-in passage, in what is known legally as 'a flying freehold'. The theatre is not attractive but it is one of the strongest buildings in London. It is the only theatre built entirely of reinforced concrete, which can be clearly seen under the coat of paint covering the façade.

Drury Lane has now become one of London's drearier streets. The southern end is dominated by the dismal yellow brick of the Peabody Buildings, erected in the

1880s to house London's poor under the will of the American philanthropist George Peabody. The street takes its name from Sir Thomas Drury who had a house here in the reign of Elizabeth I, but the neighbourhood soon became notorious. In the 1660s it had become so bad that the most stinging criticism of Nell Gwynne by the ladies of Charles II's court was that she had been born in Drury Lane.

A few yards up Drury Lane is a small recreation ground, with a tennis court, seats and a children's playground beyond. Despite the trees and bushes, it has a depressing atmosphere. This is the old Drury Lane graveyard, one of the scandals of London in the 1830s. Rotting coffins protruded from the earth and the corpses of paupers were pushed into the ground wherever a few inches of soil could be found to cover them. Dickens deliberately chose it to shock his readers in *Bleak House* when Joe brought Lady Deadlock here to see the grave of her dead lover.

The cemetery was cleared in 1851, but the tall buildings still darken it and the verger's house on one side and the mortuary house on the other do little to enhance it.

Bow Street and the Opera House

Long Acre leads from Drury Lane back towards Covent Garden. After a few yards, Broad Court passage cuts under an archway to Bow Street. The passage under the archway is for pedestrians only; two bollards dated 1816 prevent vehicles from driving through. The centre bollard, dated 1820, was added to stop vegetable barrows using the passage as a short cut to the Market.

The building immediately beside Broad Court passage is Bow Street Police Station, where the dramatist Henry Fielding and his blind brother John established the Bow Street Runners in 1750, the first effective police force in London.

The present building is Victorian and has one unusual feature. Police stations normally have a blue lamp outside for easy recognition, but the lamps outside the Bow Street Station are white. In 1870 the Sultan of Turkey came to England on a State visit and Queen Victoria brought him to a gala performance at the Royal Opera House. As they stood on the steps afterwards, acknowledging the cheers of the crowds, the Sultan asked the meaning of the blue lamps across the road. Queen Victoria told him but felt that such a blunt reminder of lawlessness was out of place in front of the Royal Opera House. The Commissioner was informed that Her Majesty would like to see white lamps outside Bow Street and white they have been ever since.

The Royal Opera House stands on the site of a house once occupied by Wycherley, the dramatist. He considered himself lucky to marry the Countess of Drogheda but soon found her jealousy to be almost unbearable. She accompanied him everywhere and did her best to see he never spoke to another woman. Her fixation became so extreme that she followed him in the streets and allowed him to attend dinners with his friends only on condition that the curtains were drawn back so that she could see from her carriage there were no women in the room.

The first theatre was built in 1732 by John Rich who had made his fortune with Gay from *The Beggar's Opera*, which 'made Gay rich and Rich gay'. Handel produced *The Messiah* here in 1743 and Dibden gave the first piano recital in 1763. In 1823 'Home, Sweet Home' was first sung here in *Clari, The Maid of Milan* and Macready introduced limelight in 1837. The second theatre, built in 1829, was modelled on the Temple of Minerva at Athens, another of London's imitations of classical buildings. In the 1840s crowds thronged here for Jullien's Promenade Concerts.

Jullien made sure his audiences saw how important he was by always having his gloves and baton brought to him on stage on a silver salver. The gloves were ceremonially changed after each piece and, if Beethoven was being performed, a special diamond-mounted baton was brought on for the occasion. Jullien was an excellent musician, but never fulfilled his crowning ambition. He confided to his friends that it was to be the greatest oratorio in the world, set to the words of the Lord's Prayer: 'Think of it! Think of it! Words by Jesus Christ, music by Jullien.'

In 1855 the theatre was taken over by John Anderson, who had lost two theatres by fire before coming to Covent Garden. On the last day of his Covent Garden lease he lost a third – and the present building dates from that period.

Floral Street leads down past the Opera House and the old eighteenth-century houses to James Street and the Covent Garden Underground Station. This is where the ghost of William Terriss has been seen since the 1950s, even though he was murdered in Maiden Lane (see Fourth Walk).

From the station we walk left along Long Acre, full of depressing new office blocks but enlivened on the right side by a series of small white busts on the wall, each showing a woman with a crown on her head. Mercer Street has half a dozen of them in twenty yards, including two that act as keystones of doorways. The busts are the badge of the Mercers' Company and mark the property in Long Acre left to them by Lady Bradbury in 1516. They finish just before No. 133 Long Acre, where a plaque on the wall commemorates John Logie Baird's first television broadcast in September 1929.

Rose Street leads down to the Lamb and Flag, here since 1620. The new wooden cladding disguises its age but it is one of London's oldest pubs. It was in the narrow alley beside the pub that Dryden was attacked by the servants of the Earl of Rochester in 1679 and would have been killed had not the landlord come to his rescue. It transpired later that Dryden had been attacked in error, because the satirical verses for which the earl had sought revenge had been written by somebody else. What really hurt Dryden's pride was that the verses were so bad, he was horrified that anybody should have thought he had written them.

The cobbles of Rose Street lead round three corners to finish in Garrick Street, named after the Garrick Club at No. 15. The club was founded in 1831 by the Duke of Sussex and the present members sometimes take exception to being reminded that the Duke's intention was to found a club where 'actors and men of education and refinement might meet on equal terms. . . .'

Garrick Street lies on the edge of Covent Garden and the boundary is marked by two small St Martin's parish badges over the windows of No. 4 and No. 7. When No. 7 was converted in the 1970s, the author found the workmen puzzling over a small circle set in the cellar floor, surrounded by tiers of wooden seats. It was a cockpit and gave every indication of recent use.

St Martin's Lane to Leicester Square

New Street around the corner has been 'new' since the time of Charles II. The White Swan has been here even longer; Pepys visited it when it was the main coaching inn for the West Country. The pavements are lit by a peculiar collection of early Victorian lamp-posts with short, stumpy bases, probably moved here from St Martin's Lane when new lamps were installed in the 1890s. Each of the New Street lamps is different from its neighbour and each is covered with the dark green paint of the Crown Commissioners.

The narrow, timber-panelled entrance to Goodwin's Court lies a few yards down Bedfordbury, around the corner from New Street. This is one of London's most delightful backwaters, a complete row of 1690 houses with bow windows that reveal small rooms and steep staircases unchanged for three hundred years. The Court leads into St Martin's Lane and the last stretch of wall on the right is all that remains of the St Martin's parish lock-up. The fittings for the bars can still be seen over the dark window in the corner.

St Martin's Lane possesses three fine theatres but its most striking building is the Salisbury, London's best Victorian pub, full of engraved glass, shining brass, polished mahogany and bevelled mirrors of every conceivable shape. It is a survivor of the great pub Gold Rush of the late nineteenth century when a drinks licence guaranteed wealth to anyone fortunate enough to secure one.

Till about 1870, most of London's pubs were small taverns like the Lamb and Flag we saw in Rose Street. In the 1880s the breweries started to build their own larger establishments which proved enormously popular. When the Conservatives were in power the building of the new pubs was encouraged, but the strong Nonconformist tradition of Liberal supporters put a brake on them during the Liberal administrations. Fortunes were made and lost as a result of General Elections. A man who had bought a licensed house for £5,000 under a Conservative Government found its price dropped to £500 under the Liberals and had to await the return of the Conservatives before he could get his investment back.

The Salisbury, originally called the Coach and Horses, became famous when Ben Caunt, 'the best known man in England', became landlord in 1830. Caunt was heavyweight champion and made the Coach and Horses the centre of boxing for twenty years. All the prize-fights and championships were organised at the pub and every visitor to London came here to admire the great man and increase his profits.

Cecil Court, lined with bookshops, leads into Charing Cross Road which runs up to Wyndham's Theatre, built in 1899 for Charles Wyndham. Every theatrical impresario had tried to persuade the landowner, the Marquess of Salisbury, to let him build a theatre on the then (1877) new street but the Marquess refused to have anything to do with them. Wyndham was a different matter. The Marquess considered him to be a gentleman and was so impressed he granted him not one lease but two.

Wyndham was certainly an unusual actor, one of the few who left home not to go on the stage, but to escape from it. Brought up by parents who wanted him to follow them in the theatre, he qualified as a doctor against their wishes. When they continued to urge him on to the boards, he ran away to America to become a surgeon in Grant's army in the Civil War. Only after more adventures in America did he return to the theatrical career in London that brought him a knighthood in 1902.

The enormous building across the road is the London Hippodrome, back under its old name after years as The Talk of The Town. The equestrian figures over the pediment advertise its original purpose, the staging of animal acts unlike any that had been seen in London before. Using the Cran Bourn stream under the theatre as its water source, the Hippodrome presented enormous aquatic spectacles, one of which included thirty polar bears while another act employed twenty divers who jumped from the roof of the theatre into the pool below the stage. It became famous for its novelty acts and one show included pygmies from Africa, giants from Russia, a boxing kangaroo and Consul, the Missing Link.

Newport Street, beside the Hippodrome, runs into Gerrard Street, now the centre of London's Chinatown. The street signs are in Chinese and English, the telephone boxes are in the shape of pagodas and every decorative surface is covered with bright red paint which the Chinese believe to be the colour of good luck. Two enormous lions stand in the middle of the street to ward off evil spirits while the community policeman has learnt to speak passable Mandarin.

Despite appearances, Gerrard Street is three hundred years old, another of the successful speculations of Nicholas Barbon. No. 43 became famous originally as the home of Dryden, who wrote his poems during his term as Poet Laureate in the front room by the window where dressed chickens now lie on a slab.

In the 1920s it became famous again as the '43' nightclub run by Kate Meyrick, who went to prison for her activities but saw three of her daughters marry members of the peerage.

Rupert Court leads into Rupert Street, where Edward VII used to change his clothes before going out incognito with the London Fire Brigade. He used the small back room of the tobacconist at No. 13; R. L. Stevenson heard the story and used it for his *New Arabian Nights*.

Lisle Street to the left is not so noisy or cheerful as Gerrard Street, but much of it is of the same date. The eastern section, marked by a plaque over the pediment of No. 18, was built in 1791 on the site of the old Leicester House, home of the Princes of Wales for nearly a hundred years. Edmund Kean lived in Lisle Street as a child and was so adventurous his parents eventually fitted him with a brass collar inscribed: 'This boy belongs to No. 9 Lisle Street, Leicester Square. Please bring him home.'

Leicester Square

Leicester Square draws crowds to its bars and enormous cinemas, but Leicester Place possesses the rotunda that pre-dates any cinema or theatre in London. In the late eighteenth century, an Irishman named Robert Barker perfected a system of drawing lines on a scenic painting that would be correct when viewed from the centre of a cylinder. This led to the development of panoramas, static exhibitions where the public were taken to a centre-point within a circular building to admire enormous scenes or landscapes painted on the circular walls around them.

Barker built London's first panorama in Leicester Place in 1793, a rotunda 90 feet in diameter divided into two rooms, with the large panorama below and a smaller one viewed at the upper level. It was a great success and the regular changes of paintings made it a popular place of resort till 1863 when the building was taken over as a French church. The church is still there, exactly the same shape as when Barker built it nearly two hundred years ago and visitors come to listen to the Mass in French or to admire the new paintings around the walls by Jean Cocteau.

Leicester Square is built around a patch of grass that is a memorial to the persistence of the residents of 1630, who fought the Earl of Leicester when he wanted to build on it. They took the matter through every court and finished with an appeal to the King himself, who ordered the Earl to leave the square as open land.

The Earl built his house on the northern side of the Square and his grandson let it to George I, who installed his eldest son there. The King was as glad to see his son go, as his son was to leave St James's; a pattern to be repeated for the next eighty years. Each Prince of Wales quarrelled with his father and each in turn was banished from the Court to the house in Leicester Square. The quarrels became so serious that anyone received by the Prince of Wales at Leicester House was banned from Court.

Londoners took a cynical view of the bad feeling in the Royal family and their general opinion is summed up in the lines that appeared when Frederick, Prince of Wales, died in 1751:

Here lies Fred
Who was alive and is dead;
Had it been his father,
I had much rather;
Had it been his brother,
Still better than another.
Had it been his sister,
No one would have missed her;
Had it been the whole generation,
Still better for the nation.
But since 'tis only Fred
Who was alive and is dead,
There's no more to be said.

The heyday of Leicester Square was from 1860 to 1914

when Daly's, the Alhambra and the Empire drew audiences from all over London. The Empire, now replaced by the Empire cinema, was famous for its Promenade, a long broad corridor where prostitutes met their clients. The Promenade became so notorious that the reformer Mrs Ormiston Chant succeeded in forcing the owners to close it off from the rest of the theatre. This led to vociferous protests from the clientele and the partition was torn down by a party of Sandhurst cadets, led by a young man called Winston Churchill. The old Empire closed in 1927 with *Lady Be Good* starring Fred and Adele Astaire, whose last night audience included four Royal Dukes.

The Odeon cinema stands on the site of the Alhambra, famous for a man who gave his name to the language. Mr Leotard amazed audiences with his skill as the original 'Daring Young Man on the Flying Trapeze' and the tight-fitting costume he wore has borne his name ever since. The theatre lost its licence in 1874 when one of the dancers became too enthusiastic and raised her foot overhead several times while facing the audience; the licensing authorities noted gravely that 'she had been much applauded each time'. In 1916, George Robey and Violet Lorraine appeared in *The Bing Boys Are Here* and sang the song the troops took back to the trenches – 'If You Were The Only Girl In The World'.

The Alhambra was demolished in 1936 but the last show was not *Tulip Time* as the records state. Max Miller is remembered nowadays as the comedian who told off-colour stories and sang songs so suggestive that the BBC banned him for years. Towards the end of his life he let it be known that his proudest moment was when he 'closed the old Alhambra'. When the theatre was being demolished in 1936, Miller arrived one lunch-time, gave the foreman a tenner to stop the work and climbed on to the stage. He entertained the workmen for an hour, jumped down and watched them knock the stage down behind him.

The statue of Shakespeare in the middle of the Square was presented by an adventurer called Gottheimer as a public relations exercise. Gottheimer was another of the company promoters who flourished in Victorian London, making his fortune by very dubious means. He changed his name to Grant and, after securing a title from the King of Italy, entered Parliament as Baron Grant. *Punch* summed up the public reaction to his title: 'Honours without honour are a barren grant'.

When the ground in the middle of the Square was put up for sale in 1874, Gottheimer bought it, erected the statue and laid out the gardens. At the official unveiling ceremony, he handed the deeds over to the Metropolitan Board of Works, which was just as well since he went bankrupt soon afterwards and his creditors could have claimed the Square.

Down at the bottom left-hand corner of the Square, an iron bollard of 1816 guards the corner of Irving Street which leads back to the Edith Cavell statue where this walk began. Amongst the sweet-shops, cafés and kebab houses on the left is a small, discreet doorway. It has no markings other than the number '9' on the plaster beside the door.

This is the entrance to the Beefsteak Club, founded by John Rich of *The Beggar's Opera* fame in 1735. Its members have included Galsworthy, Kipling and Sir Henry Irving, who once so far forgot himself as to dance on the dining table. The club has always prided itself on being discreet but this discretion proved a disadvantage in the 1920s, when a new police inspector was posted to the district.

Since the Home Office had instituted a campaign against night-clubs and brothels, the new inspector became highly suspicious when he saw four elderly gentlemen knocking at this anonymous door and being admitted after a few muttered words. He immediately secured a warrant and raided what he assumed to be a disorderly house. He found the four suspicious characters still there and greeted with derision their claims to be, respectively, the Lord Chancellor, the Archbishop of Canterbury, the Governor of the Bank of England and the Prime Minister – which is exactly who they were.

TWELFTH ♦ WALK

The Haymarket, Pall Mall and St James's

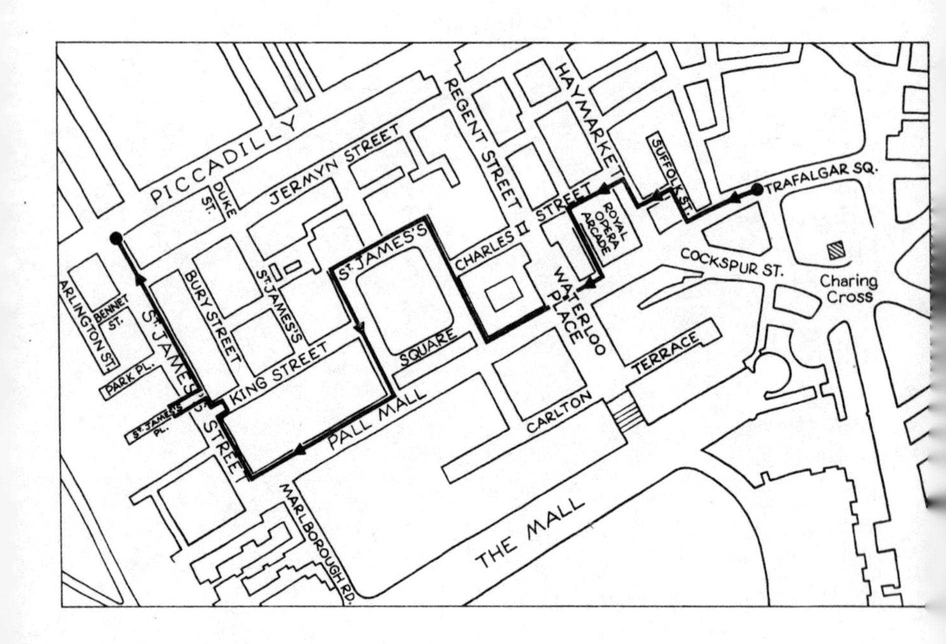

TWELFTH ♦ WALK

The Haymarket, Pall Mall and St James's

The Twelfth Walk begins at the north side of Trafalgar Square, where Pall Mall East runs in beside Canada House. This is the border of London's Clubland, considered by some to be a relic of the past and by others to be the home of the mysterious 'Establishment' that still rules Britain.

Pall Mall East and Cockspur Street run either side of a small island on which stands an equestrian statue of George III. It is an unpretentious reminder of the King who ruled for sixty years and shows him doffing his hat to reveal his hair tied in a pig-tail. It attracts little attention today but its installation caused the authorities considerable trouble.

A memorial to George III was proposed in 1820, the year of his death, but subscriptions were slow to come in. The original design was an enormous four-horse chariot driven by the King dressed in the robes of a Roman emperor. Lack of funds forced modification of the design and the second proposal was for a chariot drawn by one horse. When the subscription list was closed, it was clear that even this scheme was too ambitious and the present equestrian statue was agreed.

Immediately to the north of the statue is the office of Barclays Bank. The Bank's directors viewed the idea of the statue outside their premises with considerable alarm.

Convinced that it would become a gathering-place for beggars and vagrants, they resisted the proposal vigorously, bringing injunctions to prove it would block their light and, when this failed, seeking damages because of the harm to their business. Eventually, so rumour has it, they resorted to direct action. A workman in the foundry was bribed to sabotage the casting of the metal and the authorities had to postpone the unveiling of the statue.

It is still not known exactly how much damage was done, but Londoners believed firmly that the flowing tail on the horse was a later addition. They expressed their dislike of both the King's old-fashioned hair-style and the horse with the couplet:

Here stands a statue at which critics rail
To point a moral and to point a tail.

Suffolk Street

The graceful stuccoed buildings of Suffolk Street are by Nash, the last survivors south of Oxford Circus of the houses he built along the boulevard that stretches from St James's to Regent's Park. Half-way up the right-hand side, a gigantic portico straddles what used to be the doorway of No. 6½, the home of the Royal Society of British Artists and the United Society of Artists.

The Societies took their responsibilities to their members very seriously and, until the redevelopment of the site two years ago, the rooms of No. 6½ were constructed without any corners. Angles in walls darken a room and every corner was filled with a curved plaster coving to reduce loss of light.

The British Artists are the most senior of the various artists' societies that all seemed to begin their existence with the aim of rivalling the Royal Academy. There are now fourteen such institutes in London, though it is unlikely that many of them still express their aims in the forthright way that the British Artists did in 1850. They were described then as a body of 'artists whose works were all rejected or ill-placed at the exhibitions of the Royal Academy. No Royal Academician is, or will become, a member.'

Although Suffolk Street has always been a smart residential area, one of the problems it shared with the rest of London in the nineteenth century was noise. The din of horses' hooves and iron wheels on cobbled streets was exacerbated by the shouts of street-vendors plying their wares. The street cries of old London were not winsome verses sung by pretty country girls selling lavender. They were a cacophony of raucous bellows by fly-paper men, muffin-men, itinerant old-clothes men, beggars and costers, each trying to outshout his competitors. There were constant complaints to the authorities and one indignant Londoner wrote to *The Times* that his work had been interrupted fifty times in one morning by different street-vendors.

These were bad enough but the problem became even worse in the 1870s when troupes of German bands came to London. Their drums and brass instruments were far noisier than the single fiddler or cornet player Londoners had known before. Another letter of complaint to *The Times* was written, so the author said, to the successive accompaniment of a brass band, two organs, a Punch and Judy show, another organ pulled by a donkey, a bagpiper and another 'organ with two babies attached'.

In 1882 the novelist Anthony Trollope was staying at No. 14 Suffolk Street (now distinguished from its neighbours by the large 'XIV' on the door) when a brass band started to play outside. Rather than submit to the normal blackmail and pay them enough to move elsewhere, Trollope shouted at them to go away. The band followed their normal practice and simply played more loudly. The more he protested, the louder they played till Trollope suffered a heart attack from which he died a few days later.

The Haymarket and its Theatres

Suffolk Place joins Suffolk Street to the Haymarket, which acquired its name when Henry VIII moved the royal stables to the site of Trafalgar Square in 1534. Until the arrival of the motor-car, hay and straw were essential commodities in London and, even though this area of London was soon built over, the Haymarket remained the major market for both till 1830.

One reminder of the old market still exists in the middle of the street. One of the privileges of the old stall-holders was to park their carts in the middle of the roadway, so that they could unload straight from their cart on to the customer's. The privilege became the accepted right of any horse-drawn trade vehicle and hansom-cabs continued to park on the centre area after the market had moved elsewhere. Although the Haymarket has become one of the busiest streets in London, there is still a cab-rank in the middle, on the spot where the hay stalls stood a hundred and fifty years ago.

The Theatre Royal Haymarket is one of London's oldest theatres. The first on the site was built in 1720 when all theatres had to be licensed and approved by Royal favour. Since the original licensee could not obtain the necessary Patent, only private performances could be given and the theatre bankrupted its builder. Henry Fielding took over the management in 1735 and wrote a series of satires of the Government which infuriated the Prime Minister, Robert Walpole.

Walpole achieved some satisfaction by waiting outside the theatre door and thrashing the unfortunate actor who played him on the stage, but got even more satisfaction by persuading Parliament to pass the Licensing Act of 1737. Under the Act no play could be performed in public without the Lord Chamberlain's certificate, a restriction that held good for another two hundred years.

After Fielding left, the theatre was taken by Samuel Foote. He evaded the difficulty of a licence by charging nothing for entry to the theatre, but making the patrons pay considerable sums for the coffee served during the interval. Although insufferably conceited, he was a brilliant actor and did everything he could to secure a Royal licence for his beloved theatre.

He was boasting one evening of his skill with horses when the Duke of York, annoyed by his manner, invited him to come riding the following morning. When Foote arrived, the Duke mounted him on a horse that had never been saddled before. Within a minute Foote had been badly thrown and had his leg broken. Ashamed of the dangerous prank he had played, the Duke asked what he could do to make recompense and Foote secured the longed-for Royal licence for his theatre. The words 'Theatre Royal' appeared over the portico and, although the licence was granted only for Foote's lifetime, the theatre has kept the title ever since. The incident was probably the origin of the theatrical phrase 'Break a leg' for 'Good Luck'.

Charles Keane played his last part at the Haymarket and Ellen Terry made her debut in 1863. Like the other Theatre Royal in Drury Lane, it has a ghost. J. B. Buckstone was manager from 1853–1878 and his haunting takes the form of checking doors and locks around the theatre after performances are over. It was in the dressing-room of the Haymarket that a young actor called Herbert Blythe saw an old playbill on the wall including the name Maurice Barrymore. Blythe adopted it as a stage name, went to America and founded the theatrical dynasty that dominated the American stage for nearly a century.

Across the road is the enormous bulk of New Zealand House dominating the bottom of the Haymarket. Built in 1963 on the site of the old Carlton Hotel, it contains the only Pouihi carved in London. The Pouihi is a 54-feet-high Maori totem pole that rears up from the central hallway. It was carved by Inia Te Wiata, a Maori bass singer who came to London in 1947 on a New Zealand Government scholarship. He became a leading member of the Royal Opera House company but never forgot the help he had been given to come to London for his musical training. It took him seven years to carve the Pouihi in the cellars of the building. Cut from one giant Totara tree, it is in six sections and he was working on the final one when he died in 1971.

Her Majesty's Theatre stands across the road from the Theatre Royal. It is the second oldest theatre in London and its title changes with the sex of the monarch. Built as the Queen's Theatre in 1705 (Queen Anne), it became the King's Theatre from 1714–1837 (the four Georges) and reverted to Her Majesty's Theatre when Queen Victoria came to the throne in 1837.

The first theatre was built by one of those remarkable eighteenth-century characters who seemed to excel at anything they turned their hand to. Sir John Vanbrugh was a soldier who wrote plays while imprisoned in the Bastille, became Comptroller of the Board of Works and architect of two of the largest buildings in England, Castle Howard and Blenheim Palace. Because of the massive size of these two palaces, a rival suggested that Vanbrugh's tombstone should read:

Lie heavy on him, earth, for he
Laid many a heavy load on thee.

Handel's operas were performed here for forty years, including the first English performance of *The Messiah*. In 1790 the theatre was rebuilt as the largest opera house in England and the second largest in Europe. It was a great success and Jenny Lind made her debut here in 1847. Burnt down and restored in 1867, it remained empty for many years till it was bought by Beerbohm Tree.

Tree was one of the giants of the Victorian stage, an actor-manager who combined a sense of theatre with a gift for administration. He had made money at the Theatre Royal across the road with *Trilby* and he rebuilt Her Majesty's in 1897. He was reluctant to leave Her Majesty's even for a night and built himself a magnificent flat in the dome over the theatre. He later set up London's first school of acting which became the Royal Academy of Dramatic Art.

Tree delighted in running a successful theatre and considered that choosing the right play and the right actors was far harder than acting well oneself. At the time when theatres in London used to close for the summer, Tree kept Her Majesty's open right through the year. One day in August, he walked down the Haymarket and looked proudly at the 'House Full' notices outside his beloved theatre. He spied his colleague, the manager of the Theatre Royal across the road, and pointed out the notices to him. His colleague retorted that the Theatre Royal had 'House Full' notices up as well. He added that it didn't really matter because Tree was running both theatres at the time. Tree looked from one side of the road to the other, but his pride in Her Majesty's made him have the last word: 'Ah, yes, we both have "House Full" notices up, but we have more of them than you have!'

Tree died in 1917 but the staff at Her Majesty's are convinced his ghost is still in the theatre. He always watched rehearsals from a certain box to see the play, as he said, 'from the worst possible angle'. Customers using the box are never told of Tree's haunting and the staff are used to complaints that it is the coldest place in the theatre.

Tree was a brilliant actor and producer who used to drive his staff to distraction with the demands he made upon them. He would introduce drastic changes in the middle of a dress rehearsal, call everybody on stage to issue the necessary directions and then vanish, to be found an hour later being shaved at the barber's in the Royal Opera Arcade behind the theatre.

The vanishing trick was particularly annoying to the stage manager who suffered most from Tree's sudden changes of plan. He made it a point of honour to find out how Tree disappeared but it took him a long time to discover the secret exit.

The side of the theatre runs along Charles II Street. Just past the stage door is the entrance to the Royal Opera Arcade. Ten yards down the Arcade, the blank wall on the left is broken by an inconspicuous brown door. It opens directly on to the back of the stage and was Tree's secret escape route, especially built for him in 1897.

The Royal Opera Arcade was built by John Nash in 1816; the Regency lamps in the ceiling date from his time, converted now from gas to electricity. Tree's barber's shop was at No. 14 and enjoyed the patronage of the great Pall Mall clubs. The writer James Bone remembered walking in one day to find four dukes occupying the chairs and the Archbishop of Canterbury waiting his turn. Kipling used it regularly till the day he saw Ramsay Macdonald, the first Labour Prime Minister, in his favourite chair. This annoyed Kipling so much he never entered the place again.

Into Pall Mall

The Arcade leads into Pall Mall, a name as synonymous with dignified luxury as Whitehall is with central bureaucracy or Fleet Street with newspapers. When Edward the Confessor moved his Court down to Westminster, the nobility moved west along the Strand from the City. After the restoration of the monarchy in 1660, there was a further move westwards. The Royalists who had lost their estates were rewarded with land around London and the Great Fire of 1666 encouraged many of them to move away from the City and the Strand to the new estates around St James's Palace.

When the Palace of Whitehall burnt down in 1698, the Court moved to St James's, and Pall Mall and the streets to the north became the social centre of London. It remained a residential area for the nobility till about 1815 when the great families moved to Mayfair or to the new estates in Belgravia built by Cubitt. As the households moved away, they were replaced by the clubs that have been here ever since.

The United Service Club and the Athenaeum

Waterloo Place was originally built as a forecourt to show off the grand entrance of the Prince Regent's Carlton House, which looked out over St James's Park. When Carlton House was demolished in 1826, Carlton House Terrace was built on the site and the Crown Commissioners gave permission for two new clubhouses to stand on the corners flanking Pall Mall. The United Service Club building stands on the east side, the Athenaeum faces it on the west.

The Commissioners stipulated that the clubhouses were to be of identical design, but neither club would agree. Each had chosen its own architect and this reflected the unspoken rivalry that was to characterise the relationship between the two clubs for the next fifty years.

The United Service Club, known as 'The Senior' because its membership was restricted to officers of the Army and Navy of field rank, had been founded in 1815. Since the Duke of Wellington was a member, the club had no difficulty in securing a lease from the Crown Commissioners. Nash, the King's favourite architect, built the clubhouse in 1827 and George IV gave the club official recognition by presenting it with various fittings from the demolished Carlton House. The royal gifts were received with due gratitude, although the Carlton House staircase proved something of an embarrassment. It is far too large for the building and had to be installed facing the wrong way, which accounts for the small size of the club entrance hall.

The club possessed an excellent collection of pictures, including some presented by Earl Grey who disapproved of his heir and determined he should not inherit them. The Kaiser presented a portrait of himself when he was elected a member; the question of what to do with it exercised the committee when war was declared in 1914. The solution agreed was to take the portrait down during hostilities and replace it in peacetime, a course that was repeated in 1939–1945.

While Nash was building the Senior on the east side of Waterloo Place, Decimus Burton was engaged on the Athenaeum on the other side. The Athenaeum was founded as a club for writers, artists and scientists by John Wilson Croker. Croker was a writer and politician who coined the term 'Conservative' for the Tory party. He became Secretary to the Navy and set the tone of the club from the start by naming it after the Athenaeum of Rome, a university of science and literature founded by the Emperor Hadrian.

Croker kept tight control of the club and had no doubt that he knew what was best for the members. It was he who decided the club should have the gilded figure of Athene over its entrance and he commissioned the frieze that runs above the main windows. The members wanted the money to be spent on an ice-house to keep meat fresh, but Croker decided otherwise:

I'm John Wilson Croker,
I do as I please.
They ask for an ice-house,
I'll give them a frieze.

Although the Duke of Wellington was a member of both clubs (a mounting-block for his use still stands outside both), the Senior and the Athenaeum made no secret of their mutual antipathy. The Athenaeum members envied the favour shown to the Senior by George IV and stressed the intellectual content of their club compared with the brute force they considered to be the hallmark of the soldiers and sailors across the road.

There are countless anecdotes of the rivalry between the two clubs. One records the reluctance of an aesthetic member of the Athenaeum to enter the Senior 'because of all those red, beefy, brutal faces'. The equal antipathy of the Senior was expressed by an elderly general who swore his umbrella would never be safe in the Athenaeum 'at the hands of all those clergymen'.

As more and more bishops joined the Athenaeum, the Senior began to refer to it as 'Bishopsgate'. The Athenaeum's response was to name the Senior 'Cripplesgate' because of the preponderance of elderly generals and admirals amongst its members. The Senior noted the large number of Athenaeum members who wore horn-rimmed spectacles and referred to them as 'Athene's owls'; the Athenaeum replied with the comment that the barn-like architecture of the Senior was intended to remind its inmates of their life in barracks.

If there ever was any serious rivalry between the two clubs, the Athenaeum can be said to have won. In 1858 Burton, who had built the Athenaeum, was called in to remodel the exterior of the Senior – and make it resemble the Athenaeum in the process. In 1976, the Senior was forced to close and the Institute of Directors now occupies the building.

The Athenaeum was the last club in London to instal a bar. The view was that if a member wanted to lean on a counter to drink, he could go to a pub. The committee was eventually persuaded to instal one, but did so in keeping with the tradition of the club. On the left of the building are steps leading down to the basement. This is the bar entrance but the wording over the top is in Greek, a line from the *Odyssey*, where Nausicaa welcomes Odysseus to her father's court: 'Follow me so that I can offer you hospitality.'

The most popular member of the Athenaeum in its early days was Theodore Hook (1788–1841). Having written thirteen successful comic operas before he was 23, he spent the rest of his life alternating between successful journalism and bankruptcy. Hook held court every day in the Athenaeum coffee-room in what became known as Temperance Corner. Because of the number of clergymen who came to listen to his stories, Hook did not like to offend their susceptibilities by his consumption of alcohol. He therefore ordered 'lemonade' when he wanted champagne and 'toast and water' or 'cold tea' when he wanted brandy. The club steward noted that the number of members taking lunch always dropped considerably when it was known Hook was out of London.

Hook was a great practical joker who perpetrated the Berners Street Hoax of 1809. He was walking along Berners Street, just north of Oxford Street, with a friend who commented on the inconspicuous appearance of No. 54. Hook bet him a guinea that he would make it the most famous house in London within a month.

He sat down with some friends and wrote 1000 letters all addressed from No. 54 Berners Street. On the appointed day, he hired a room in the house opposite and waited for results. At 10 o'clock, twelve chimney sweeps arrived at No. 54 in reply to Hook's letters. They were followed by twenty coal drays each carrying a ton of coal, furniture drays, brewers' wagons loaded with beer, a hearse and three mourning-coaches and several hundred other tradesmen, all intent on delivering the goods ordered by Hook.

The friend admitted he had lost the bet but Hook told him there was more to come. The hundreds of indignant tradesmen filling the street were joined by the Lord Mayor of London, the Archbishop of Canterbury, the Lord Chief Justice, the Governor of the Bank of England and the Duke of York, who arrived with an escort of cavalry befitting his position as Commander-in-Chief. Each of them came in response to a letter from an old friend who was dying at No. 54 and craved a last interview.

Hook was never prosecuted but found it advisable to leave London for some time, a prudent measure that gave rise to the expression 'to hook it'.

By the end of the nineteenth century, the Athenaeum had achieved the reputation for intellectual eminence it enjoys today. It possessed three libraries (plus another for the servants) and numbered Dickens, Thackeray and Trollope among its members. It was in the Athenaeum that Trollope heard two clergymen discussing the appalling behaviour of Mrs Proudie in his latest Barchester novel. They agreed she would be better dead, at which Trollope sprang to his feet, thanked them for the idea and killed her off in the next episode.

With the exception of men like Theodore Hook, the Athenaeum has always been renowned for the respectability of its members. In the 1890s the Bishop of Rochester returned to his palace from a visit to London deeply disturbed. He confided to his household that he had suffered a grievous loss in the library of the Athenaeum. He had laid down his gold-rimmed spectacles on a table and, when he looked for them a minute later, they had vanished.

His family expressed surprise at his gloom over such a minor loss, but it transpired that what really worried the good bishop was the identity of the thief. 'That,' he said, 'is the dreadful part. There were only four other people in the room – the Bishop of London, the Bishop of St David's, the Archdeacon of Rochester and – and Mr Gladstone!'

The sombre building next door to the Athenaeum at 106 Pall Mall is the Travellers' Club. Built by Barry in 1832, it is a copy of the Palazzo Pandolfini in Florence, another of the many buildings in London that imitated the architecture of Florence and Rome. It was the custom of the club for members to eat their meals in silence, with a book on the table beside them. When the club was closed for cleaning in the summer, the members were temporarily accommodated at the Garrick, where conversation was the rule at mealtimes. Those members of the Travellers' who had brought their books with them had them confiscated by the head porter with the firm remark, 'Not done at the Garrick, Sir.'

The Reform Club next door, at No. 104 Pall Mall, was also built by Barry. This time the design used was that of the Farnese Palace in Rome. The club was founded by the Radical Whigs who supported the Reform Bill of 1832. The enormous central hallway, surrounded by the largest mirrors in Europe, was intended to have been an open piazza, but the members took the practical view that what might be appropriate for the climate of Rome was not really suitable for London.

The kitchens of the Reform were designed by the famous chef Alexis Soyer, the inventor of the bain-marie. He was the first to use gas-stoves in kitchens and the Government borrowed him from the Reform Club to assist with the problems of feeding the Irish during the famine of 1847. In 1855 he was sent to the Crimea to advise the British Army on cooking in the field, where he invented the Soyer stove that is still found in some Army barracks. He and his wife were buried under a headstone with the inscription *Soyez tranquilles*.

Another chef at the Reform was sacked by the committee after he was found in a compromising position with one of the maids. The members were furious and insisted on his reinstatement with a formal acknowledgement of his rights to try his luck with the female members of staff. Perhaps it was this determination of the Reform Club to enjoy good food that led to the clerihew:

The Savage Club
Is a good pub
But the soup is warm
At the Reform.

The stretch of road outside the Reform Club saw the first gas-lamps in London. A German named Winsor set up a small plant in Pall Mall and manufactured enough gas to illuminate the street for the King's birthday in 1807. London was 'much amused and delighted by this novel exhibition' and Winsor started the first gas-lighting company. Because of the difficulty of producing pipes to withstand the pressure, he converted barrels of surplus

Army muskets which is why the term 'gas barrel' piping is still used today.

St James's Square

Across the road from the Reform Club is a small section of roadway connecting Pall Mall to St James's Square. It is now counted as part of the Square but used to be John Street, the shortest street in London.

St James's Square was planned by Henry Jermyn, Earl of St Albans, to be exactly what it became, the most fashionable address in London. Built in 1670, its thirty-one houses contained six dukes and seven earls by 1700. By 1730 every house had a titled occupant. The luxury of the Square aroused criticism in some quarters and the Nonconformist preacher Richard Baxter conducted a public prayer service in the street because: 'The residents of St James's Square are like the Americans; they have not heard a sermon for years.'

No. 10, on the north side of the Square, dates from 1736 and was home to three Prime Ministers: Pitt, Derby and Gladstone. No. 14, in the corner, has been the home of the London Library since 1845. The Library was started by Carlyle after he had spent a frustrating morning waiting for a book in the Reading Room of the British Museum. What particularly annoyed him was that he could see Macaulay in a private room with an attendant on call to fetch books for him quickly.

Although Carlyle was the guiding spirit behind the Library, he was not the best of members. He broke all the rules he had helped to formulate, refused to return books when asked and scribbled rude remarks in the margins.

No. 16 is now the home of the East India, Devonshire, Sports and Public Schools Club. In 1815 it was the setting for Mrs Boehm's famous dinner party. By spending money recklessly, Mr and Mrs Boehm had managed to work their way into London Society and achieved their ambition when the Prince Regent accepted an invitation to dinner. As the guests were being presented to the Prince in the drawing-room, they heard shouts in the distance. The noise grew louder and Mr Boehm and his guests stepped out on to the balcony to see what was happening.

There was a rattle of hooves and a carriage swung into the Square with a crowd of people shouting and cheering behind it. The coach drew up outside Lord Castlereagh's house across the Square, a man exchanged a few words with the porter, re-entered the coach and directed it to No. 16. As the guests watched, an officer in dishevelled uniform ran up the steps with a soldier behind him carrying half a dozen tattered French banners. The officer was Major Percy with the dispatch announcing the news of Waterloo. The Square filled with a cheering throng, the Prince addressed the crowd from the balcony and departed for a Privy Council meeting, leaving Mrs Boehm 'much annoyed with the battle of Waterloo since it quite spoilt her party'.

Although the Square was renowned for the nobility of its inhabitants, the gardens in the middle became notorious for their neglected appearance. No one would accept responsibility for them and they became a refuse heap for the households around the Square. Eventually a tradesman decided that, since no one exercised any authority over the gardens, he might as well make use of them and started to build a timber warehouse on the site.

This was a very different matter and the residents of the Square promptly rallied to evict him. To ensure it did not happen again, the gardens were laid out as we see them today, although their maintenance continued to be haphazard. During the Gordon Riots of 1780 the great key of Newgate Prison was stolen by the mob and thrown in the fountain in the middle of the gardens. It was not discovered till the fountain was cleaned seventy years later in 1850.

The equestrian statue of William III in the gardens shows the famous molehill on which William's horse stumbled, causing his death. This was the origin of the Jacobite toast used for many years: 'To the little gentleman in black velvet.' The statue had been proposed in 1697 by a merchant who had made money from William's accession, but received little support. In 1705 the merchant died and left money for the statue to be erected but the bequest was contested. Nothing was done till 1735, when the lawyers released sufficient funds from the estate to put up the plinth. The will was then lost and the plinth remained vacant for seventy years. The will reappeared in 1805 and the statue was eventually completed in 1806, a century late.

Because of its proximity to St James's Palace, the Square was a convenient place of residence for the royal mistresses. In 1676 No. 21 was the home of Arabella Churchill, mistress of James II, and her neighbour at No. 22 was Moll Davis, mistress of Charles II. Arabella Churchill was succeeded at No. 21 by Catherine Sedley, another of James II's mistresses. She purported to be puzzled why he chose her: 'It cannot be for my beauty, because I have none; it cannot be for my wit since he has not enough to know I have any.'

The street in the south-west corner of the Square enters Pall Mall opposite the Royal Automobile Club, the biggest clubhouse in London. Sometimes referred to disparagingly by its more senior neighbours as 'Charing Cross Station', it has a membership of 8000. The club has its own post office, Turkish baths, swimming pool and rifle range, but its size makes it so impersonal that Burgess and Maclean chose it as a suitable venue for lunch when laying their plans to flee the country.

The club was founded in imitation of the French Automobile Club and French workmen were employed by the architects. The result is that the interior is decorated in the Second Empire style and one of the cherubs above the portico is driving an early Renault motor car. It has given rise to sardonic comments over the years on the inability of British car manufacturers to resist foreign competition.

The dignified red-brick building at Nos. 80–82 Pall Mall is Schomberg House which dates from the 1690s. Gainsborough lived here till his death and painted the 'Blue Boy' in the saloon. One wing was rebuilt by the Victorians but restored to its original appearance in the 1950s by Cecil Elsom. Elsom was better known as an architect in the modern style and his admirers were startled to learn that he regarded the Schomberg House restoration as his finest work. He took particular pride in the fact that it is extremely difficult to tell which wing he restored (he rebuilt the eastern wing).

The house immediately beyond Schomberg House, No. 79, is unique in Pall Mall. It is the only freehold site; all the rest are on Crown lease. The freehold has been in private hands since 1676 when Nell Gwynne lived here. Charles II offered her a long lease of the property which she rejected, insisting on a freehold because she 'had always conveyed free under the Crown and always would'. The house saw further royal embarrassment a century later. George III's brother, the Duke of Gloucester, was secretly married here against the King's wishes, an act that led to the passing of the Royal Marriages Act of 1772. The connection with royal peccadilloes continued with Mrs Fitzherbert, George IV's morganatic wife, after which the house was occupied, somewhat inappropriately, by the Society for the Propagation of the Gospel in Foreign Parts.

The Oxford and Cambridge Club at No. 76 has a classical frieze along its front and the badges of both universities over the doorway. It is easy to recognise which is which. The Oxford coat of arms shows the book of knowledge lying open with three crowns around it; the Cambridge coat of arms shows the same book tightly shut with three lions to ensure it is never opened. The Cambridge version of the story is that the Oxford book is open because no one has yet managed to finish it.

Marlborough House

The gateway on the corner beyond the Oxford and Cambridge Club leads to Marlborough House, designed by Wren for the first Duke of Marlborough. It reverted to the Crown in 1817 and became the London house of the Prince of Wales, later Edward VII. George V lived here when he was heir to the throne and Queen Mary made it her home during her widowhood. It is now the Commonwealth Conference Centre.

Marlborough House was built under the supervision of Sarah Churchill, the formidable Duchess of Marlborough who fought the Duke's political enemies in England as vigorously as he fought the French at Blenheim and Malplaquet. Marlborough House is built of Dutch bricks which the Duke sent back as ballast for his ships, thus saving the cost of carriage. The Duchess laid the foundation stone in 1709 and soon dismissed Wren because she considered the contractors were cheating him. She was probably right to do so, especially as she knew no contractor would dare to cheat her.

The Duchess stood no nonsense from anybody and her sharp tongue was famous. On one occasion she called at her lawyer's office to find he was away. She refused to leave her name but the porter had no doubt of her status: 'She swore so very dreadfully, I knew she must be a lady of quality.' She stayed on in Marlborough House after the Duke died, living in great state and regarding herself as the first lady of the land. She had little opinion of the Hanoverians and referred to King George I in St James's Palace as 'my neighbour George'.

She loathed the Prime Minister, Robert Walpole, who was one of the few people who ever got the better of her. In 1733 the Duchess decided that Marlborough House should have a grand entrance from Pall Mall, where the Oxford and Cambridge Club stands today. Walpole heard of the proposal and promptly bought in the leases of the Pall Mall sites. He also ordered the wall on the Park side to be strengthened, so she could not use that either. The Duchess was forced to make do with the narrow gateway on the corner that is still the only entrance.

She lived till the age of eighty-four, feared and respected, if not loved, by the whole of London. A year before her death, her doctor told her she must be blistered (have a poultice applied) or she would certainly die. The Duchess's reply was typical: 'I won't be blistered and I won't die'; and she made no secret of her satisfaction when the physician himself fell ill and died a few months later.

The occupancy of Marlborough House by the Prince of Wales in 1863 produced some problems for the houses at this end of Pall Mall. To ensure privacy for the Prince's household, the Crown Commissioners insisted that the windows on the south walls of Nos. 66 and 68 be blocked up and that the Oxford and Cambridge Club replace their southern windows with frosted glass. When the club wanted to build an extension in 1928, the Commissioners dismissed the proposal out of hand.

The Club made an informal approach directly to the Royal Family, inviting them to see what was proposed. The invitation was accepted, Queen Mary being delighted, it was said, to have the chance of seeing inside a gentlemen's club. The Royal party toured the Club, were pleased with what they saw and approval was given for the new extension.

St James's Palace

Marlborough Road, which separates Marlborough House from St James's Palace, has only been open to the public for a century. Officially it is the private royal entrance from the Palace to the Park and the gates can be closed whenever the Sovereign wishes. The gates themselves date from the time of George IV and consist of railings cast in the form of partisans, the ceremonial pike carried by the Gentlemen at Arms, who have their headquarters in the Palace.

The palace was built by Henry VIII and the superb gatehouse and octagonal turrets date from his day. When the Palace of Whitehall was burnt down in 1698, it became the main royal residence and the four Georges had their Court here.

Although Buckingham Palace has been the royal residence since 1830, ambassadors are still accredited to the Court of St James. The first proclamation of the accession of a new sovereign is made at St James's and the present Queen held her first Privy Council here in 1952.

Despite the constitutional importance of accession proclamations, mistakes can be made. The proclamation made at St James's when Queen Victoria came to the throne was one such occasion. The herald should have read out the words: 'Our Sovereign Lady, Queen Alexandrine Victoria', but omitted the first name. Once the proclamation was made, it could not be rescinded, so we now speak of 'great Victorians' rather than 'great Alexandrinians'.

A small dark stable in the corner of the Palace used to be known as 'Hell'. George I and George II used to escape from the boredom of Court etiquette by using it for private gambling sessions with their friends. Its squalor and gloom was soon applied to every other 'gambling hell' in London.

The clock over the gatehouse was restored in the reign of William IV. His advisers had little respect for his intelligence (he is reputed to have been the original 'Silly Billy') and told him the tower was too weak to take the clock's weight. The King retorted that he had seen twenty-five of them on the balcony watching his Coronation procession and if the tower could take their weight, it could bear one clock.

St James's Street

St James's Street, the old road from the Palace to the north, became the centre of London's club life when the Court moved to St James's Palace. Few notables lived here and it became famous for its fashionable shops and clubs rather than for its residents. Berry Brothers have been at No. 3 since 1703 when they bought the premises from William Pickering, the coffee merchant whose trade sign of a coffee-mill still hangs in front of the shop.

Berry Brothers have an enormous weighing-machine in the middle of the floor on which famous customers have been weighed, from the Prince Regent to the Aga Khan. It is so finely balanced that it will swing for half an hour after use.

A small passage beside the shop leads to Pickering Place, a delightful Georgian backwater set around a small courtyard with a plaque to Lord Palmerston in the centre. There was some controversy on the reason for the plaque's position in the courtyard till someone discovered that it had simply been left here by a workman who could not be bothered to put it anywhere else.

The seclusion of Pickering Place made it a favourite place for duels in the early nineteenth century but some historians consider its most interesting feature is the covered passage that leads to it. The half-timbered wall and roof are the last of the cowshed built to provide fresh milk for Henry VIII's Court at the Palace across the road.

No. 6 St James's also dates from around 1700 and Lock's have sold hats here since 1765 to such customers as Byron, Nelson and Wellington. One of their more short-tempered patrons was the Earl of Rosebery who had little time for the niceties of shopping. When he decided he needed a new top-hat, he just opened the shop-door, shouted 'Hat!' as loudly as he could and expected a perfectly-fitting new model to be placed in his hand before the echoes died away.

Lock's made the first bowler hat for William Coke, who wanted something strong enough to cope with the demands of the hunting field. He accepted the model they produced after standing on it to test its strength. The name 'bowler' comes from the firm of William

Bowler who made it to Lock's specifications, but Lock's always invoice it as a 'Coke'.

King Street, on the right, has been the home of Christie's, the auctioneers, since 1823. Across the road from Christie's is Almack House, built on the site of Almack's Assembly Rooms. Almack's was the most exclusive resort in eighteenth-century London and entry was strictly controlled by seven ladies of rank who used their position to blackball anyone who had offended them. It became a commonplace for dukes and their duchesses to dine with their sovereign but be refused entry to Almack's. Henry Luttrell wrote:

If once to Almack's you belong,
Like monarchs you can do no wrong;
But banished thence on Wednesday night,
By Jove, you can do nothing right.

Their regime was so strict that the Duke of Wellington was refused admission twice. On the first occasion he was not admitted because he was wearing trousers rather than the required knee-breeches. On the second occasion he arrived late after a Privy Council. The hostesses felt that midnight was the latest time anybody should be allowed entry and the Duke arrived too late. The Prince Regent himself arrived a few minutes later and was similarly excluded.

Almack's made two important contributions to London's social life. In 1815 the Marquis of Worcester, Clanranald Macdonald, Lady Jersey and Lady Worcester danced the first quadrille seen in England. Six months later, the same quartet gave the first performance in this country of the waltz.

No. 69 St James's Street, across the road from King Street, is the Carlton Club and the television camera outside the door shows the security measures that are now necessary for the club where the Prime Minister is a member. The building was originally Arthur's Club, founded in 1811. The members paid a joint subscription for the upkeep of Kitty Fischer, London's leading prostitute, although the term courtesan was preferred by her clients.

It was a member of Arthur's Club who looked back from the respectability of Victorian England to the full-blooded emotions of the St James's Street he had known in the eighteenth century:

The dear old street of clubs and cribs,
As north and south it stretches,
Still smacks of William's pungent quips
And Gillray's fiercer sketches.
The quaint old dress, the grand old style,
The mots, the racy stories,
The wine, the dice – the wit, the bile,
The hate of Whigs and Tories.

The Carlton Club moved here in 1941 after their old clubhouse in Pall Mall was bombed. It is one of the few clubs that has remained strongly political. Bonar Law was elected leader of the Conservative Party in the Carlton in 1911; the famous decision to withdraw from Lloyd George's Coalition Government was made here in 1922. Balfour told Lord Curzon: 'The Carlton is a beastly club, infected by the worst of the species, i.e. the bore political. But you are quite right to belong to it. It must be suffered like long hours and constituents as a necessary, though disagreeable accompaniment to a political career.'

St James's Place, like Buckingham Street off the Strand, is one of those London backwaters that can claim a famous resident for every house. Chopin stayed at No. 4, Cruikshank lived at No. 11 and Gibbon complained bitterly at the £2 a week rent he was asked for No. 10. Lord Cochrane, the original of C. S. Forester's 'Captain Hornblower', lived at No. 34, Elgar at No. 37 and Captain Marryat at No. 38. No. 28 was the residence of William Huskisson, the politician renowned as the finest economist but most awkward man in London. His contemporaries felt it appropriate that he should have the unhappy distinction of being the first man to be killed by a railway engine, an incident caused by his tripping over a rail and falling into the path of a train at the opening of the Liverpool and Manchester Railway in 1830.

No. 22 (now rebuilt) was the home of Samuel Rogers, the banker, poet and novelist. Rogers lived from 1760 till 1855 and spent the latter years of his life gathering around him all the writers of the time. He provided a link between the London of Dr Johnson and Boswell through the Regency and Napoleonic Wars to the age of Dickens and the Great Exhibition.

Rogers's dinner parties were famous. Wellington traced out his dispositions at Waterloo on the table that a fellow guest, Chantrey, proudly announced he had made as an apprentice fifty years before. Byron met Thomas Moore for the first time at Rogers's house and Madame de Stael had her famous argument with Sheridan there. At one dinner Rogers sat down with Sydney Smith, Tom Moore, Wordsworth, Washington Irving and Walter Scott, keeping them enthralled with his stories of Dr Johnson and the men who had led the literature of the eighteenth century as his audience were doing in the nineteenth.

Rogers was offered the post of Poet Laureate but refused it on the grounds of age. He encouraged others who qualified for the honour, and gave practical assistance when it was needed. When Wordsworth accepted the Laureateship, he was very concerned to learn that the ceremony involved wearing Court dress with knee breeches, which he did not possess. Rogers immediately lent Wordsworth his own Court dress, sending him off to the Palace with a sword borrowed from Sir Humphrey Davy.

When Tennyson succeeded to the position on Wordsworth's death, he found himself in the same difficulty. He came to Rogers for advice, who immediately produced the same suit that Wordsworth had worn seven years previously. Tennyson was a good deal larger than

Rogers but a few judicious cuttings of seams enabled him to squeeze into the coat and breeches. He left for the Palace with the good wishes of his friends and dire warnings on what would happen if he bowed too deeply to his sovereign.

Brooks's Club stands between No. 60 and No. 61 St James's Street but has no number of its own. It is simply 'Brooks's Club, St James's Street'. Founded in 1764 by Almack, Brooks's soon became famous for heavy gambling. Fortunes were won or lost in a night and Charles James Fox once had to borrow money from the waiters to get home. Black velvet (a drink made from champagne and stout) is reputed to have been invented at Brooks's Club in 1861 to mourn the death of the Prince Consort. The betting book is still in use although the wagers nowadays are for modest amounts. A modern bet was whether the maître d'hotel of the Royal Spithead Club had or had not been educated at Eton and was the son of a bishop. (He had been and he was.)

The splendidly-named Boodle's Club at No. 28 was also founded by Almack although its elegant clubhouse was rebuilt in 1775. Almack made a fortune from the clubs he founded, mostly from the percentage all winners were expected to pay the house. He made a second income from his habit of always cleaning the main rooms himself and picking up the coins that had rolled into corners. Boodle's became a popular club with country squires; it was said that anyone calling for 'Sir John' would immediately find himself surrounded by members.

In common with every other large street in London, St James's has traffic islands in the middle of the road for pedestrians to take refuge from the vehicles whirling by on either side. Those we see today were installed in the 1930s but the first was erected by Colonel Pierrepoint in 1864. Annoyed by the heavy traffic that hindered his crossing St James's to his club, the colonel paid for an island to be built in the middle of the road and boasted to his friends how much safer he had made the crossing.

Three weeks later, as he walked the final few yards, his pride became his undoing. He looked fondly over his shoulder at his invention and was run over by a hansom-cab.

Our last club is White's at No. 37, the oldest and grandest club of all. Lord Boothby once said that being elected to White's as a young man was as great an honour as being awarded the Garter. The famous bow window, installed in 1811, was the favourite spot for Beau Brummell to show off his elegance to an admiring London. Brummell confirmed his break with the Prince Regent outside White's as he was walking with Lord Alvanley. The Prince Regent walked towards them and Alvanley left Brummell to exchange a few words with him. On his return, Brummell asked him in tones clearly intended to be heard by the Prince: 'Who is your fat friend?'

White's reputation for heavy gambling spread across the Atlantic. In 1820 the American ambassador remarked that he had heard that the lights of White's burned all night. 'Yes,' said a member, 'I do not think they have been out since the reign of Charles II.' The members had the reputation of betting on anything no matter how ridiculous it might be. Lord Arlington bet £3000 on which of two raindrops would reach the bottom of the window first; on another occasion a man collapsed on the club steps and the members immediately started betting on whether he would live or die. A surgeon trying to assist the sick man was furiously assailed by the members who said they would allow no foul play of that kind and he was to leave the man alone.

The White's tradition is still alive. One post-war bet was whether a member could hit a golf ball from the Royal Exchange to the steps of White's in less than 1000 strokes. He did it in 279. Another wager depended on the aerofoil properties of the club's saucers; a member bet that he could skim them from the steps of White's through the windows of the building across the road.

This walk ends with the moral that even a club as

old and exclusive as White's can make mistakes. In the nineteenth century the freehold of the site came up for sale and the members tried to buy it. They were outbid by the first Lord Cheylesmore whom the members had blackballed some years before. He allowed them to stay but increased their rent considerably. When he died his son was immediately elected a member but, out of loyalty to his father, refused to join and put up the rent yet again. It was not until 1927, when the first Lord Cheylesmore's grandson went to live in Canada, that the members were able to buy their clubhouse.

THIRTEENTH ♦ WALK

Trafalgar Square, The Mall and St James's Park

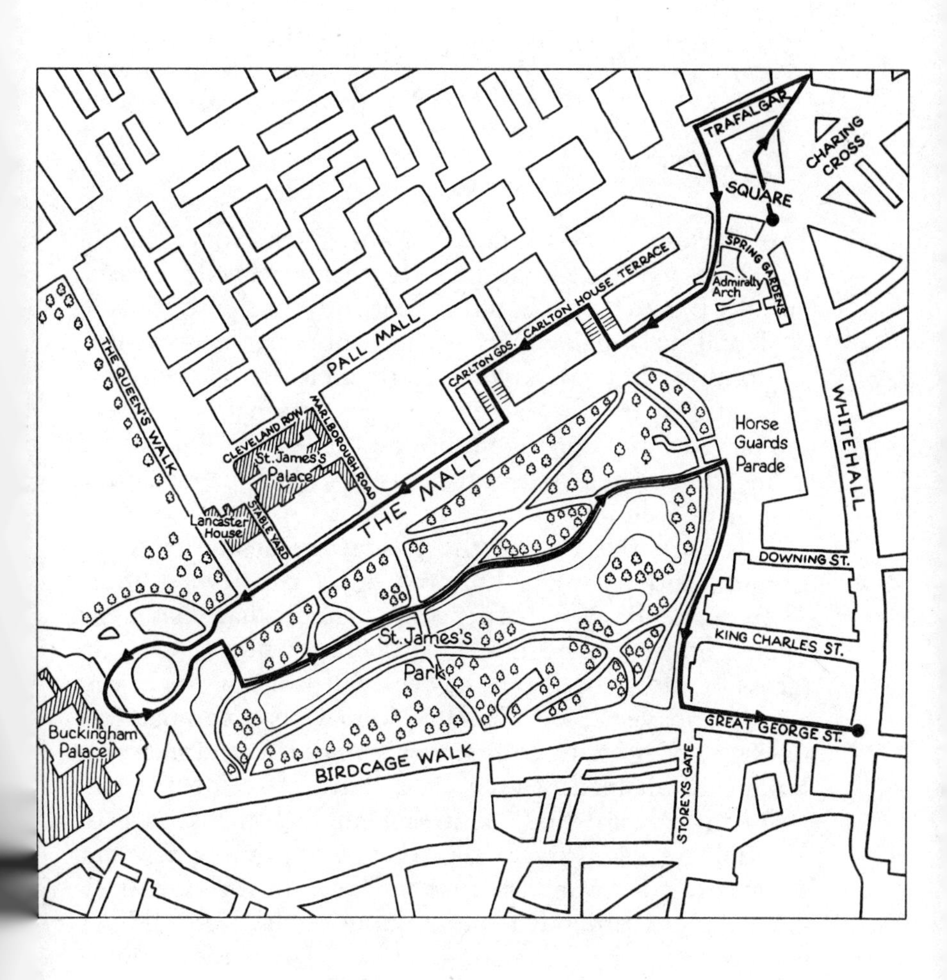

THIRTEENTH ♦ WALK

Trafalgar Square, The Mall and St James's Park

The Thirteenth Walk follows another route from Charing Cross to Parliament Square. It begins outside Drummond's Bank (Royal Bank of Scotland) on the south side of Trafalgar Square. This is the panorama every visitor to London remembers: South Africa House on the right, St Martin-in-the-Fields beyond, the National Gallery on the far side and Canada House on the left. In the middle is the Square itself, where tourists feed the pigeons beside Nelson's Column.

This corner is one of the busiest traffic junctions of London and over five hundred buses pass every hour. They make it even harder to imagine what the scene looked like at the beginning of the last century. Charing Cross beside us has been the centre of London for nearly a thousand years, but Trafalgar Square is a comparative newcomer. As with so many of London's landmarks, it was never planned; it grew by a series of accidents.

When Edward the Confessor moved the Court to Westminster (see First Walk), there was nothing here but a few cottages around the road junction. In 1377 Geoffrey Chaucer superintended the building of the Royal Mews to house Richard II's falcons and hawks. The Mews occupied the site where the National Gallery stands now and was extended in 1534 when Henry VIII transferred his horses here after their stables at St John's Wood were burnt down. Londoners saw no reason to stop using the old name, so the word 'mews' gradually changed to its present meaning as somewhere to keep horses.

St Martin-in-the-Fields came next, the parish church authorised by Henry VIII when he grew tired of funeral processions passing through Whitehall Palace on their way to St Margaret's at Westminster. As the new estates of St James's and Mayfair became fashionable, this section of London was left behind. The Royal stables became a barracks and the area in front of it gradually filled up with squalid shanties and taverns, interspersed with dark alleys and courtyards. Londoners called it 'The Bermudas' from the lawlessness of those who lived there, or 'Porridge Island', the supposed diet of the beggars who made it their home.

The National Gallery

The first change came in 1829, when John Nash proposed opening the site to make it easier to get from Charing Cross to the new Regent Street he was building north from St James's Park. He also suggested that such an open site would be suitable for the National Gallery which had been established a few years before. The idea received Government approval and the site was cleared. It was the start of the Square we see today, but planners and architects have argued over it ever since – and the Square is still unfinished one hundred and sixty years later.

The commission for the National Gallery was given to William Wilkins who completed it in 1838. The Gallery was immediately derided by every architect and designer in London and the newspapers vied with each other in the scorn they poured upon it. The expressions of outrage continued for years, and concentrated on the roof-line with its 'pepper-pots' which everybody agreed looked like 'the clock and vases on a suburban mantelpiece, but far less useful'. In 1862, Dickens' weekly paper *All The Year Round* renewed the attack with an article which concluded: 'This unhappy structure may be said to have everything it ought not to have, and nothing which it ought to have. It possesses windows without glass, a cupola without size, a portico without height, pepper-boxes without pepper, and the finest site in Europe without anything to show upon it.'

From the south side of the Square it is easy to see why the critics disliked the Gallery, but Londoners have grown accustomed to it and Wilkins did have certain problems. He was commissioned to build a picture gallery in any way he liked, with only six provisos.

Firstly, it must have a roof-line similar in appearance to the old stables it replaced. (This accounts for the 'pepper-pots' at either end which had been foul-air vents from the old stables.)

Secondly, the roof-line was to be the same height as that of St Martin's church across the road. (This meant Wilkins was unable to add the extra floor he had proposed to give the building the correct proportional height.)

Thirdly, the Gallery was to be built further back than the old stables it had replaced, to give a clear view of the front of St Martin's church.

Fourthly, the Gallery was to leave room behind for a new barracks. (This forced Wilkins to design a thin structure half the depth he had proposed.)

Fifthly, he was to make use of the pillars from the recently demolished Carlton House in whatever manner he could devise.

Sixthly, he was to leave a right of way for the public up one side of the Gallery and a passage for the Guards to reach the barracks on the other. (This meant he could not compensate for the lack of height or depth of the building.)

The arguments have been revived in the 1980s by the proposal to build an extension to the Gallery. The Prince of Wales voiced the views of many when he described the first plans as 'a monstrous carbuncle on the face of a much loved and elegant friend'. The Prince saw what the planners and architects had ignored. It is not mentioned in any of the hundreds of guide-books about London, but it is the feature that makes the Square so attractive to visitors and Londoners alike.

Around the roof of St Martin's church is a balustrade. The National Gallery to its left has the same balustrade at a matching height running along the north side of the Square. To the right of the church, South Africa House continues the balustrade down the eastern side, while Canada House matches it on the west. Each of the four buildings has columns overlooking the Square. It is this combination of balustrade and pillars around three sides that gives the Square the visual unity so much admired.

Nelson's Column

While all the fuss was being made about the Gallery, the Square was being laid out. The newspapers began to ask what it was to be used for and it became clear that the authorities were not sure. Those who had travelled to Europe spoke of it as London's answer to the Piazza San Marco in Venice or to the great Places that adorned Paris. One idea that received support was that it should be a memorial to the reigning monarch, William IV. Another proposal was to fill the entire Square with a pyramid of the same height as St Paul's (twice the height of the present column) as a memorial to the dead of the Napoleonic Wars.

A third suggestion developed the theme of the National Gallery and proposed building a Colosseum of the Arts in the Square. This was to be the same shape and dimensions as the Colosseum at Rome and all the learned societies were to share it (whether they liked it or not). This propinquity, it was felt, would produce friendship and common understanding amongst the rival artists, sculptors, surgeons, scientists and architects, which would soon bring about a new Golden Age of educational progress and advancement in every field of human endeavour.

It was not until 1837, four years after the Square had

been laid out, that the suggestion was made to erect a memorial to Nelson. It received immediate support and no fewer than 120 designs were submitted. They included rebuilding the Parthenon with Nelson on the top, a Gothic cathedral also with Nelson on the top, and a stone globe so positioned that Britain appeared on the top surface with Nelson standing on the spot where London should be. The most imaginative idea was to rebuild Nelson's ship, the *Victory*, in stone, twice life-size with every member of the crew depicted in bronze in the position he was at the moment Nelson was hit.

It took a year to decide on the present column, copied from the pillars of the temple of Mars Ultor in Rome. The Committee accepted the design by William Railton, but made one stipulation. A few years before, the Duke of York's Column had been erected in Pall Mall; although the Duke had been Commander-in-Chief of the Army, the Committee wanted to ensure no one could compare his ability with Nelson's. Railton was therefore instructed to design a column on which Nelson would be at least 30 feet higher than the Duke. Railton agreed and, to be on the safe side, added a few more feet on his own account. The result is that Nelson now stands 170 feet up in the air, compared with the Duke's 120 feet.

From then on matters proceeded at a leisurely pace. Some of the delay arose from the decision to split the task amongst half a dozen artists but *Punch* had good cause to criticise progress. The design was agreed in 1838, but the column was not built till 1842. The capital, completed the same year, was made of bronze from the guns of the *Royal George*.

This decision caused some sardonic comment in the Navy, because the *Royal George* was the most inappropriate ship that could have been chosen. The ship had sunk in the most ignominious of circumstances; she had capsized while tied up in harbour. This usually meant automatic court-martial for the captain – and in this case the captain of the unfortunate ship had been Nelson himself. Nevertheless, the designer of the capital, happy to see his part completed, celebrated by holding a dinner party for fourteen guests on top of the capital. (One can only admire their courage in accepting.)

The statue of Nelson was put up the following year (1843) amidst great publicity, but was hurriedly taken down again because the sections did not fit. It was finally set in position a few months later but the authorities kept the event quiet till they were sure it was successful.

Things then slowed even further and London had to wait another six years, till 1849, for the panels to be placed in position around the base. There was some excuse for this delay, because bronze panels of this size had never been done before. They represent Nelson's four great battles: Cape St Vincent, the Nile, Copenhagen and Trafalgar. The Trafalgar panel, by Carew, is larger than the others; for twenty years it was the largest bronze panel in Europe.

The four lions at the base arrived eighteen years after the panels, in 1867. Cartoonists and music-hall comedians made jokes about the delay, but the authorities could do little about it. They had rejected the lions produced in 1859 by the chosen sculptor and had given the commission to Sir Edwin Landseer, the most popular artist of the day.

Landseer was most reluctant to undertake the job because, as he pointed out repeatedly to the authorities, he was a painter, not a sculptor. Eventually the matter was decided by the Queen herself, who let Landseer know she 'was most anxious' that he should accept. Landseer was a brilliant animal painter and had shown his first picture at the Royal Academy when he was thirteen. He had acquired much of his skill from dissecting animals as a child and decided to do the same with the lions. The authorities were a trifle taken aback since it meant more delay, but Landseer was firm. He placed an order with the London Zoo for the next dead lion that became available and warned the authorities that nothing would happen till it arrived.

Two years went by before the Zoo was able to deliver the dead lion he had asked for. During that time Landseer practised modelling figures but also started to show signs of the mental instability that was to stay with him till his death. He began work on the lion at once but his powers of concentration were fading rapidly. Reports vary as to how long his family had to endure the sight and smell of the decaying carcass, but it was certainly long enough for his friends to become extremely reluctant to visit him. The lion was modelled and remodelled before Landseer would let it be cast. He finished it in 1866 and the lions appeared the following year.

Trafalgar Square had been laid out thirty years before Landseer's lions arrived, but it was still incomplete – and it is still incomplete today. At the right-hand end of the balustrade around the Square is an equestrian statue of George IV. The matching left-hand plinth is empty, as it has been since 1836.

There are two more things to look at before we leave this corner of Drummond's Bank. This the best angle to admire St Martin-in-the-Fields, the oldest building in the Square. The architectural motif of the balustrade on its roof has been faithfully repeated around the square by later architects, but this is only one of its features.

Built by James Gibbs in 1724, it replaced the old church that Henry VIII had upgraded to become the parish church for those who lived north of Charing Cross. Gibbs built three others in London at the same period, all on the same basic design. They caused a sensation. We are used to the design today but St Martin's, like Inigo Jones's Banqueting Hall in Whitehall, is the first of its kind. And, like the Banqueting Hall, it has been copied up and down the country ever since.

What Gibbs did was to build the steeple over the west end of the church, rather than the east end, and place it over a temple portico of tall columns. It became the talk of London and every architect in the country adopted the design. It became even more popular in America, when three of Gibbs's assistants went to New England and introduced 'the new English style' of church. As the settlers moved west across the United States, they took the design with them. It was simple to construct and could be built as easily in timber as in stone or brick. There are now thousands of churches across America in this style, all of them imitations of St Martin's.

Drummond's Bank

The bank immediately beside us stands on the site of Oliver Cromwell's house. Andrew Drummond started banking at Charing Cross in 1717. The business began inauspiciously because Scotsmen had become unpopular in London after the Jacobite Rising of 1715. He persevered and, by 1740, had acquired the bank account of George II. Ironically, he lost the Royal account a few years later and made his fortune by doing so.

When Bonnie Prince Charlie landed to lead the second Jacobite Rising in 1745, Drummond's were suspected of being sympathetic to the Jacobite cause. King George withdrew his money from the bank, an example followed by others, and Drummond's were on the verge of bankruptcy. The outcome proved very different. All the Scotsmen in London saw the King's action as an attack on them and proceeded to pour their money into Drummond's as a sign of support. Within a week it had become one of the richest banks in London and never looked back.

Although Drummond's has been taken over by a larger group, it sticks to the old ways. The banking hall is a dignified room with a splendid long-case clock, walnut furniture and portraits of the Drummond family around the walls. It is the last bank in London to provide quill pens for its customers. Ballpoint pens are available at the cashiers' counters but the centre table has pewter inkwells and goose-quill pens. They do not write smoothly though they are sharpened regularly (and the author always uses them).

A request to a bank attendant to see the lion's bones will be met by an invitation to step around the corner from the banking hall. In the adjoining room are glass cases containing the remains of Trafalgar Square's earliest inhabitants. They are the bones of the prehistoric animals discovered when the present building was constructed in 1877. They include a mammoth, a rhinoceros and a lion, which came to drink at the watercourse that still flows under Trafalgar Square.

Across the Square

Walk across the road to the middle of the Square. The balustrade running down the slope on the left ends with a pillar surmounted by a peculiar twelve-sided lamp. The tradition has grown up that it came from the *Victory*, Nelson's flag-ship. It is a nice story but untrue. The lamps are another example of the dilatoriness that has characterised the planning of the Square. This is one of the ten Panopticon lamps set around the Square in 1842. The inventor claimed the twelve-sided glass lanterns would give the maximum amount of light and the authorities put them here as an experiment. A decision is still awaited.

The matching Panopticon lamp on the right-hand side stands on top of London's smallest police station. In 1887 the Square was the scene of the Bloody Sunday riot when a Socialist rally was held in defiance of the Home Secretary's ban. Two people were killed and Londoners thought a revolution was about to break out. The police had the pillar bored out to provide them with a secure point of observation over the Square.

The bollards around the base of Nelson's column repeat the naval theme. They are carved in the shape of ships' capstans, interspersed with iron bollards in the shape of gun-barrels. There are pigeons everywhere, descendants of the rock doves the Romans brought to

England. They soon learnt to build their nests on the ledges and crevices of London's buildings and in 1389 Chaucer found them a nuisance when he was in charge of the Mews here.

A large scar defaces the western side of the stone plinth of Nelson's Column. It looks like bomb-damage but was caused by some Australian soldiers who set fire to a watchman's hut here on Armistice Night in 1918.

The statue to the left of the column is of Sir Charles Napier, who fought bravely in India and telegraphed his victory at Hyderabad in 1843 with the famous one-word message '*Peccavi*' ('I have Sinde'). Behind Napier are the two fountains, originally supplied by the stream under the Square, but now fed by mains water. They are turned on every day at ten o'clock after the attendant has checked the weather; a combination of full jets from the fountains and a windy day can clear the Square in seconds.

Set against the wall on the north side of the Square are busts to three other Naval heroes. Admirals Jellicoe and Beatty won fame in the First World War and their busts were set up here together in 1948. Because Jellicoe was the senior of the two, he is on the right of Beatty. Cunningham won his victories in the Second War and there were some protests when his bust was placed on Jellicoe's right. It was pointed out that Cunningham would never have agreed to such a breach of Service etiquette.

Immediately below the three busts is a set of Imperial measures of length, set out in brass along the pavement. They show the old inch, foot, yard and the now legendary rod, pole or perch (5½ yards).

At the top of the steps is the controversial statue of George IV, dressed in a Roman toga and looking most uncomfortable on his horse. Many guide-books point out the sculptor's error in omitting the stirrups, but the sculptor was right. George IV followed the practice of having himself portrayed as a Roman emperor of the Augustan period; stirrups were not used by the Romans till two hundred years later.

The pose of the horse is another matter. Equestrian statues normally portray the rider reining in a spirited steed, but George IV's horse is clearly not intending to go anywhere. The reason is that the King was fat and bloated when he posed for the statue and was unwilling to sit on any horse that would need physical effort to control it.

When the sculptor, Chantrey, accepted the commission from the King, the agreement was that one third of the fee should be paid immediately, the remaining two thirds on completion. The King died in 1830, just as Chantrey finished the statue, and he found that the King's legal obligations had died with him. George IV had become unpopular in his last years and nobody saw any reason to honour agreements incurred by his vanity.

Chantrey took the matter to the courts, but received no satisfaction till 1840, when the Government reluctantly agreed to pay another third of the fee. Chantrey died the following year and his widow continued the battle. Eventually, in 1843, the outstanding money was paid on the personal orders of Queen Victoria.

The next question was where to put the statue. George IV had intended it to stand on the top of Marble Arch. The Arch was built as the ceremonial entrance to the Palace, but proved too narrow for the State Coach and was moved to the corner of Oxford Street and Hyde Park. The authorities therefore placed the statue in Trafalgar Square, where it was greeted with derision by every art critic. An official statement was hurriedly issued saying the location was a temporary measure; the statue would be moved to a more suitable position as soon as one was found. The only action taken in the next fifty years was the placing of an identification tablet on the plinth in 1908. As with the Panopticon lamps, a decision is still awaited.

South Africa House, running down the east side of the Square, was built in 1935 by Sir Herbert Baker, who seems to have cornered the market in Imperial buildings.

He helped Lutyens design New Delhi, built the Government Building in Pretoria, three cathedrals in South Africa, and India House along the Strand as well as the Bank of England. He liked identifying his buildings with appropriate symbols and the keystones of South Africa House are decorated with elephants, lions and gazelles.

St Martin-in-the-Fields

St Martin's was once the centre of the largest parish in London, stretching from Covent Garden to Hyde Park. Separate parishes were created within its boundaries later but it saw the burials of such people as Nell Gwynn, who left a legacy to the bell-ringers, Thomas Chippendale, Jack Shepherd the famous highwayman and the first Sir Winston Churchill, whose son became Duke of Marlborough.

Soon after the present church was built in 1724, a trapeze-artist called Violante persuaded the vestry to let him use the steeple to demonstrate his 'death-slide'. He tied a rope from the top of the steeple across the road to where the statue of George IV now stands. In front of an enormous crowd, which included the Royal Family, he slid all the way down head first, arms outstretched. It is often seen today at military displays, but it caused a sensation then. Violante made a fortune repeating the feat around the country until the rash of imitators spoiled the novelty.

The pediment is decorated with the coat of arms of George I because St Martin's is the parish church of St James's Palace where George I had his Court. A small crown on the steeple is another assertion of royal status and the clock face is blue and gilt, following an edict laid down by Henry VIII. As with most clocks, the figure four is represented by 'IIII', not 'IV', a fashion set by Louis XIV to avoid confusion with the 'VI' of six. Gibbs 'signed' the church by inscribing his name in small letters across the portico.

The link with royalty still exists. Although most royal

ceremonies take place at St Paul's or Westminster Abbey, this is still the parish church for Buckingham Palace and St James's. The births, deaths and marriages in both palaces are recorded in the registers here.

George I did go some way to earning the coat of arms on the pediment. He gave £100 to help with the building and accepted the post of churchwarden. On the advice of his ministers he attended parish meetings, which must have been extremely tedious because he spoke no English. He resigned after a short time but found that being King did him little good in trying to escape his parochial responsibilities. The parish vestry fined him £1500 for resigning and bought a splendid organ with the money.

On the north side of the church are steps leading up to a side doorway. This is the entrance used by the Royal Family when they attend the church; the crown over the doorway was placed there in the 1920s at the suggestion of Queen Mary. Apart from being the parish church for Buckingham Palace and St James's, St Martin's is one of the three churches in England entitled to fly the White Ensign. It is the official church of the Admiralty, a tradition started when the Admiralty moved to Whitehall and the Lords Commissioner came to give thanks after naval victories.

St Martin's became famous in the 1920s when the rector, Dick Sheppard, opened the crypt as a shelter for vagrants. The BBC gave their first broadcast of a church service here in 1924 and Myra Hess inaugurated the famous lunch-time concerts during the last war, a tradition that continues today.

Over the last century the road in front of the church was widened so much that the pavement now encroaches on St Martin's broad steps. Because of the legal implications, the church authorities threatened to enclose the steps with railings, which would make the pavement unusable. After lengthy negotiations a compromise was reached whereby the local authority accepted responsibility for maintaining the lower flights. Cynical parishioners assert it is only too easy to recognise the boundary by the well-maintained steps above it and the poorly-kept stones below.

St Martin's looks across to the wall of the National Portrait Gallery with its pediment adorned by a seated figure. Like the statue of George IV nearby, it was carved for the Marble Arch. The original figure represented naval power and showed Britannia in her glory, with Nelson's head carved on the shield. When the Marble Arch was moved to Hyde Park, Britannia was taken down and given a few tactful alterations before reappearing here as Minerva, patron of the arts.

The statue of George Washington in front of the National Gallery is a copy of one done from life. Washington is shown as the civil leader of his country, with his general's sword discarded beside him. Although he is shown in contemporary dress, the sculptor could not resist one classical tradition. Washington's hand rests on a bundle of fasces, the sign of authority of a Roman magistrate. There are thirteen sticks in the bundle, one for each of the States Washington led to independence.

The National Gallery

Ruskin believed the view from the top of the National Gallery steps equalled that of the Piazza San Marco in Venice. Few would agree with him today, but it does provide a superb view down Whitehall to the Palace of Westminster at the end.

This walk does not include a tour of the National Gallery, but one section is all too often overlooked, literally. Although walked on by hundreds every day, few people stop to admire it. The steps behind the ticket kiosk inside the Gallery lead up to a central landing. From here three more sets of steps lead to the east, north and west vestibules. Each landing has a mosaic floor laid by Boris Anrep illustrating subjects from every section of English life.

Anrep started in 1928 with the North Vestibule mosaic

which shows The Labours of Life. The panels include a sculptor representing Art and a man washing a pig to illustrate Farming. A child's slate with various book titles stands for Letters, while a student looking at a skeleton of a dinosaur in the South Kensington Museum depicts Science. The East Vestibule opposite shows The Pleasures of Life and includes a Christmas pudding, cricket, football, a mud pie (for children) and a girl cyclist representing Speed.

The lower landing contains The Awakening of the Muses and the eleven panels include Greta Garbo as Melpomene, Countess Jowitt as Thalia, Virginia Woolf as Clio, Sir Osbert Sitwell as Apollo and Clive Bell as Bacchus.

The most amusing mosaics are those on the North Landing: The Modern Virtues. Compromise is shown by the actress Loretta Young wearing the cap of Liberty as well as a crown; Curiosity has Lord Rutherford splitting the atom; Sir Winston Churchill on the cliffs of Dover is Defiance and Sixth Sense is portrayed by Dame Edith Sitwell, reading a book of poems while crossing a chasm full of terrifying animals.

The statue on the right of the National Gallery steps is of James II. It is one of the two bronze statues in London by the greatest English wood-carver, Grinling Gibbons. It was paid for by Tobias Rustat, surgeon-barber to three kings, who was honest enough to admit his wealth owed more to royal patronage than to any skill he had. Such candour was unusual and he was known at Court as: 'a very simple, ignorant but honestly loyal creature'.

We turn left beside Canada House, built in 1827 to house the College of Physicians at one end and the Union Club at the other. The railings are interrupted a little way along by two squat pillars seeming to serve no purpose. They are a survival from the bombing of 1941 which destroyed the side entrance to the Physicians' College. The pillars stood on either side of a bridge which led over the sunken area. During the repair work, the door was replaced by a window and all the facing stonework was replaced at the same time. The work was done so well that the pillars are now the only clue that a doorway ever existed.

Through Admiralty Arch to St James's Park

Admiralty Arch is the official start of the Victoria Memorial, the processional way which runs down to the statue of the Queen in front of Buckingham Palace. Until the Arch was erected in 1910, the only access to this end of the Park was by following the twists of Spring Gardens that still cuts across and behind the Arch.

Spring Gardens was the beat of one of London's legendary characters – the crossing-sweeper who became a millionaire. The story did not come out till around 1870, when a wealthy landowner died and his will revealed that he had been the famous 'Ha'penny crossing-sweeper'. Educated as a barrister, he had no success at his profession and looked for another career. He had noticed that no matter how poor he was, he was still expected to give something to a crossing-sweeper every time he crossed the road and decided to adopt the calling himself.

He became wealthy by refusing any sum of money larger than a halfpenny. If more was offered he refused it or insisted on giving change. People came from all over London to see this phenomenon and bets were laid on whether he could be tempted to break his rule. He refused sovereigns and guineas, even bank-notes; every visitor to London came to see him, each offering a penny or more so they could tell their friends they had also had money returned. After fifteen years the barrister retired to an estate in the country with enough money to keep him for the rest of his life.

The Arch is decorated on the Park side with naval symbols. Navigation is represented on the left by a female figure holding a sextant; Gunnery on the right, cradles a gun-barrel which bears an unfortunate resemblance to a brandy-bottle. The similarity is due to the thickness of the early Armstrong gun-barrel, reinforced to cope with the new explosives.

The Admiralty Arch is another of London's boundaries, separating the Royal Parks from the rest of London. The Parks have their own staff and a separate police force. Their royal status goes back to the time of Henry VIII, who took the land belonging to Westminster Abbey and turned it into four royal hunting parks: St James's Park, Green Park, Hyde Park and Kensington Gardens. A hundred years later, Charles II used St James's Park as the 'royal back-garden' between Whitehall Palace and St James's Palace.

Like the pubs in Whitehall (see First Walk), St James's Park lies 'within the verge of the Palace of Whitehall' and is controlled by the Board of Green Cloth. Until a few years ago it was patrolled by the Green Cloth beadles, dressed in green tail-coats and braided top-hats. Tourist coaches were stopped at Admiralty Arch to ensure their drivers had a pass to enter the Royal Park and ice-cream sellers were forbidden. The last beadle retired ten years ago, but trade vehicles are still not allowed in The Mall, a restriction now enforced by the new Royal Parks Constabulary. Ice-cream can be bought in the Park, but only at the kiosk by the lake – and even that concession is an accident of history.

The Milk Fair

Until well into this century, fresh milk was a luxury in London. It was easy to dilute, difficult to keep fresh (refrigerators were rare) and many of the larger households guaranteed a fresh supply by keeping their own cow in the stables. Before the Admiralty Arch was built, this corner of the Park was occupied by the famous milk-stall, run by two old ladies. They entered the Park every day with three or four cows, set up their stall and sold milk 'fresh from the cow' at a penny a cup. Nobody knew where they came from and nobody queried their right; they were just a traditional London treat for the children.

When plans were being made for the Arch in 1905, officialdom gave the old ladies notice to quit. They refused and sought public support. Every newspaper took up their cause; elderly MPs and peers remembered their own enjoyment of a cup of milk from the stall; even Edward VII, it was said, let it be known that he would be sorry to see the stall go.

Officialdom stuck to its decision; the old ladies had no legal rights whatsoever. If they had, then things might be arranged differently, but, since they did not. . . . The two old ladies then produced their trump card. They did have a legal right, granted by King Charles II himself. They claimed that an ancestor had given Charles I a cup of milk on the way to his execution and his son had given them the licence in gratitude.

Officialdom regarded the tale as highly suspect but found that the family had certainly sold milk at the corner for at least two hundred and fifty years. A compromise was found. Officialdom did not accept the story of Charles I, but allowed the stall to be moved down to the lake – only for the lifetime of the two ladies, however. Everybody was delighted with the happy ending and the stall continued by the lake for another fifteen years. It was replaced by the present refreshment kiosk, still the only place in the Park where a cup of milk can be bought.

The statue of Captain Cook outside the Admiralty was erected as a tribute to his skill and bravery as a sailor and explorer. Cook is portrayed in a heroic pose, one foot on a coil of rope, his eyes fixed on the horizon. It has always been regarded with some cynicism by sailors, who know that Cook would never have been so stupid as to stand on a coil of rope; it is a very dangerous thing to do on board a sailing-ship.

The enormous, windowless red-brick block at the end of the Admiralty has given rise to dozens of rumours since it was built in 1941. One theory is that it was Churchill's secret headquarters, another suggestion is that it was the bomb-proof shelter for the Royal Family. Neither is correct; it was built solely as protection for the Admiralty's communications centre during the last war.

The Royal Parks staff had difficulty trying to disguise its bare walls and eventually resorted to Russian vine, which now covers most of the brickwork. To conceal its presence from German bombers the roof was covered in grass, which has to be cut twice a year. The author, who once worked in the Admiralty, remembers the procedure vividly. A knock on the office door was followed by a workman waving a pass and towing a large lawn-mower behind him. This was pulled across the office floor, out through the window and up metal steps to the roof. At the end of the day, the process was reversed, leaving a trail of grass across the office floor.

The stretch of gravel that runs down the right-hand side of the road is the real Mall, the second of that name. The game of Pall Mall takes its name from *pallo a maglio* (ball to mallet) that originated in Italy. Mary, Queen of Scots brought it from France and her son, James I, passed on his enthusiasm for the game to Charles I.

The game, a mixture of golf and croquet, was played on an alley half a mile long. Charles I laid out a course along the north side of St James's Park which became known as the Pall Mall Alley. After Charles II came to the throne in 1660, houses were built beside the Alley and the King decided to move the course. The old course kept the name Pall Mall and the new course, inside the Park boundary, was given the shorter name of the Mall. As the whole of London society flocked to watch the King play, The Mall became the fashionable name for any open-air promenade and was given to dozens of walks, avenues and parks up and down the country.

Charles II was an excellent player, although it is unlikely that he was as good as Waller portrayed him.

Waller was a poet who had written adulatory verses to Cromwell in a successful attempt to be allowed to return to England. He was equally quick to write sycophantic verses to the new King:

> Here a well-polished Mall gives us the joy,
> To see our Prince his matchless force employ;
> His manly posture and his graceful mien;
> Vigour and youth in all his motions seen.
> No sooner has he touched the flying ball
> But 'tis already halfway down The Mall,
> And such a fury from his arm has got,
> As from a smoking culverin 'twere shot.

The Mall remained the centre of London Fashion for a century. Because it counted as an annexe to the Court, debtors could not be arrested here and young men thronged to the Mall, looking for rich wives or a loan from a friend. It went out of fashion about 1760, superseded by Bond Street and Hyde Park. In 1910, when the new road was built from the Admiralty Arch to Buckingham Palace, the old Mall was left as it is now, a gravelled horse-ride lined with the old gas-lamps that bear the badge of George IV. The new Mall has tall bronze lamps along its length, each surmounted by a model of the *Golden Hind*; Londoners promptly christened them 'Queen Victoria's fleet'.

The pavement at the bottom of the Duke of York's Steps is the best place to see three things that make the Mall different from other roads in London. The first is the unusual red colour of the roadway. This is not to emphasise its royalty nor, as some guides will tell you, to act as a marker for helicopters landing at Buckingham Palace. It is merely the colour of the special material used to make the surface safer for the horses of the Household Cavalry. Horse-shoes slip easily on wet tarmac and this surface is always renewed before major parades.

The second thing to notice is the traffic island in the middle of the road. It looks the same as any other, but it is portable. It is secured to the roadway by large screw-bolts and can be removed easily for State processions.

The third symbol of the Mall's special function is difficult to spot, but plays a vital part in the smooth running of royal ceremonial. Trooping the Colour takes place in June each year and involves hundreds of soldiers, who march to Horse Guards Parade from different barracks around London. The contingents have to assemble on the parade-ground in the correct order and arrive to an exact time-table. To enable them to check their progress, the Mall is divided by markers set in the ground. Directly in line with the Duke of York's Column is a small white metal disc, set beside the kerb. It has the letter 'F' on it; 'C', 'D' and 'E' lie further along the Mall.

Carlton House Terrace

The top of the steps by the Column gives a view up to Piccadilly Circus. This is the first section of the Regent Street scheme of John Nash. Nash became the Prince Regent's favourite architect and had the same grandiose ideas as his patron. He designed three palaces for the Prince and convinced him that London needed a broad avenue that would connect Carlton House to Regent's Park. The Prince agreed and Nash laid out the wide street that sweeps north through London. It aroused opposition from every other architect and builder, mainly because Nash ensured that he designed all the houses along the new route. The famous Nash terraces were built, covered in stucco, and were promptly satirised:

> Augustus at Rome was for building renowned,
> And of marble he left what of bricks he had found.
> But is not our Nash too, a very great master?
> He found us all brick and leaves us all plaster.

Most of Nash's buildings have gone, but he set a precedent that the Crown Commissioners have followed since. All the buildings up Regent Street lie on Crown land and the Commissioners still ensure they are of uniform height and faced with the same material. They provide the same satisfactory uniformity that Nash envisaged nearly two hundred years ago.

The Duke of York's Column commemorates George III's second son, who commanded an expedition against the French in the early part of the Napoleonic Wars. He was the original of the nursery rhyme:

The grand old Duke of York,
He had ten thousand men,
He marched them up to the top of the hill
Then he marched them down again.

The rhyme is an unfair criticism of the Duke's tactics in the Netherlands. He did not win any battles, but managed to bring back his army intact, something which few commanders before him had achieved. The Duke realised that any army camping in the damp marshlands of the Netherlands soon suffered disease. Every previous British expedition to the Netherlands had lost far more men through illness than through battle. The Duke moved his army every few days and kept his troops healthy, although his method of doing so exasperated them.

He became Commander-in-Chief but resigned when his mistress was found to be selling Army commissions, supposedly on his behalf. He died in debt and when the lightning conductor was fitted to the Column, every newspaper asserted it had been put there so he could file his unpaid bills on the spike. The base of the Column should have had a decorative panel on each side, but the money ran out and they were never installed. The newspapers took delight in pointing out that the Duke's memorial was as insolvent as he had been.

The top of the steps beside the Column is guarded by black iron gates, installed here as a safety measure on the orders of Mr Gladstone. In 1852 Gladstone was standing on the steps of the Athenaeum Club, the large building on the left of Waterloo Place in front of us. He heard screams and shouts up Regent Street and saw a runaway horse galloping down the slope, pulling a carriage containing a terrified woman clutching a baby. Gladstone dashed across the road, caught the horse's reins and dragged it to a stop just before it reached the steps. After making sure the woman and baby were safe and the horse under control, he returned to the House of Commons to have a quiet word with the senior Crown Commissioner. The gates were installed a week later.

Proposals have recently been made to remove the gates, but the Crown Commissioners refused. They pointed out that children are still left in cars parked up the slope of Regent Street, handbrakes can still slip, so the gates had better remain.

The left edge of the gates finishes at a low grey wall, on the other side of which is a small open space with a stone in front of a tree. It marks the grave of Giro, the pet dog of Von Ribbentrop, Hitler's Minister for Information, who was appointed ambassador to Britain in 1938. During the war an American writer used the gravestone in an attempt to explain the British character to his readers. He pointed out that, although Von Ribbentrop had become a figure of hatred in Britain, no one would dream of disturbing his dog's gravestone.

The Terrace is lit by a collection of street lamps marked with the cyphers of every sovereign since George IV, painted in the peculiar green shade used by the Crown Commissioners. The Terrace is now the home of learned institutions and public bodies but was once famous for its private residents. To the right, Lady Astor lived at No. 18; No. 16 was Crockford's gambling club; Lord Lonsdale considered he needed both Nos. 14 and 15 to keep up appearances. Earl Grey (of tea fame) was at No. 13 and Gladstone lived at No. 11.

In the 1930s No. 10 was the home of the Union Club, whose members found the great staircase ideal for tobogganing down on tea-trays. The membership included Philip ('Fill-up') Atkinson, who acquired the nickname from his capacity for drink. He entered the club every day at 11 o'clock, drank whisky till 6, then switched to gin till 7 o'clock, when he went home. He died in 1941, not from drink, but from a German bomb attack.

The square in front of the Terrace is Waterloo Place, which has become a gallery for London statues. There are six within a few yards, including Captain Scott whose statue was sculpted by his widow. Another explorer, Franklin, faces him on the other side, who is flanked by Sir John Burgoyne who served in the Army for seventy years.

Follow the terrace to the left, past No. 9 which used to be the German Embassy and No. 6, now the home of the Royal Society founded by Charles II. Palmerston lived at No. 5 and the august Turf Club followed him. No. 1 was the home of Lord Curzon, whose statue stands across the road. Curzon was a brilliant statesman, who would have become Prime Minister if George V had not consided the Premier should be a member of the Commons. He was appointed Viceroy of India at 39, was Foreign Secretary twice and received a marquisate and the Garter.

His personal habits were austere, but he believed in living as a nobleman should. After the First World War he made what he saw as a great concession to the new world around him. He instructed his butler that the footmen might wear trousers if twelve people or less dined at the house. For more than twelve, of course, full livery and knee breeches were *de rigeur*.

His curt manner, caused by the permanent pain he suffered, offended many of his colleagues and he is best remembered now by the rhyme composed by his fellow undergraduates at Oxford:

My name is George Nathaniel Curzon,
I am a most superior person.

My face is pink, my hair is sleek,
I dine at Blenheim once a week.

Curzon's house stands next to Carlton Gardens, which has four houses around it. Napoleon III lived at No. 1 as did Lord Northcliffe after him; Lord Kitchener lived at No. 2 till his death in 1916 and No. 4 was home to both Palmerston and Balfour.

Steps lead down from the Gardens back into the Mall, past a statue of George VI. At the bottom, a few yards to the right, is a mounting-block beside the railings. It stands opposite another of the discreet parade-markers along the kerb of the Mall, the letter 'E' set in a small disc.

The mounting-block has a Government arrowhead just visible on one side, similar to those we saw in Whitehall. The block is here because the lane behind the gateway runs up to the back of what used to be the War Office, before the Royal Automobile Club occupied the site. Queen Victoria insisted on regular reports from the Commander-in-Chief so, every Tuesday, the officer would walk down the lane, mount his horse here and ride down to Buckingham Palace.

For much of Victoria's reign the Commander-in-Chief was the Duke of Cambridge who was renowned for his strong language, although he deplored the habit in others. He once brought a school speech-day to a hilarious conclusion when he finished an impassioned address on the evils of bad language with the words: 'Damn it all, boys – never swear!'

The long wall on the right, guarding the grounds of Marlborough House, has been here for three hundred years. When Nell Gwynne lived in Pall Mall she built a mound against the wall, from which she used to watch the crowds promenading in the Mall. Charles II used to pay his respects to her here and shocked John Evelyn by his public acknowledgement of the woman who cheerfully introduced herself as 'the King's Protestant whore'.

Evelyn's diary records his deep misgivings as he watched them 'have a very familiar discourse'.

Marlborough Road leads off to the right, between St James's Palace and Marlborough House, described in the Twelfth Walk. A plaque on the corner commemorates Queen Mary, and the ornate fountain-monument opposite the Palace courtyard was done by Alfred Gilbert, the creator of Eros. The fountain is in memory of Queen Alexandra, Gilbert's last commission after George V had persuaded him to return from exile on the Continent.

The next opening on the right is Stable Yard which runs up to Clarence House, the home of the Queen Mother. Every morning a little ceremony takes place in this section of the Mall when the mounted Guard come by on their way to Horse Guards Parade. As they pass Clarence House the order of 'Royal Salute' is given, the trumpeter blows the call and, if she is in residence, the Queen Mother acknowledges the salute from her balcony.

The last house along the Mall is Lancaster House, built in 1807 for the Duke of York, whose column we saw earlier. It was bought by the Duke of Sutherland, whose Duchess made it the centre of London's social life. Queen Victoria was a frequent visitor, telling the Duchess: 'I have come from my house to your palace.' It was presented to the nation by Lord Leverhulme and the Queen gave her Coronation Banquet here in 1953.

Queen's Walk, just beyond Lancaster House, is named after Queen Caroline, wife of George II. The Queen, who laid out Kensington Gardens as we see them today, wanted to turn Green Park and St James's Park back into private gardens for the Royal Family. She consulted the Prime Minister, Robert Walpole, and asked how much it would cost. She received the famous reply: 'Three crowns, Madam; England, Scotland and Wales'. She built a pavilion in the middle of Queen's Walk and took breakfast there regularly, much to the discomfort of her ladies-in-waiting. Her liking for fresh air proved her undoing, because it was during a draughty breakfast in the pavilion that she caught the chill which killed her a few days later.

It was on the corner of Queen's Walk that Charlie Chaplin made his first appearance on film. It happened in 1896, when a very early newsreel was being made of the Life Guards trotting down the Mall from Buckingham Palace. Chaplin, then seven years old, waited till the camera started turning and jumped in front of it to give a demonstration of his acrobatic skill before the photographer managed to drive him away.

Green Park, stretching up to Piccadilly, used to be known as Upper St James's Park. It was a popular spot for duels in the eighteenth century, though sometimes they seem to have been fought for the look of the thing rather than to inflict serious injury. One of the more civilised bouts was between Count Alfieri and Lord Ligonier, whose wife was Alfieri's mistress. The duel was a brief one. The challenge was issued at the start of the performance in the Opera House and Alfieri arrived back with his arm in a sling, in time to see the last act. He dismissed inquiries airily: 'My view is that Ligonier did not kill me because he did not want to, and I did not kill him because I did not know how.'

At the end of the Mall is the Victoria Monument, sculpted by Thomas Brock from 2300 tons of marble. The Queen wears her wedding-ring on her right hand in the German manner, in deference to Prince Albert's wishes. She sits surrounded by figures representing such ideals as Victory, Peace, Manufacturing and Agriculture. Most of them are unexceptional, but the sculptor had some difficulty in idealising the Army and Navy on the south side. The effeminate figures portrayed do not inspire thoughts of martial glory.

The present Buckingham Palace, named after the Duke of Buckingham, is the third on the site. James I planted mulberry trees in the grounds, some of which survive, and it is appropriate that the Palace grounds saw the first cup of tea drunk in England in 1663. The Palace was rebuilt by George IV and remodelled again by Queen Victoria. The famous façade in front of us with the balcony where the royal family waves to the crowds, is really the back of the building, which faces towards the gardens on the west.

The balcony was not built till 1912, when the whole of this wing was restyled. The job was accomplished in four months and George V and Queen Mary were delighted with the speed at which it had been done. The entire work-force was invited to lunch and the King insisted on the senior foreman being placed on his right, while the senior brick-layer sat beside the Queen.

Too many people look through the great gates of the Palace and never bother to look at the gates themselves. They are works of art in their own right. The decorative locks show a cheerful imp astride a dragon, whose body vanishes through the top of the lock and reappears with a scaly tail at the bottom.

It was in a first-floor room on the right of this wing that Edward VII had the encounter he joked about for the rest of his reign. In 1905 a porter from a famous art gallery delivered a picture to the Palace and was left alone in the room to unwrap it from its packing. He finished the job and, since no one came to show him out, he seated himself at a writing desk in the corner. The sight of so much stationery, heavily embossed with the awesome words 'Buckingham Palace', was too much for him and he started to write a letter.

As he paused in his writing, he found the King behind him, having come to inspect the new picture. The porter jumped to his feet and stammered out explanations. The King looked at the letter, burst into a shout of laughter and dismissed him with a sovereign. The porter had not written very much, but it was enough to amuse the King:

'Dear Father, Please note change of address. . . .'

Turn back along the Mall and follow the path to the right down to the lake in St James's Park. The lake was laid out originally by Charles II and given its 'romantick' curves by George IV. Like St Martin-in-the-Fields, it helped George I to realise the difference between being an autocratic King of Hanover and a constitutional King of Britain.

On his first morning in England, he was presented with a pair of carp by a servant of the Steward of St James's Park. The King accepted them and, in response to his courtiers' advice, reluctantly gave the man two guineas. He then inquired where the fish had come from. He was horrified to learn they had been caught in the St James's Park lake in front of his own windows. 'What! Am I really expected to give two guineas to the servant of my steward who gives me my carp from my lake in my park?'

The view from the middle of the bridge over the lake is the most romantic in London. The water stretches east towards the fountains and a view of the Horse Guards which has the turrets, towers and pinnacles of the Old War Office and Whitehall Court directly behind it. On a sunny October morning the whole horizon shimmers, an effect produced by the particles in the Portland stone of the three buildings.

This is the second bridge to be installed. Its predecessor, a wooden suspension bridge erected in 1867, lasted a hundred years and its removal dismayed Londoners. The building of the present bridge revived the old question – who was the donor? The Office of Works and the Crown Commissioners have always been reticent on the subject. One historian traced a payment for the first bridge to a firm of solicitors, but got no further. He subsequently discovered that the solicitors handled Queen Victoria's private affairs but the Royal connection has never been confirmed or denied.

The path on the north side of the lake passes the refreshment kiosk, on the site of the old milk-stall where the two old ladies moved in 1905. They stayed till 1922 and then gave up the business, fading out of the history of the Park after nearly three hundred years.

This end of the lake is home to hundreds of wild-fowl, collected from all over the world. The most famous are the pelicans whose well-being occupies the attention of the House of Commons at regular intervals. The first pelicans were presented by the Czar of Russia in 1660 and there have been pelicans at St James's ever since. In 1970 their numbers had fallen to one bird, nicknamed the Lady of the Lake by the newspapers, but known to the bird-keeper more familiarly as Daphne.

During the discussions on the procurement of new pelicans, someone remembered where the first birds had come from. The Russian Ambassador was informed that a brace of pelicans would be as welcome as their predecessors had been three hundred years before and, in due course, some new Russian pelicans arrived.

Unfortunately the new arrivals found difficulty in coping with their new environment. Within a few months they had learnt that small birds were just as tasty as the fish they were supposed to eat. The newspapers spoke of 'Russian aggression' and a Member of Parliament reported that his children had nightmares after seeing a pigeon they were feeding being itself gulped down by a pelican. Diplomacy prevented any drastic measures being taken and the Russian pelicans were discreetly retired to the Zoo 'for a rest'.

The picturesque cottage at the end of the lake stands on Duck Island, where injured birds are cared for. When the poet, St Evremond, was forced to flee France because of his attacks on Mazarin's government, he came to London looking for an appointment at Court. He had powerful friends in London but Charles II relied on the French for financial support and was reluctant to offend Mazarin needlessly. He compromised by giving St Evremond the title of Governor of Duck Island. The appointment saved him further appeals from St Evremond's supporters and amused the French ambassador, who was able to reassure Mazarin on the real significance of St Evremond's grandiose new title.

The path bends right around the end of the lake, leaving Horse Guards Parade on the left. The dark red brick wall on the corner of the Parade protects the garden of No. 10 Downing Street. In 1872 Gladstone was persuaded to allow the garden to be used for the demonstration of a new explosive, whose sponsors asserted it would revolutionise warfare. They claimed it was completely silent and insisted on the demonstration being held in secret.

While Gladstone and his Cabinet watched, the explosive was fastened to a tree and detonated. There was a tremendous bang that shattered every window in Downing Street and nearly produced a dozen vacancies in the House of Commons. Gladstone said nothing, walked over to the Minister who had persuaded him to attend the trial, grunted expressively and went indoors.

In the middle of the patch of grass beside the Downing Street wall is the statue of Lord Mountbatten. If the statue is ever destroyed, there will be no difficulty in tracing its history. The sculptor, Franta Belsky, has left a 'time-capsule' inside Mountbatten's left leg; it consists of a jam-jar containing her bill, newspaper cuttings about the statue and a set of coins.

Behind Mountbatten's statue, in the far corner of the grass is a single lamp-post, the only autographed lamp-post in London. It dates back to the Arts and Crafts movement of William Morris and the Aesthetic movement that followed. The artistic world became concerned with the need to improve the appearance of London's streets and decided to demonstrate how a lamp-post could be both functional and beautiful. They commissioned an artist to design this model and placed it at the bottom of the Downing Street steps where, they hoped, it would inspire Ministers as they walked by on their way to Cabinet meetings. The plinth has cherubs and dolphins on it and the artist's signature can be seen under the dolphin on the Downing Street side.

The next building on the left is the Foreign Office, where the Secretary of State sits behind the large window on the corner of the first floor. The Foreign Office ends at the steps up to King Charles Street, beside the entrance to Churchill's War Rooms. It was the opening of the War Rooms that settled a long-standing argument between Royal Parks staff and the London Tourist Board.

The argument was over the name of the road we are walking along. The Royal Parks do not carry street signs and some maps call it Horse Guards Approach, others Horse Guards Road. Some maps simply ignore it. A senior Whitehall official spent years trying to sort out the problem. Eventually, the opening of the War Rooms gave her the argument she wanted – how can people be expected to find the War Rooms if the road they are in is not marked? The Parks authority accepted her point – but only grudgingly. At the end of the road is a small police lodge on the right. On the railing beside it is (in 1988) a small, discreet wooden sign that reluctantly admits that this is Horse Guards Road. But the map inside the police lodge still calls it Horse Guards Approach!

This corner of the Park is Storey's Gate, the junction of Birdcage Walk, Great George Street, Horse Guards Road (or Approach) and Storey's Gate, running south. A few yards along Great George Street is the old gatekeeper's shelter, a small stone building looking like a petrified telephone box.

Great George Street's short length contains the headquarters of the Institute of Civil Engineers, the Institution of Mechanical Engineers and the Institution of Chartered Surveyors. They are here for a very good reason.

When the Industrial Revolution and the invention of railways transformed the landscape in the nineteenth century, a separate Act of Parliament was required for every new river bridge and every new length of railway line, dock and harbour. The result was that every developer who wanted to promote a new railway company (there were 200 at one time) had to persuade a Member of Parliament to sponsor a Bill. Every Bill needed engineering specifications and land surveys and any amendments needed the same professional attention. From 1840 onwards, so many engineers and surveyors found it worthwhile to have their offices near the House of Commons that Great George Street was the natural place to have their headquarters.

A few more yards brings us to Parliament Square, which is described in the Fourteenth Walk.

FOURTEENTH ♦ WALK

Around Parliament Square

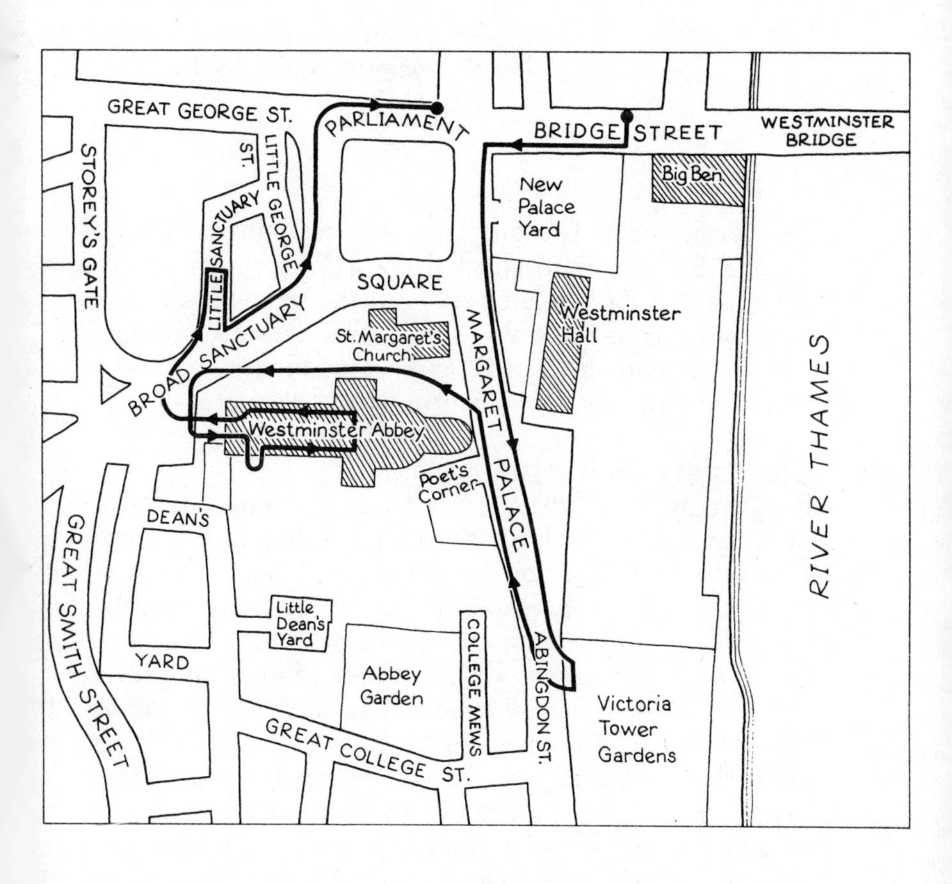

FOURTEENTH ♦ WALK

Around Parliament Square

The Fourteenth Walk begins at Westminster Underground Station, with the Palace of Westminster across the road and Parliament Square to the right. Books have been written about every one of the famous buildings that lie around the Square and we confine ourselves on this walk to some of their more unusual aspects.

The Palace of Westminster

People come from all over the world to admire the Palace of Westminster, the largest Gothic building in the world. Edward the Confessor built the first Palace when he brought the Court here in 1040, so that he could supervise the building of the new Abbey of St Peter. The Palace grew over the years, with the Great Hall as its centre, and was the main Royal residence till Henry VIII moved the Court to Whitehall. The King's councillors, the Houses of Lords and Commons remained and the palace became known as the Houses of Parliament. That form of address will not be found in official publications; although no king has lived here for four hundred years, this is still the Royal Palace of Westminster.

In October 1834 a fire destroyed the old Palace; only the old Hall and the Jewel Tower survived. Months were spent in trying to decide whether the Palace should be rebuilt here or on another site. One party suggested Hyde Park or Green Park, where the Commons could keep an eye on the King; King William IV offered Buckingham Palace itself, while other suggestions were Trafalgar Square or the Temple. The final decision was made, as so many decisions were made at the time, by the Duke of Wellington. The Duke, a realist in everything, pointed out that this site by the river had one great advantage – it could not be surrounded by the London mob – and his advice was followed.

A competition was opened for a new Palace and ninety-seven entries were received although the competitors were only given four months in which to produce complete sets of plans. The competition was won by Charles Barry, who had an assistant called Augustus Pugin, a genius at Gothic design. Nobody knows how much of the final design was Barry's and how much was Pugin's but, in four months, they produced the plans for this tremendous edifice which the whole world comes to admire.

Looking at the Palace from this angle, it is possible to see how nearly Pugin realised his ambition that not a single square foot of space should go undecorated. Every section of wall, tower or roof has ornament on it somewhere and statues of the Kings and Queens of England are set along the walls. The figures on the north wall facing us are the Saxon Kings of England; the remainder, every sovereign from William the Conqueror to Victoria, overlook the river.

The Palace has over 1000 rooms, eleven quadrangles and courtyards, a hundred staircases and two miles of corridors. Legend has it that no single person has ever managed to see them all. In front of us now is London's most famous landmark, the Clock Tower – commonly and incorrectly called Big Ben. Big Ben is not the tower nor is it the clock above the tower, it is the bell that strikes the hours.

Big Ben and the Clock Tower

The Clock Tower, 316 feet high, was intended to be the first section of the Palace to be completed. After the first hundred feet had been built it was realised that no allowance had been made for the five tons of clock mechanism to be lifted up to the top, so the tower had to be taken down and started all over again. It was the beginning of a saga that amused Londoners and infuriated officialdom for the next ten years.

The clock that we see now, with each face 22½ feet in diameter, was to have been made by Mr Vulliamy, a friend of Barry's. Unfortunately for Mr Vulliamy, the matter became public knowledge and a Commission was set up to decide what sort of clock the new Palace should have. The Commission decided that the clock should be accurate to one second in each twenty-four hours, a decision that plunged the clockmakers into gloom because none of them felt capable of achieving it. The matter rested for six years until a Mr Denison developed the machinery and escapement required and made the clock to the specified standard. He then had to wait another five years for the Tower to be completed.

When the clock was eventually installed the whole of London turned out to admire it but, unfortunately, Mr Denison had concentrated too much on its accuracy and not enough on the strength of the mechanism. The minute hands, fourteen feet long and made of cast iron, weighed 2½ tons each and the machinery could not move them. New hands were hurriedly made in gun-metal and the clock was tried again. This time the machinery was able to lift them to the top of the face, but was unable to stop them falling down to the 3 o'clock position on the other side.

In desperation Mr Denison tried hands made of hollow copper tubing, one tenth of the original weight. These proved successful and have been used ever since. The clock is still one of the most accurate in the world; any necessary adjustment is made by placing a small coin on the pendulum which alters the accuracy by ⅖ths of a second per day.

While the clockmakers were agonising over the mechanism of the clock, the bell that was to go inside it was also causing problems. The original specification could have been met by any bell-founder but Mr Denison considered that, if he was competent to design the clock, he could design the bell too. He specified a mixture of copper and tin in proportions that no bellmaker would accept. A firm eventually undertook the casting but refused to take any liability, and the bell was installed in the courtyard here for tests.

The bellfounders had recommended that the weight of the clapper should not exceed 4 cwt but Denison knew better and installed a clapper of 7 cwt that promptly cracked the bell so badly it had to be melted down and recast.

The firm who recast it made sure that it was tested before leaving their works, made equally sure that Mr Denison gave it his official approval, and let it go with a final warning that the weight of the clapper should not exceed 4 cwt. The bell travelled through the streets of London followed by an admiring crowd. It was hung in the tower and at last, in May 1859, the clock and bell began their long partnership. It comes as no surprise to learn that, within a few months, the bell cracked again. Mr Denison, despite all that had happened and all the warnings he had been given, had installed another clapper weighing 7 cwt instead of the 4 cwt that the bellfounders advised. This time the crack was small enough to accept and gave the bell the peculiar tone that the whole world recognises as the sound of Big Ben.

The final episode of the saga was the name 'Big Ben' itself which started as a joke in the House of Commons. Although he had no direct involvement in casting or hanging the bell, the Commissioner of Works, a large gentleman named Sir Benjamin Hall, had to accept all the criticism over the affair. His embarrassment was a constant source of amusement to his political rivals and the matter was raised so often that his nickname became synonymous with the bell itself.

Westminster Hall

On the south side of the courtyard is a building with a steeply pitched roof. This is Westminster Hall, a survival from the old Palace; it escaped the fire of 1834 and the bombing of 1941. The Hall was begun by William Rufus in 1090 and completed by Richard II in 1399, when the work was supervised by Geoffrey Chaucer. State trials were held in the Hall for nearly five hundred years, including the trial of Charles I.

The great feature of the Hall is its mighty hammer-beam roof timbers which give it a span of 67½ feet, the widest span of any unsupported wooden roof in the world. Some of the beams were replaced in 1819 by ships' timbers and in 1913, when the Hall was over 500 years old, it became clear the others needed replacement. Oak beams of that size were and are difficult to procure and there was considerable anxiety over their availability, till someone thought of looking at the invoice of 1394.

The invoice showed that the original beams had been supplied by Courthorpe of Wadhurst in Sussex. The MP for Rye in Sussex in 1913 was Sir George Courthorpe of Wadhurst who informed the authorities that his ancestors had planned for the future. Having sold the original timbers in 1394, they had set aside a plantation to replace them when it became necessary. The trees had been grown, cut and seasoned and were ready for use whenever they were needed.

A common sight in this part of London is tall, impressive gentlemen wearing full evening dress with a large gilt badge suspended around the neck. These are the 'Badge Messengers' of the Houses of Parliament. Their black dress is common to all Parliamentary officials save one. The doorkeeper of the House of Lords wears a bright red frock-coat and is officially known as 'Redcoat'. His is the only Royal appointment in the Palace. It dates from the day Charles I came to Parliament and found no one at the door to greet him. He promptly appointed his own coachman as doorkeeper and the appointment has been considered Royal ever since.

There are hundreds of anecdotes about the Palace and its inhabitants, but space allows room for two only. At a certain time every day, the Lord Chancellor walks through the Palace in solemn procession to preside over the House of Lords. He wears eighteenth-century dress, a gown of black and gold, and has a retinue of attendants to escort him. One day, when Lord Hailsham was Chancellor, his procession approached a group of awed American visitors. As he drew near them, the Chancellor spotted a friend and called to him, using his Christian name. 'Neil!' the Chancellor shouted – and all the Americans did.

A few years ago, a small kiosk was opened in the Palace to sell souvenirs to Members and their visitors. It has become one of the most successful shops in London but it has one problem. Many of the items sold are very small and stock disappears faster than it ought to. Because these are the Houses of Parliament, the committees who discuss the problem never use the world pilfering or theft; that would be far too rude to Members of Parliament and their constituents. The euphemism employed is 'shrinkage of stock'.

The railings surround New Palace Yard, which has been called 'New' since 1098 because Old Palace Yard already existed around the corner. On the pillar at the corner is a yellow lamp, shaped like a lantern. This is the Palace's special system for summoning taxis; if the light is flashing, a Member of Parliament is waiting.

The corner by the railings has always been one of the busiest in London and the first traffic-signals were installed here back in 1858. They were based on the semaphore system which worked very well on the railways but proved to be a failure on the roads. The next experiment in 1926 proved more successful, when Parliament Square saw England's first one-way system.

The Statue of Oliver Cromwell

The railings on the Parliament Square side finish at a low balustrade, overlooking a small patch of grass. In the middle is a statue to Oliver Cromwell, matching the statue of King Charles I that we saw at the other end of Whitehall in the First Walk. Royalists lay wreaths at the foot of King Charles every January 30th; those who believe in the supremacy of Parliament come here to lay wreaths on September 3rd. It is an excellent representation of Cromwell, although the sculptor made an error with the spurs which are upside down.

Cromwell died more than three hundred years ago but his influence lingered a long time. He brought down a Government in 1649; his statue did the same thing three hundred and fifty years later.

In 1895 a Liberal Government was in power led by Lord Rosebery. Rosebery admired Cromwell as a great Parliamentarian and he introduced a Bill proposing that the Government should erect this statue. The idea seemed innocuous enough, but Rosebery had forgotten one important factor – the Irish Members of Parliament. The Liberals had only a small majority in the Commons and relied on the Irish Nationalist MPs to support them against the Conservatives. The Irish Members were prepared to support Rosebery in most things, but they were not prepared to agree to a statue of Cromwell, whose atrocities in Ireland were still vividly remembered.

Rosebery was unwise enough to press the point and the Irish Members took their revenge by voting against the Government or abstaining from voting at all. A series of Bills was defeated and Rosebery realised it was impossible to carry out policies when their success, as it was said at the time, depended on whether Tim Healy had had a good dinner.

Rosebery's administration fell, an election was held and the Conservatives came to power. A year later Rosebery introduced the idea again, but this time the motion included the information that the statue was to be placed on this small patch of grass. This was an entirely different matter so far as the Irish Members were concerned. This patch of grass is known as the Pit and the thought of Cromwell being officially consigned to the Pit struck them as being a splendid idea. The motion was greeted in the Commons with acclamation, especially when they learnt that it was to be paid for by an anonymous donor.

What the Irish Members forgot was that statues have plinths. Rosebery, discovered later to be the anonymous donor, made sure that Cromwell is seen today rising out of the Pit, not sunk in it. But then Rosebery had a habit of getting what he wanted. He may not be especially remembered today as one of the giants of the Victorian age like Disraeli, Palmerston or Gladstone but he died a happy man. When he was at Oxford, he told his friends he had three ambitions: to marry an heiress, to win the Derby and to become Prime Minister.

He got the Premiership, married Baron Rothschild's only daughter and won the Derby three times.

Another few yards brings us to the public entrance of the House of Commons and Old Palace Yard, laid out in the time of Edward the Confessor. Guy Fawkes and his fellow conspirators were executed here, just about where the statue of Richard Coeur de Lion stands.

The statue of Richard has always been very popular, yet it was done originally as a purely speculative venture by Baron Carlo Marocchetti. He had achieved great success on the Continent with statues of royalty but the revolutions of 1848 gave European monarchs something else to think about and his commissions faded away. He came to England and had little success until a friend advised him to study English taste. He did so, produced a plaster cast of this statue and exhibited it at the Great Exhibition of 1851. The speculation paid off. The public was delighted, the Queen herself enraptured, and Marocchetti was told to produce this version in bronze. He went on to enjoy a lucrative career in England, assisted by a series of well-publicised Royal commissions.

At the end of the Palace is the Victoria Tower, thirty feet higher than the Clock Tower, and the tallest Gothic tower in the world. In the gardens immediately beyond is a statue of the famous suffragette, Mrs Emmeline Pankhurst. It represents her accurately as a strong-minded Victorian who was every inch a lady. She is shown as a refined feminine figure, clad in a long coat with fur collar, clasping in her hand the only pair of lorgnettes on any statue in London. At the sides of the memorial are copies of the Suffragettes' badge, a convict's arrow-head superimposed on the portcullis of Westminster.

Although Mrs Pankhurst's Movement had secured votes for women in 1918, this was restricted to women over thirty, and the Suffragettes continued to fight for equality and the right to vote at twenty-one. Mrs Pankhurst, who was herself elected to Parliament, led the struggle and lived just long enough to see the House of Lords approve the Bill.

Over the years the Suffragettes had become bitter enemies of the police but, such was the respect in which Mrs Pankhurst was held, this memorial brought them together. The address at the unveiling was given by Stanley Baldwin and the music was provided, at their own request, by the Metropolitan Police Band. They played under the baton of the ardent feminist composer Dame Ethel Smyth who had conducted her own marches with a toothbrush from her cell in Holloway prison.

The stretch of road from the statue back to Parliament Square confuses tourists because it contains five separate streets without a house number amongst them. This confusion was once common all over London when streets changed their names every hundred yards, depending on the whim of the landowner. Rationalisation was not achieved till 1855 when the Board of Works, to give one example, took a dozen Lanes, Ways and Terraces and made them into Oxford Street.

Perhaps because of their proximity to Parliament, these

streets have kept their identity. The section of road by Mrs Pankhurst's statue is the start of Millbank; the section from Mrs Pankhurst to the corner of the House of Lords is Abingdon Street. From the corner of the House of Lords to a spot twenty yards past Richard I on his horse is Old Palace Yard, while the roadway up to Oliver Cromwell's statue is St Margaret Street. The final section, to the corner of Bridge Street, is either Old Palace Yard (on the right side) or Parliament Square (on the left).

The old Jewel Tower, on the patch of grass to the left of the road, is a survivor from the old Palace. The Tower dates from 1365 and, although its moat has recently been re-dug, it is still watered by one of the streams that separated the old Isle of Thorney from London a thousand years ago.

St Margaret's Church

A path beyond the Jewel Tower leads off to the left between St Margaret's Church and the Abbey. St Margaret's, the parish church for Westminster, maintained its independence as a separate establishment from the Abbey till 1973. Its parish boundary marks march across Westminster and there is another assertion of its ancient independence at the corner of the path by St Margaret's west door: an old black lamp-post with the initials 'St M IW' on its base. The 'St M' stands for St Margaret's but nobody, not even the archivist of the Abbey, is sure what 'IW' stand for. The best guess so far is that they stand for James Wyatt, the man who refurbished the Abbey in the early nineteenth century.

Until it was cleared in the 1840s, the grass around St Margaret's was the old parish burial ground. It was on a tombstone here that William Cowper saw the name 'John Gilpin' that he used in his best-known poem.

Many of Cowper's contemporaries traced his emotional problems to another event that occurred here. For a long time Cowper suffered from religious mania and fits of despair during which he was convinced that he was excluded from salvation. His friends attributed this to the incident in Cowper's schooldays when, walking through this graveyard on a dark night, he was suddenly struck on the head by a skull thrown from a deep pit by a careless grave-digger. His obituary noted solemnly: 'The awful circumstance made a great impression on him and much affected his later life.'

Every corner and angle of the church is protected by the waist-high 'Commit No Nuisance' railings we saw in Whitehall. On the tower is a splendid new sundial with blue dials and stainless steel gnomons, which was presented in 1981. The colouring is unusual because, although most public clocks are black and white, church clocks and timepieces are still governed by the regulations laid down by Henry VIII. He specified colours of blue and gold for all church 'clockes and planettes with dialles', the clock faces to 'be enamelled blew and the signs on them gilt'. Although the tradition is dying, a surprising number of church clocks still follow his edict.

St Margaret's became the official House of Commons church in 1614, when the Parliamentary party took exception to the High Church ritual and pro-Royalist preaching at the Abbey and came to St Margaret's to hear preaching more to their liking.

The Speaker has a pew at the front of the church, all MPs are counted as members of the parish and St Margaret's bells are rung for the opening of Parliament and the election of a new Speaker.

Milton, Pepys and Churchill were married here, although only Churchill would have seen St Margaret's greatest treasure – the superb piece of sixteenth-century stained glass that a Victorian romantic called 'The Wandering Window'. It is another London landmark that arrived by accident. The history of this landmark, however, seems to have involved every historical figure in Tudor and Stuart England.

After he won the throne from Richard III at the Battle of Bosworth in 1485, Henry VII consolidated his position by a series of diplomatic moves to ally himself and his new dynasty with the reigning powers of Europe. Under one of these alliances, Henry arranged a marriage between his eldest son Arthur and Catherine of Aragon, daughter of Ferdinand and Isabella of Spain. To celebrate the event Ferdinand and Isabella commissioned this superb window to be placed in the new chapel Henry was building in Westminster Abbey. Prince Arthur is represented by the kneeling figure at one side, with St George above him; Catherine kneels on the other side, with St Catherine above her.

By the time the window was completed, Arthur had died and Catherine had married his younger brother Henry. By the time it arrived in England, Henry VIII had succeeded to his father's throne. The window had now become an embarrassing reminder of past events but, since it was far too valuable to waste, Henry sent it to the monks at Waltham Abbey in Essex for safe-keeping.

When Henry broke with Rome over his divorce from Catherine and his remarriage to Anne Boleyn, the monasteries were dissolved and the last Abbot of Waltham moved the window for safety to the chapel at New Hall in Essex. There it passed into the hands, ironically enough, of the father of Anne Boleyn. His granddaughter, Queen Elizabeth I, inherited it and gave it to the Earl of Sussex. The Duke of Buckingham, James I's favourite, bought it from him, after which it came into the possession of Cromwell who had enough sensibility to bury it so that it would not be destroyed by the Puritans.

After Cromwell's death and the restoration of the monarchy, the window was reclaimed by the second Duke of Buckingham. He sold it to General Monk who left it to his wife. After she died the next owner of the property, John Olmius, destroyed the chapel but kept the window in the hope of selling it. It lay packed in chests for some years till a Mr Conyers bought it and moved it to his chapel at Copthall. Conyers' son then sold it to the churchwardens of St Margaret's in 1758, during the restoration of the church. And that should have been the end of the saga.

For some reason the Abbey authorities were against the window being installed in St Margaret's; perhaps they remembered that it was originally intended for them. They claimed that St Margaret's had no right to the window; that they had no permission to install it or, if they did, the permission had not been properly obtained. It took St Margaret's seven years to win the case but the window is still here just a few yards from the Abbey for which it was originally intended.

In front of the west door of St Margaret's is a stretch of grass with a seat beside it. A few feet from the seat is a flat stone slab with the letters 'TR' on it. It has no marker or plaque yet it is one of the oldest relics in London. It is a Roman milestone or boundary mark, probably indicating the distance from the old Roman city of Londinium. It has been here for nearly two thousand years.

The Abbey

The path from St Margaret's runs down the side of the Abbey to the West Door. The Abbey does not form part of the normal ecclesiastical jurisdiction and the Dean of the Abbey is appointed by the Crown. It is the Dean who greets Royalty at this door; he meets bishops there as well although he would not dream of reminding them that he does so, in law, as a formal protest against their intrusion into his jurisdiction.

This has been a Royal church since the Conquest, and the Earl Marshal exercises the Crown's authority by claiming the Abbey keys the night before a Coronation – though he always hands them back afterwards. Its Royal status proved useful when it provided the setting for one of the historic decisions of the English church – the seniority of the Archbishops of Canterbury and York.

The rivalry of the two prelates went back to the Dark

Ages. Canterbury claimed precedence from St Augustine, who came from Rome, while York claimed seniority through the old northern church that had come from Ireland. In 1176 the Papal Legate called a synod at the Abbey and both Archbishops attended. When the Archbishop of York arrived, he found Canterbury seated on the Legate's right. Infuriated by the affront he promptly sat down on Canterbury's lap, asserting his right as senior archbishop. After a most unseemly squabble, in which the retainers of both archbishops became involved, the Papal Legate settled the question by a masterpiece of terminology that has been followed ever since. The Archbishop of York is indeed Primate of England, but the Archbishop of Canterbury is Primate of All England.

Visitors come to the Abbey to see the Coronation Chair with the Stone of Scone beneath it, the tomb of Edward the Confessor, Henry V's tomb with his helmet, shield and saddle still on the beam above, where he ordered them to be placed and – the glory of the Abbey – the Henry VII chapel with the most beautiful roof in England.

One of the monuments often missed amongst so much grandeur is the tomb in the centre of the nave, midway between the organ and the west door, not far from the tomb of the Unknown Soldier. It is the grave of Admiral Cochrane, the extraordinary sailor who was the origin of the fictional Hornblower and whose feats of daring make Nelson's seem insipid. Sailor, adventurer, Member of Parliament, inventor and scientist, he fought Napoleon and went on to help Peru, Chile, Brazil and Greece win their independence. At the age of fifty, he commanded a single ship against a Portuguese fleet so successfully that he captured over sixty merchant ships and chased their escorting thirteen warships all the way across the Atlantic to Portugal. He earns a mention in the history of Westminster by being its MP for twenty years, as well as being the first man to lay tarmac on its streets in the 1840s.

There are thousands of monuments in the Abbey, but six deserve particular attention. Three of them commemorate one man, the only person in the Abbey to be so remembered. He is not a king or statesman, but a professional boxer named John Broughton. Broughton achieved fame in the eighteenth century by being unbeaten for sixteen years, inventing boxing gloves and introducing rules of boxing that stood for a hundred years. After retiring from the ring, he became a Yeoman of the Guard and spent his last years as verger in the Abbey.

Along the South Aisle wall, on the right as one enters by the West Door, is a doorway to the Cloisters. Halfway down the right-hand Cloister wall is a tablet commemorating Mrs Elizabeth Broughton and Mr John Broughton, a Yeoman of the Guard.

Broughton is commemorated by a second stone on the ground, with an empty space below his name. The gap is there because the stone should read 'John Broughton – Champion of England'. The Dean and Chapter forbade the addition because they considered that boxing was a disreputable pursuit and saw no reason to recognise its existence. (N.B. At the time of writing, this section of the Cloisters wall has been repaired and Broughton's plaque has not yet been replaced.)

On the right-hand wall of the Abbey, near the Choir, is the monument to Major André, which includes a dramatic bas-relief of a soldier with a flag handing a letter to George Washington.

It is a sad story. During the American Revolution Benedict Arnold, an American traitor, decided to hand over the plans of an important American fort to the British. André was given the job of meeting Arnold and made the journey disguised in civilian clothes. He collected the plans but was caught on the way back and tried as a spy by the Americans. He did not attempt to conceal what he had done but asked that he be shot rather than hanged. The plaque shows the request being made to Washington who, reluctant though he was to do it, confirmed the order of hanging. There was tremendous outrage in England and André's body was brought back after the war for a hero's burial in the Abbey, paid for by the King himself.

Look closely at the head on the figure of Washington. Indignant Londoners knocked it off almost as soon as this memorial was erected and, although the head was replaced, it was promptly struck off again. The second replacement lasted about thirty years till England fought America again in the War of 1812 when the head was knocked off for a third time. The territorial dispute of the 1840s seems to have provoked more violence against Washington but the present, fourth replacement has been undisturbed for the last hundred years.

The next memorial to look at is nearby, on the wall near the doorway beside the organ. It shows the famous murder of Tom Thynne (Tom of Ten Thousand) in Pall Mall in 1682. It was the sensation of the time. A wealthy landowner (Tom Thynne) engaged to a beautiful heiress, Lady Elizabeth Percy, was assassinated in his coach by a rival in love. The rival was that most dramatic of figures, a foreign adventurer with the splendid name of Count Koningsmark.

The whole affair reflected little credit on anybody. Koningsmark was acquitted by ferocious bribery of the jury although his servants, who had committed the murder on his orders, were all hanged in Pall Mall where the murder had occurred. Even the murdered man came out of it badly. He was so notorious a rake that the Dean and Chapter felt unable to allow the proposed wording of his memorial. That is why there is an empty space where the normal panegyric ought to be. The only person to come out of the incident with any advantage was the coachman depicted on the plaque who escaped unhurt. He returned to Wales and founded a long line of hill-farmers, all of whom took great pride in their ancestor's being commemorated in the Abbey.

The next monument to see, the third to John Broughton, is straight across the Choir in the North Transept. On the right hand side is a monument to Admiral Sir Peter Warren which depicts an enormous figure of Hercules setting the admiral's bust on a pedestal. The sculptor could think of no one better than the muscular Broughton to represent Hercules and asked him to pose for the figure.

On the way back to the West Door, a plaque under one of the windows of the North Aisle shows the second assassination depicted in the Abbey. It is the memorial to Spencer Perceval and shows him being shot in the lobby of the House of Commons in 1812.

The Abbey museum contains the effigies that were carried at the funerals of kings and queens. One of them, Queen Elizabeth of York, wife of Henry VII, is the original of the Queen on English playing cards. She was directly related to no fewer than ten kings and queens – daughter of Edward IV, sister to Edward V, niece of Richard III, wife of Henry VII, mother of Henry VIII, Margaret, Queen of Scotland and Mary, Queen of France and grandmother to Edward VI, Queen Mary and Queen Elizabeth.

The figure of Nelson in the museum is an accurate representation. When Lady Hamilton came to see it she fainted from shock. After she had recovered, she moved some of the hair away from the eyes, the only improvement she felt was necessary. The Nelson effigy was put here to try and win visitors back from St Paul's where Nelson is buried, another tactic in the lengthy competition between the Abbey and its rival in the City.

The rivalry was particularly fierce after the Reformation when the monastic establishments lost their property. The Abbey was retained as a royal church but St Paul's asserted its rights as the cathedral for London. The struggle by both establishments for endowments was widely discussed. When Edward VI took the revenues of the Manor of Paddington away from the Abbey, whose official title is the Collegiate Church of St Peter in

Westminster, and gave them to St Paul's, the language acquired a new metaphor – 'robbing Peter to pay Paul'.

A line of buildings outside the West Door of the Abbey leads to the archway into Dean's Yard. The first building is the Faculty Office of the Archbishop of Canterbury where it is possible to procure an immediate marriage licence. One of the Archbishop of Canterbury's powers is the authority to grant a licence of marriage without the normal period of notice and there is a surprisingly heavy demand. The special licences cater for emergencies and are sought by couples injured in car crashes or by people in hospital wishing to regularise their relationship before it is too late.

A gateway off Dean's Yard leads into Westminster School. One of the school's headmasters, Nicholas Udall, is remembered as the author of *Ralph Roister Doister* the first English comedy. There were doubts about his suitability since his previous appointment as headmaster of Eton had ended in a term of imprisonment for stealing the school's silver.

Another memorable headmaster was Dr Busby who advocated flogging as a normal method of discipline, but who was a man of strong principles. At great risk to his own life, he led the school into the Abbey on the day of Charles I's execution and led them in prayer for the King.

He managed to keep his post during the Protectorate and was delighted to welcome Charles II on a royal visit after the Restoration. Though he was a fervent Royalist, Busby was very conscious of his position. He greeted the King with every respect but refused to doff his hat. When Charles asked the reason for this discourtesy, Busby explained that he intended no disrespect, but the interests of the school meant '. . . the boys must not see that there is anyone greater than I.'

During a discussion on the number of his boys who had fathers in Parliament, someone cast doubt on his importance as headmaster. Busby crushed him instantly: 'The fathers of my boys rule the country. The mothers rule the fathers, the boys rule the mothers – and I rule the boys.'

From Dean's Yard, Broad Sanctuary swings round to the right to the red-brick Middlesex Guildhall across the road. Broad Sanctuary takes its name from the old Norman City of Refuge that stood where the Guildhall is today. It had walls twenty-five feet thick and came under the protection of the Abbey beside it. It was a common refuge for the families of noblemen engaged in civil wars, since not even the most desperate opponent would commit the sacrilege of attempting to take them from the Sanctuary building.

Over the years the right of sanctuary was dropped and the thick walls made the building ideal for use as a prison, the Westminster Bridewell, which became notorious for its treadmill. It was demolished in 1834 but, if one walks round the back of the Guildhall, the Victorian red brick is interrupted half-way along by the old prison doorway that has been here since 1665, the year of the Great Plague.

The panels on the front of the Middlesex Guildhall provide an extraordinary mixture of allegory and history. The keystone of the doorway is a small plaque depicting the Great Hall of Hampton Court, flanked by two niches with small figures representing the Law. Immediately above the keystone is a crowded scene showing Henry III presenting a charter to the Abbey. The panel has two more figures flanking it, Prudence and Justice (with the sword). On one side, Magna Carta is being signed, while the other has the unhappy Lady Jane Grey accepting the crown which she was to wear for only nine days.

The figures in a semi-circle above the panels are Wisdom, Architecture, Literature, Government, Sculpture and Music, Truth, Law, Shipping and Education, with Britannia in the centre. As on the Eleanor Cross at Charing Cross Station, it is the hands of the statues that identify which is which.

The Statues of Parliament Square

Cross the road to the centre of the Square to look at the statues grouped there. The first is Robert Peel, the man who founded the Metropolitan Police (hence the familiar term 'Bobbies'). He was a brilliant politician although his absorption in his work left him little time for the social graces. Wellington summed up fashionable London's view of him with the comment: 'I have no small talk and Peel has no manners.'

Peel seemed to spend his time splitting his party on grounds of conscience, conduct that got him heartily disliked by those of his colleagues who put power before principle. He was, however, prepared to accept reality and made what must be the frankest statement of policy uttered by a politician:

> As a Minister of the Crown, I reserve to myself, distinctly and unequivocably, the right of adapting my conduct to the exigency of the moment.

Next to Peel is Benjamin Disraeli, who became Lord Beaconsfield. It was Disraeli who reorganised the Conservative Party in the nineteenth century and kept Queen Victoria on his side by flattering her outrageously. In 1867 the Queen published, with some nervousness, her *Leaves from a Journal of Our Life in the Highlands*. Disraeli, who had published nine popular novels before he entered Parliament, delighted her by opening a conversation with the words, 'We authors, Ma'am . . .'.

The statue of Abraham Lincoln across the road is a copy of the original in Chicago, and historians like pointing out that the number of stars (32) around the plinth is the same as there were States during his presidency.

A few yards from Lincoln is the statue of Canning (1770–1827) which with the Law Courts clock and the Standing Stone in Hyde Park shares the unfortunate distinction of killing somebody. The victim in this case was a Mr Reilly who, when the statue was being lifted on to the cart to bring it here, thought the ropes holding it were secure when they weren't.

Canning served in the Government during the Napoleonic Wars and was Prime Minister for the last year of his life. He had a strong sense of humour which came out even in his official dispatches. During a long and complicated dispute with the European nations on what Customs duties they should pay when they sent goods to England, the British Ambassador at The Hague received a cypher that read:

> In matters of commerce the fault of the Dutch
> Is offering too little and asking too much,
> The French are with equal advantage content
> So we clap on Dutch bottoms just twenty per cent.

The next statue, of the 14th Earl of Derby (1799–1869), is noteworthy for the detailed carving of the plaques around the plinth. Historians have been able to identify many of the figures in the panel depicting the Chamber of the House of Commons; it is one of the very few places where it is possible to see what the old House of Commons looked like before the fire of 1834.

Perhaps the sculptor's greatest feat is the three-dimensional carving of the two-dimensional picture over the fireplace in the plaque showing the Cabinet Room, still much as it is shown here.

The next statue, to the right, is Palmerston (1784–1865), Conservative Prime Minister from 1855 till his death ten years later. He was the original of Lord Brock in the Palliser novels of Trollope and the election victory that gave him his second term of office was completely unexpected. Rumour has it that he was voted back into power on a wave of popular admiration at his being cited as co-respondent at the age of seventy-five.

The essayist Desmond McCarthy always maintained that Palmerston's is the best-dressed statue in London and 'ought to be an object of pilgrimage to all the tailors of England. The frock coat fits like a glove, and though the trousers do not break on the instep to suit modern taste, the hang of them is magnificent.'

The next figure, that of Field-Marshal Smuts, has probably received more puzzled glances than any other statue in the Square. Was Smuts's head really that size, or is it a trick of perspective? The puzzled glances are justified because the proportions are wrong; the optical illusion was deliberately created but was carried too far. It is common practice to make the head disproportionately large on a standing figure like this to ensure it does not look too small to the spectator below. In this case the sculptor, Jacob Epstein, was misled on the height of the plinth to be used. He over-compensated the proportion and was furious when he saw the final result.

On the balustrade of the Government offices across the road from Smuts's statue is a small brass plaque. It marks the site of the old King Street that ran from this angle through to the Cockpit that became Downing Street. It also marks the end of our walk round Parliament Square, beside the statue of Winston Churchill. It has none of the detail seen in the other statues around the Square, but it conveys perfectly the brooding power and strength that led us through the Second World War.

FIFTEENTH ♦ WALK

Piccadilly Circus, Piccadilly and Mayfair

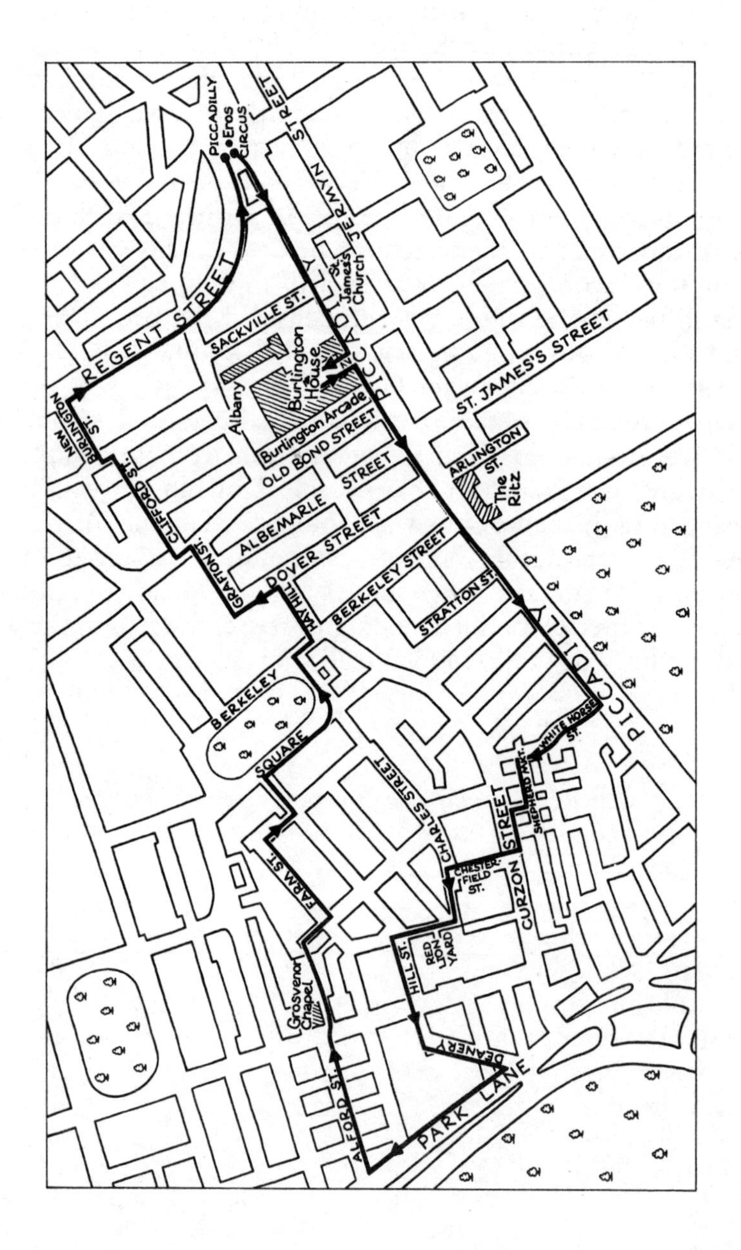

FIFTEENTH ♦ WALK

Piccadilly Circus, Piccadilly and Mayfair

The Fifteenth Walk begins at Piccadilly Circus, to which every visitor to London comes at least once. In the minds of millions it has become the centre of London in the same way that Charing Cross, at the junction of Whitehall and the Strand, was the centre of things in the days of the Stuart and Hanoverian kings.

The Circus, half-way up the boulevard of Regent Street built by John Nash to connect St James's Park with Regent's Park to the north, stands at the borders of five different areas of London.

On the east side, Coventry Street introduces the raffishness of Leicester Square, where teenagers munch hot-dogs outside the cinemas. In the north-east corner Shaftesbury Avenue with its six theatres marks the edge of Soho, which has been the foreign quarter of London since the Huguenots were expelled from France in the sixteenth century and where there have been Greeks in Greek Street since 1671. On the northern side, the shops along Regent Street separate Soho from the dignity of Mayfair, while Piccadilly to the west still clings to some of its old smartness as Mayfair's southern border. To the south, Lower Regent Street and the Haymarket lead to the expensive shops and gentlemen's clubs of St James's.

The heyday of the Circus was from 1851, when the Great Exhibition brought the whole world to London, till 1914. This was the age of wealth and elegance when top hats and sovereigns were commonplace and London's social life revolved around the Circus's most famous landmark, the statue of Angelo Colorossi, better known as Eros.

The Eros Monument

Like Cleopatra's Needle, Eros is another of London's landmarks to which officialdom gave one name and Londoners promptly gave another. In this case the name they chose was extremely inapposite because the statue is meant to represent the Angel of Christian Charity, while Eros gave his name to erotic love.

The monument, the first aluminium figure of this size in the country, was erected in 1893 as a memorial to the seventh Earl of Shaftesbury, in whose honour Shaftesbury Avenue was named. He was a great social reformer who spent his life alleviating the conditions of the poor in factories and in improving housing conditions. The monument is meant to be a pun on his name and the sculptor, Alfred Gilbert, designed it to stand facing Shaftesbury Avenue so that the angel could be shown 'burying a shaft of Christianity' in that direction. The authorities took a different view and, although it has pointed three different ways in its ninety years, it has never faced in the direction that Gilbert intended.

Gilbert was a brilliant sculptor who had come to prominence in the 1880s, but he had the bad habit of taking on too many commissions and then failing to complete them. This was not due to idleness, but a sense of perfectionism which led him to complete many sculptures and then destroy them since he was not satisfied. He had poor financial sense, accepted the Eros commission for far too small a sum and then argued for months with the committee on the siting and proportions of the plinth for the statue. He refused to attend the opening ceremony, telling the committee that they should: 'Take it down, melt it and turn it into pence and give it to the unfortunate people who nightly find a resting place on the Thames

Embankment, to the everlasting shame and disgrace of the metropolis in the world. . . .'

He resigned from the Royal Academy just before they were about to expel him for not fulfilling his commissions, became bankrupt and fled to the Continent in 1901. He left unfinished the sculptures for the tomb of the Duke of Clarence which had been commissioned by Edward VII, but returned to complete them in 1926, in response to a a personal request from King George V.

Eros was modelled on Angelo Colorossi, a 16-year-old assistant in Gilbert's studio. After Gilbert fled the country, Colorossi became a solicitor's clerk and finished his life working in an aircraft factory, but always took a great pride in being the original Eros. The statue has its critics who point out the bow is strung the wrong way round, and that the susceptibility of aluminium to corrosion made it a poor choice, but it is still admired and photographed by hundreds every day.

The 'Cri', the 'Pav' and the 'Troc'

Immediately beside Eros is the Criterion, built in 1874 as an 'all-in-one' entertainment centre with restaurant and dance-floor upstairs, the famous Long Bar at ground level and London's first underground theatre below, where the Victorian mosaics still decorate the walls. The 'Cri' met every need of London's Bohemian set and, in the 1880s and 1890s, they mingled with card-sharps, confidence tricksters and prostitutes in the Long Bar that has now been restored and reopened.

The London Pavilion stands on the north-east corner of the Circus, with the Trocadero immediately behind. Both were built as variety theatres and brought the boisterousness of the old music-halls into the West End. The Trocadero opened as the Argyll Rooms in the 1850s, but became so notorious that its licence was not renewed and J. J. Lyons rebuilt it as the Trocadero Music Hall some years later. The 'Troc' was made famous by the music-hall star Charles Coburn, whose especial property was 'Two Lovely Black Eyes', the song he introduced and sang for years in a long life that stretched from the Crimea to the end of the Second World War.

The 'Troc' 's rival, the London Pavilion, became even more famous when, in one evening in 1878, it changed the history of Europe and added a new word to the English language. After the Crimean War had finished in 1856, Britain, France and Germany had tried to keep peace in the Balkans amongst the three eastern powers of Austria-Hungary, Russia and the Turkish Empire. Despite their efforts, Russia and Turkey went to war in 1878 and a Russian army advanced on Constantinople.

Although Britain took no official part in the conflict, the Mediterranean Fleet was sent to the area. If the Fleet took station outside Constantinople, the Russians could not cross the Straits; the question was – should the British Government give the order to intervene or not? Intervention or non-intervention was the burning issue of the day and the Government could not secure sufficient support in Parliament for either course. One night, as the House of Commons once again tried to reach a decision, the audience at the Pavilion were told that one of the turns, G. H. Macdermott ('The Great Macdermott') was to sing a new patriotic song. Macdermott strode out on to the stage and launched into:

> We don't want to fight, but by Jingo if we do,
> We've got the ships, we've got the men, we've got the money too. . .

concluding each verse fortissimo with the rousing lines:

> We've fought the Bear before, and while we're Britons true
> The Russians shall not have Constantinople.

The Pavilion audience went wild. Macdermott sang it again and again, the audience took it up, sang it with him and then forced Macdermott on to the balcony to sing it to the crowds outside. People poured out of the pubs

Suffolk
NR32 1UL
UK
44(0)1502 539194

Ship via:

Payment: Prepaid

Ship To:

Robin Butcher
2 Brookhurst Close

CHELMSFORD Essex CM2 6DX Great Britain

Bill To:

66dgr1vw2866mjm@marketplace.amazon.co.uk
Robin Butcher

QTY	SKU/ISBN/UPC	Condition	Loc	Description	Media	Price
1	13153col011 0091737117	Used; Good Hardcover, English language, good condition, with good dust jacket	[Lowestoft, Suffolk, UK]	One Man's London ... N.T.P. Murphy	Hardcover	£59.99

and theatres nearby to see what the noise was about and joined in until the whole of Leicester Square and Piccadilly Circus was filled. With Macdermott in their midst, the crowd made its way down Whitehall, growing all the time. By the time they reached the Houses of Parliament, the crowd had grown to twenty thousand and they sang the song for two hours, until word came out that the Government had decided to intervene. The crowd cheered their heads off and dispersed, singing as they went the Fleet received its orders and steamed into the Straits, the Russians withdrew their forces and the war came to an end.

Macdermott's Pavilion was rebuilt in 1885, and the new owners decided it would be enhanced by a series of semi-nude goddesses over the pediment; a step which Londoners insisted was merely an advertisement for the Pavilion's chorus-line. The figures were replaced in 1987 by new carvings and, if the goddesses seem similar in appearance, it is because they were all modelled on Miss Michelle Derrick, who has joined Mr Colorossi in becoming a feature of the Circus.

The famous garish lights of the advertisements beside the Pavilion have never equalled those of New York's Broadway, but the Circus got theirs first. A Bovril advertisement of six hundred light bulbs astonished the crowds of Piccadilly in 1890, a year before Broadway put up its first electric sign. The signs are restricted to the eastern side of the Circus because the buildings here are privately owned. The western side belongs to the Crown Commissioners, which is why Nash was able to develop Regent Street as one thoroughfare, and the Commissioners have always refused to allow their buildings to be disfigured with such commercialism.

The large block on the northern corner, surmounted by Britannia, is a relic of Nash's original design of 1816. The section of Regent Street curving north from the Circus is known as the Quadrant and Nash built a colonnade along the front of the shops that stood there.

Although the colonnade sheltered pedestrians from the rain, which was Nash's intention, it proved unpopular with the shopkeepers who had to keep their lights on all day. It was eventually dismantled with the exception of the section at the corner.

The building has always been an insurance office and the strong resemblance to Inigo Jones's Piazza in Covent Garden and the frontage of Somerset House is intentional. When Nash published his original plans, there was considerable reluctance to take up leases of the new shops, but one far-sighted insurance director realised this corner building would dominate the Circus and paid the asking price without question. Nash was delighted to let the site so quickly and readily agreed to alter the design to meet the buyer's request that the façade should resemble as closely as possible Inigo Jones's design for the old Somerset House.

Over on the left is the old Swan and Edgar building that has been the favourite rendez-vous for Londoners for more than a century. The firm traded here from 1813 to 1982 and made its reputation by supplying drapery to Queen Victoria and her numerous children for fifty years.

Immediately beside Eros, the wall of the Criterion bends back to form an angle with Lillywhite's, who have been involved with cricket since James Lillywhite led England against Australia in 1876. In the short stretch of blank wall can be seen four small holes, where screws have been removed. These mark the site of the plaque, stolen by vandals, erected to commemorate the meeting in the Criterion Bar of Dr Watson and Stamford in the opening chapter of the first Sherlock Holmes story, *A Study In Scarlet.*

St James's Church and the Albany

Cross the Circus to walk down Piccadilly, past the fluted bronze traffic lights which were presented to the Circus by the city of Chicago in the 1930s. Piccadilly takes its name from a draper who made a fortune in the reign of

Charles I from selling the stiff ruffed collars called pickadils. He built himself a large mansion on this corner which derisive Londoners promptly christened 'Pickadill Hall', the name which has stuck ever since.

In the 1660s houses began to be built along the road and, by the start of the nineteenth century, the street had become as smart as St James's had been the century before.

St James's church on the left was designed by Wren in 1674 to cater for the new district of St James being built by his patron Henry Jermyn. That is why the main entrance faces Jermyn Street in St James's and not Piccadilly. It is the only one of Wren's London churches built on a new site and he was very proud of it, although he was slightly put out when the local vestry rejected the spire he designed, preferring one built by their own carpenter. They realised their mistake when the weight of the carpenter's spire caused the tower to buckle and, although they replaced it in 1699, they found it could carry the weight of only two bells. The problem was eventually solved by the invention of plastics and the church is one of the very few whose spire is protected from the elements by reinforced nylon.

The reredos and the font were carved by Grinling Gibbons; the organ was built in 1685 by Renatus Harris for the Chapel Royal. After James II fled the throne in 1688, the organ was deemed to be a Catholic relic and was going to be destroyed, but the vicar of St James's persuaded Queen Mary to give it to the church where it was installed by Henry Purcell.

One of the graves in St James's is that of 'Old Q', the infamous Duke of Queensberry who spent his old age in Piccadilly scandalising his neighbours with his open lechery. He spent his days looking out from his window at pretty women as they walked along Piccadilly and a footman waited in readiness below to pursue anybody the Duke fancied. He was reputed to bathe in milk in an attempt to keep his youth and he re-enacted the Judgement of Paris in proper costume – or lack of it – with three of the most beautiful women in London, presenting an apple of gold to the winner. His house, at the western end of Piccadilly, later became the Ladies' Lyceum Club where, it is said, the members did not take kindly to any reference to the scenes their drawing room had previously witnessed.

A few years before the Duke's death in 1810, the church had seen the burial of Mrs Margaret Thompson, perhaps the greatest devotee of snuff that London has seen. Snuff became popular in England through one accident and finished with another. In 1702 Admiral Rooke captured a Spanish fleet in which one of the prizes contained fifty tons of snuff. Although snuff-taking had been practised in England for some time, the expense had restricted it to a wealthy few. The sale by the Government of such an enormous amount brought the price down to a level everybody could afford and snuff became a national habit.

Snuff's popularity died just as quickly in 1861, with the death of Prince Albert. Victoria and her Court went into deepest mourning; their example was followed by the upper and middle classes who went into the black and dark grey clothes that remained standard dress for men for the rest of the century. The adoption of such sombre dress meant coloured handkerchiefs were no longer worn and, since white handkerchiefs were soon ruined by snuff-taking, the habit died nearly as quickly as it had started.

Mrs Thompson considered snuff to be God's greatest gift to mankind and left specific instructions that she was to be buried wearing snuff-coloured clothes in a coffin filled to the brim with her favourite brand. The coffin was followed by two of her maids who distributed snuff by the handful to passers-by, while the mourners qualified for their bequests only if they took snuff every twenty yards along the funeral's route.

Hatchard's bookshop, just beyond the church, opened in 1797. Up to a few years ago the upstairs floor was still laid out as Mr Hatchard's private library, a popular meeting-place for social reformers in the early nineteenth century. The Royal Horticultural Society was founded here and the room saw the meetings that led to Wilberforce's successful anti-slavery campaign.

Much of Hatchard's trade came from the Albany across the way, which stands just west of Sackville Street, the longest street in London without a turning out of it. The Albany, like the Inns of Court, is a survival. It stands at the end of a quiet quadrangle and is unchanged after two hundred years. Built as a town house for the first Lord Melbourne in 1770, it was redesigned in 1802 as sets of chambers for bachelors, still its role today.

It has always been one of London's smartest addresses. The residents have included Byron, Canning, Gladstone, Macaulay and Edward Heath, though probably its most famous occupant was the gentleman cracksman A. J. Raffles of the Hornung novels.

When Macaulay was writing his history of England here, his niece sent him an anonymous letter warning him of a burglary. Macaulay took the matter very seriously and promptly had the spiked gates and doorway erected at the back entrance as a precaution. Although she admitted the prank some time later, the railing and postern door are still there. Bulwer Lytton, the politician and author, took rooms here because, as he told his wife, he needed peace and quiet to write the novels on whose profits they lived. One letter he sent her said that he was 'at the Albany with Solitude'. His suspicious wife called on him unexpectedly and found, as a Victorian commentator states drily: 'Solitude well deserved the dignity of a capital letter because the personification was sustained by a fair creature, fashionably dressed in white muslin and perched upon his knee.'

It was on the pavement of Piccadilly, just outside the Albany, that the Baron Meyer de Rothschild was walking with a group of friends when he dropped a penny into the gutter. Seizing the opportunity to reinforce his remarks on the fleeting nature of riches, the Baron made a tremendous to-do of searching for the lost coin. It was eventually found but the Baron's moral lesson lost some of its force when it was discovered his watch had been stolen in the confusion.

The next building on the right, Burlington House, is the only survivor of the original Piccadilly mansions of the 1660s. Built for the Earl of Burlington, it was refaced in the eighteenth century and the quadrangle and frontage were reconstructed in 1872. In 1854 it became the home of half a dozen learned societies including the Royal Academy. They had been in Somerset House but the Government required it for offices and persuaded them to move west to Piccadilly. Some of the learned bodies needed more persuasion than others and the Society of Antiquaries proved particularly obdurate. It needed a metal workshop and steam-drill installed over their library to convince them the move might be politic.

The Societies are still here grouped around the courtyard, although most people ignore them on their way to the Royal Academy on the far side. The Antiquaries, in the left-hand corner, are the oldest and recently received a bequest appropriate to both their seniority and interests. A member left money in trust for use by his family with the stipulation that, if the family died out, the capital should revert to the Society. The bequest was made in 1776; the Society received the windfall two hundred years later.

An enormous wooden gateway stands beside the Piccadilly frontage of Burlington House. When the gate is open, it affords a view of London's highest wall stretching down to Burlington Gardens two hundred yards away. Lord Cavendish built the first wall to protect the gardens of Burlington House from the rubbish thrown into them by passers-by, but it had little effect. The wall was built higher and higher, but this was merely taken as a challenge by London's vandals and missiles continued to arrive. Eventually Lord Cavendish decided the only thing to do was to fill in the lane which the vandals used so he built the Burlington Arcade along it in 1819.

The Burlington Arcade is where the commercialism of Piccadilly Circus changes to the luxury and dignified wealth of Mayfair. It is as discreet and luxurious as Lord Cavendish intended, although its reputation in the early years was marred by the equally discreet and luxurious brothels that were established in the small upstairs rooms.

It has become one of London's best shopping centres and Sullivan's cigarettes, made famous by Hornung's A. J. Raffles, can still be bought at the tobacconist at the far end.

The beadles in their famous tall hats are all ex-warrant officers, whose duty is to ensure the dignity of the Arcade is not disturbed by people whistling, singing, running or carrying large parcels. (The last rule is not so strictly observed nowadays since there are fewer servants to collect their mistresses' shopping.)

The title of beadle is not an honorary one. These dignified gentlemen are not police constables, but they are legally appointed and can be called to do duty in London courts. One of them had to exercise his authority recently when an admiral in full dress and sword belt came to do some shopping on his way back from an investiture at Buckingham Palace. The rules of the Arcade forbid the wearing of swords and the admiral was allowed in only after he had divested himself of the weapon and left it outside in Piccadilly with his aide-de-camp.

Opposite the Arcade is Fortnum and Mason's, who have been here since 1756. The founders are represented by the two figures beside the clock over the entrance, who come out and bow to each other on the hour. Mr Fortnum wears the red coat that indicates he was a footman in the Royal Household, where his duties included placing new candles in the State Rooms every day. By selling the used candles to the ladies of the Court, he made enough money to go into partnership with Mason, who was already in business as a grocer. With Fortnum's knowledge of the Court and Mason's commercial skill, the shop soon became the best-known grocery in London. The staff still wear tail-coats and their bakery is supervised by the Groom of the Pastry.

They made their reputation with food of the highest quality and their jars of potted meat accompanied Wellington's army to the Peninsula. Queen Victoria sent their beef-tea concentrate to Florence Nightingale's hospitals in the Crimea and their famous hampers are still sent all over the world. In 1886 young Mr Heinz called on them with his new range of tinned foods and they made his reputation in England by buying the entire stock.

Immediately beyond the Burlington Arcade is Bond Street, or more specifically, Old Bond Street and its extension, New Bond Street, whose numbering system has confused visitors for two hundred years. Old Bond Street was built in the 1680s by Sir Thomas Bond, while New Bond Street came into existence forty years later, when Mayfair started to become as fashionable as St James's. It is the only road running from Piccadilly to Oxford Street and the authorities have made several attempts to renumber it as one street, a move always decisively defeated by the residents, who prefer things as they are.

Bond Street became established as a residential street when the Duchess of Devonshire persuaded those of her acquaintances who lived in Covent Garden to move here so they could vote for her friend James Fox. The shops for which Bond Street is now famous moved in to cater for the aristocratic residents and have been here ever since. Window-shopping or 'the Bond Street promenade' became the fashion and the Prince Regent strolled here every day, although it sometimes proved more expensive than he had expected. James Fox used to stroll with him and won a sizeable amount from the Prince by betting that they would see more cats on one side of the street than the other. The Prince took the bet, but lost by 13 to 1 because Fox had taken care to choose the sunnier side of the street.

Dean Swift, Gibbon, Pitt the Elder, Boswell and Nelson all lived in Bond Street and some of their houses still exist. Yardley's at No. 33 started in 1801, when they had the good sense to purchase the firm that had had the monopoly of making soap in London for two hundred years. Atkinson's, their rivals across the road, possess London's only carillon of 23 bells that are rung on special occasions. The old Aeolian Hall at 135 New Bond Street still bears the frontage of its predecessor, the Grosvenor Gallery which W. S. Gilbert satirised unmercifully in *Patience* with his 'greenery-yallery, Grosvenor Gallery, foot-in-the-grave young man'. Sotheby's at No. 34 New Bond Street have been auctioneers since 1744 and the head of the Egyptian goddess Sekhet over their doorway dates from 1600 BC; it is the oldest outdoor sculpture in London.

Albermarle Street is famous for its art galleries and for the Royal Institution which was founded in 1799. Humphry Davy made his discoveries on alkalis and earths here and took on Michael Faraday as his assistant in 1813, who carried out his experiments into electro-magnetism in the Institution laboratory. Robert, James and William Adam, the three brothers who revolutionised architectural design in England, lived together at No. 13, and No. 50 has been the offices of the publisher John Murray since 1812. This was the centre of literary London in the early nineteenth century, when Murray's guests included Jane Austen, Moore, Southey and Walter Scott who met Byron here for the first time. It was in the fireplace of No. 50 that Murray and Thomas Moore burnt Byron's memoirs after his death, considering them too dangerous to publish.

Dover Street is best known nowadays for Brown's Hotel, opened by James Brown in 1837. It became famous for its 'private house' atmosphere and its guests have included Theodore Roosevelt, who came to London to get married in 1886 and whose nephew, Franklin Roosevelt, spent his honeymoon here twenty years later. Cecil Rhodes and Kipling were frequent guests but Brown's are probably proudest of their visitor of 1876, Alexander Graham Bell, who made the first successful telephone call in England from the hotel.

Opposite Brown's, at No. 37, is Ely House with the bishop's mitre that was placed on its wall in 1772. This is the house built for the Bishop of Ely when he finally lost the battle with the Crown over his old palace at Hatton Garden (see Tenth Walk) and was awarded this site by way of compensation.

At the beginning of this century, Dover Street had become a 'club street' second only to Pall Mall. Its short length contained twenty clubs, of which the most famous was the Bath Club that used to stand at No. 34.

The Bath Club, founded in 1894 by two gentlemen who wanted a club where they could swim, became famous when the present Queen and Princess Margaret learned to swim there. In the 1930s Johnny Weissmuller, the star of the Tarzan films, was invited as a guest, and impressed the members with his prowess in the pool and with the gymnasium ropes and swings that hung over it. It was probably this incident that gave P. G. Wodehouse the idea of using it as one of the sources of his immortal Drones Club, home to Bertie Wooster and Gussie Fink-nottle.

No. 35 next door was the Empress Club, the first ladies' club in London, whose original committee included a princess, a duchess and several countesses. It began with the encouragement of Queen Victoria herself who had often heard her ladies-in-waiting complain of the treatment they received at the clubs to which their husbands belonged. It is not certain what prompted the idea of starting their own club. One possible explanation is the famous incident when a titled lady, blessed with blonde hair and unusually good looks, called for her husband at his club and found the porter reluctant to go and look for him. 'Fetch him at once; I'm his wife!' 'Ah, yes, Madam. That's what they all say.' With the foundation of the Empress Club the ladies were able to get their own back and, for the first year or so, made it a point of principle to keep any male visitor waiting for at least ten minutes in the vestibule.

The only club in Dover Street now is the Arts Club at No. 40. Dickens, Du Maurier, Whistler and Rossetti were members as was Charles Keene, the *Punch* cartoonist, who made the club rooms familiar to millions by using them as background in his sketches. The club has an excellent collection of pictures presented by its members, but to save possible argument on their artistic merit, no member is allowed to present one of his own pictures until after his death.

Arlington Street and the Ritz

Dover Street looks across Piccadilly to Arlington Street, the last section of St James's to be completed in the 1680s. In the early eighteenth century, when St James's Square had a duke or earl in every house, Arlington Street became known as the 'Ministerial Street' because of the number of politicians who lived there. Robert Walpole and his son Horace occupied No. 5, and it was Horace Walpole who recorded that at one time there were twelve Government or ex-Government Ministers living there. The east side of the street was favoured by those out of office, while those in office enjoyed the more desirable houses on the west with a view over the Park.

No. 5 is still there and the drawing-room upstairs was the scene of the death of Walpole's pet cat Selina in 1747 exactly as Thomas Gray described it in his 'Ode on the Death of a Favourite Cat, Drowned in a Tub of Goldfishes'.

The Ritz Hotel at the corner of Arlington Street and Piccadilly was built in 1906 and its colonnades are an imitation of the Rue de Rivoli in Paris. It was London's first steel-framed building and was designed by César Ritz himself, who had originally come to London to manage the Savoy. Ritz moved on to the Carlton a few years later, taking the famous chef Escoffier with him, and crowned his career by building this hotel overlooking Green Park.

Its luxury and smartness gave the word 'ritzy' to the language and its guests between the wars included Edwina Mountbatten, whose sheer silk stockings shocked London in the 1920s, John Barrymore, Elinor Glyn, Tallulah Bankhead and Barbara Hutton the Woolworth heiress, who was the original of Noel Coward's 'Poor Little Rich Girl'. It was in the corner of the Ritz Bar that Cole Porter scribbled:

> The world admits,
> Even bears in pits do it,
> Even Pekingese at the Ritz do it,
> Let's do it, let's fall in love.

The Aga Khan had a suite here for forty years and King Boris of Bulgaria always used the Ritz for his London visits, although he sometimes caused the hotel embarrassment by his appearance. He was an enthusiastic engine-driver and had great difficulty in establishing his identity with the hall porter one morning when he returned covered in soot and oil, after driving the night express into Euston.

Because of its steel construction, the hotel became even more popular during the Blitz and two babies were born during the air-raids. The hotel is quietly proud of the fact that one mother was a duchess, the other a marchioness and that one of the infants is now a director of the hotel.

One wartime guest the Ritz was not glad to see was the 'Duchess of Jermyn Street', the redoubtable Rosa Lewis, owner of the Cavendish Hotel around the corner, who stayed here when her own hotel was bombed. Renowned for her sharp tongue, Mrs Lewis saw no reason to ignore the friends of her youth and scandalised the Ritz with her shout across the dining-room to an eldery duke lunching with his grand-daughters: 'Hullo, old mutton-chops. Still fancy a nice clean whore?'

Eventually she was asked to leave after she had interrupted a senior Cabinet Minister and his colleagues with her strident inquiry: 'How are the old waterworks? Still as unreliable as ever?'

The Ritz stands beside the Green Park, a patch of meadowland that Charles II enclosed and added to St James's Park to form a continuous strip of parkland nearly three miles long from Parliament Square to Notting Hill.

The sunken area immediately beside the Underground Station was once a reservoir, built by the Chelsea Waterworks Company in 1775. Our old acquaintance Benjamin Franklin came here one windy day with the members of the Royal Society to demonstrate how to calm troubled waters by pouring oil on them, a practice quickly adopted by the Royal Navy in the stormy waters of the Channel.

Beyond the station are the Green Park Gates, which were moved here in 1925 from Devonshire House across the road. Their age is a matter of argument, but they have certainly outlasted the four great houses they guarded in various parts of southern England; it is probable they were designed by Inigo Jones in the 1630s.

Inside the gates is a path running parallel to the roadway. Opposite the Park Lane Hotel is Dead Man's Tree, a large plane tree standing ten yards from the junction of the paths, recognisable by the large hole in its trunk twelve feet up from the ground. A man shot himself here in 1820 and rumours of his ghost began to spread a year later. The authorities found nothing to concern them, but had to take official notice when the Guardsmen who patrolled the park refused to walk here on their own. The duty was changed to a two-man patrol and remained so till the police took over the duty this century.

Stratton Street, on the northern side of Piccadilly, was laid out by John Evelyn. Its most famous resident was

Baroness Burdett-Coutts, the Victorian millionairess, whose philanthropy earned her the then rare honours of a peerage in her own right and the freedom of the City of London. She encouraged Dickens in his social reforms and offered to marry the Duke of Wellington to look after him in his old age.

The Baroness's house stood at the western corner of Stratton Street and Queen Victoria liked to visit her here because she said it was the only place in London where she could watch the traffic moving normally. A feature of the house was a china cockatoo that stood in the window looking down on Piccadilly. Every Londoner knew it and in 1885 it stopped a riot, when a large crowd held a meeting in Hyde Park and decided to march on Parliament with their grievances. As they came to the house with the cockatoo in the window, someone in the procession bet another it was real. Each sought support for his views and the whole procession debated the matter hotly for nearly half an hour, by which time the police had drawn a cordon across Piccadilly and were able to disperse them.

No. 81 Piccadilly, just past Stratton Street, was the home of Watier's Club, a famous Regency gambling club founded by George IV's cook. It was renowned for its high stakes and one night Beau Brummell, after losing heavily, made a great point of asking for the loan of a pistol so he could shoot himself.

Although he was admired as the best-dressed man in London, Brummell's sharp tongue had won him few friends. He was a trifle disconcerted to receive, in place of the sympathy he expected, the prompt offer not just of one pistol but of two, so he 'could make sure of it'.

Piccadilly's Clubland

No. 85 Piccadilly was the home of the Turf Club till 1975, a club so exclusive that it is rumoured the Aga Khan was blackballed for membership. For many years a cabmen's coffee-stall stood on the other side of Piccadilly and acquired the nickname of the Junior Turf Club, from its use by West End clubmen who patronised it in the early hours. One London historian records a story of letters being delivered there in mistake for the august institution across the road and the pride the coffee-stall owner took in the error. His reported comment was 'They may know over there what races to put the horses in, but it's over here that you find out why they didn't win.'

No. 94 Piccadilly is the address of the Naval and Military Club, popularly known as the 'In and Out' from the signs on its gateposts. When built in 1761 it was the westernmost house in London and became the home of the Duke of Cambridge, George III's youngest son, and of Palmerston after him.

Into Mayfair

White Horse Street curves round to enter Shepherd Market, the site of the original 'May Fair' authorised by Edward I to raise funds for the leper hospital at St James's which later became St James's Palace. The Fair lasted till the middle of the eighteenth century, when the complaints of the residents brought about its closure.

Shepherd Market was the idea of Edward Shepherd, who had built much of Mayfair. He realised the great houses around him might buy their luxuries in Bond Street and Piccadilly, but would need a local source of supply for such staples as bread, candles, meat and fodder for their carriage horses. The result is that Shepherd Market still possesses a village atmosphere as well as the pubs, rare in Mayfair, where the servants of the nearby mansions could meet in their spare time.

Mayfair's great days were the eighteenth and nineteenth centuries, when some of the mansions employed more than thirty servants and a dozen horses. This gave it the combination of buildings peculiar to Mayfair and Belgravia: long broad avenues of spacious houses with small narrow cobbled streets behind where the coachmen, grooms and horses lived.

After the 1914 War, taxation and the shortage of servants meant that many of the mansions had to be given up. It became fashionable to sell one's house to an American, or turn it into a block of flats and move into the mews cottage where your coachman had lived before the war. The process was repeated after the Second War. In 1988 only a dozen or so families still live in the Mayfair houses of their grandfathers.

Trebeck Street runs from the middle of Shepherd Market to Curzon Street. When the cartoonist Pellegrini, the famous 'Ape' of *Vanity Fair*, discovered Disraeli was unwilling to sit for him, he persuaded Lord Rowton to accost Disraeli in Curzon Street and engage him in conversation while Pellegrini sketched him from a shop window on this corner.

Lombard House, on the left, stands on the site of the famous Curzon Street Chapel, where the Rev. Alexander Keith performed marriages without banns or licence, before the horrified fathers and mothers of London forced through the Marriage Act of 1753. The Chapel was one of London's scandals, but very popular with young couples who thereby evaded all the restrictions placed on them by their parents. There was a move to declare all the marriages illegal but this idea was hurriedly dropped when it was realised how many Government Ministers and members of the House of Lords would find themselves with illegitimate grandchildren. The 1753 Act stopped Mr Keith's activities but, since he kept no records of the marriages he performed, he left a fruitful source of litigation behind him. As late as 1923, the succession to the Dukedom of Somerset depended on the validity of a Curzon Street marriage.

Chesterfield Street on the right is the least altered of Mayfair's streets; nearly every house dates from the eighteenth century. This is the old Mayfair, of discreet houses set in quiet terraces, built before the Victorian millionaires arrived with their new money. There are no stables here because the Chesterfield Street residents would have found it cheaper to hire a carriage than to keep one.

From the time of Dr Johnson till the turn of this century, a horse in London cost as much as a servant. Each cost about £50 a year, but a horse needed a coachman to drive it and a stable to live in. In a large household a two-horse carriage needed a groom as well and Thackeray wrote once that the desire to become 'carriage folk' was the commonest cause of bankruptcy in London.

Beau Brummell, who set the standard of elegance in Regency London, lived at No. 4 Chesterfield Street and the Prince of Wales came here to take lessons in tying a cravat. Other would-be exquisites followed to have their clothes critically examined by Brummell. He gave his sartorial advice for nothing but looked for 'assistance' with his gambling debts from those he advised. Somerset Maugham celebrated his financial success as a writer by moving to No. 6 in 1911 and Admiral Cochrane lived here in the 1840s.

Chesterfield Street ends at Charles Street where a plaque marks the birthplace of Lord Rosebery. No. 20 beside it was the modest home of the Duke of Clarence until he succeeded to the throne as William IV in 1830. It is a surprisingly small dwelling for an heir to the throne but the Duke, who had no children by his wife, spent much of his income in supporting the nine children he had by the actress Mrs Jordan.

This western end of Charles Street narrows abruptly because it goes nowhere or, to be exact, nowhere the Charles Street residents would want to go. It leads to the old stables of Hay's Mews where the Charles Street horses and carriages were kept. Opposite the small pub in the corner, built to cater for grooms and coachmen, is a house that belongs to the depths of the countryside rather than the middle of Mayfair. It is a wood-lapped building resembling a rustic barn. It is the original workshop of

John Philips, the carpenter who helped to build Charles Street in 1745–1750 when this was open country.

Park Lane

Hill Street and Deanery Street lead down to the Dorchester Hotel and Park Lane. Park Lane was the last section of Mayfair to be built and soon acquired a reputation as the smartest address in London. A house in Park Lane became the ambition of every Victorian millionaire and South African diamond magnate who used their wealth to fight their way into London Society. They vied with each other in the splendour of the palaces they built along its length and *Punch* satirised them often. One cartoon by Du Maurier showed an indignant magnate arriving home at three in the morning to find the butler and four liveried footmen in the hall awaiting his return:

> Wot's all this, then? Only five of you to let me in? Supposing I'd brought a friend home?

Most of the Park Lane palaces have been replaced by hotels and blocks of flats, but one survivor is Stanhope House, on the left, at No. 47. Built in Forest of Dean sandstone in 1898 for Hudson 'the Soap King', the architect squeezed every Gothic feature he could on to its façade and embellished its interior with Flemish panelling from the seventeenth century. An idea of what this section of Park Lane once looked like can be deduced from the description of Stanhope House in 1902 as 'a modest house, whose restraint both in size and decoration is a reproach to its larger and more vulgar neighbours'.

Our walk continues up Park Lane past the Dorchester Hotel on the right, which was built in 1930 on the site of Dorchester House. The Hotel's architects went to extraordinary lengths to sound-proof its bedrooms, lining the floors with sea-weed and the ceilings with cork. The original Dorchester House, an incredible Victorian building that copied the Villa Farnese in Rome in style and size, possessed drawing rooms and saloons deliberately designed to be larger than those at Buckingham Palace.

The list of residents of South Street resembles a *Who's Who* of the nineteenth century. Charles James Fox, Florence Nightingale, Beau Brummell, the Duke of Orleans ('Philip Egalité') all lived here, as did Lord and Lady Holland and Lord Melbourne during his premiership. Lord Lucan of Light Brigade fame came here after the Crimea and Sir Alec Douglas-Home was born at No. 28.

The most exotic resident was undoubtedly Catherine Walters, whose residence at No. 15 is now commemorated with a blue plaque. Catherine Walters, universally known as 'Skittles', was the most famous courtesan in Victorian London. Her early conquests included the Marquis of Hartington, who later became leader of the Liberal Party, and the Duke of Devonshire whose mournful, if statesmanlike, statue stands in Whitehall. 'Skittles'' success was an affront to respectable society and she shocked London even more by riding with her admirers every morning in Rotten Row in a costume so finely made and well-fitting that, as someone said, she was more naked than if she had been in her bath.

Apart from her looks and forceful language, 'Skittles' attracted male admiration by her horsemanship and appeared often with the hard-riding Quorn. She was regularly first at the kill and one Master, after presenting her with the brush, ventured a compliment on the fine colour of her cheeks after a long run. 'Skittles'' typical response was: 'Huh! That's nothing. You ought to see my ruddy arse.' She lived till 1921, on an annuity of £2000 a year given to her by the Marquis of Hartington and achieved sufficient respectability in her old age to entertain Mr Gladstone to tea and to have her wheelchair pushed through Hyde Park by Lord Kitchener and Admiral Fisher.

The Grosvenor Estate

At Aldford Street we turn right, back into Mayfair, leaving the older section of Park Lane to the north. The Grosvenor House Hotel, on the site of the Duke of Westminster's mansion, was the first hotel in London to have a swimming-bath, while its Great Room beside Park Lane was originally a roller-skating rink built during the skating craze of 1930.

Beyond the hotel are the original Park Lane houses of the 1820s, built with their backs to the Park which had not yet become fashionable. Disraeli lived at No. 93 for many years; No. 96 was the home of Rufus Isaacs, the brilliant lawyer who rose from humble beginnings to become the only man ever to occupy successively the posts of Solicitor-General, Attorney-General, Lord Chief Justice, Viceroy of India and Foreign Secretary. Lily Langtry was introduced to Edward VII at Dudley House, No. 100 Park Lane; forty years later it was a rendez-vous for Edward VIII and Mrs Simpson.

The Earl of Dudley, who built the house in the 1820s, was a well-meaning man who reluctantly accepted the post of Foreign Secretary even though he knew it was well beyond his powers. At the height of a crisis with the French and Russians which could have led to war, the Earl set out Britain's views in two letters to the Foreign Ministers of both nations – and put them in the wrong envelopes!

The error proved to be a diplomatic coup. Working on the basis that no one could be so stupid, the Foreign Ministers in Paris and St Petersburg immediately assumed it was a tremendous bluff and a masterpiece of diplomatic finesse. Each Foreign Minister returned his letter with a polite note, upon which the Earl promptly redirected them to the correct capital. The original letters were received with even more respect as a double-bluff and both nations accepted the British view, with awed admiration at the incredible subtlety of perfidious Albion.

At the end of Aldford Street is the Grosvenor Chapel,

built in 1730 for use by the residents of the Grosvenor estate, who have owned this section of London since 1677 when Sir Richard Grosvenor married the owner Miss Mary Davies.

The Grosvenor estates centre around Grosvenor Square a few hundred yards to the north, now dominated by the enormous American Embassy building. The Americans have never been happy with the situation because Grosvenor Square is the only American embassy in the world held on lease; all the others are held on freehold as sovereign American property.

Repeated approaches were made to the Grosvenor Estates to sell the site but they always refused to do so, even when Parliamentary pressure was applied. In the 1930s the Ambassador met the Duke of Westminster and made a final appeal. The Duke listened to him and made a counter-offer; America could buy the freehold if they returned the Grosvenor property in America that had been confiscated after the American War of Independence. The Ambassador was delighted – until he realised the estate in question included the city of Miami and half the State of Florida.

The gardens behind the Grosvenor Chapel are full of seats presented by Americans whose Forces adopted it as their chapel during the war. Somewhere in the gardens is the grave of Ambrose Phillips who died in 1749. He was a poet who would be completely forgotten today were he not the original 'Namby-Pamby', a name given him by Pope because of his infantile style of writing. When he died, a friend summed up his career as: 'a good Whig and a middling poet'.

Tombstones have disappeared from most of the old London graveyards, but in this one they have been retained to buttress the grass banking. With unusual consideration for those who like looking at such things, they have been placed upside down, so that they can be read by those walking on the grass above.

The trees in the garden are, officially, the highest in

London. One of them, estimated to be nearly two hundred feet high, was climbed last year by the entrepreneur Richard Branson to publicise his campaign to keep London tidy.

A narrow path leads from the gardens into Farm Street, best known for the Jesuit Church that was built here after the Catholic Emancipation Act of 1829. In the 1920s Lloyd George and some other politicians came here to attend the funeral of a colleague, seating themselves in the choir stalls beside the coffin. The sacristan took a firm line; if they wished to sit in the choir, they must be properly dressed. When they decided to stay where they were, he promptly directed them to the vestry where he fitted them with cassocks.

Farm Street was built on the site of the Hay Hill Farm which stood here in the seventeenth century. Under an old leasing agreement, one of the houses still has to keep a passageway clear for cows to walk through to their long-gone pastures. While much of the street consists of garages with small flats above, there is one group of houses that resembles the back-cloth for a pastoral scene in a musical comedy. In the 1920s William Clough-Ellis designed a rustic folly for a famous actor and half a dozen imitations were promptly built alongside it. The best, or worst, example was pulled down only a few months ago, a full-size replica of Anne Hathaway's cottage at Stratford, complete with old-fashioned water-pump, 1930s leaded windows and 'antique' wooden beams.

Through Berkeley Square

The street bends round into Berkeley Square, whose heyday came to an end in the 1920s when it saw the last receptions in the grand manner. Royalty attended with Garter ribbons and tiaras and every male guest was expected to wear Court dress which included knee-breeches and swords.

The last recorded nightingale was heard in 1850 in the plane trees in the middle of the Square, which are the oldest in London. They were planted in 1789 as an experiment which proved extremely successful. Because the plane sheds its bark as well as its leaves, it proved ideal for London's smoky atmosphere and has become a standard feature of London's streets.

Berkeley Square came about by accident when this part of London was given to the Earl of Berkeley in the 1660s by Charles II, who repaid his supporters with grants of land. In 1696, the Earl sold his house to the Earl of Devonshire but made it a condition of sale that nothing be built on Berkeley land north of the house. Since the Grosvenor Estate starts two hundred yards to the north, the space in between was left open and became the Square we know today.

The row of buildings on the western side are the only survivors of the great houses of the 1740s that once stood all around the Square. Horace Walpole considered the staircase of No. 44, built in 1742, to be the most beautiful he had ever seen. Pevsner goes further and says it has the grandest interior of any eighteenth-century house in London.

No. 45 was the home of Clive of India. He committed suicide here but the house remained in his family's possession till 1950. The extraordinary ceilings of the first floor salon can be seen through the windows, although those at No. 47 are even more impressive. No. 48 belonged to the Prime Minister, Earl Grey, who rented it to the then Lord Chancellor, Lord Brougham. Brougham had little time for housekeeping and left behind what Lord Grey's indignant estate agent called 'the dirtiest house in London'.

In the 1860s the rumour spread that No. 50 was haunted. The house had been empty for years but mysterious lights were seen late at night. Eventually a newspaper reporter carried out an investigation and managed to find a man who had been caretaker in the house for ten years. The caretaker pooh-poohed the whole thing, but the reporter asked what his duties had been.

As the reporter had suspected, the ghost turned out to be the caretaker himself. He had been under strict orders to admit nobody to the house and to check the security of the doors and windows every night. It was his candle, carried through the empty house at night, that had caused all the fuss.

Like its neighbours, No. 52 was built in the eighteenth century, but the panelling in the drawing room pre-dates the house by six hundred years. When William the Conqueror was establishing his authority after Hastings, he made great efforts to conciliate the clergy, who might have led opposition to his rule. He awarded land to the Dean of Winchester Cathedral and sent a baulk of oak from the New Forest to help in rebuilding the cathedral roof. The timber was labelled as the gift of the King and stored in the cathedral workshop to season.

Time went by but no specific use was found for the wood. Eventually, in the nineteenth century, the Dean decided that it had been lying there long enough and allowed the cathedral carpenter to take it away. The carpenter sold it to a Mr Cloete in the 1880s, who had it made into panelling and installed in the drawing-room of No. 52.

The new building at the bottom of the Square stands on the site of the old Lansdowne House, where Joseph Priestley discovered oxygen in 1774. The vast hallway covers the space where the gardens used to be and should have a blue plaque somewhere, since it was on this spot that the first game of lawn tennis in the world was played in 1869.

In the summer of that year, Major Wingfield came to lunch at Lansdowne House and told Lord Lansdowne of an idea he had for a new game that four players could enjoy on a small piece of grass. Lord Lansdowne was interested, asked him back the following day and invited two other young men along to make up the party, one of whom was A. J. Balfour, later to become Prime Minister. The game was a great success, although all the players had differing views on the rules to be adopted. That is why the first published regulations did not appear till 1874, when they were called the rules of 'Sphairistike'. The name 'lawn tennis' was adopted later at the suggestion of Balfour who took pride in coining the term.

The small black gate by the entrance to Lansdowne Row, at the corner of Berkeley Street, was placed here two hundred years ago. It was put up by the residents after a highwayman held up a coach in Curzon Street in 1760 and made his escape through this narrow entry. The gate is still here to ensure that he cannot escape this way again.

Hay Hill is one of those slopes that seem imperceptible till one walks up it in a hurry. Queen Mary Tudor stationed her troops here to meet Wyatt's rebellion and had his head exhibited on a pole afterwards to dissuade others from following his example. By the 1790s it was surrounded by houses but was near enough the open country to be a favourite spot for footpads. One night the Prince of Wales and three of his friends were held up on Hay Hill by a robber whose expectations of rich pickings from such a wealthy-looking group were quickly dispelled. The Prince and his friends had spent the evening at a gambling den and had not a snuff-box, ring or tie-pin left amongst them. The disgruntled footpad finished up with a solitary half-crown found in the lining of a coat.

Hay Hill finishes at the point where Dover Street, for no apparent reason, suddenly becomes Grafton Street, which used to belong to the City of London. The City water-supply came through the conduit of Conduit Street just to the north and two of the Grafton Street houses still have the badge of the City of London on their walls.

No. 4 Grafton Street was the home of Lord Brougham from 1839 till his death in 1868. Brougham was a Scots lawyer who came to London to make his fortune but had little success till he was overheard in a tavern expressing his views on the famous divorce case of George IV and

Queen Caroline. The men who overheard him were the Queen's solicitors and they promptly offered him the case, after which Brougham never looked back.

He became Lord Chancellor in 1830 and carried through the great Reform Bill of 1832 as well as becoming a leading member of the Royal Society, an advocate of the abolition of slavery and a supporter of compulsory education. His interest in such diverse subjects as mathematics, theology, science and metaphysics was the talk of London and his reputation was summed up by an acquaintance who watched him drive by: 'There goes Solon, Lycurgus, Demosthenes, Archimedes, Sir Isaac Newton, Lord Chesterfield and a good many more in one post-chaise.' His most lasting memorial is the caricature showing him as a satyr being drawn along in a chariot that appeared on the front of *Punch* for a hundred and twenty years.

No. 7A, in the corner, has the second smallest frontage of any house in London (we look at the smallest in the next Walk), and Grafton Street bends around to join Bond Street, at the corner where Henry Irving lived. Cross Bond Street and walk down Clifford Street to No. 18, the dark building that has been Buck's Club since Captain Buckmaster founded it in 1919. Buck's Fizz was invented here and, with the Bath Club of Dover Street, it is a major source of P. G. Wodehouse's immortal Drones' Club.

At the end of Clifford Street is Savile Row, whose reputation for fine tailoring started in the 1860s, when the death of Prince Albert put the whole of London Society into mourning. The adoption of sombre blacks and greys made cut and fit the important aspects of men's clothes and they have been the hallmark of Savile Row ever since. Hawkes, at No. 1 on the corner, celebrated their bi-centenary in 1971 and the unusual spaciousness of their showrooms stems from the fact that the building was originally the headquarters of the Royal Geographic

Society where Livingstone's body lay in state before its burial in the Abbey in 1874.

Sheridan, whose brilliance as a dramatist and politician was equalled only by the scale of his financial disasters, died at No. 14 Savile Row. Tradition has it that his ghost haunts his previous house, No. 17, where his pen can be heard scratching in the early hours in the room where he wrote most of his plays.

Down Regent Street

New Burlington Street takes us into Regent Street and the last section of our walk. Up to the left is Liberty's, the shop that dictated fashion in England from the 1880s till the 1920s. The first Mr Liberty was fascinated by the Orient and imported the Chinese fabrics and patterns that made the firm's name. D'Oyly Carte came here to buy the Japanese fabrics to be worn in *The Mikado*. *Punch* lampooned Liberty's often but paid them the compliment of the famous cartoon in which a lady proudly stated her dress was: 'as good as anything Liberty's could produce'. Her listener murmured sadly: 'Ah, Liberty's! What sins are committed in thy name.' Like all the other buildings in Regent Street, Liberty's stands on land belonging to the Crown Commissioners. That is why, like its neighbours, its frontage onto Regent Street is faced with Portland stone.

The shop overcame that restriction on its individuality by the frieze across its front which shows the process of bringing Liberty's goods to London. Coolies, camels, elephants and ships are represented, all struggling to bring their produce to the benign Britannia at one end, while three carved figures on the roof-line watch the process with interest.

Around the corner of Liberty's in Great Marlborough Street is the frontage that Liberty's would have erected on Regent Street had it been allowed. It is an amazingly accurate imitation of Tudor timber-framing and even the windows and lead drain-pipes are made by hand. The splendid clock has a St George who comes out to chase the dragon at every quarter-hour; he catches him on the hour and delivers a number of jerky blows. Other shops in London have timber-framing on the outside of their buildings, but the Liberty's timbers are genuinely old. They come from the old warships *Impregnable* and *Hindustan*, the same ships which provided the wooden floors and staircases of which this wing is constructed. While the decorative effect is splendid, the staircases run in such unusual directions that in 1970 the firm issued a booklet entitled *How not to get lost in Liberty's*.

No. 112 Regent Street is Garrard's the jewellers, who cut the Koh-i-Noor diamond for Queen Victoria and asked the Duke of Wellington to strike the first blow. It stands at the start of the Quadrant which swings down into Piccadilly Circus past the Café Royal.

The Café Royal occupied a special place in London's life for nearly eighty years. Opened in 1865 by Daniel Nicols, it was the first large French restaurant to flourish in the West End. Oscar Wilde held court here till his disgrace, followed by Max Beerbohm and Augustus John, whose presencc always ensured a large crowd around them. Royalty and the Stage followed in their wake and the staff of the Grill Room, which recently had its famous ceiling cleaned and restored with 60,000 sheets of gold leaf, took a pride in the contrasting customers they served.

One regular customer for nearly forty years was a small, shabby man who came in every day and ordered a soda-water, drank it quietly and left. Nobody knew who he was till one night in the 1920s when a race-gang crowd came in and started threatening the other customers. The shabby man walked over to the ring-leader, whispered in his ear and watched quietly as the whole gang left the bar. The manager thanked him, asked his name and how he had cleared the bar. The man turned out to be Jim Carey, the last bare-fist middle-weight champion, and he had simply told the ringleader that unless he left, every pugilist in London would be there in ten minutes to ensure he was never able to enter it again.

The Café Royal developed a strong sense of discretion, and not even the waiter who had been her fiancé showed any emotion when a chorus girl came to celebrate her engagement to a marquis. That was the same night that a bishop entertained a lady whom the Café staff knew had 'admirers' at every level of society and the occasion prompted the manager to compose:

There once was a bishop of Brum,
A jovial clerical sport.
He enjoyed his Baba au Rhum
As well as a lady from Court.
And although I won't tell her name,
Because that would be very disloyal,
On the stage she enjoyed quite a fame
With others who dined at the Royal.

The management of the Café Royal prided themselves on meeting all their customers' wishes, although they had great difficulty, in 1902, in convincing the Shah of Persia that he could not take the entire chorus line of the Empire Theatre back home with him.

The last story of this walk concerns the famous symbol on the windows of the Café Royal – an 'N' surmounted by a coronet. Although Nicols himself was an ardent Republican, his brother-in-law was an equally fervent supporter of Napoleon III and took every means of expressing his loyalty. In 1870, Nicols's wife persuaded him to take a holiday and he left his brother-in-law in charge. He returned to find the windows decorated with the Napoleonic symbol which, his brother-in-law knew, he would be too parsimonious to remove. Nicols was furious but his brother-in-law managed to placate him by persuading him he was far better known in London than the Emperor; every Londoner would automatically assume the N stood for Nicols – which most of them did.

SIXTEENTH ♦ WALK

From Marble Arch through Kensington Gardens to Hyde Park Corner

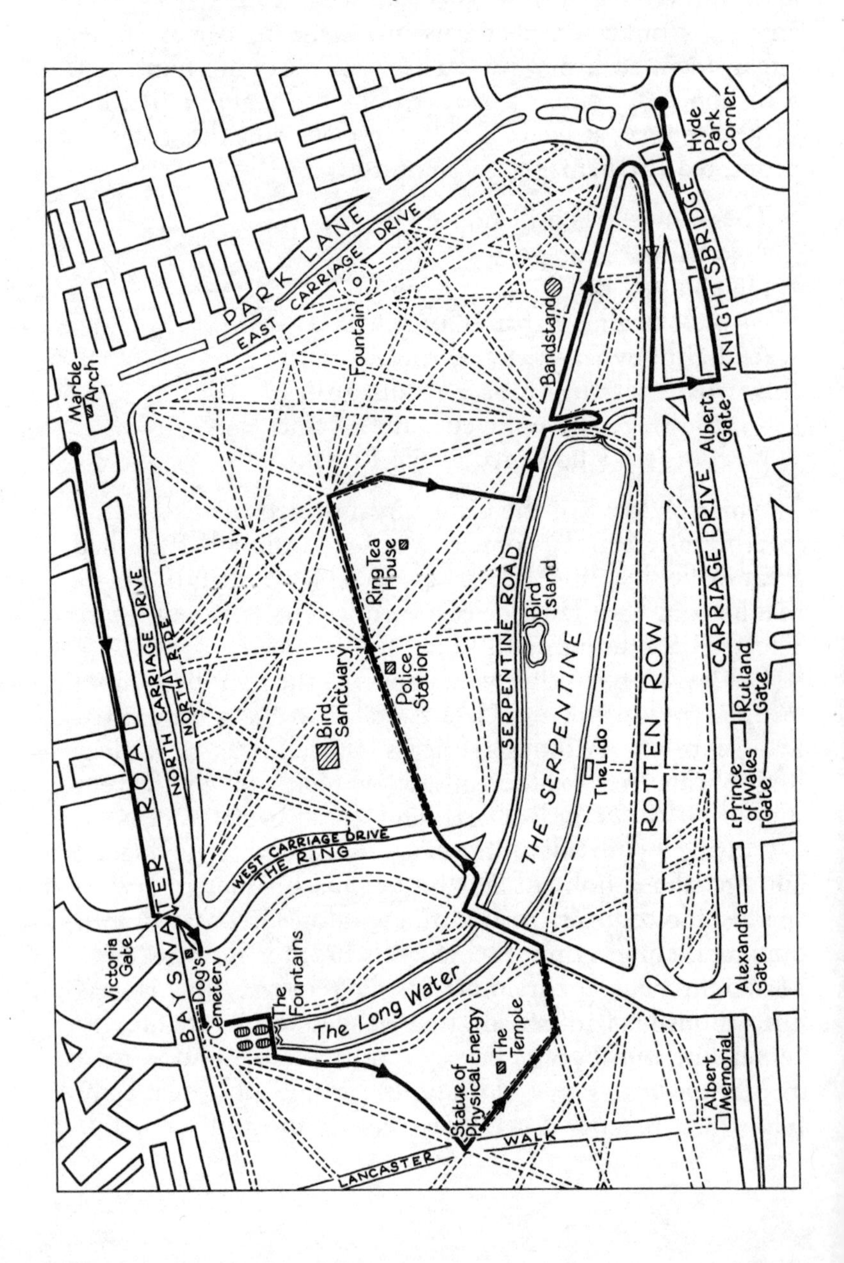

SIXTEENTH ♦ WALK

From Marble Arch through Kensington Gardens to Hyde Park Corner

This walk begins at Marble Arch at the bottom of Edgware Road, where the traffic from the north meets the flow of vehicles from the west along the Bayswater Road to make this corner one of London's busiest junctions.

It saw the first omnibuses in 1829 introduced by George Shillibeer, when he brought to England the new long coaches he had seen in France. He also brought over the French name for them coined by a shopkeeper in Nantes called Mr Omnes. Seeing the success enjoyed by the local coaches that specialised in carrying passengers for short distances, Mr Omnes entered the business himself. He had new vehicles designed to carry more passengers for short journeys, advertising them with a pun on his own name; *omnes* is Latin for 'all', *omnibus* means 'for all' or 'for everybody'. It remained the official name for the vehicles till the 1920s when London Transport adopted the shortened version of 'bus'.

This same stretch of road saw London's first trams, operated by an American with the appropriate name of Mr Train. The theory of reducing friction was sound, but the idea failed because the steel rails for Mr Train's vehicles projected from the road, causing so much damage to other vehicles that the scheme was soon abandoned. It was another ten years before someone thought of setting the rails below the surface, enabling London trams to run successfully for nearly a hundred years.

To the east is Oxford Street which has now become the busiest shopping street in Europe and accounts for a quarter of the retail sales in London. It lies along the old Roman road that led from the City to the west and its position as London's leading shopping street was confirmed by the arrival of Gordon Selfridge in 1909.

Selfridge was an extraordinary character who had become a partner in America's largest store, Marshall Field, before he was 28, and believed he could create a store in London that would outsell even William Whiteley who had earned the nickname of 'the Universal Provider'. With financial backing from Waring of Waring & Gillow's, lent with the proviso that Selfridge did not sell furniture, a condition the store still honours, he opened his enormous building in 1909.

He combined selling with showmanship, employing four Royal Academicians to design the grand entrance which is surmounted by the extraordinary figure holding the famous clock. It astonished Londoners and led *Punch* to write:

Hickory-dickory-dock,
A mouse ran up Selfridge's clock.
It didn't expect
Such a bizarre effect,
And never got over the shock.

Selfridge brought in thousands of customers with his publicity stunts. The store was opened with fanfares of trumpets by as many Army musicians as he was able to hire, which led Harrod's to reply with similar musical attractions for their customers, though theirs took the more discreet form of a series of concerts by the London Symphony Orchestra. When Blériot flew the Channel for the first time, his aeroplane was in Selfridge's front window the following day and Signor Marconi was similarly persuaded to give personal demonstrations of his new wireless equipment.

The Marble Arch and Tyburn Tree

Oxford Street ends at the Marble Arch, the London landmark which stands at the junction of Mayfair and Hyde Park to the south and Marylebone and Bayswater to the north. The Arch, which is made from Carrara marble, was originally erected outside Buckingham Palace in 1827 when George IV and his architect John Nash were intent on changing the appearance of London (see Thirteenth Walk). The Arch, however, cannot be considered one of their successes.

It was intended to be a glorious reminder of the victory over the French in the Napoleonic Wars and it bore representations of the battle of Waterloo on one side and of Trafalgar on the other. George IV commissioned an impressive equestrian statue of himself to stand on top, but he died before the statue was finished. Since no one respected his memory enough to ensure that his wishes were carried out, the statue was eventually erected in Trafalgar Square to occupy an empty plinth.

The main difficulty, however, lay in George's desire to recreate the grandeur of Imperial Rome and the Arch, a copy of the Triumphal Arch of Constantine, was intended to be the grand entrance to Buckingham Palace. Unfortunately the copy was made too accurately and, although the width of the centre arch may have been correct for a Roman chariot, it proved too narrow for the State Coach and could not be used for the royal processions for which it was intended. It remained in front of the Palace as an embarrassing reminder of George IV's grandiose ideas till 1851, when London underwent an enormous spring-clean in readiness for the Great Exhibition and the Arch was taken down and rebuilt on its present site.

The authorities took the opportunity of the move to make a few discreet changes to the Arch to emphasise what they saw as Britain's role in 1851 – a nation of traders rather than a nation of soldiers. The figure of Britannia whose shield bore the head of Nelson underwent some tactful alterations and reappeared on the portico of the National Portrait Gallery as Minerva, while the panels of Waterloo and Trafalgar were replaced with the more uplifting figures of England inspiring Youth and Valour, Virtue, Peace and Plenty. It still counts as a Royal Arch, however, and the only people allowed to drive through it are Royalty and the King's Troop of the Royal Horse Artillery when they come down to Hyde Park to fire salutes.

The arrival of the Arch was welcomed by the residents of this part of London because they had been trying to acquire a new name for the area for thirty years. This cross-roads is the site of Tyburn Tree where executions were carried out for six hundred years, giving the area an evil reputation that the owners of the newly-built houses of genteel Bayswater and Marylebone were anxious to dispel. The difficulty was that the rest of London persisted in using the old name, but the installation of the Marble Arch in 1851 went a long way to improving the status of the area.

Over the centuries executions were carried out in different parts of London. Smithfield in the City had been the popular place for burning heretics in the sixteenth and seventeenth centuries although it was common practice to execute murderers as near as possible to the scene of the crime. For most offences, executions were carried out at official sites; since public executions were thought to be a deterrent, the authorities made it as easy as possible for people to see them. Tyburn was chosen since it lay in open country enabling large crowds to assemble. As a further incentive, execution days were official public holidays.

Because of the tremendous flow of traffic, it is difficult to see the actual site of the Tyburn gallows but it is marked by a small circular plaque in the middle of the railed traffic island in the Edgware Road at the point where it runs into the Bayswater Road. Executions were carried out at Tyburn from 1388 till 1783, when they moved back to the City, outside Newgate Prison (see Ninth Walk). Over the years Tyburn gave rise to dozens of legends, spread by the enormous sale of broadsheets and pamphlets that recounted either the grisly crimes of the man about to die or, even more popular, his so-called confessions – a ghoulish fashion still popular today.

Among those who died at Tyburn were Claude Duval the romantic highwayman, Jack Sheppard whose death in 1714 was watched by a crowd of nearly 200,000 and Jonathan Wild, the thief-catcher who himself became London's greatest criminal and whose last act was to pick the hangman's pocket. Derricks, the large lifting cranes used in docks today, take their name from a Tyburn hangman in the seventeenth century who devised a new form of gibbet, while the original Jack Ketch was a Tyburn executioner for thirty years.

Bayswater Road

Walk west along the northern side of Bayswater Road, where the numbering of the houses reflects the reluctance of the residents to admit they lived on what was called the Tyburn Road. The result is that each Terrace, Place or Gate along the Bayswater Road has its own postal address and set of house numbers.

Twenty yards brings us to the Convent of the Holy Martyrs, built to commemorate the Catholics who died for their faith at Tyburn. A few doors further on is London's smallest and narrowest house at No. 10 Hyde Park Place. It is four feet wide and, although it is officially a house, it was originally built because the owner of No. 9 wanted to close the alley that ran beside his house and found the only way to do so was to build on it.

The open space on the right beyond the smallest house is St George's Fields, once the burial ground for St George's Hanover Square and now a housing estate. Laurence Sterne was buried here in 1768 but his corpse was stolen by body-snatchers two days later and sold to a Professor of Anatomy for dissection. The theft was only discovered when one of the Professor's audience fainted with horror on recognising the corpse. The authorities were fully aware that this burial ground, set in open country, was vulnerable to body-snatching and made efforts to stop the practice though these were often ineffective. The local newspaper reported that: 'a Watchman was placed there, attended by a large mastiff Dog; notwithstanding which, on Sunday night last, some villains found means to steal out another Body and carried off the very Dog.'

The Dogs' Cemetery

Victoria Gate, opposite Brook Street, is one of the twenty-three entrances to the Park. Beside it is the famous Dogs' Cemetery, which can be seen best through the Park railings from the outside. It is here because a pet dog was run over just outside the Lodge gate in 1880 and the owner insisted on it being buried as near as possible to where the accident had occurred.

The Park authorities would normally have refused the request out of hand, but the distraught owner was the Duchess of Cambridge whose husband was not only a cousin of Queen Victoria and Commander-in-Chief of the British Army, but also happened to hold the appointment of Ranger of Hyde Park.

The story spread round London and set a fashion, since to tell your friends that your departed pet lay in the graveyard implied either an acquaintance with the Duchess or at least some sort of influence with the Park authorities. There are over three hundred graves in the small plot because, although the Park officials resisted strongly, they were unable to stop the practice till 1915 when they were able to plead lack of space. Even then, some owners managed to convince the authorities they had some form of legal right and an interment certainly took place as late as 1953.

Hyde Park and Kensington Gardens

Walk the few yards back past the Lodge and enter the Park through the Victoria Gate, where the lamp has a spiked cresset and crown to show you are entering Crown property and a notice-board tells you the ninety-two things you are not allowed to do in the Royal Parks. The path to the right, parallel to the Bayswater Road, runs down to the next lodge at Westbourne Gate.

Westbourne Gate lies on another of London's invisible boundaries. It is the border between Hyde Park and Kensington Gardens, a border still recognised today by the Metropolitan Police who patrol Hyde Park, while the Gardens are the responsibility of the Royal Parks Constabulary. From the Lodge, built in 1858 to guard the Buckhill Gate that separated the two parks, the boundary runs south along Buck Hill Walk, across the bridge over the Serpentine, and on to Alexandra Gate.

Hyde Park and Kensington Gardens have been open country since they were given to the monks of Westminster after the Conquest. When Henry VIII seized the Church's property in 1536, he retained the park as a hunting ground and deer were hunted here on Buck Hill till 1768. As London grew westward after the Fire of 1666, St James's Park and the Green Park beside the Court at Whitehall became the fashionable places to stroll in the evening, but Hyde Park was the place to show off your horsemanship.

Samuel Pepys came here in 1663 to try and impress Charles II and recounts how he dressed carefully for the occasion and rode his own old horse to Charing Cross, where he hired a younger, more spirited animal to show off before the Court in the Park. Unfortunately the hireling was too high-spirited and Pepys had to retreat ignominiously without having either his finery or his horse noticed by the King.

The separation of Kensington Gardens from Hyde Park began when William III came to the throne in 1688. William suffered badly from asthma and set up his Court in what is now Kensington Palace to escape from the riverside damp of Whitehall. Queen Anne who succeeded him preferred Kensington as well, but the layout of the Gardens that we see today was carried out by Queen Caroline, wife of George II, who had strong views on what the Royal Parks should look like.

She set about extending the small formal gardens around the Palace to the present 275 acres and laid out the Round Pond, the Broad Walk and the long lines of elms that give the Gardens the formality absent from Hyde Park. Her greatest improvement was the creation of the Serpentine, made by digging out the marshy ground that lay beside the Westbourne stream running diagonally across the Park. Since it kept her occupied and cost him nothing, the King did not interfere. It was only after her death that he discovered he had been paying for all the improvements and that the £26,000 to pay for the creation of the Serpentine had come from the Privy Purse, by means of a private arrangement between the Queen and Walpole, the Prime Minister.

Although Hyde Park remained open to the public at specified times, Kensington Gardens was considered private property and access was for a long time restricted to members of the Court and their friends. The privilege became more general and by the start of the nineteenth century 'all respectably dressed persons' were admitted.

It was this restriction of entry that gave Kensington Gardens its reputation for exclusivity and the famous Nannies' Walk got its name as a safe and respectable place for aristocratic babies to have their airing. The more plebeian Hyde Park was a different matter; it was open to the 'soldiers, sailors and servants' who were forbidden the Gardens. In the nineteenth century, when soldiers still wore scarlet, Hyde Park was the place for servant girls to impress their friends by being seen with a handsome warrior in full dress. There was a regular tariff for the afternoon escort duty; a soldier from a Line regiment cost sixpence, an artilleryman or sapper charged ninepence for his company while a lordly Guardsman refused anything less than a shilling.

The Long Water and Peter Pan

The path parallel to the Bayswater Road leads down into the valley of the Westbourne and Queen Anne's Alcove, an enormous open-sided summer house with a high shell canopy and the Queen's monogram over the arch. Wren built it for her in 1708 and it stood beside Kensington Palace till the last century. Facing south, it is the most sheltered spot in the gardens, keeping out the wind effectively just as Wren designed it to.

Beyond the Alcove are the Fountains, an Italian water garden laid out in 1861, with the pumping station on the right that controls the level of the Serpentine. The water is supplied by the Westbourne, one of London's 'lost rivers' which makes a rare appearance just behind the building, on its way from Hampstead to the Thames. If the pumping station looks vaguely familiar, it is because Prince Albert specified the building should look like the Petit Trianon at Versailles.

Albert had a good eye for architecture and coupled it with an appreciation for the practical aspects of domestic life. He said once that if he had not been born a prince, he would like to have been a plumber since that trade provided more benefits to humanity than any other. It was because of his interest in the subject that so many sanitary and plumbing devices were shown at the Great Exhibition, which led in turn to the adoption of modern plumbing in the 1850s and 1860s. (See Sixth Walk.)

The balcony beyond the fountains looks south over the lake. On the left is a medallion of Victoria with a matching one of Albert on the other side. The other two plaques are of cherubs presumably showing the pleasures to be enjoyed in the Gardens. One plaque shows two cherubs manning a sailing boat and cheering on another who is swimming alongside; the other plaque strikes a more bloodthirsty note and commemorates the time when the Gardens were the royal hunting-ground. One cherub holds a dead pheasant while another with dog and gun is clearly on the lookout for more.

In the middle of the balustrade are three boundary marks set in the paving stones: SGHS, 9A PP and MBP 1900. They were almost the last to be erected in London and represent the end of the struggle for jurisdiction between the secular and Church authorities.

The Manor of Paddington was granted to the monks of Westminster Abbey in the tenth century and was seized by the Crown after the Reformation. Twenty years later in response to a request for support from St Paul's, a non-monastic foundation, Edward VI gave the revenues of Paddington to the Bishop of London – the 'robbing Peter to pay Paul' described in the Fourteenth Walk. At the end of the nineteenth century Paddington became an independent parish and put its boundary mark (PP) here to show its border with St George's Hanover Square (SGHS).

The third mark, MBP 1900 (Metropolitan Borough of Paddington), stems from the Local Government Act of 1899 that created the Metropolitan Boroughs we know today. The new Boroughs followed the general boundaries of the old parishes but it transpired that the Borough of Chelsea had a claim, through an old bequest, to part of the Borough of Paddington. Both Boroughs were jealous of their new authority and it needed a Royal Commission and a Board of Inquiry before the final compromise was reached. Chelsea received a slice of Kensington, who in turn received a small area of Paddington. Paddington promptly laid out this further set of boundary marks in 1900 in an attempt to stop any future claims.

Follow the path southwards with the water immediately on your left. This is the Long Water, one half of the lake which Queen Caroline created by damming the Westbourne at the far end. The Long Water has become a sanctuary for wildfowl because it lies within the Royal

Gardens where no boating, swimming or sailing is allowed.

The path runs beside the lake to the Leaf Yard, a thick copse that comes down to the water's edge. A small open space contains the Peter Pan statue, which has the double distinction of being the most popular statue in the Gardens and having no right to be here at all.

J. M. Barrie lived nearby at No. 100 Bayswater Road and spent much of his time in the Gardens. The success of his play *Peter Pan* had given him the idea of commissioning the statue and he asked a senior Parks official for permission to place it here. Since statues in the Royal Parks are normally a matter for Royal Commissions or Parliamentary committees, the official was taken aback but made discreet inquiries. He found that no official recognition could be given to the matter but neither would there be any official objection, so long as the matter was kept quiet. Since this was exactly what Barrie wanted, he went ahead, although the secret leaked out and questions were asked in Parliament on who had authorised this departure from normal practice.

At Barrie's insistence there was no unveiling ceremony. The statue was placed in position under a shroud on 30 April 1912 and at midnight Barrie came down and uncovered it so that: 'Children will come here tomorrow on May Morning and find Peter Pan has just grown out of the ground.'

As soon as it was unveiled it was attacked by every art critic in London, but they missed the point Barrie was making. It was not designed to be seen and criticised by adults; it was designed for small children. If one bends down and looks at it from the height they do, it becomes a very different thing. It has fairies, squirrels, rabbits and mice; even the small snail at the base is polished from the tiny hands that have reached up to stroke it. Sculpted by Sir George Frampton, it was voted the most popular statue in London in 1921.

When the author visited the statue in 1988 there was a

mother assuring her child that 'Yes, this is Peter Pan.' She was right in every sense. In 1897 Barrie met the young Llewelyn-Davies boys in Kensington Gardens and took them under his wing. He became friends with their parents, whom he drew as Mr and Mrs Darling in *Peter Pan* and became the boys' guardian after their parents had died of cancer. He brought them here to feed bread to the ducks and squirrels and, in 1910, he changed the script of *Peter Pan* to introduce the sleep-walking and nightmares suffered by Michael Llewelyn-Davies (1900–1921).He told them later: 'I made Peter Pan by rubbing the five of you violently together, as savages with two sticks produce a flame.' When Sir George Frampton did the statue, he used Michael Llewelyn-Davies as his model.

Behind the Leaf Yard copse, the spire of Kensington Church on the horizon stands just to the right of Kensington Palace, where Queen Victoria spent the first seventeen years of her life. Spread along a line from the Leaf Yard to the Palace are five pairs of stones set in the grass, each marked 'PP' to show the Paddington parish boundaries. It is from these that Barrie got the name Peter Pan and he acknowledged his debt to the Gardens by installing the children's swings in the playground at the northern end of the Broad Walk.

The path towards the Palace joins Lancaster Walk at the Statue of Physical Energy. A long open avenue of trees leads to the Broad Walk and the statue of Queen Victoria sculpted by her fourth daughter Princess Louise. The Princess was unhappily married to the Duke of Argyll and spent much of her life in the Palace where she wrote under the pseudonym of Myra Fontenoy, perhaps a reference to the great elm trees around the Gardens which, so tradition says, were planted in the formation adopted by the Guards regiments in the French wars. She became a competent sculptor under the tuition of Sir Joseph Boehm and, although the inscription shows the statue was presented by the Borough of Kensington, the back is signed with a bold 'Louise fecit'.

North of the statue of Physical Energy, further up the Lancaster Walk, is the obelisk commemorating the African explorer John Speke. His discoveries were the sensation of England but his fellow-explorer Burton doubted his claim to have found the source of the Nile and challenged him to a public debate. Speke went out to shoot partridge on the morning of the meeting and was found dead. Because of the public esteem in which he was held, a verdict of accidental death was pronounced, but the feeling amongst his friends was that he had committed suicide rather than face Burton's accusations.

The wording on the obelisk is deliberately ambiguous. His family wanted the words 'In memory of Speke, the discoverer of Victoria, Nyanza and the source of the Nile.' The Royal Geographic Society which erected the monument took a slightly more cautious view and their wording simply reads: 'In memory of Speke. Victoria, Nyanza and the Nile 1864.'

The dramatic figure of Physical Energy by G. F. Watts was erected in 1904 and Cecil Rhodes was so impressed by it that he asked for a second copy to be made for his own grave. Watts agreed and completed the casting just as news of Rhodes's death reached London.

Two paths lead south from the Statue of Physical Energy. One points due south to the Albert Memorial, the other leads half-left towards the Serpentine Gallery. Half-way along the path towards the Gallery is a small white building a few yards off the path. This is the Temple, a folly built around 1728, probably as a summer-house for Queen Caroline and her ladies.

The Temple has been stripped of most of its fittings, but is worth a visit to admire the care with which our forefathers scratched their graffiti. There are hundreds of names carved in the stone, but the vandals of the early nineteenth century took far more trouble with their signatures. Could anybody today equal the carvings on the eastern corner by John Hedgins of Chepstow, E. Lucas who cut his name in 1821, or 'IC' or 'PP' who inscribed their initials in flowing copper-plate in 1799?

From the Temple the path turns left towards the bridge across the Long Water, leaving the Serpentine Gallery to the right. The restaurant by the bridge was built in 1963 (a black hexagonal slab in front records the date) amidst protests that it would ruin the Gardens. Although it is built on the 'public' Hyde Park side of the road, it was felt it would attract the 'wrong sort' of people to the Gardens. The authorities were able to point out that the Serpentine Gallery in Kensington Gardens had been a refreshment house originally; the new one was built only because so many people had protested when the Gallery restaurant had been closed.

The Serpentine and the Achilles Statue

The Rennie bridge of 1826 separates the Long Water of Kensington Gardens from the Serpentine of Hyde Park. The bridge, offering superb views across to Westminster Abbey and the Houses of Parliament, looks down on the Lido, known for thirty years as 'Lansbury's Lido', after the Labour politician who opened it officially as a swimming place in the 1930s.

Over the bridge the road curves right and left around the Magazine, built in 1803 to store ammunition for the London Militia who stood by to repel Napoleon's invasion, which seemed just as likely then as Hitler's did in 1940. It served its purpose for over a hundred and fifty years, storing ammunition in both World Wars. The Parks gardeners use it now but the left-hand wall still bears a stern warning from its previous role: 'No Smoking – 3 Mile Limit'.

Cross the busy road by the Magazine and take the path half-right to the north-west, past the horse-trough that, with the others around the Park, seem to be the only ones left in London fulfilling their original purpose. The

Bird Sanctuary lies a few yards to the left of the path with the famous, or infamous, monument to the naturalist W. H. Hudson. Epstein's carving of 'Rima' from Hudson's *Green Mansions* aroused even more protest than his nude figures in the Strand (see Fourth Walk). The unveiling by Stanley Baldwin in 1925 was followed by uproar in the Press; a newspaper started a fund to buy the monument so that it could be demolished; it was tarred and feathered within a week and regularly daubed with black paint for years afterwards.

The path runs between the Superintendent's Lodge on the left and the Police Station on the right, to a shrubbery two hundred yards ahead that conceals a public lavatory. On the far side of the shrubbery is a drinking fountain erected 'To Commemorate the International Year of the Child' when two hundred thousand children came to Hyde Park. The plinth bears an inscription: 'The Great Childrens' Party in Hyde Park 30–31 May 1979' and adds: 'The Queen came and so did the Duke of Edinburgh and Princess Anne and many other famous people.' The fountain has fifty childrens' toys cast in brass. There are model aeroplanes, boats, motor cars and Teddy bears, while the figures include Pinky and Perky, Basil Brush, the Beatrix Potter characters and Mickey Mouse.

This area of the Park is known as the Ring, from the original cattle pound that the monks used, and was the fashionable spot in Charles II's day to show off one's new horse or coach. In the eighteenth century it became the favourite spot for duellists and, at the height of the fashion, combatants queued up for their turn to try and shed each other's blood.

Although many of the duels were serious and were fought to the death, some seemed to have been fought for appearance's sake and ingenious tricks were devised to lessen the risk or to even the chances between the combatants. One young man, faced with an opponent whom he knew to be an expert shot, claimed the right to nominate the distance at which shots were to be exchanged. Thinking he was going to claim thirty yards instead of the normal twenty, his opponent readily agreed but hurriedly decided to apologise when the young man specified a distance of three feet – which meant certain death for both of them.

Another more cautious duellist opted for a distance of four hundred yards to which his equally cautious opponent readily agreed. The last formal duel was fought here in 1817 although the Park authorities have a record of two elderly gentlemen in 1871 who decided to settle a dispute with their walking-sticks and succeeded in reducing these to matchwood, before they were separated by the Park keepers.

Follow the path due south to the Serpentine and turn left along the horse track at the water's edge. At the end of the lake is the Dell restaurant and immediately behind it a balustrade with an urn on the corner. It informs the passer-by that:

> A supply of water by conduit from this spot was granted to the Abbey of Westminster, with the manor of Hyde, by King Edward the Confessor.
>
> The Manor was resumed by the Crown in 1536 but the Springs as a head and original fountain of water were preserved to the Abbey by the Charter of Queen Elizabeth in 1560.

The ground drops sharply to the right to the Dell, one of the few formal gardens in the Park. The Westbourne makes its last appearance here, flowing over the end of the dam before it vanishes underground on its journey to the Thames.

The monolith on the right of the path is the famous Standing Stone. Tradition holds that it is a Druid stone brought here by Charles I, but its true history is more prosaic. It is a seven-ton piece of Cornish granite brought here by Nancy Mitford's grandfather as a support for a long-vanished drinking-fountain. It shares with the Law Courts' clock and Canning's statue the melancholy distinction of having killed someone, a Mr Sandby, who was unfortunate enough to be underneath when it fell over while being placed in position.

The Achilles Statue

Continue along the horse-ride, leaving the Dell on the right and the Cavalry Monument (St George and the Dragon) on the left. At the end of the track is the Achilles statue, a sculptural confidence trick. The plinth states that it was erected by 'The Women of England to Arthur Duke of Wellington and his brave companions in arms'. It looks towards Apsley House, the large building on the corner of the Park which was, and still is, the home of the Duke of Wellington, although as Leigh Hunt said, it seems 'to be manifesting the most furious intentions of self defence against the hero it commemorates'.

It was the first nude statue to be seen in public in England and it was received with fury by Londoners, one of whom wrote to *The Times* to say that if his mother 'had seen any of her children looking at such an object, she would have soundly whipped them'. It was originally completely nude and the fig leaf was added later after some necessary mutilation of the carving beneath, like that suffered by the Epstein figures in the Strand.

The confidence trick of the Achilles statue lies not in its nudity but in its origins. It is not Achilles, it is not an original work and it was certainly not chosen by the women of England. What happened was that the Countess Spencer and a few friends, including the sculptor Richard Westmacott, decided that London needed a copy of the statue in Rome by Phidias, the greatest sculptor of ancient Greece, which showed Alexander the Great taming Bucephalus.

They opened a subscription list but, since very little money came in, they decided to take advantage of the current adulation of the Duke of Wellington, starting the project all over again in a new guise. Instead of being a subscription to buy a copy of an unknown statue, the new advertisement sought money to erect a monument to the Duke in the form of a statue of Achilles, made from the metal of French guns captured during his campaigns.

This was a very different matter and the money poured in; the Pope made the statue available for a cast to be made, the Army provided thirty French guns to provide the metal for the statue and Richard Westmacott started work. He completed the casting, made a few tactful alterations to the figure and the promoters of the project had the satisfaction of seeing their 'Achilles' unveiled by George IV on the anniversary of Waterloo.

It has subsequently come to light that the committee were almost as mistaken as the women of England they had persuaded to contribute. The figure provided by the Pope was not that of Alexander by Phidias since no such thing existed; Phidias died over a century before Alexander was born. It was of Castor, son of Zeus, by an unknown mediaeval sculptor. The metal from the French guns proved unsatisfactory and had to be quietly disposed of and replaced with ordinary statue metal, while Westmacott's 'tactful' alterations included putting a sword and shield in Achilles' hands instead of Castor's reins and whip and finishing off the Alexander/Castor/Achilles figure by putting Wellington's head on top. The Duke made no public comment but his friends record that he was not happy at being portrayed as the rudest and nudest man in England.

Albert Gate and Knightsbridge

The Achilles statue is separated from Rotten Row by a narrow stretch of grass where William Friese-Greene took the first ever cinematograph film of his cousin and his young son in 1889. Rotten Row was the centre of London's fashion for over a century. From the 1820s till 1939, to ride in 'The Row' was a mark of social distinction and, in its heyday in the late nineteenth century, peers and peeresses, generals and admirals came here and stood on their chairs to watch the beauties of London ride by. Parisians came to admire the scene of fashion and wealth and someone once calculated that 'Rotten Row on a good morning in Spring contained over half the money, half the land and most of the beauty of England.'

Turn right along the Row to Albert Gate, passing the small tablet commemorating the vicious bomb attack on the contingent of Life Guards in 1982. The Life Guards are based at Knightsbridge Barracks further along the Row where Disraeli made the famous speech in 1878 when he described his opponent Gladstone as:

> A sophistical rhetorician, inebriated with the exuberance of his own verbosity, gifted with an egotistical imagination that can at all times command an interminable and inconsistent series of arguments to malign his opponents and glorify himself.

Two enormous buildings stand beside Albert Gate. They were erected in 1841 and were promptly nicknamed 'Gibraltar' and 'Malta', since like those Imperial outposts 'they would never be taken'. Ironically the building on the left was 'taken' by our oldest enemy and has been the French Embassy for more than a century.

The Embassy had one previous tenant, George Hudson 'the Railway King', who made Albert Gate famous. In the 1840s England was at the height of the railway fever as speculators opened new lines all over the country. Some stretches of line were only a few miles long but every new company seemed to make money for its promoters; at one stage there were over 270 railway companies all issuing prospectuses and Hudson was involved in most of them.

At about the time Hudson's wealth enabled him to move into this enormous building, the Ranger's Lodge in Green Park was demolished and there was much concern over the famous statues of the two stags that had stood beside the Lodge gates. Hudson saw a way of improving his public image and had them set up where they are today, on the pillars of Albert Gate. Because Hudson made his fortune by promoting companies and then selling the shares at a premium, and his association with the stags, the process became known as 'stagging', the term used on the Stock Exchange today.

Albert Gate leads into the traffic of Knightsbridge, which grew in a hundred years from market gardens to become the byword for luxurious respectability we know today. Knightsbridge is a Victorian creation but many of its buildings date from the Edwardian era, like the block that faces us across the road. It was completed in 1901, the year Edward VII came to the throne, and the architects celebrated the event accordingly. At the left-hand end facing Wilton Place, King Edward in his Coronation robes looks down on the roadway, while the portico above No. 55 shows Queen Alexandra in her finery. To her left at No. 69, Lord Roberts, Kipling's 'Bobs Bahadur', manages to display one of his rows of medals and seems as uncomfortable as Lord Kitchener who occupies a similar position above the window of No. 73.

Hyde Park Corner

Hyde Park Corner lies to the left, dominated by the enormous building across the road occupied from 1733 till 1980 by St George's Hospital. The hospital's most famous physician was John Hunter who ran the establishment with a rod of iron and founded the Hunterian Museum of anatomical specimens. The museum still exists and includes the skeleton of the unfortunate Mr O'Brien, the Irish Giant, who was eight feet tall, suffered from ill health and who knew perfectly well that Hunter was after his body. O'Brien made every effort to escape Hunter's clutches and left specific instructions that he was to be buried at sea, but Hunter bribed the undertaker to leave the coffin in London for one night. He made the undertaker's assistants hopelessly drunk, stole the body and replaced it with stones that were in due course dropped into the Channel with appropriate religious rites.

Hunter was a man of quick temper and used to get his own way in the hospital by letting it be known that such rages were dangerous to his health. The trick worked for many years but at last his fellow Governors refused to give way to him any more, voted against his advice and ignored the outburst that followed. Hunter left the room in a fury and fell down dead outside, just as he had always threatened to do.

Hunter caused problems even after his death. He was buried in the crypt of St Martin-in-the-Fields in 1793 but, in 1859, the anatomist Frank Buckland secured approval for his reburial in Westminster Abbey and went to St Martin's to collect the coffin. Since no records existed, Buckland had to search the entire crypt containing 2,266 coffins. Hunter, contrary to the last, eluded him for sixteen days and was eventually found in the 2,264th.

The old hospital building stands at the corner of Belgravia, the area of London of which an admiring visitor once said: 'the squares are broad, the houses are gracious and nothing can ever go wrong'. Most of it is still owned by the Grosvenors and it was for hundreds of years a useless swampy marsh known as the Five Fields. The transformation was brought about by one of London's greatest builders Thomas Cubitt, who asked the Earl of Grosvenor for a building lease for the area. The Earl was reluctant to grant him one but eventually gave way after warning Cubitt that the ground was of soft clay unsuitable for building of any sort.

Cubitt knew the marshy land could not take houses as it was, but he had secured the contract to dig out the East India Docks at the other side of London and found he was excavating thousands of tons of gravel. He dug out the clay from the Five Fields, refilled them with gravel carried upstream from the docks and used the clay to make bricks for the estate that stands there today.

The subsequent fate of the St George's Hospital building is another example of the efficiency of the Grosvenor Estates records office that we saw in Grosvenor Square in the Fifteenth Walk. When the hospital was closed in 1980, the Government looked forward to a healthy profit from the sale of what is one of London's finest sites. They were more than taken aback to receive a discreet notification from the Grosvenor Estates that it might be worth looking at the hospital's 1733 lease before proceeding any further.

Whether the Government ever found the documents is not known, but the Grosvenor Estate copies showed clearly that it had no rights over the hospital at all. The lease of 1733 had been granted on condition that the land was used as a hospital; if it ceased to be so used, the land reverted to the Grosvenors. There was a certain amount of chagrin in Parliament but the documents were binding and, like the American Embassy before them, the British Government had to make other arrangements.

In front of the old hospital is the large traffic island carved out of Green Park to make a roundabout. The enormous stone howitzer in front of the hospital is the Royal Artillery Memorial by C. S. Jagger who was himself an artilleryman in the First War. The elevation and angle of the gun is so designed that a shell fired from it would land on the River Somme where so many lost their lives in the First World War.

The dominating feature of the area is the archway in front of Constitution Hill. The arch is a source of some irritation to visitors because it appears in maps and guidebooks under three different names: the Wellington Arch (still the name it bears on Government publications), the Green Park Arch (the name given to it when it was moved here in 1883), and the Constitution Arch (the name by which it appears in most guides). It was erected in 1828 directly in front of Apsley House, the Duke of Wellington's house on our left, and carried an enormous 40-ton statue of Wellington of such hideousness that a French veteran visiting London muttered, 'We are avenged.'

In 1883 the Arch was moved back to its present site and the old statue was taken down to be replaced with the smaller statue that faces Apsley House today. Like the arch on which it stands, the present sculpture on the top has three different names. It is officially a memorial to Edward VII presented to London by Lord Michelham, one of the financiers whom King Edward had ennobled. It was unveiled as the 'Peace Monument', yet all the guide-books call it the Quadriga, from the four horses who pull the chariot. It was done by Adrian Jones, a sculptor who specialised in equestrian statues, a task for which he was well qualified since he started life as a vet and then served in the cavalry for twenty years before he took up sculpture.

The figures of the horses are twice life-size and Jones and eight friends took dinner inside one of them before the statue was unveiled. The small boy attempting to rein in the horses was modelled on Lord Michelham's eleven-year-old son and the whole thing was officially unveiled as a monument to the hundred years of peace Europe had enjoyed since the battle of Waterloo in 1815. For some reason the monument was unveiled in 1914, in the ninety-ninth year, just in time to witness the outbreak of the First World War when more people were killed than in all thc European conflicts of the previous five hundred years – and the Kaiser attended the unveiling.

The building beside the gateway into Hyde Park is Apsley House, presented by the nation to the first Duke of Wellington. The Wellington Museum inside contains the finest array of Marshal's batons ever presented to one man, examples of nearly every order of chivalry in Europe and the Great George. The Great George is a collar of the Order of the Garter with the pendant badge of St George and the Dragon made twice the normal size. It was commissioned originally by Queen Anne to present as a mark of special honour to the Duke of Marlborough, whose victories in the early eighteenth century at Blenheim, Ramillies, Oudenard and Malplaquet were as glorious as those of Wellington a hundred years later. It reverted to royal ownership after Marlborough's death but was given to Wellington by George IV. It has been worn only once since Wellington's death; at the special request of the Queen it was worn by Sir Winston Churchill at her Coronation in 1953.

Apsley House is full of Wellington memorabilia but perhaps the most unusual is the Goya portrait of the Duke. The proportion of the neck and shoulders puzzled art experts for years until X-rays taken in 1960 showed that Goya had painted Wellington's features on top of a previous portrait – of Joseph Napoleon, the Emperor's elder brother.

Goya did the painting of Joseph Napoleon, King of Spain, in Madrid in 1812 and it was nearly completed when Wellington's armies captured the city and forced King Joseph to flee. The sudden change in political power brought an equally sudden change in Goya's patrons and the features of the late King were hurriedly covered by those of the victorious Duke. It is a pleasant irony on which to end these walks, at the last of London's ducal mansions.

These sixteen walks have covered only a fraction of London. Every one of its streets has a story and an anecdote can be told of every church, pub and statue.

London is changing fast but the traces of a thousand years can be seen everywhere. They are in the bend of a road, the shape of a doorway or an old archway over a forgotten alley, all there for those with eyes to see.

INDEX